D0214799

MICHELET, HISTORIAN

MICHELET, HISTORIAN

Rebirth and Romanticism in Nineteenth-Century France

ARTHUR MITZMAN

Yale University Press   *New Haven and London*

*Published with assistance from the
Louis Stern Memorial Fund.*

*Designed by James J. Johnson.
Set in Fournier Roman types by
Brevis Press, Bethany, Connecticut.*

*Printed in the United States of America by BookCrafters, Inc.,
Chelsea, Michigan.*

Library of Congress Cataloging-in-Publication Data

Mitzman, Arthur, 1931–
  *Michelet, historian : rebirth and romanticism in nineteenth-
century France / Arthur Mitzman.*
      p.   cm.
  Includes bibliographical references (p.).
  ISBN 0-300-04551-4 (alk. paper)
  *1. Michelet, Jules, 1798–1874.   2. Historians—France—
Biography.   3. France—History—19th century.
4. Romanticism—France—History—19th century.
I. Title.
DC36.98.M5M54   1990
944'.007202—dc20   89-27244
                                                        CIP*

*The paper in this book meets the guidelines for permanence and
durability of the Committee on Production Guidelines for Book
Longevity of the Council on Library Resources.*

10 9 8 7 6 5 4 3 2 1

An individual destiny, when one penetrates it, is more than the life of a nation.

MICHELET, *Journal*

Why do you think I date everything I do? Because it is not sufficient to know an artist's works—it is also necessary to know when he did them, why, how, under what circumstances. . . . Some day there will undoubtedly be a science—it may be called the science of man—which will seek to learn more about man in general through the study of creative man. I often think about such a science, and I want to leave to posterity a documentation that will be as complete as possible. That's why I put a date on everything I do.

PABLO PICASSO

CONTENTS

PREFACE

This book was originally intended as part of a more extensive study dealing with generational mentalities in nineteenth-century French cultural history: the focus was to be on three figures from the birth cohort of 1798–1802—Jules Michelet, Victor Hugo, and Hector Berlioz—and two from the birth cohort of the 1820s—Gustave Flaubert and Gustave Moreau. It became evident in the course of a decade and a half of work toward this goal that the clarity and specificity needed to accomplish it could best be built up by detailed studies of the individuals concerned, studies in which their personality development and their social-cultural contexts were jointly studied for the purpose of mutual illumination. The first result of this is *Michelet, Historian,* a work that continues and broadens the approach I used in *The Iron Cage: An Historical Interpretation of Max Weber.*

Both time and shifting historical paradigms have nonetheless led to significant departures from the method applied there. In the course of the twenty years since I wrote *The Iron Cage,* the psychohistorical enterprise has been constrained to respond to criticism both intemperate and measured. Within psychoanalytic theory, moreover, has grown an increasing realization of the limitations of Freud's view of the Oedipus complex and a corresponding integration of Kleinian and Eriksonian perspectives, among others, on the pre-Oedipal phase and the social construction of the ego. Both perspectives have improved the possibilities for integrating psychoanalytic history writing into the broader concerns of historians of mentalities and cultures, an integration that I am convinced holds the best promise for the future of psychohistory and that I have attempted to implement in this book.

In this task, I have been considerably assisted by others—in the Netherlands, very broadly and importantly by my seminar students at the University of Amsterdam, whose healthy skepticism was a frequent spur to rethinking my assumptions. A sabbatical year (1982–83) at the Netherlands Institute for Advanced Study in Wassenaar made possible an initial phase of research and writing, and the Faculty of Letters and the Historisch Seminarium of the University of Amsterdam assisted me by providing research time and generous use of their copying facilities. Colleagues and friends at Dutch universities—Willem Frijhoff, Jan Aarts, Peter de Back, and Laurens van der Heijden—have helped more specifically by their comments on the manuscript. Ann Rigney deserves special thanks for her subtle commentary on an early draft of the manuscript. My wife, Marleen Mitzman-Wessel, has been an indispensable source of reasoned complaint and constructive criticism of everything from my capricious use of diacritics to the theoretical foundations of my approach.

In France, Mona Ozouf, Eric Fauquet, and Nicole Taillade read and commented with expert knowledge on major sections of the manuscript, and Michelle Perrot offered a constant stimulus and a link to French research on private life in the nineteenth century. The staff of the Bibliothèque Historique de la Ville de Paris and its director, Jean Derens, provided me with a uniquely pleasurable and efficient work environment to examine Michelet's unpublished letters and papers; their assistance over the years in deciphering the indecipherable has been *sans pareil.*

In the United States, I received helpful criticism and support at difficult moments from Sidney Monas, Donald Kelley, and Lewis Coser. Phyllis Mitzman offered good suggestions for revising Parts V and VI. My largest debt of all is to the stylistic and organizational wisdom of Peter Gay, who is principally responsible for the transformation of the penultimate version from garrulousness and repetitiveness to whatever virtues of concision it may now possess.

All these institutional and intellectual midwives are, of course, no more responsible for persisting defects in *Michelet, Historian* than members of the obstetrical trade normally are for the deficiencies of the young.

INTRODUCTION: BIOGRAPHY AND THEORY

History: violent moral chemistry in which my individual passions become generalities, in which my self turns back to bring life to the peoples.

MICHELET

Why Michelet?

Jules Michelet's stature in the historical tradition of France is indisputable.[1] Since roughly the beginning of the Third Republic around 1870, one can speak of an era of "scientific" history, with a multitude of university chairs and journals.[2] Although Michelet's romanticism was largely antipathetic to the purveyors of the new disciplinary rigor, in the half century before this era he was its John the Baptist: his prophetic pathos became the bad conscience of many of the future popes of the new faith in science. His career extended through five regimes and was punctuated by three revolutionary outbursts and a coup d'état: the governments of the Restoration, the July Monarchy, the Second Republic, the Second Empire, and the early Third Republic; the outbursts of 1830 and 1848, which filled him with hope, as well as that of 1870–71, which inspired dread; and Louis-Napoléon's coup of December 1851, which pushed him into exile. During this half century there were, of course, other writers of history, but most were either politician-scholars, like François Guizot and Adolphe Thiers, or radical journalists and men of letters, like Alphonse de Lamartine and Louis Blanc.

Michelet's fame gradually waned after his death in 1874. His students aged and passed on, and the discipline of history embraced with increasing conviction the antiromantic tenets of scientific positivism. In the early twentieth century, most historians had dismissed and forgotten Michelet; if they looked for predecessors from the mid-nineteenth century, they preferred the sober vision of Numa Denis Fustel de Coulanges or Alexis de Tocqueville to Michelet's populist-nationalist one. Nonetheless, it was Michelet and not Fustel or Tocqueville who focused attention on central problems in the methodology of history and on its ideological significance for the nation, and it is for this reason that he has been picked up again in the past fifty years by Lucien Febvre and Marc Bloch, as well as by many of the contemporary historians associated with the all-important journal they founded, the *Annales*.[3]

In this introduction, I survey Michelet's significance for the history of culture and mentalities in his own time and the basis for the renewed interest in him. In the chapters that follow, I discuss intensively the fifteen years of his life from 1840 to 1854. Extending from the apogee of French social romanticism during the July Monarchy through the Second Republic to the first years of the Second Empire, these years show Michelet at his most creative and politically engaged. Paralleling the curve of increasing republican militancy before 1848 and of radicalization and reaction after that year, Michelet's life in this decade and a half was framed at the beginning by his first wife's death and at the end by the writing of *Le Banquet*, his unfinished manifesto for a humanitarian social religion, the high point and conclusion of Michelet's engagement as populist socialist. In between, Michelet lost one great love in 1842 and gained another in 1848; contributed to the undermining of the July Monarchy by feuding publicly with the order of Jesuits; wrote two volumes of his *Histoire de France*, his populist masterpiece *Le Peuple*, and his seven-volume *Histoire de la Révolution française*, as well as several lesser works; was twice suspended from his chair at the Collège de France; and saw his public career definitively smashed in 1852 when he refused to swear loyalty to Louis-Napoléon's dictatorship. My method will be to trace the social and intellectual problems discussed by Michelet back to their personal and historical context, to illuminate, through Michelet's personality and work, the achievements and dilemmas of both social romanticism and republicanism in mid-nineteenth-century France.

Michelet's contribution to the historical tradition was situated at the confluence of four contemporary intellectual currents, which sometimes moved in opposing directions. The liberalism and eclecticism of his mentors, Victor Cousin and Abel-François Villemain, shaped his early thinking. Second, he looked to the new natural sciences, primarily chemistry and biology, as an intellectually liberating force and a model for thinking about society. Third—and here he was borne by a largely contrary tide—he was strongly influenced by the social romanticism of the July Monarchy. Similarly reacting against the dryness of Enlightenment rationalism, the obsolescence of Catholic beliefs, and the cold individualism of the new social order, Michelet took from the social romantics the belief that a redemptive social harmony could be created by integrating the emotional warmth of the people with the rationality of middle-class intellectuals, and he tended to interpret history and write for the future in light of that ideal. Finally, there was the tradition of the French Revolution: he saw himself, because of his popular origins and intellectual gifts, as the inheritor and prophet incarnate of the revolutionary legend.

These shifting tides, in one combination or another, carried Michelet's historical approach through its various phases. His orientation toward the scientific thought of his day probably encouraged him in his reliance on primary sources—original documents wherever they could be found rather than existing chronicles and narratives. As head of the historical section of the Archives nationales, he was better placed than most of his colleagues to do this: it was a matter of professional pride for him and made him the predecessor of the rigorous "scientific" study of sources that began toward his life's end. His vital ties to the revolutionary tradition, expressed through his "Introduction à l'histoire universelle," his *Histoire de la Révolution française,* and *Nos Fils*[4] made him a central figure in the creation and maintenance of French republican consciousness in the nineteenth century. If his first major historical statement, the "Introduction à l'histoire universelle," revealed in its dominating theme of individual *liberté* versus natural and social *fatalité,* primarily the liberal interpretation of the Revolution common to the middle-class scholar-politicians of the Revolution of 1830, his "French Revolution," written when he was under the influence of the social romanticism of the 1840s, showed an almost mystical devotion to the causes of social justice and fraternity.

In this role as apostle of the revolutionary tradition, he and his contemporaries saw his educational mission—via his chair at the Collège de France and his widely read books—more as that of a prophet than a pedagogue. Indeed, through the political positions a few of his disciples attained, some of his impassioned pleading for a republican reform of education was translated into reality. His former secretary, Victor Duruy, was minister of education under the liberal Empire; another former disciple, Emile Ollivier, was its head. Jules Ferry, a radical, anti-Bonapartist republican and protégé of Michelet's friend Edgar Quinet, received Michelet's ardent support in the elections of 1869 and in the late 1870s laid the foundation of the Third Republic's anticlerical system of public education.

Distinct from these practical services to French democracy, Michelet's most important contribution to modern historiography has less to do with the republican side of his character than with his near mystical, social romantic side. Through his evolution to this position in the 1840s he developed two perspectives that have been discussed considerably in modern historiography: one is the powerful role of popular consciousness in history, expressed in the histories of sociability and mentalities—that is, of witchcraft and popular religion, of women, children, and working people—that have proliferated in the French historical schools of the past few decades. Michelet's work clearly anticipates all of these.[5] The other is the question of the historian's subjectivity and how it can be used to draw out the hidden motivations of his subject matter: a point of view echoed between 1870 and 1940 in the theories of Wilhelm Dilthey, Benedetto Croce, and R. G. Collingwood and discussed anew in the past two decades by psychohistorians, intellectual historians, and philosophers of history.[6] The result of this multiple significance is that Michelet, though sometimes scorned for his romanticism and emotionality, has remained the titular deity of an important current in French historiography, and some of the approaches he initiated—the search for popular mentalities, the use of oral testimony, and the self-inquiry of the historian into his relation to his subject—seem to have come into their own primarily in recent decades.[7] One might expect, in light of this renewed relevance, that literature discussing Michelet's contribution and its historical setting would be extensive, and indeed there is no shortage of titles on him. Nonetheless, because of the firm French custom of relegating the history of ideas to literary historians and the tendency of literary scholars since Roland Barthes to focus on Michelet's psychological richness in a way that eschews biographical questions, the literature of the past thirty years on Michelet is little more than a collection of brilliant fragments—fragments that in general fail to respond to the concerns of contemporary historians to link the individual and the collective, to integrate the cultural and the social.[8] A study of the interdependence of work, personality, and historical context has remained absent from scholarship on Michelet.

Filling this gap through a psychohistorical analysis and relating this inquiry to the sociocultural context is an enterprise very much in the spirit of the historian himself. For Michelet emphasized the common psychological denominators of a historical epoch and its representative individuals, and his strong introspective bent led him to the edge of what would later be called psychoanalytic awareness. Indeed, through his frequent inclination to interpret history as a family drama, he is particularly susceptible to psychohistorical interpretation: Michelet often glimpses fathers, mothers, sons, and daughters symbolically, both in his own situation and in the relations between historical collectivities. And as we shall see, the question of whether nature should be viewed as a beneficent mother or a wicked stepmother recurs at crucial moments in his evolution and stands metaphorically for a determined effort to come to terms with his own largely unconscious sexual impulses.

Yet Michelet's panoply of family symbols should not deceive us. There is another historical lesson hidden behind them, as there is behind the ideological hegemony of the nuclear family in the nineteenth century: the persistence of networks of sociability that pervaded the social life of the old regime and provided, at the level of mentalities, a powerful supplement to the educative force of fathers and mothers—the peer groups, youth associations, and other collective solidarities, masked and hypostatized in the ideas of French republicanism as *fraternité* and *patrie*.

The book that follows is not a comprehensive "life and works" of Michelet. As indicated, I part company with him when he is fifty-six, in 1854. Moreover, I have good reasons to deal rather summarily both with his early career and with his childhood. Although my approach is, to borrow Peter Gay's expression, psychoanalytically informed, I believe the course of adult life, with its conflicts and tragedies, can be understood in many cases largely—if not exclusively—on its own terms. In the instances of some of Michelet's literary compatriots, such as Hugo, Baudelaire, and Flaubert, the forms that adult creativity took can be directly related to childhood and adolescent experience. Michelet is different. His most impressive contributions seem to be responses to the political events and personal experiences of his maturity and are related only marginally to his upbringing and early object-relations. Nonetheless, a most interesting *re*working of his childhood is evident during the repeated self-proclaimed rebirths and renewals that were the mature Michelet's responses to the emotional shocks he endured after age forty. Furthermore, though Michelet's twenty-fifth to fortieth years contain much to interest historians, he became a truly fascinating figure politically, psychologically, and even historiographically—in his contributions to French republican mythology, discovery of the traditional popular culture, and unashamed subjectivity—only after his fourth decade.

Practical considerations of source materials also justify focusing on the later Michelet. Information on his childhood, scholarly apprenticeship, and early career is skimpy, and even his autobiographical journal became consistently self-revelatory only after he began, at age forty-two, the emotional adventure that transformed his life.

For these reasons I offer only a sketch of the first forty years of Michelet's life in the pages to come. After a survey of the framework for those years, I summarize the most relevant information about his childhood, youth, and early career and focus for the rest on Michelet at mid-life and after. Further details about Michelet's early years will, of course, emerge where the later Michelet is found to be thinking, puzzling, or obsessing about them at critical moments—a not infrequent occurrence.

Reflections on Method

This book, a psychobiographical approach to Jules Michelet's middle years, shows the interdependence of personality development, social-cultural setting, and creative achievement. In so doing, it draws on a storehouse of theory that is by no means universally accepted among historians. I would therefore like to clarify here what I view as the relevance to the ongoing concerns of the historical profession—particularly as regards biography, psychohistory, and mentalities—of my use of various concepts and methods.

There are basically two issues: First, what is the wisdom of devoting several years of a historian's life—and several days of the reader's—to the analysis of a single person from the minuscule stratum of famous individuals? To pose the problem more positively: What is the potential relevance of a biographical approach to the current interest in social-cultural history? Second, what is the usefulness of psychoanalytic concepts in this enterprise?

Until recently, few serious historians viewed biography positively, and the recent return to favor of the genre probably owes more to its commercial possibilities and to the decline of faith in more "structured" historical perspectives than to real conviction. Carlo Ginzburg's well thought-out use of individual "traces" to illuminate broader historical problems may constitute an important exception to this judgment; moreover, the recent occurrence of a French "colloque" on the subject and the appearance in 1989 of a number of the Dutch *Journal of Social History* (*Tijdschrift voor sociale geschiedenis*) devoted to historical biography surely reflect a groundswell of learned interest. Nonetheless, most historians, now as in the past half century, continue to associate biographies with assumptions that history is shaped by the acts of powerful individuals. Such individuals were supposed to have decisively influenced both the political-social existence of humanity and its cultural horizons.

Historians rightly rejected these assumptions, which may have had their source in the fact that their forebears, usually born into the professional elites and trained in universities to which no more than 1 or 2 percent of the population had access, identified with hegemonic political structures that were led by a similarly thin stratum of notables. Although these structures survived by several decades the spread of universal male—and then female—suffrage in North America and Western Europe, somewhere in the middle third of the twentieth century, the control of politics and culture by traditional elites broke down, and the notables had to surrender hegemony to parties, organizations, and movements that were broadly based on the new mass electorate. Violently negative aspects of these were to be seen in the rise of fascism, more benign versions in the evolution of democratic socialism and the welfare state. In any case, all manifestations of political, social, and economic modernism presupposed advanced technologies, giant corporate entities, and a large, well-trained bureaucratic, managerial, and technocratic elite, for which the mass universities of the second half of the twentieth century have become the indispensable training ground.

Thus, between the democratic political evolution toward a mass society and the needs of modern industry for university-trained personnel, the foundations of traditional social control by coteries of notables crumbled in both politics and universities, as did the naive assumption that the world was shaped by the actions of powerful individuals. In an exaggerated response to the new state of affairs, the historical discipline tended to exclude individuals altogether from scholarly consideration. At a supra-individual level, social history increasingly encroached on political history and the history of mentalities more and more took over that part of cultural and intellectual history that related individuals to their social and political environments. At an infra-individual level, study of the history of ideas, which used to put these ideas in some relation to their authors, has been replaced by a rigorous study of the products or "artifacts" of intellectual production, which has usually meant a study of texts to the *exclusion* of their authors.

These tendencies were partially justified by the weaknesses of the traditional approaches. Intellectual historians who sought a social context for thinkers and their ideas frequently did so quite amateurishly, presupposing "Zeitgeists" as an explanatory framework without seriously considering ethnic, religious, class, or status differences within a period, without making the necessary distinctions between traditional and modern, urban and rural cultures, among regional, national, and international frameworks, among elite, popular, and mass cultures or the gradations within them. Historians of ideas had become expert in the history of philosophy or other branches of intellectual endeavor (science, theology, literary structures, and so on) but too often dealt with the work of a thinker as a purely rational elaboration of an existing tendency, a shining link in another "great chain of being." Both the nonintellectual context and the possibility that ideas could have nonrational sources in their authors' values and emotions vanished in the process.

In reacting against these positions, however, cultural and intellectual historians have left a painful gap between the generalizations about "mentalities" and the specificity of "artifacts": the individual, who is the concrete embodiment of the first and the specific creator of the second. The present return to biography can fill that gap, but the way in which it may do so needs critical examination.

It is, of course, true that a focus on individual existence does restrict the historian to a tiny minority of the human race, nearly all of it from the well-educated elite, that expressed its daily sentiments in diaries and letters and reflected on its childhood and later development in autobiographies.[9] Nonetheless, one need not maintain an obsolete faith in "great men" as the movers of history to view such biographic studies as valuable building blocks for generalizations about elite mentalities and as a crucial basis for the understanding of textual "artifacts." Even if we are restricted to the thin stratum of the elite, a serious, comprehensive view of individuals for whom the necessary documents are available can shed great light on a variety of questions. How is the relation between elite and popular culture articulated in an individual from a specific ethnic, social, religious, and generational background at a specific moment in history? What are the intellectual, ideological, and ethical options available to someone like Michelet, and how are they integrated into a personality shaped by a specific mentality and a particular familial and social background? What relation do we discern between a historically and personally concrete family constellation and extrafamilial agencies of socialization and identification: school, church, and national or class consciousness? Historians who have learned to generalize about the social components of these questions but regard the personal component as impenetrable or irrelevant abandon the one historical object which, as thinking, feeling, and self-reflecting subjects, they are uniquely capable of comprehending in the totality of its personal and social dimensions—the historical individual.

The use of psychoanalytic constructs follows from the decision to pursue a biographical line of inquiry. Many of the questions that now fascinate historians of cultures and mentalities arise from a view of human personality as moved by nonrational needs and impulses: attitudes toward nature and especially toward human nature, the rituals through which individual emotions find social expression, the ways in which anxieties, aggression, and sexual impulses are channeled and legitimized or forbidden and suppressed—

all are matters that should link serious biographers and social historians in a community of interest. This book is premised on the notion that psychoanalytic theory, used judiciously, offers the clearest theoretical entry to these and other important questions, particularly concerning the relation between a man's (or woman's) personal development and the character of his (or her) intellectual production and career.

A number of distinctions are in order between Freudian and post-Freudian psychoanalytic theory. Freud's own ideas, whatever their therapeutic value, have objectionable aspects for most historians. Freud had little feeling for the personalities of the female half of the human race; he offered little perspective for the study of personality growth beyond childhood; he professed a normative notion of personality development, bound up with his own cultural environment, that made maturity contingent on a properly fought-out Oedipus complex and he saw only limited importance in pre-Oedipal stages of development. In all of these areas, Freud's successors, such as Erik Erikson, Melanie Klein, and even the notoriously obscure Jacques Lacan have improved his concepts and made them more accessible for historians. Accordingly, I find a number of psychoanalytic ideas useful[10] but not always in the form that Freud gave them.

The notion that personality develops through phases of psychosexual development focused on oral, anal, and genital needs and expressions, for example, is valuable,[11] but the idea that this development must culminate in a phase of Oedipal conflict with the father, implicitly and unconsciously centered around possession of the mother, and that a "healthy" or "mature" personality depends on the successful resolution of this conflict, is a normative notion applicable in therapy and perhaps valid for certain bourgeois cultures of this and the preceding century but often a hindrance to the historical understanding of cultures with other norms. I elaborate on this problem in the Conclusion.

Another point: the idea that personality is shaped through the integration and internalization by a budding consciousness, or "ego," of social norms and values is essential to understanding the relation of individual to society, but Freud's formulation of this process requires emendation. Freud assumed that those norms and values, which everyday speech refers to as conscience and which the founder of psychoanalysis called "superego," were transmitted in early years by the parents. Historians and anthropologists have had to modify Freud's notion, since substitutes for the parents in extended kin or household networks are known to occur, especially before the modern era and beyond the confines of the bourgeois family that was Freud's model.

Furthermore, even if the basic notion of a necessary internalization of norms and values, tied in good measure to parental influences, is sound, the notion needs historicizing to account for the broader social sources of such values. Freud himself laid the basis for such historicizing. He distinguished between "superego" as the more coercive, punitive, primitive, and biologically based internalization of parental mandates and "ego-ideal" as the model for positive aspirations.[12] And he suggested that the concept of such a normative model could easily be extended outside the zone of parental influence into the cultural sphere. Teachers and friends at a level of personal influence, charismatic political or religious leaders at a level of public influence, could supplement—or contradict— the parental model.

Freud's extension of this notion had two problems. In a clear case of terminological confusion, he referred to it as a "cultural superego," though the exemplary and noncoercive model he was referring to corresponded to his concept of ego-ideal. To set matters straight, I shall employ in this book the concept of "cultural ego-ideal." And Freud did not go far enough, since this concept could be applied not just to important individuals but to normative mentalities and ideologies as well. In my chapter on the young Michelet, I discuss the relation between, on the one hand, his adaptation to the various ego-ideals—parental and otherwise—available to him and, on the other, the development of his social and political awareness.

Finally, throughout this book I make use of the large post-Freudian literature that illuminates the importance for Michelet's personality of the pre-Oedipal tie to the mother, in order to clarify his repeated personal "re-naissances."

If I turn back from these psychoanalytic structures to a more precise look at the social-cultural matrix in which they are embedded in this study, then four concepts demand at least a cursory definition and an indication of how they enter my narrative: *mentality, ideology, generation,* and *civilizing offensive.* Taken together, these concepts constitute a sociological counterpoint to my psychoanalytic perspective.[13]

Mentality refers to the collectively established and not necessarily conscious attitudes, concepts, norms, and values of a particular social group concerning nature, the supernatural, social order, and disorder, and the desired degree of inhibition over basic impulse (sex, aggression, greed, and so on). The group may be constituted by rural villagers, a religious sect or church, a social class or subclass, or a nation. Because mentalities convey to parents the customs and rituals by which they guide their offspring through the phases of psychosexual development and establish the emphases within those phases characteristic of different cultures, they are an important influence on character formation. And because they govern individual notions of good and evil and have a censoring effect on perception, they may also be considered as the diffuse background of the cultural ego-ideal. Relevant to Michelet's early career was his parents' petit-bourgeois artisan mentality—a mentality that combined a bourgeois work ethic with the austere ideals of Jacobin democracy and elements of the popular culture. Later, in the 1840s, Michelet was to be powerfully influenced by the social-romantic mentality of the period. Mentalities relate to ideologies as oceans to the fish that inhabit them.

By *ideology* I mean the organization or "codification" of a mentality into discrete propositions by an individual or individuals. Ideologies can be seen as the replacement, in more or less mobile, literate, and pluriform societies, of the traditional lore that spelled out mentalities in stable, oral, homogeneous cultures. In one sense they simply rationalize and perpetuate the nonrational character structure and values of a society, class, or subclass. In another, they can express the concrete interests—economic, political, religious, or aesthetic—of a subgroup of those who share the mentality, and may be used as an instrument of war by this subgroup, to impose its views and interests on related or competing groups. Examples would be the doctrines of Calvinism, of English classical economics, of Marxism.

The relation between an ideology and an individual expression of ideas that may support or contradict it is the relation between what German sociology has called objective and subjective mind. Objective mind—ideologies—constitutes the already made intellectual world, embodied in books or institutions external to the subjective, creative mind that reacts to them.[14] Michelet's work can well be viewed in terms of the creative reaction against ideology as objective mind. His *Introduction à l'histoire universelle* was a riposte to the ideology of Cousinian philosophy, too deterministic for the young historian. His *Le Peuple* was a broader reaction against the antinatural asceticism and "machinism" of the ideologies and mentalities that shaped his early years. Yet in both these works there is also an element of adaptation to and support of the prevailing ideologies and mentalities, in the first instance of liberalism, in the second of social romanticism.

A *generation* is a group whose mentality has been shaped by certain common influences or experiences of childhood and youth. The age-cohorts that have been influenced in such a way as to form a generation have usually been born within less than fifteen years of one another. They can arise from the impact of a war or a depression or a revolution or a wave of reaction or a natural catastrophe.

To belong to a generation does not necessarily imply conflict with the generations senior or junior, but feelings of being misunderstood or of being barred from access to power and status can lead to such conflict. Moreover, shared generational experience is frequently in tension, at the individual level, with the familial sources of superego formation. An obvious example is the American student generation of the 1960s: molded by the childhood experience of World War II and the youth experiences of the Vietnam War and the massification of higher education, this generation translated its group consciousness into social alienation and personal withdrawal from adult authority, as the watchword "Don't trust anyone over thirty" made clear.

An essential question is the dimension and social characteristics of the group affected by generational experience. Alan Spitzer, in a most useful work on Michelet's generation,[15] specifies that he is dealing with an age-cohort of educated young men born between 1792 and 1803; the 183 individuals in his sample—those who left some record of their existence—stand for a larger group, but at least 98 percent of the French population born in the same period does not belong to it. The formative experiences of Spitzer's "generation of 1820" were a childhood in the Napoleonic era, an adolescence or youth marked by the national defeats of 1814–15, and a young adulthood in the repressive atmosphere of the 1820s. Class, education, and gender led this group to react differently to those experiences than the vast majority of their age cohort, forced early into manual labor in farms and towns and without access to higher education; their birth-dates insured that their experience set them off from members of the educated class born before or after them. Because this was a generation whose ideological options influenced much of the course of French history in the decades before 1848, it merits study despite its small size.

The *civilizing offensive* refers to European elite culture's imposition on the lower orders of standards of belief, moral behavior, and emotional discipline—particularly the repression of aggressive and sexual impulses—that were deemed necessary, from about 1580 on, for the inner acceptance of centralized religious and secular authority. Norbert Elias's *The Civilizing Process* (1939) showed how the aristocratic elites of Western Europe, under court pressure, gradually internalized this mentality in the early modern era, and historians since then have studied its diffusion downward. In many ways the mentalities of the traditional popular cultures—expressed in festive outbursts of violence and license and in local beliefs that merged the natural and the supernatural—were indeed incompatible with such internalization of centralized authority. The "civilizing offensive," an attack on "disruptive" aspects of the popular cultures, thus produced sustained tension within those cultures between "traditional" and "modern" ways of thinking and doing. It also served the elites themselves as a continual reinforcement of their own superego defenses against "immoral," "irrational," and "undignified" behavior, all of which were projected onto the presumably superstitious, lazy, mendacious, and criminal lower orders of society. In chapter 1 and in the Conclusion I deal with the vicissitudes of the civilizing offensive during Michelet's lifetime.

Let us turn now to the history of nineteenth-century France, the framework for the life and the creative contribution of Jules Michelet.

PART I

PRELUDE,
1789 – 1831

My master, the blessed Hegel, once said to me: "If one had written down the dreams which people had dreamt during a particular period, the reading of these collected dreams would provide a quite accurate picture of the spirit of that period." Michelet's *History of France* is such a collection of dreams, such a dream book from which the entire dreaming Middle Ages gazes at us with its deeply suffering eyes and its ghostly smile. We are almost frightened by the gaudy truth of color and form. In fact, for the depiction of that somnambulistic age, you need a somnambulistic historian like Michelet.

HEINE
Lutetia (*Sämtliche Werke,* Insel Verlag, 9:348)

CHAPTER 1

MICHELET'S WORLD

The French Nineteenth Century

Today's French historians, handsomely seconded by their British and American colleagues, have explored with great sensitivity the new problems of mentalities that Michelet had signaled. They have subtly uncovered the conflicts of modern and traditional ways of thinking and have related these conflicts to the complex relations between elite and popular cultures, the rivalry of centralizing powers and regional cultures since the Middle Ages, the sources and significance of demographic and economic change, and the interpenetration of pre-Christian, Christian, and post-Christian modes of looking at the world. Forgotten ways of thinking and feeling have been resurrected; existing sources, scrutinized by modern intelligence, have generated a new past.

Illuminated by the innovative brilliance of these scholars, nineteenth-century France has come to signify something quite different to the historical imagination than the bond, assumed by earlier generations, between the Enlightenment promise of emancipated Reason and the twentieth-century fulfillment of that vow. That we can recognize ourselves in the social and political values that link Voltaire and the Declaration of the Rights of Man to Zola, Camus, and modern democracy, as well as in the cultural "modernism" that ties Flaubert, Gide, and Proust to Sartre and Foucault, has proven rather deceptive. Certainly, when we look more closely at the French culture of the first half of the nineteenth century, the environment that was the seedbed for Michelet's life and work, then another world emerges, a world in which such harbingers of modernism as Stendhal, Baudelaire, and Flaubert were anomalies. We now know that, in general, the literature and ideas, like the politics, of the period before 1850 were embedded in a sociocultural matrix remote from Enlightenment or modernist perspectives: a large peasant majority, living mainly by archaic folkways in near-medieval conditions, industry still at the artisanal level of the eighteenth century, the predominance of aristocratic, landholding values in the new bourgeoisie, clans of rural notables dominating the local social and political structures, and enormous regional differences.[1] To enter this world requires the patience of an anthropologist discovering a strange ethnicity. Yet the intellectual, literary, and artistic creativity of France in the nineteenth century was second to none.

In fact, the brilliance of France's cultural achievement between Waterloo and World War I arises paradoxically from the fact that its history in this period lacked in the political and economic realms the dynamism we associate with modern England, the United States, or Germany. There was much political movement, of course, but it was of the convulsive sort that characterized the repeated efforts to escape the constricting restorations of obsolete systems. The European-wide dominance of French revolutionary ideals and Napoleonic arms gave way following the imperial debacle to an uneasy sixty years' effort to regain and stabilize the transient achievement of 1792; an enduring French Republic emerged in the 1870s only after two monarchies and a second empire. Intellectuals, recognizing their country's loss of prerevolutionary power and cultural dominance, increasingly accepted English and German models. Before 1848, German thought, transmitted by Victor Cousin and Madame de Staël, powerfully influenced French romanticism, as did the English models of Byron and Shakespeare. After France's defeat in the Franco-Prussian War, Wagnerism and Darwinism were received as invigorating and liberating winds from abroad, viewed by French pessimists as salutary medicine against the national trend to entropy and decadence.[2]

In the realm of economics, liberals and Saint-Simonians hailed prematurely, after 1830, the spread of an English-style Industrial Revolution. Contrary to what some hoped and others feared, no rapid transformation of the French economy occurred in the nineteenth century. This non-fact is crucial if we are to penetrate the opacity of French culture to its anthropological "otherness." Change was steady but slow compared to the English, German, and American take-off periods; brief accelerations were never rapid and thorough enough to uproot the peasant majority and to industrialize and multiply the urban masses, as happened elsewhere.[3]

The result of this lack of industrial dynamism was that the modernist transformations heralded by the Enlightenment and the Revolution touched only a thin stratum of seers and intellectuals in nineteenth-century France, were bitterly opposed by many, and, most important, only marginally affected the crucial spheres of family and social existence. Slow population growth and industrial progress meant that the occupational structure and the distribution of wealth altered more gradually than elsewhere. This relative stability had consequences. Parvenus did attract literary attention; some sons outstripped and derided their fathers; but French parents had considerably better prospects of retaining status and authority over their offspring than did parents in countries where occupational skills rapidly became obsolete and fortunes had to be divided among a population that was three times larger by the end of the century than at its beginning (the population of France increased by only 50 percent in the nineteenth century, compared with 300 percent in England).

Traditional authority was thus not a value rigidly imposed— as in Prussianized Germany after 1870—by a conservative political elite that had to prevent rapid economic change from undermining traditional social power. Such authority was, in spite of the violent rivalries of French political factions, built into the barely changing relations between peasants and markets, between artisan producers and consumers, and, at the most personal level, between sons and fathers. We see these constancies in the political weight of France's peasant majority until after the First World War, in the persistently small-scale character of most industrial production, and in the relative scarcity of overt generational conflict within families. This last is indicated by the absence of the theme in literature (Theodor Zeldin informs us that only 10 percent of French novels on adolescence between 1880 and 1910 even touch on parent-child conflict; German literature of this period is suffused with it). It is also, according to Alan Spitzer, a striking characteristic of the age-cohort of Jules Michelet, which, in spite of its social and cultural rebelliousness against the "gerontocracy" of the Restoration, maintained a filial piety in the personal sphere that the most hidebound moralists could only approve.[4] In fact, during the 1820s, as in later generations, the stormy rebelliousness of radical youth against those in power was often expressed in the name of the father's ideals.

We are then, in nineteenth-century France, dealing with a different world than what we might expect from an orientation toward Enlightenment models of Reason and personal autonomy or toward Anglo-American and German ones of rapid economic and social change. In spite of the political saturation of the century with the problems and perspectives born in the French Revolution, French cultures and mentalities before 1914 were traditional in ways that require a great leap of the imagination to comprehend. The two main expressions of this traditionalism are the French aristocratic heritage and the regional and local popular cultures; popular culture interacted more powerfully with elite culture in the generations after the Revolution than it had for centuries before.

Excluded from trade by a rigid social code that allowed no English-style gentry as a link to middle-class values, the aristocracy was also, from the administrative reforms of Cardinal Richelieu onward, pushed out of the political power structure, its functions given to royal appointees. Never compelled, as the Prussian aristocracy had been, to rationalize its domains and to accept permanent burdens of military and administrative discipline, it devoted itself to luxury, the hunt, and a rare fling at military glory. Its gift to the French bourgeoisie was its model of the leisured life, which, given the lack of opportunities for capital investment, inspired successful merchants to avoid the exertions of their Anglo-American analogues by spending their profits on art, fine food and furniture, and early rural retirements. Its gifts to the artists were its values of beauty and luxury, taken over as ends in themselves by acolytes of "art for art's sake," and of "prowess" as a way of life, and its disdain for bourgeois utilitarianism and commerce. Its gift to French generals, conspirators, and insurrectionists was its audacity, its refusal to temper action to reflections on consequences, which is the main reason for the noisy failure of all three groups (1830 and 1848 excepted) from Waterloo to the twentieth century.

French popular culture, with its festivals, rituals, *abbayes de jeunesse,* and *veillées,* was repressed by royal and religious absolutism during the two centuries from the Council of Trent to the Revolution and equally denigrated by the new bourgeois powers after 1789. Nonetheless, the total dependence of the Revolutionaries on popular muscle to unseat the Old Regime, a dependence that recurred under the restored monarchies after 1815, forced the bourgeois to tolerate many previously tabooed aspects of the *culture populaire.* From about 1820 on, urban varieties of popular culture—carnival, street theater, *compagnonnages*—became for the republican bourgeoisie an early nineteenth-century version of what a more recent generation has called "radical chic." Class as well as cultural lines were more fluid, especially during the July Monarchy, than before or after. Higher and lower orders mingled freely in the theater of the boulevard du Temple and disguised their social identities altogether at Carnival. The children of doctors, lawyers, and bureaucrats lived as Bohemian students alongside low-paid artisans, conspired with the wretched of the earth in the secret societies, and courted working-class "grisettes" in garrets. George Sand hobnobbed with the *compagnon* organizer Agricol Perdiguier and jointly set up the socialist *Revue indépendante* with Pierre Leroux, ex-typographer and one-time Saint-Simonian. (Leroux himself was skilled in crossing class lines. Of respectable family, he became a typographer—and mason—after lack of funds forced him to drop out of the Ecole polytechnique. He built his publishing career on his experience as a printer and his intellectual one on his scholarly background.)

After 1850, this pattern of cultural mixture and the social-romantic ideologies that celebrated and supported it largely disappeared. As a result of the workers' rising of June 1848, the French bourgeoisie decided for once and for all that it had more to fear than to hope for from the *canaille* of the *faubourgs* and gradually prepared itself for the embrace of its Bonapartist savior. The Third Republic, which began with the extermination of the Commune, continued this hostile mood. From mid-century on, the openness of bourgeois radicals to the "people," and through them to the popular culture and to nature, was largely replaced by the sour hostility of the hegemonic class to all three, a continuation of the "civilizing offensive" of the prerevolutionary elites, the moralizing and disciplining attitude to the culture populaire of Old Regime church and state. The cultural effects were subtle and far-reaching. It is probably due to this resumption of the civilizing offensive, which imposed a stricter disciplining of bourgeois radicals as well as popular emotional expression, that what Spitzer refers to as "the deep, tender, and romantic friendships between young males" of the first half of the century, characterized by "a rhetoric . . . that would in our day be confined to lovers," had by 1900 largely disappeared.[5]

The vicissitudes of popular culture and of the social romanticism that celebrated it before 1850 are comprehensible in political terms. These terms were established by a third, more recent aspect of the nineteenth-century's heritage: the Revolution of 1789. The Revolution haunted the consciousness of nineteenth-century France in ways that are today scarcely imaginable. It posed problems that would take a hundred years and more to resolve. From the French students of 1820, protesting a reactionary electoral law, to Zola's lonely crusade for truth and justice in the Dreyfus Affair, hardly a single important political event does not echo the ideals or models of the Revolution. It is difficult to find a major novelist who did not express the national trauma, either directly or through one of its many echoes, in his work. The heroes of both of Stendhal's best novels, *Le Rouge et le noir* and *La Chartreuse de Parme,* show the grip of the revolutionary and Napoleonic legends on the French imagination. Balzac—"Napoleon of the pen"—writes extensively on their consequences in *La Comédie humaine.* Hugo's *Les Misérables* takes us through one of the Revolution's lesser known replays, the abortive rising of 1832. A third of Flaubert's *Education sentimentale* concerns the Revolution of 1848. Zola's *Rougon-Macquart* begins with rebellious peasant and artisan masses in Provence reenacting the *levée en masse* of 1792 against Louis-Napoléon's coup d'état while singing the "Marseillaise."

The Generation of 1820

No novel has been written on the student riots of June 1820, but they were the beginning of the revived revolutionary consciousness of many of those born around 1800, including the subject of this book. For five years Louis XVIII had governed according to the liberal charter of 1814: a parliament based on a severely limited suffrage constituted a middle way between the vengeful demands of ultraroyalists and the revolutionary impulses of a populace whose loyalty to the defeated emperor had been demonstrated in the Hundred Days. Moderate constitutional monarchists ran the government, the liberal Pierre-Paul Royer-Collard presided over the education system, and Victor Cousin, the liberal philosopher of "eclecticism," dominated the Ecole normale. In February 1820, a saddler, a secret worshiper of the exiled Napoléon, assassinated Louis's nephew and successor, Charles-Ferdinand, duc de Berry. Because Saint-Simon had just published a brochure that questioned the utility of the aristocracy, paranoid ultras immediately identified a conspiracy and demanded countermeasures. The assassination inaugurated the reactionary decade of the 1820s: among other measures to curb the increasing weight of the liberals in the electorate, the government pushed through an electoral law that increased the representation of the wealthiest voters. Extensive protest demonstrations and riots by student idealists failed to move either the artisan masses of the faubourgs or the regime, but they strengthened the government's resolve to eliminate liberal influence in the university; besides giving the educated young men of Michelet's generation their first reminder of what 1789 had been about, they also laid the basis for four of the five major oppositional currents of the decade to come.

The first current was the revolutionary conspiracy, which blossomed after the abject failure of the student demonstrations in June. An abortive attempt in August 1820 to raise the garrison at Vincennes was followed in 1821 by a more serious and sustained effort. A dozen or so student militants and young professionals secured the aid of Cousin, then age twenty-eight, and idealistic scholars from his circle; with older republicans, they formed the Carbonari, a tightly organized conspiracy whose idea was imported from Italy and which did its best to subvert the army until effectively repressed in 1823. The ranks of the Carbonari included three of the most prominent Republican leaders of the July Monarchy, Eugène and Godefroy Cavaignàc and François-Vincent Raspail, the future Saint-Simonians Saint-Amand Bazard and Philippe Buchez, the author of the pamphlet against the gerontocracy, James Fazy, and, from Cousin's circle, the future liberal luminaries Paul Dubois, Theodore Jouffroy, and Augustin Thierry (briefly Saint-Simon's secretary).

After the collapse of the Carbonari, several of its conspirators, led by Bazard and Buchez, formed the Saint-Simonian sect, the second important oppositional current in the 1820s. Cousin, who saw the Ecole normale closed and the university purged by zealous ultra politicians soon after the student riots, continued to be the center of a third, academic oppositional wing, though the most his liberal acolytes could hope for in the mid-twenties was the kind of lycée professor's post enjoyed by Michelet and his friend Hector Poret. (Michelet, vaguely liberal but usually apolitical in his youth, gravitated into Cousin's circle in 1824.) The fourth voice for the opposition, also led by two ex-Carbonari, was the vigorous and open liberal daily *Le Globe*; Paul Dubois and Pierre Leroux founded it in 1824, the year after the failure of the Carbonari taught them the hopelessness of conspiratorial politics.

All these fragments of the original oppositional movement that had been crushed in its revolutionary phase shifted the labor of subversion from politics to intellectual critique. Spitzer has shown how, in spite of internal rivalries and ideological differences, all shared a need to surpass the materialism and sensualism that was the last echo, under the Empire, of Enlightenment philosophy, to reconstruct the theoretical basis of political opposition and to establish the moral foundation of a new society. The Saint-Simonians may have been more dogmatic and authoritarian than the others, both in their ideas and in their organization—the *Globe* group, originally close to Cousin, doubted his eclecticism and wanted to air all new ideas—nonetheless, in Spitzer's view, the common goal outweighed the differences.

The fifth group of oppositionists in Michelet's generation was not at all in opposition during the Carbonari period but ultimately became the most important: the romantic literary movement led by the young Victor Hugo. Pillars of Catholic royalism at the beginning of the 1820s, the group around Hugo discovered that their impeccable credentials gave them little artistic freedom. Most early romantics rejected the Revolution, along with the Enlightenment and classicism, as based on principles of rationality and irreligion that impeded the necessary reconstruction of an organic Christian society. They failed to realize how deeply embedded in the classical literary tradition their aristocratic friends were and how fearfully those friends identified imagination with rebellion, innovation in aesthetics with social subversion. The romantics' desire to revive a preclassical Gothic style in literature, to break through the desiccated verse models of Corneille and Racine, and to look to Shakespeare and Byron for inspiration, irritated their patrons; this irritation in turn divided the romantics, led them to abandon their review, *La Muse française,* and soon provoked Hugo and some of his mates to question their royalist premises. Hugo himself underwent a personal conversion in the mid-1820s from the model of his royalist mother to that of his father, the ex-general of Napoléon, and as the field marshal of the new movement was then sought out and coddled by the critics of *Le Globe,* always on the lookout for new allies against Bourbon despotism. The result was Hugo's rebirth as a liberal and *Le Globe's* romance with romanticism, a rapprochement consecrated in the *grand cénacle* of 1828, where *Le Globe's* Charles-Auguste Sainte-Beuve and Prosper Mérimée were to be found with Hugo, Vigny, Nodier, and Dumas.

The overlap between the mutually hostile groups of the youthful opposition is most evident in Leroux's career. Leroux had his ties to the group around Cousin through his Cousinian co-founder of *Le Globe,* Paul Dubois. Having befriended the romantics, *Le Globe*—and Leroux—became Saint-Simonian in 1831. A decade later, now an ex-Saint-Simonian, Leroux founded, with George Sand, the *Revue indépendante,* the most important exponent of that merger of romanticism, republicanism, and humanitarian socialism we call social romanticism.

The phenomenon of social romanticism in the 1840s is striking evidence for Spitzer's argument: the "shared assumptions" of the antagonistic oppositional currents of the 1820s.[6] The liberalism of those years, emphasizing individual freedom against social and material determinism, clearly opposed Saint-Simonian dogmatism and hierarchy, as well as romantic excess and irrationalism. Yet the romantics also valued individual freedom, and the Saint-Simonians had early identified a problem of the nineteenth century that many liberals recognized but could not respond to: the need to integrate the impoverished urban workers into a new social order.

The coming of the Orleanist regime presented excellent opportunities for the co-optation of all the oppositional groups of the twenties. A number of romantics and liberals had been on the Orleanist payroll before the July Revolution, and the new government was quickly staffed by former liberal oppositionists: Cousin, Adolphe Thiers, and François Guizot. The question confronting all the idealists of the Restoration Left was whether and where career building under the new dispensation entailed the surrender of principles they had cherished while in opposition. Some romantics exchanged their innovative genius for the dependable and lucrative writing of popular drama and feuilletons. Some liberals joined the government or became editors of establishment dailies. Some Saint-Simonians became capitalists. And some intellectuals reentered the universities and maneuvered for election to the Collège de France.[7] Whether the intellectuals were inside or outside the Orleanist establishment, fundamental political and social problems, first posed during the Revolution of 1789 to 1794, remained unresolved: the exclusion of the vast majority of Frenchmen from political participation, and the social alienation and economic exploitation of the urban workers. In the first four years of the July Monarchy, dedicated republicans fomented insurrections against the undemocratic monarchy, and underfed artisans struck and rioted to protest social injustice. But the two groups had little in common—the artisans were apolitical when they were not Bonapartist—and the new regime handily suppressed their separate revolts. Within the government, a "party of movement" favored concessions to the movements from below but quickly lost out to a conservative "party of resistance." The late 1830s were a period of stalemate; the revolutionary energies of the first years of the monarchy were exhausted, but neither a new radicalism nor a reinvigorated Right took their place. The conservative Juste-Milieu reigned uncontested in these years.

Nonetheless, an economic depression in 1837, producing unemployment and wage reductions, set the stage for a new and more profound wave of dissatisfaction in the 1840s. In 1840 itself, strikes and street demonstrations revealed the renewed militancy of the artisan strata, and a foreign policy debacle in the Middle East shook the regime's prestige. A sudden flood of books and periodicals posed the social question: Pierre Joseph Proudhon's *Qu'est-ce que la propriété?*, Louis Blanc's *Organisation du travail,* Etienne Cabet's *Voyage en Icarie,* and Leroux's *De l'humanité* were echoed by the first literary expression of social romanticism, Sand's *Le Compagnon du tour de France.*[8] All appeared in 1840. The first major workers' paper, *La Ruche populaire,* founded by Saint-Simonian artisans, began in December 1839 and was followed in 1841 by Cabet's *Le Populaire,* by the Christian Socialist Buchez's *L'Atelier,* and by the dissident Cabetist *La Fraternité.* And Sand and Leroux launched *La Revue indépendante* in 1841.

These reverberations of popular dissatisfaction and intellectual critique, in which republican, Jacobin, and Christian socialist motifs merged, together with the suddenly revealed fragility of the narrowly based regime, formed the background for the loose intellectual coalition of social romanticism. In it, the most committed elements of the generation of young Restoration liberals, Saint-

Simonians, and romantics found themselves again and made the decisive transition to humanitarian socialism. Social romanticism formed the setting for Michelet's turn to the Left, for his adoption of new values concerning nature, the common people, women, and history in the years after his encounter with Madame Dumesnil. To illuminate Michelet's mid-life metamorphosis, a closer look at this setting, at its social presuppositions and its implicit psychology, is warranted.

Saint-Simonians and other radicals had since 1830 been preaching the harmonious reconciliation of the common people and the upper classes. In doing so, they reinforced a crucial aspect of French romanticism which, in the dramas and novels of Hugo, Alexandre Dumas, Sand, and Eugène Sue, had similarly striven to merge elements of popular culture, such as melodrama, with cultural forms of the elite to create a new art and a new audience. Although, as Paul Bénichou has shown, radicals and romantics were often at loggerheads over the artists' insistence on their freedom, the social romanticism of the 1840s allied the most dedicated and the least dogmatic elements of both groups.[9]

The similar goals of the two main components of social romanticism reflected a corresponding historical point of departure: the sporadic alliance between popular classes and the middle layers of the bourgeoisie that had characterized the euphoric beginnings of the Revolutions of 1789 and 1830 and reappear in February 1848 and 1869.[10] The material base of this alliance was its weak point: the class interest of the preindustrial artisan and shopkeeper strata of Paris was opposed to that of the bourgeois of the professional and economic elite. The alliance could produce revolutions when these classes joined forces because they felt threatened by aristocratic reaction or royal arbitrariness, but it was mined with contradictions that exploded into civil war once revolution had ended the threat. For the preindustrial strata were impelled by a reactionary utopia—the return to a premodern system of corporate protection—whereas the bourgeois elites anticipated complete economic freedom.[11] To the small independent producers and their artisan assistants, the unfettered economy advocated by the bourgeois elite was bound to wipe them out or subjugate them to the new "feudal" yoke of high finance. Moreover, the political solution traditionally supported by the bourgeois elites—constitutional monarchy based on restricted suffrage—deprived them of political as well as economic prospects.

As a result, every time a revolution eliminated the oppressive Old Regime, the new regime was savagely attacked by the group excluded from power. This dialectic of exclusion and attack had occurred repeatedly between 1789 and 1794. In 1830, no popular solution was permitted. After the celebrated unity of the July Days shook off a reactionary Bourbon regime that threatened both groups, the bourgeois elite of landowners and bankers immediately established its constitutional monarchy, with a somewhat broader electorate, under Guizot's motto of "enrichissez-vous" and the guidance of liberal economic principles. The result, as noted, was several years of intermittent rioting and attempts at insurrection in Paris by radical artisans and republicans, ending, by 1835, in repression and quiescence.[12] But meanwhile the principles of laissez-faire, the obvious egotism of the bourgeois solution, and the disinterest in traditional religion of the urban masses led to the attempts of sectarian radicals and romantics to create quasi-theological, redemptive models of harmony for society and the arts. Again, the social-historical point of departure was that intermittent alliance of bourgeois and people that had created those rare but unforgettable moments of national euphoria, the revolutionary epiphanies of 1789 and 1830. But the new movements of the 1830s added a religious element that was rooted not only in the prevailing intellectual and aesthetic reactions to the age of reason and the spirit of liberalism but in a depth-psychological reaction as well.

The Saint-Simonian sect, whose idealism attracted Michelet almost as much as its authoritarianism repelled him, was the largest such movement; in the early 1830s, it combined social ideas and insights into psychological needs that, but for their dogmatic form, were strikingly similar to those in Michelet's *Le Peuple* (1846). Indeed, it was probably no accident that the social romanticism of the 1840s was fueled by that dissident Saint-Simonian Pierre Leroux, since many Saint-Simonian ideals and values reappeared, minus their sectarian trappings, in social romanticism. As the sect's leaders saw it around 1830, harmony between the productive classes of the new France was to replace the cold isolation, the exclusively critical and abstract spirit liberalism engendered in the nineteenth century. A secular religion of humanity, in which artists would take the place of priests, would replace Christianity. Transmitting these ideas to ever wider circles were the many young followers of the movement's spiritual leaders: these leaders regularly lectured their disciples in Parisian meeting halls.

Like other sectarian movements and ideologies of the July Monarchy, the Saint-Simonian organization consciously combined the gender of symbols of the celebrated family life of the July Monarchy with traditional religious forms. The group's leaders were all "fathers" (*pères*), and by a masterpiece of providential design, the père who took over the movement after a schism in 1831 bore the surname Enfantin. Apart from the fact that the followers of père

Enfantin were organized in a "family," the association followed a number of sectarian ideologies in striving to rehabilitate women as equal partners of men, and it searched for a supreme *mère,* a female pope (*papesse*) for the movement.[13]

The feminism of the Saint-Simonians and of their social-romantic successors, as well as the attempt of both to build a harmonious society on the model of family relations, reflected specific social tensions and the psychological adaptation to them of a specific generation. The social stresses were those of an urban population that, because of a successful revolution, saw itself denied the protection of traditional social networks and the psychological comforts of traditional belief in monarchy and Christianity. Stated broadly and simply: those traditional networks and beliefs had muted the shocks to physical existence and self-esteem caused by social injustice and physical misery. Instead of eliminating injustice and misery, the Revolution had simply changed their character while destroying the traditional protections that softened their impact. The only improvement to emerge from a quarter-century of revolution and empire was the awareness that human action could change the future, and many under the new dispensation would understandably use the greater margin of mental freedom it permitted to fantasize new protections—new kinds of communal sociability and new belief systems. Many aspects of these protections were predictable. The new social utopias frequently combined the preindustrial "greengrocers' paradise" of artisans and shopkeepers with a yearning for the harmony between bourgeois and peuple that had emerged early in the revolutions of 1789 and 1830. They also contained a modernized form of Christian belief, in which natural progress took the place of divine providence and suffering humanity that of the crucified Christ.[14]

In keeping with this secularization of religious conviction and with the generational psychology of those born during the Napoleonic era—the generation of Michelet, Hugo, Hector Berlioz, Dumas, Sand, and most other romantic writers and artists—were the keynotes of the new social gospel: the rehabilitation of the mother, and human brotherhood. Many in this generation grew up seeing a discrepancy between the Napoleonic public ideology of martial valor, which made of every military hero a father figure for the children, and the domestic enfeeblement of immediate paternal authority. Although many fathers were exempt from military service, those who stayed home could hardly be viewed as heroes in a land where children were being taught to adore uniforms. In a sense, the only good fathers were the absent, and the best were the martyred dead. Which left the mothers. And their status was even greater than it would normally have been in fatherless families, since the Revolution and the multiple waves of political terror had broken through the traditional networks of kin and social relations that had, under the Old Regime, afforded so many potential substitute parents for young children.[15]

The feminism and familialism of Saint-Simonians and of other ideologists of social redemption between 1830 and 1848 was, then, in part a response to this altered family equilibrium, in part an answer to the liberal individualism rampant after the July Revolution, and in part an extension of the ideal of social harmony engendered by the ephemeral, if indispensable and dramatic, class alliances of the revolutionary epoch: a celebration of the harmony of men and women and, more broadly, of humanity and nature.

CHAPTER 2

THE YOUNG MICHELET: LIBERALISM VERSUS ROMANTICISM

Michelet found Saint-Simonian doctrine repellent in 1830, both for its dogmatic embrace of the principles of harmony and for its glorification of women and motherhood. His initial vision of history, expressed in the "Introduction à l'histoire universelle" of 1831, exalted human freedom as the immortal antagonist of a suffocating "mother" nature. In the next decade, he gradually modified these views, but it was only after 1840, impelled both by his personal development and by the emergence of social romanticism as a nondogmatic successor to the Saint-Simonian dispensation, that he clearly reversed course.

The social-philosophical assumptions of the young Michelet were thus born amid the ideological infighting among liberals under the Restoration and can be understood only in this context. Though the July Revolution gave wings to Michelet's view that the free spirit was in eternal conflict with the material "fatality" in which human history was embedded—geography, climate, and race—he had expressed the basic idea three weeks before the uprising that ended the Restoration. Condemning the Saint-Simonian attempt to replace Christianity by what he viewed as "pantheism," he said:

> Everywhere that the hand of pantheism appears, it freezes the moral faculty. Some have said that life tends to reconcile soul and body, spirit and matter, and this reconciliation, this peace between spirit and matter, is the work which pantheism attempts to accomplish. I do not think that man can ever make a treaty of eternal peace with the body. The body is always the enemy of human liberty. The most ingenious means used by sensual nature to deceive us, is to say that it is at peace

with the soul. There is no need for it to exist, this peace; there is a need for the soul to struggle until the body is its slave. One inebriates the monster and says to oneself: Peace with the body! No, what is necessary is that the latter should be vanquished, not sated.[1]

As Paul Bénichou has demonstrated, the liberalism of 1830 was a highly unstable mixture based on deist and "scientific" principles.[2] It could accept neither the Christian orthodoxy of the restored church and state nor the purely materialistic determinism and utilitarianism of the radical Enlightenment. Like Michelet, who inherited much of his intellectual baggage from liberalism, it espoused a moral imperative to transcend the deterministic realm of nature by free will.

In "Introduction à l'histoire universelle," Michelet mixed this transcendent liberal voluntarism with a modest dose of nationalism, explicitly inspired by the Revolution of 1830. The chances of the free spirit to gain the upper hand over material destiny, to liberate itself from natural necessity, appeared to be directly proportional to this spirit's proximity to Paris; in India, submerged in warm, fecund nature, its chances were nil; in England and Germany they were better, but nowhere were they as good as on the plains of north-central France. Although Michelet wrote under the influence of the Revolution of 1830, France entered his scheme largely as a metaphysical abstraction. His emphasis was clearly on individual liberty as the highest good. With his individualism and his unremitting work ethic, the young scholar despised sensual gratification and was hostile toward womankind as the shackle of freedom and heroism. This hostility manifested itself in metaphorical references to motherhood, identified with the tyranny of all-powerful Nature in the Orient: because in India, the source of human civilization, mankind was "bent, prostrated under the omnipotence of nature," Michelet called it "the womb of the world." Continuing the metaphor, he described the human race in India as "a poor child at the breast of its mother, a weak and dependent creature, spoiled and beaten in turn, less nourished than intoxicated by a milk too strong for it." Later in the "Introduction" he wrote of the painful rupture needed in later civilizations "from the fatal destiny on whose bosom it [mankind] was so long suspended. . . . Nonetheless, it must occur, the child must leave its mother must walk forward by itself. . . . This last step, far from the fatal order of nature . . . takes it towards the social God."[3]

The equations and antitheses are clear: nature equals mother equals bondage. Only by breaking with maternal nature could men find freedom and "the social God," which was a mythical way of referring to human fraternity. Fifteen years later, in *Le Peuple,* Michelet continued to equate nature and motherhood, but the rest was different. Here he saw the social God, the source of fraternity, precisely in the original tie to the mother and to nature. At birth, the child "leaves a society already quite old." The quest for the social was a search for "a shadow of the precious union he had and lost."[4]

Accordingly, the values that Michelet associated in *Le Peuple* with humankind's historical origins in India, with nature, and with motherhood differed greatly from what they had earlier been. Instead of seeing them as the enemies of the free spirit, Michelet associated all three with "universal fraternity." Love for society, he said, was evident at birth and came from the fetus's nine-month union with the mother. If, in 1831, the social God could be attained only by fleeing the suffocating maternal paradise—of both man's phylogenetic origins in India and its ontogenetic beginnings in the mother's womb—in 1846, Michelet saw society, universal fraternity, as inherent in both the historical and the individual beginnings of man. The "precious union that he had and lost"—union with the mother—had become for him both the source and the goal of the social impulse.[5] Clearly, Michelet's attitude toward women and the relationship he postulated among women, freedom, and human fraternity were crucial for his changing historical vision: for his close ties to liberalism in 1831 and to romanticism in 1846.

Michelet wrote an autobiography about his childhood and adolescence when he was in his early twenties.[6] Though in it he referred more often to his father, friends, and school experiences than to his mother, a few disconnected remarks about his mother and other women who took her place stand out. Michelet went to school only when he was twelve. Until then, he writes of himself: "Too clumsy to play with the other children, who would have made fun of me, and forced to lead a sedentary life with mama, I read, I learned poorly, but I learned alone."[7] The material difficulties of Michelet's father in the Napoleonic era, perhaps combined with political adversities, made life very uncertain for the young Michelet: his family moved to ten locations in Paris in his first twenty years, sometimes to escape creditors. Michelet's father, Furcy, was a printer who, at the start of his career in 1796, seems to have printed leaflets for a Jacobin rising against the Directory. Under Napoléon, his press was sporadically closed because of a regulation that limited the number of printers in the capital. He appears to have been naive, unable to resist apparently generous offers that turned out to be swindles, and the family's position deteriorated.

Before school at age twelve, then, the future historian could never strike roots deep enough to make friends and was restricted to the emotional resources of his parents and extended family network. In the face of Michelet's father's problems, his mother gives the impression of being strong, picking up the pieces and often resenting it. Michelet writes of his family's situation after a move at age ten: "What aggravated our position at that time was the irritable character of mama, exasperated by so many sorrows and privations, and who attributed everything to papa's negligence. As to him, he listened with a goodness and patience worthy of Epictetus. I should have kept silent; my impetuous character led me to side now with the one, now with the other and I aggravated the dispute. It is certain that my poor mother found in me little consolation."[8]

It is not too surprising that Michelet reports a juvenile enthusiasm for the "satire against women" of the seventeenth-century poet Nicolas Boileau. We get a clear impression from these remarks that Madame Michelet was a dominant woman, perhaps as much a mother to her husband as to her son, and this impression is strengthened when we discover that, apart from being apparently more practical than her husband, she was nine years older than he.

After his mother died in 1815 Michelet continued to have relationships with this kind of woman. In that year, he became more or less an adoptive son to a Madame Fourcy, the housekeeper in a doctor's home where Michelet's father worked as a concierge and errand runner. Under the influence of Madame Fourcy Michelet had himself baptized as a Catholic—something his Jacobin father had neglected in 1798—and, when he heard about her daughter's suicide after an unhappy love affair, he cut short a budding relationship with a fifteen-year-old girl.[9] When he began his career in teaching, he developed a relationship with an assistant to Madame Fourcy, Pauline Rousseau, and married her in 1824, shortly after the older woman had died. Like Michelet's mother, Pauline was much older than her spouse (six years), and Michelet admitted later that he desired her in spite of the age difference because she resembled his mother. In fact, his explanation to his aunts of his coming marriage was a model of his mother's hard-headed practicality. Economic benefits, not emotional or intellectual affinities, were the sole justifications he advanced for his union with Pauline:

> She is neither young nor beautiful, and you will nonetheless see that for a man who only seeks something solid, it's a suitable match. Mlle Rousseau, besides her establishment, has ... private means.... [Six sentences on the income of her mother and aunts and how they might set up a lucrative nursing home for foreigners.] Mademoiselle Rousseau is 28 years old (I am 26). [In fact, she was 31 and he 25 at the time of

writing.] She is no longer in the age of pleasures and expenses. She is not what is called a "Parisienne." She is an excellent housekeeper; she is very capable of supervising and directing a considerable household since if necessary she can do everything herself. She is more economical than I, and that's saying a lot. Finally, what seems to be very important in the choice of a wife, her health is unfailing. For five years I have had occasion to observe all this. Now you ask me why I am in such a hurry to marry. First, the desire to live more economically. . . . The mending of clothes, the cleaning of them, etc.: married, I have nothing at all to pay. . . . I will spend less and besides I will earn more. Several times I could have taken as boarders young and wealthy foreigners who came to study in France, on desirable conditions. There was but one obstacle, I was neither married nor a priest. These two statuses alone present a sufficient guarantee of moral probity and I feel no vocation for the latter. One must also be a priest or a married man to occupy certain university positions that require a certain stability and paternal character, such as prefect, headmaster of a lycée, etc. For all positions in the university or elsewhere, if there are several competitors, one prefers the married man.[10]

Michelet neglected, understandably, to inform his aunts that the decisive reason for marrying Mademoiselle Rousseau at that moment was to legitimize the child she bore him a few months later. And we might assume that in stressing exclusively the material advantages of marriage, he was using the only language he thought his rural aunts could understand. Nonetheless, even his admiring biographer, Paul Viallaneix, concedes that such language betrays "a certain sympathy" for their outlook; that his impoverished childhood left him with a hard-headed desire to avoid future privations wherever possible; that he was, in short, "the worthy nephew of his parsimonious aunts."[11]

Michelet's ascetic practicality and evident hostility to "maternal" nature indicate his essentially puritanical character and thus give a broader dimension to his articulation of the heroic struggle against "fatality" in his "Introduction." Puritanism is associated in the history of culture with two apparently divergent phenomena: the heroic age of English Protestantism—the seventeenth-century resistance to Absolutism and Catholicism—and personal asceticism, which psychoanalysis views in terms of anal eroticism.[12] One can join these points by seeing the heroic character as built overtly on asceticism and unconsciously on the predominance of anal traits.

Puritan anality and puritan heroism are undoubtedly closely

linked, but neither could be expected to coexist happily with "the womb of the world" or any other symbol of motherhood. Yet we have seen enough signs of Michelet's discomfiture with the dominance of his mother to suspect that identifying this petty-bourgeois puritanism with her gave him additional unconscious motives for fearing both motherhood and nature.

Michelet's intellectual gifts, combined with the lonely puritanism of his years at the Lycée Charlemagne, led him to concentrate single-mindedly on his studies and afterward to rise rapidly through the educational establishment. The ambition evident in the letter to his aunts was not wasted. At the lycée, he had been the star pupil of Abel François Villemain (1790–1867), later minister of education under Louis-Philippe. Later, he attracted the attention and support of a number of slightly older liberal scholar-politicians: Victor Cousin, Adolphe Thiers, and François Guizot.[13] Upward mobility and continued vertical dependencies on mother and father substitutes contributed to Michelet's growing identification with *la patrie* as the source of the transcendent free spirit: it was, after all, the emergent, postrevolutionary French nation that offered young men from the popular classes the chance of social ascent. A second pattern of relationships in Michelet's adolescence, however, to his peers, was initially perhaps of little importance, but when catalyzed by the personal evolution and the historical currents that bore his career along in the early 1840s, it made possible the fundamental shift toward romantic values evident in *Le Peuple.*

Michelet is very clear about this second pattern. He mentions in the *Mémorial* the close ties of his early and late adolescence with his friends Paul Poinsot and Hector Poret, as well as friendships with youths in the tutoring pensions he attended in the years before the Lycée Charlemagne. With the peer group, however, just as with his mother, he felt a profound ambivalence. Before he attended the tutoring groups, he was alone with "mama." After them, he entered the Lycée Charlemagne, where because of his impoverished background and timidity he was the butt of his schoolmates' cruel jokes.[14] The lycée boys refused to accept him; his maternal ego ideal was dominant but threatening, since it allowed him no adult male identity; his paternal ego ideal was a weak model. Michelet's solution was to immerse himself in his studies, in the world of culture—in other words, to trade off the problematic paternal ego ideal for the powerful cultural ego ideal of the educational establishment while mixing with it the puritan inheritance from his mother.

This caused certain problems, disjunctions in Michelet's personality between what his upbringing gave him as potential sources of ego strength and what he was striving after. For, given the cultural ego ideal he was accepting at the beginning of his career, around 1820, little integration was possible either with the model of his father or with the ideals of friendship embodied in his relations with Poinsot and Poret. The political and ideological mainstream of the times worked against such a synthesis.

This was clearly so under the authoritarian empire that lasted until Michelet's sixteenth year and under which his father, partly because of Jacobin convictions, was repeatedly pushed out of his trade and spent nearly a year in jail for debt. In fact, the *Mémorial* hints strongly that Michelet identified his father's persecution under the press laws of the Empire with his own persecution by his schoolmates.[15] That his identification with his father was largely negative—identification as a victim—made it especially difficult to connect the paternal model to the cultural ego ideal implanted by his intellectual models, and the political temper of the Restoration made such an integration yet more unlikely.

The lack of a strong paternal model undermines any obvious application of the theory of Oedipal conflict to Michelet's evolution. At a personal level, the basis for such conflict with his biological father seems to have been missing. Nonetheless, the social conflicts of the nineteenth century did offer a stage for the impersonal and ideological expression of such rebelliousness, for example, in those conflicts of liberals against aristocratic reaction that culminated in France in the Revolution of 1830 (sometimes depicted as an uprising of "youth" against "gerontocracy"). It is arguable, then, that in Michelet's case—and in that of many other young men—where personal conditions for becoming conscious of and expressing Oedipal resentment were dormant, social ones were abundantly present and took their place. At this level, we can trace a certain reflection of Oedipal conflict in Michelet's early work. It is probably one of the mainsprings for his celebration of the struggle of "liberty" against "fatality." Fatality, however, signified not merely the fossilized Old Regime, which the revolutionaries of 1830 had to vanquish, but in a larger sense the realms of nature, in which such biological or physical determinants as climate, race, and geography were viewed as offering even more serious obstacles to the free spirit than "gerontocratic" reaction. In general, Michelet's anxious projections onto the natural world reflected his disquiet about his own biological determinants, from which, he subsequently indicated, he wanted very much to escape (see chapter 14, below). His identification of a maternally defined nature as a suffocating, wicked mother betrayed a profound ambivalence about his "mama." Although Michelet had assimilated her ascetic ethos to the cultural ego ideal of the liberal educational establishment, he feared and mistrusted her more typically "maternal" qualities as dominating, destructive to the élan of his young ego.

This leads us to the realization that, judging by the ideological precipitation of his "Oedipal" impulses in the "Introduction" of 1831, Michelet feared and rebelled against "maternal" restraints on his liberty at least as much as "paternal" ones; that if the paternal sources of anxiety were present primarily at the level of social and political experience, the maternal wellsprings of anxiety and hostility went far back into his childhood.

At one level, in fact, his paternal inheritance, mixed with his peer-friendships, armed the young scholar for battle against the entropic manifestations of "fatality." For the heritage of the French Revolution remained as a seed beneath the snow of the restored Bourbon monarchy. Michelet's early career, though overtly apolitical, shows repeatedly the confluence of his intellectual development with the politics of Restoration scholarship; both currents were mediated through his most intimate friendships. We see this confluence in the way Michelet's evolution during the 1820s was shaped by the turmoil that terminated the liberal phase of the Restoration in 1820: a consequence of the duc de Berry's assassination. In the course of the demonstrations protesting the government's proposed restriction of the already very limited suffrage, a student was killed. Riots ensued, and the young Michelet, though he clearly feared the intervention of "le peuple" in the political process, hoped ardently for a revolution of young idealists: "What glory for the youth of France if, alone, it could make this sublime revolution." In a letter to Poinsot dated "5 juin, 3e jour de la révolution,"[16] he wrote that his "papa" had left for the action, that he was being locked in by "ces dames" (presumably Madame Fourcy and Pauline), and that he very much wanted to learn to use a rifle.

The riots seem to have triggered his nascent historical consciousness, leading him to relate his personal history to the history of his age: On June 4, the day after the rioting began, Michelet started his autobiographic *Mémorial,* intended for Paul Poinsot. Significantly, among the reasons the twenty-two-year-old gave for writing this account of his as yet brief existence was the desire "to improve the future by the past," which we cannot help but view as his personal contribution to the hoped-for "sublime revolution." As was frequently to be the case in Michelet's life, the personal and the political claims he felt were mutually reinforcing.[17]

So were the personal and the scholarly aspects of his life. Alongside Poinsot, who died of consumption in 1821, Michelet had another friend, Hector Poret. Unlike Poinsot, Poret was philosophically inclined. A classmate in the Lycée Charlemagne, he helped the twenty-four-year-old Michelet into a chair in history at the Lycée Sainte-Barbe and two years later (1824) introduced Michelet to Victor Cousin.[18]

Cousin, only six years older than Michelet, already occupied a central place among the liberal scholars of the Restoration. As the inspired transmitter to his students of Hegel and the German idealist philosophers, he was viewed as having rescued French philosophy from the radical sensualism of Condillac and the *idéologues.* Yet, as the substitute for the liberal Royer-Collard in the Sorbonne and as the leading light of the Ecole normale, founded under Napoléon, he was hated by Catholic and legitimist ultras and was one of the first to be purged after the duc de Berry's assassination: In 1820, the government refused to continue him in the Sorbonne as Royer-Collard's substitute, and in 1822, Monseigneur Frayssinous closed the Ecole normale when he became head of the university system. Cousin's election to the Collège de France at about this time was nullified by the government.[19]

Nonetheless, for less conspicuous young men like Poret and Michelet, employment as lycée teachers remained possible; indeed, the Lycée Sainte-Barbe, where the not very outspoken Michelet was assigned to teach, was a bulwark of Restoration royalism. In spite of this sign of favor by the ultras, Poret's friend could become part of the blacklisted Cousin's circle in April 1824. Michelet had already discovered the work of the remarkable Neapolitan philosopher Giambiattista Vico (1668–1744), and his brief contact with Cousin in the spring and summer of 1824 was decisive in the execution of his first major scholarly work, his translation of, and introduction to, Vico's *Scienza nuova.* It was fortunate that Michelet did not delay his first visit to Cousin. A few months later, in September, Cousin journeyed to Germany, and the police of Charles X, fearing that Cousin intended to make contact between French and German revolutionaries, had the Prussian government arrest and imprison him. He remained incarcerated in Berlin until February 1825, when the protests of Hegel and others procured his release, and it was May before he could return to France.

Back in Paris, Cousin introduced Michelet, now twenty-six and working on Vico, to an even younger disciple, Edgar Quinet, who had taken it on himself to translate and present the work of the eighteenth-century German philosopher of history Johann Gottfried von Herder. Cousin's stimulus encouraged the younger men to integrate into the liberal heritage of the French Enlightenment philosophies of history that were later of great value, through their amalgams of liberal nationalism and romanticism, in preparing the way for the Revolution of 1848. Vico, through his emphasis on man as the maker of his own history, helped to bury lingering Christian notions that history was the working out of an immutable providential design. The obscure Neapolitan powerfully stimulated Michelet's liberal voluntarism after the Revolution of 1830—his view of world history in 1831 as the eternal combat of liberty and fatality. Later in the 1830s Vico's notion of historical evolution as a cycle that began in a stage of primitive aristocracy and mythic poetry primed Michelet's receptivity to folk culture in his *Origins of Law*; in the following decade, this notion was decisive in shaping Michelet's views on traditional popular culture in *Le Peuple*.[20]

Michelet fully absorbed Vico's message only over a twenty-year period. For some time after his work on Vico he retained the ascetic hostility to nature of militant liberalism. Nonetheless, as the Revolution of 1830 made clear, even the liberalism of the age was revolutionary under the Restoration. The ideal of human liberty that Michelet associated with the French Revolution (and indirectly with his father) was from 1830 on restored to the national value structure; the terms of the "Introduction à l'histoire universelle" make this unmistakable.

Michelet's ascendancy was continuous after his initial appointment as a lycée teacher. During a liberal interlude in the late 1820s, the teacher training school, the Ecole normale, reopened, and in January 1827, Michelet was appointed there to lecture on history and philosophy. Within a few years he became a rival of his mentor, Cousin, and his "Introduction" of 1831, a rejection of Cousin's Hegelian historical determinism, can be seen as his declaration of independence from his master.[21] In September 1828, he became tutor to Charles X's nine-year-old granddaughter, and Louis-Philippe, Charles's successor, appointed him as tutor to his daughter just two months after the Revolution of 1830 sent the last of the Bourbon monarchs into exile. Shortly after, Michelet foundered in an initial attempt to enter the Collège de France, the mecca of French intellectuals.[22] In 1831, however, the appearance of his "Introduction" and his *Histoire de la République romaine* brought him wide acclaim, especially among liberals and republicans. In 1833, he published the first two volumes of his *Histoire de France,* the beginning of a labor that stretched, with a ten-year hiatus between 1844 and 1854, over thirty-five years. In 1834, he became the substitute of François Guizot, Louis-Philippe's minister of education, at the Sorbonne.

Finally, in 1838, Michelet was elected to the Collège de France, whose public lectures were the summit of French intellectual life. There Michelet discovered the historical and political significance of the bonds of fraternity that had tied him to Poinsot and Poret and then to Quinet. This significance became incarnated for him not only in his militant alliance with his friends and colleagues Quinet and Adam Mickiewicz but also in the support he received from the mass of radical and romantic students who attended his courses. It was a totally different experience from being the object of his classmates' ridicule in the Lycée Charlemagne, which had created within Michelet a profound tension between peer-relations and the life of the mind. From the perspective of his own evolving career, Michelet thus tended around 1840 to join his intellectual values more in the horizontal peer dimension than in the vertical substitute-parent dimension he had adopted earlier. This is almost certainly one of the factors behind the stress on universal fraternity in *Le Peuple.*

Michelet's celebration of fraternity as the cornerstone of his new philosophy of history was much more than a reflection of his new career status; it was part of the sea-change in the elite mentalities of the 1830s and 1840s that I have discussed above. And this change in mentalities must in turn be comprehended in terms of its integration with Michelet's personality. During the July Monarchy, Michelet seems to have undergone a process we can describe only as a second adolescence, with a new identity as the result. The positive sides of Michelet's ambivalence, about his peers and about womanhood, were powerfully encouraged by both social ideologies and his career experiences. But the central experiences were internal.

Michelet seems to have felt a genuine sensation of rebirth as a result of the July Revolution, but around 1830 he still expressed it largely in terms of abstractions. As if echoing that revolution, the first parts of his *Histoire de France* underline the historical role of the French people in creating a centralized national monarchy. This first act of rebirth prepared Michelet for subsequent, more personal ones. In 1839, a year after he entered the Collège de France, his wife, Pauline, died, and the following year he began a relationship with Madame Françoise-Adèle Dumesnil, the mother of a student. An earthquake in Michelet's emotional existence accompanied the most profound love of his life. Because of this love, his feelings and values concerning nature and womanhood changed radically. With Madame Dumesnil, he was able to share his spiritual and intellectual affinities in a way that had been impossible with his mother and her two successors, Madame Fourcy and Pauline.

To Michelet's immense sorrow, Madame Dumesnil died in 1842, but the ideal of woman as a spiritual and intellectual companion and not simply as a dominant and dangerous force of nature, a satisfier of sensual needs, had come to Michelet for good. Notations in his journal about her trace a broad spectrum of changes in his views, not only about nature and womanhood but about religion, ethics, politics, and history as well.

PART II

THE RESONANCES OF MADAME DUMESNIL, 1831–1843

The completely abstract culture they gave us desiccated me for a long time. I needed many years to efface the sophist they had made of me. I only arrived at myself by letting go of this alien accessory. I only discovered myself by a negative path.

MICHELET
Le Peuple

CHAPTER 3

THE BACKGROUND OF AN AFFAIR: MICHELET AND FEMININE NATURE

Mentalities and Individual Experience

As I have suggested, various overlapping mentalities and ideologies coexisted in the character of the young Michelet. At the most elementary level, the petit-bourgeois mentality of his parents, especially his mother's, conveyed a stubborn, puritanical work ethic. The Lycée Charlemagne and the Sorbonne exposed him to the Restoration liberalism of Benjamin Constant and Victor Cousin, an ideological current compatible both with the ascetic individualism he inherited from his mother and with the sympathy for the French Revolution that his father shared with most other skilled workers. Reinforcing his asceticism was the Christianity of the Restoration, absorbed through the personal influence of Madame de Fourcy and the doctrinal impact of Felicité de Lamennais's *Essai sur l'indifférence.* Both his "Introduction" of 1831 and the early volumes of the *Histoire de France* contain handsome encomiums to Christianity's heroic cultural defense against the temptations of sensual nature. Thus, Michelet's early emphasis on individual freedom and his concomitant allergy to the natural world and the "suffocating" maternal grasp can be explained in this larger framework as well as in the personal one.

What, however, are we to make of Michelet's shift in the 1840s to a social-romantic view of the world, revering natural fecundity and maternity as the source of human brotherhood? To say that here too he is following a "mentality" begs the question of how he moves from one such mentality to another. Let us return, then, to Michelet's changing character and follow its evolution, respectfully, in its own terms, with due regard for the mentalities and ideologies of the period. We can hear the conceptual echoes of this evolution most clearly in his shifting evaluation of nature and motherhood.

Mothers and Stepmothers

The question of whether nature should be viewed as beneficent mother or wicked stepmother (*mère* or *marâtre*) recurred repeatedly in Michelet's writing between the appearance of his "Introduction" in 1831 and Madame Dumesnil's death in 1842. He clearly viewed nature early in this period as a hostile marâtre and at the end, after Pauline's death and under Madame Dumesnil's influence, as the good mother.

Particularly noteworthy in this evolution is that Michelet's view of Christianity, though becoming feminized, remained positive. His well-known anticlericalism did not emerge until 1843. Before then, he altered his earlier celebration of Christian values only to the extent that he perceived and honored an essentially matriarchal and naturalist core in the religion of Jesus. This evolution to a feminized concept of Christianity paralleled his gradual abandonment of the belief that conflict was eternal between the free spirit and the fatal destiny dictated by "stepmother" nature. Conditioned by the romantic social ideologies of the July Monarchy and impelled by personal experience, Michelet slowly retreated from the misogynist assumptions about motherhood implicit in the metaphors of his "Introduction." As late as 1834, however, he was restating the original antithesis in strikingly personal terms.

Thus in a summary chapter to book IV of the *Histoire de France,* which he wrote in 1833, he continued to postulate the opposition of nature and liberty, which had been the key theme of the "Introduction à l'histoire universelle": "This is the oriental Passion, the immolation of the soul to nature, the suicide of liberty. But liberty is vigorous, he does not want to die. He revolts against nature and first of all repulses her threats. He stands firm against the lions of Nemea and the hydras of Lerna. All the tests that the stepmother [*marâtre*] imposes on him, he accomplishes. He tames and pacifies the world."[1]

A summer vacation the following year in the forest of Fontainebleau led Michelet to a similar but more sexually and personally revealing view of nature: "There is a singular sensuality in solitude. It is a tête à tête with the all-lovable and all-fecund, but also dangerous, resistant, homicidal feminine ... incestuous mother who creates us and proposes our seduction, makes us enjoy her, caresses us, stupefies us and kills us: Nature. *O marâtre.* ... Must it be that

so many years wept in the desert have not yet purified this incestuous Circe? .... What! Is there then adultery and incest with
God?"[2]

Three years later the equation of nature with marâtre recurred
in Michelet's "Introduction" to his *Origines du droit français,* but,
perhaps through the influence of Jacob Grimm's romantic histori-
cism, the paranoid bite was gone. Nature was a marâtre only for
northern peoples, among whom the values of heroism and fraternity
dominated. India continued to be immersed in feminine nature, but
in Persia, the state dominated nature, and the Greeks simply disdained it as alien to the city.

An attenuated version of the nature-stepmother equation occurred to him once more the following year. Again on summer
vacation, this time in Switzerland, Michelet found "a cold rationalism under the heavy and glacial hand of nature": "She will inspire
little enthusiasm. Rousseau's words, when lying in his boat on the
Lake of Bienne—'nature, oh my mother'—will be incomprehensi-
ble. People will shake their heads. This mother who freezes her
infants eight months of the year with her breath does seem to be a
marâtre. They will rather say, with Zwingli: 'Since original sin, nature is like a fruit stricken by the hail.' They will neither bless nature
like Rousseau, nor curse it like Byron."[3]

A year later, Pauline had died of drink, tuberculosis, and neglect, and Michelet, in agonized and guilty reflections jotted down
the day of her death, began to question his attitudes toward nature
and women. He felt that in her extreme possessiveness Pauline had
been estranged and irritated at the least sign of his devotion to
anything or anyone else. Yet,

> What a hard and denatured thing is art and science, that we
> desert for it those who love us. How many long Sundays I left
> her alone, while all other families went together to find decent
> amusements. .... Alas, it's at the expense of her happiness and
> her life that I did all that I did. If I had some glory it would
> be at her expense. I bitterly rediscover the compensation on
> the day of her death. ... This poor self [*moi*] who has died
> today, I had reduced to being my *sensual self* [*moi sensuel*]; if I
> had put her in contact with my whole soul, she would have
> been happy, would have lived.[4]

The self-reproaches were more general seven weeks later: "She
was for me nature in its lively spontaneity, devoted to my individuality, which was beyond nature, against nature."[5]

Madame Dumesnil

During this time Alfred Dumesnil, age eighteen, was preparing to begin legal studies in Paris. His mother, probably motivated by a desire to escape both the boredom of provincial life and her much older husband, had brought him there from Rouen in 1837, when he was sixteen. After finishing his secondary studies in Paris, Alfred, accompanied by his mother, attended Michelet's renowned lectures at the Collège de France. Since Alfred had studied at Rouen's Collège royale with Michelet's disciple, Adolphe Chéruel, he—or his mother—took the trouble to obtain a letter of introduction from Chéruel to the master.[6]

Through this introduction, Alfred quickly developed a privileged relationship with Michelet, benefiting from private discussions with him. In May 1840, at the end of the academic year, Madame Dumesnil visited the historian to request his assistance on a personal matter. To improve her son's health, a doctor had suggested a long walking trip, and because he could not make the trip alone, Madame Dumesnil asked Michelet if he could recommend a young man to accompany him.

Alfred's health was probably more pretext than reason for Madame Dumesnil's visit to the historian. She had been attending Michelet's lectures all year and almost certainly wanted to develop a personal friendship with him. In any case, the visit conveyed her considerable trust in Michelet's integrity and probity, and he replied in kind: In two or three years, Alfred would be mature enough to socialize freely, but now he needed his mother more than anyone else; if a travel companion was necessary, it should be she. Maternal care would not weaken her son; for "tender natures" like Alfred's, it was indispensable.[7]

Twelve days later, on Sunday, May 17, Michelet returned the visit, and though Madame Dumesnil's letter on the subject to her son stressed the historian's elevated moral intentions, a seed of intense mutual involvement was being planted in the two forty-year-olds. In his journal notation the following Sunday, in which Michelet mentioned Madame Dumesnil's visit earlier in the month, we see several reflections of the powerful impression her maternal devotion seems to have made on him. He had just visited Pauline's grave with his children, for the first time in a long while, and his thoughts wandered through the theme of mothers and children, ultimately returning to his courtship and marriage. He noted that lately he had spent more time than usual with his children, especially his daughter, taking them almost daily to their gymnastic exercises. Then he remarked on having found something "touching" at Père-Lachaise: the graves of a twenty-four-year-old mother and her daughter of five, dead within three months of each other. And he noticed the inscription on another child's tomb: "It was much desired." Finally, he recalled parts of the cemetery he had seen twenty years earlier, when his relation with Pauline was beginning: "In the middle, my two walnut trees, where I sat in 1819 with her on that stormy day. . . . It was the beginning of this long union, also stormy, and nonetheless so tender. . . . She is buried at the level of the two walnut trees, as far as I can judge, and with her, twenty years of my life and the youth and gentlest emotions of my heart."

A month later, bitter comments about his attitude to nature and his emotional life appear in the context of reactions to accusations from Catholic critics that he was a pantheist: "If the pantheist is someone who willingly lets himself be absorbed in nature, I am not that man. What reason do I have to be pleased with her? And why should I love her? On the other hand, if God is a moral God, it must be admitted that he likes to hide his ways."

Following this confession is one, slightly masked, about his personal life. He had been considering entering a new relationship, apparently with a married woman, and had discussed the matter with Edgar Quinet's wife, who advised him not to become involved. Apart from noting the scabrous character of such liaisons, she pointed out the inevitable lack of balance in them: you are attached to someone of an inferior educational level from whom you are always divorced intellectually, and she either loves you too little, which makes you wretched, or too much, which makes her miserable.

Yet, wrote Michelet—and here he suggests that the woman in question was married—"marriage is impossible for a long time." Even if it were not, he doubts the relationship would be compatible "with the great work which is my life's destiny." For: "Such a work allows of no sharing of time or energy. One must live and die as a book, not a man." What then should he do? "Suffer, work, forget if possible. But I cannot love and thank the One who has made the world so. I know full well that he can strike me again, deprive me of all that remains. I have something to fear, but I do not love any more. When I want to bless and thank, it sticks in my throat. I have no reason to love nature. I will be silent about Providence."[8]

Clearly, though Michelet did not then feel ready to start a new relationship, he needed one and was dissatisfied with the beast of labor he had become. Amid his disconsolate carping at God and nature, he was ripe for a change.

Later that summer, Michelet traveled through Belgium and the Ardennes to see and take notes on the remains of the Burgundian realm for the next part of his *Histoire de France.* His final stop was Renwez, in the Ardennes, where his mother's sister and favorite aunt, Célestine, had died the year before. His complaints about the world of nature continued, but in a different vein from those of the early 1830s, when he had viewed nature as a suffocating, homicidal mother. The problem haunting him in 1840 was simply that what nature gave, it took away, capriciously and mercilessly: "When we think of the barbaric and quiet way that nature incessantly weaves living threads only to break them, it is difficult to be thankful." While traveling along the Meuse earlier in his trip, he had reconsidered the mother-stepmother question in nature: "I saw it again, this nature. . . . The bones of the great mother appeared to me momentarily; mother? Yes, and not stepmother. I was less angry with nature and my bitterness was assuaged."[9]

Madame Dumesnil and Alfred, meanwhile, had returned to Rouen. Alfred came to Paris again in autumn 1840 and, armed with another letter from Chéruel, obtained an invitation to visit Michelet at home on December 23. The following month, Michelet went to Rouen to view the site of Joan of Arc's trial; while there, he was a guest in the Dumesnil home in Sente Bihorel. At the end of February, Madame Dumesnil returned to Paris to rejoin Alfred. According to Viallaneix, during her nine months in Rouen her attitude to Michelet had "ripened into a discreet and lively affection." A similar evolution on the historian's part seems probable.[10]

Journal entries from April 1841 suggest more or less simultaneous changes in Michelet's personal situation, his attitude toward nature and his historical perspective. As the pain caused by his wife's death healed and he began to cherish the hope of new love, his rancor toward nature as the deceiving bearer of death receded, replaced by a vision of eternal rebirth in both nature and history. "I need to prove, both to myself and to this humanity whose ephemeral appearances I sketch, that one is reborn, that one does not die. I need it, feeling myself die. I enumerate in vain the serious comforts of my present situation, I only really rejoin life by this sort of faculty of enlivening something, of giving life, in my own way."[11]

The humanity he envisioned overcame the cruelty of death and nature not by blind opposition but by a dialectical interaction with them. The metaphor of nature as the weaver who broke the threads of life returned, but now Michelet saw the possibility of overcoming death by human will: "We draw from ourselves, from our will, the wherewithal to rebind the bloody tissue." He set himself in nature's place when he wrote that it was his task "to weave the web of ideas by which men perpetuated themselves, continued to live, denied death and derided nature." A note at the end of April pinpointed what he had been saying by specifying the relationship between his pain after Pauline's death and his historical vision:

My wife died and my heart was tormented. But from this very

torment emerged a violent and almost frenetic energy. I plunged with somber pleasure into the death of France in the XVth century, merging in it passions of ferocious sensuality that I found both in me and in my subject. It is not without reason that someone wrote that the fourth volume of the *Histoire de France* was the result of an immoral inspiration. That is what gives it its strange force. Never has a bad epoch been recounted in a worse agitation of the mind.[12]

In spite of the bleak character of the example, what Michelet was describing was the process that, in the very period of this notation, enabled him to extrapolate from the personal renaissance he was experiencing with Madame Dumesnil to the European Renaissance of the sixteenth century. In fact, this reference to Pauline's death was the last to be accompanied by a feeling of desolation. The period of mourning was coming to a close, and Michelet's outlook in following months was increasingly dominated by love for Madame Dumesnil. His reference to human will as a means of overcoming nature's murderous impulse to kill off its creations, moreover, though it superficially mirrored Michelet's earlier juxtaposition of liberty against natural fatality, brought him close to a total revaluation of nature. For the rebirth that he saw, the role of the hero in rescuing new life from the claws of morbid nature could just as well be seen as the task of the maternal side of nature itself. All he needed to make this short but crucial step was a small push; he was to receive it that summer from Madame Dumesnil, who in Michelet's eyes was the good mother incarnate.

On June 11, 1841, Michelet wrote to Madame Dumesnil's husband to explain that for reasons of health, she had moved into his house for a few days. Although the days became a year, the reason given was genuine: she had cancer, and her year in Michelet's house would be her last. Moreover, as Michelet explained to Monsieur Dumesnil, her son, Alfred, had already returned to Rouen, and the servant in Madame Dumesnil's flat was incapable of caring properly for her; to resolve the problem, Michelet's sixteen-year-old daughter had volunteered her services as nurse. Michelet himself "seized with eagerness this occasion to return to your family the most kind hospitality which I have received from you." "She will have all possible care," he wrote, "in the midst of a family which loves her and is devoted to you." Nonetheless, if Madame Dumesnil entered Michelet's household in a state of health that made long-run hopes unrealistic and expectations of physical intimacy improbable, it was critical for Michelet's development that she did move in and that he was able to enjoy her company and her spirit during her final year of life.[13]

On July 24, the second anniversary of his wife's death, Michelet visited Pauline's grave with his children, Alfred, and Madame Dumesnil, who attempted to console him. The next day, the couple seem to have discussed their relationship; he quotes her as saying, "Why not some years of compensation after so many bad ones?"

In August they all spent five days in Fontainebleau. He had two reasons for going there. He used the occasion to examine the art in the château for his chapters on Henry II and the French Renaissance. But in connection with a project on Napoléon, he also wanted to examine the site of the emperor's abdication. He wrote that everything before the modern world—antiquity, the Middle Ages—had died for him: "Today, action, action! The only places that attract me are those with which the great interests of modern crises have been bound up, the points of articulation in which these great matters have been arranged and tied together, from Louis XIV to Napoleon: London, Amsterdam, Vienna. . . ."

The project on Napoléon, probably inspired by the recent return of the emperor's ashes to Paris, was postponed for more than twenty years; it ultimately became the *Histoire du XIXe siècle,* Michelet's last book. But the historian's activist impulse, a sign of his renewed energy, was in 1843 to be satisfied by the savage conflict with the Jesuits, caused by his and Quinet's lectures at the Collège de France. Meanwhile, more significant for his future than either of his historical concerns were long walks in the forest of Fontainebleau with Madame Dumesnil. "We were talking about the influence which the study of nature would have on my work: 'She is coming to you with full breasts and her hands full of flowers.' To which I said: 'Oh nature, you are beautiful, charming, fecund, but on condition that your Epic will not interrupt my drama. For I too am a nature for myself alone, a world in which the world and nature may not intervene too much.'"[14]

What a difference from his anguished experience of the forest of Fontainebleau seven years earlier, where he described the marâtre, nature, as "the incestuous mother who . . . caresses us, stupefies us, and kills us." This alone suggests the magnitude of Madame Dumesnil's influence on him. The journal gives little further evidence of Michelet's relationship with Madame Dumesnil in 1841.[15] If we examine his historical writings from this period in the context of his journal notes and letters, however, we cannot doubt that this friendship cast its shadow on many of his attitudes toward religion, nature, and history.

Michelet's early attitude toward nature, freedom, and history was burdened by a profound ambivalence toward his mother. Not only was she the source of his fears of nature as a punitive wicked stepmother; she was also the model for the puritan asceticism that enabled him to suppress his own sensual nature. In fact, we can view his idea that world history was the stage of a grand combat between individual "liberty" and the "fatality" of nature and reified social institutions as the projection of a corresponding inner conflict between two parts of the internalized maternal heritage: the ascetic ego ideal of the work ethic and the deeper-seated—and feared— recollection of an earlier symbiotic relation to the mother. To the extent that Pauline, his first wife, was intended to satisfy those natural needs he could not altogether suppress, needs whose first satisfaction was in the infantile relation to the mother, he must have hated her, as he feared and hated those needs. When Pauline died, Michelet reacted with so much remorse and guilt that it was almost as if he had killed her. There was also, though, the potentiality of release—release from the seductive and punitive maternal imago he had projected onto her and had intuited with horror in nature. Pauline's death was in a sense the second death of Michelet's mother. Having internalized and expressed his view of nature as a "stepmother," he could now exorcise it and reach back to the earlier, symbiotic relationship to rescue it from the weight of his paranoid fantasies of the incestuous, homicidal marâtre. In Madame Dumesnil, he rediscovered the pure, good mother with which he was able, from 1841 on, to identify nature, God, and historical development.

CHAPTER 4

JOAN OF ARC AND THE RESURRECTION OF NATURE, 1840–1841

Michelet's "maternalized" view of history is evident in two texts that date from the first half of 1841: his concluding pages on Joan of Arc in book X of the *Histoire de France* and a draft of what more than a decade later became his "Introduction to the Renaissance." He seems to have written the pages on Joan after he visited the Dumesnils in Rouen in January 1841. He gave he draft on the Renaissance to Madame Dumesnil's son, Alfred, in Rouen during another brief visit to the Dumesnils that May. Known among Paris intellectuals, according to Heinrich Heine, as Monsieur Symbole, Michelet had long been inclined to view Joan of Arc as a pivotal figure who incarnated in the late Middle Ages the beginning of French national consciousness. She appeared more than once in his books of the 1830s; he had lectured on her in the Collège de France and had written most of his chapters dealing with her in his *Histoire de France* before his visit to Rouen in 1841 and his friendship with his disciple's mother. But his treatment of Joan before meeting Madame Dumesnil focused on her and France's quality as a virgin— that is, as nonmother: "Each town had a maiden in its coat of arms, who was claimed to be a virgin. The English, in burning The Maid and wanting to violate her, thought they were deflowering France."[1]

Paul Viallaneix has pointed out that Michelet's view of Joan was profoundly influenced by his relationship with Madame Dumesnil. "He encounters her," writes Viallaneix, "while another woman is preoccupying him, who saved France from despair. Would it be, in his own destiny, after the incursion of death, the annunciation of a new renaissance? From the singular harmony of what he lives, writes and teaches, Monsieur Symbole cannot help but extract a comforting portent."[2] In fact, Michelet probably saw a parallel between the "spirit of sacrifice" in Madame Dumesnil (for her son, Alfred) and that of La Pucelle for France. What is clear is that in the passage in book X written after he visited Rouen in January 1841, he identified the French nation as "the people of love and grace" and then wrote two significant sentences: "The savior of France had to be a woman. France was a woman itself."[3]

It was in the context of his study of the Renaissance that Michelet removed Joan of Arc from the symbolic realm of virginity and placed her in "the epoch of fecundity, of maternity." The draft on the Renaissance in which this line appeared was written during May 1841, in what the historian referred to three months later as "a moment of exaltation."[4] Like his work on La Pucelle, the sketch was intended for the *Histoire de France*. Since 1839 the Renaissance had been a theme of Michelet's lectures: in his lectures of 1839, he still believed that the progress of liberty occurred in a line that went from the natural fatalities of India to the triumph of liberty in France.[5] Nonetheless, he saw a historical necessity for a return to the natural sources of life, and he comprehended the Italian Renaissance, whose germ lay in the revival of ancient culture through commercial and political contacts with the Middle East, as such a return. A long notation of July 1839 on this subject includes the following remarks:

> Renaissance, that is, resurrection of Nature, rapprochement of man and nature, of Christianity and ancient paganism, of Europe and Asia. For a long time, the renaturalization of Europe was being accomplished, not only in history and politics, but in science: 1. by the direct study of Nature (alchemy, arab, etc.); 2. by the philological and philosophical study of a paganism that adored nature. . . . The North has to go to the South, to Italy, that is, to the past, to paganism, to Nature; the Occident has to go to the Orient, to the Turks, that is, to the past, to Nature. . . . Always we swear not to return, always we return.[6]

His course on the Renaissance the following year stressed the inner connection between Christian mysticism in the fifteenth century and the breakthrough of Italian artists to a realistic understanding of nature. "Christianity," he said, and he might have been talking about himself, "in its struggle against the adoration of nature had condemned nature too much." The ossified Christianity of the Middle Ages was liberated by the Christian mysticism of the followers of Saint Francis and Dante. Michelet saw in the paintings of the Franciscan Fra Angelico and, more generally, of the Umbrian school a union of mystical reverie and nature, the revelation of "the grace of God in nature." The breakthrough of nature in art subsequently occurred when the Medicis encouraged the painting of non-Christian subjects, but the first impetus came from within the Christian tradition.[7]

Michelet's return to nature, then, was prepared in the years before he met Madame Dumesnil. The decisive year of that meeting, however, signals an intensification of this return and an infusion of it and its projections onto history with outspoken ideas of womanhood and fecundity.

Thus Michelet's draft introduction to the Renaissance, written in 1841, bore the title "Renaissance, fécundité, maternité." He showed it to Alfred and Alfred's mother in Rouen just five days after he wrote it—in "exaltation"—on May 17. Continuing his thoughts of the previous year on the relation of Christianity to the Renaissance, he saw that period as a turning point in the development of Christianity's view of women and, through this view, of its understanding of the Imitation of Christ, one of Michelet's central religious conceptions. As a mediating force that linked humanity and nature and tied the family together, Christianity had in Michelet's eyes a basically feminine character, and its essential idea was thus womanhood. The Christian Middle Ages, he argued, understood only the Virgin; it was left to the Renaissance and to the modern era to comprehend and value the Mother. Antiquity—for convenience reduced to Greece and Rome—had no concept of motherhood, according to Michelet. Christ, by contrast, not only had a mother, "he has a woman's soul: he weeps over Lazarus, he calls the children to him. He was born of a woman alone, through the Divine Spirit." Nonetheless, for well over a millennium, burdened by notions of celibacy and purity, Christianity saw in the Virgin birth only the Virgin and denied the Mother. Even if Christian practice remained well below the Christian ideal, the ideal strove to rise above vulgar nature, in which motherhood was the reality. Thus Beatrice was absorbed by the quest for eternal wisdom and Heloïse rejected marriage. The reality of femininity caused anxiety: under Philip Augustus, Michelet noted, the fear of femininity led to a prohibition on teaching women to read.

The art and literature of the Renaissance and later periods broke through this sterile view of women. From the moment that painters put the Infant Jesus into the arms of his Mother, she began to supersede the ideal of the Virgin, of celibacy. In profane literature, the incarnation of love was no longer Beatrice but Laure, the mother of a family. In the iconography of the High Renaissance, Michelet saw a sculpture like Michelangelo's *Pietà* as an example of the imitation of the feminine Christ: the Virgin Mother became "the daughter of her son."

At this historical moment, in which all traditional values and institutions were shaking, Michelet saw in the idealization of motherhood a "profound progress": the strengthening of family ties. He believed, moreover, that all aspects of culture were becoming suffused with the idea of natural fecundity, which he viewed as flowing out of the new celebration of maternity. He found the significance of the "Agneau mystique" of Jan van Eyck to lie in the fact that, according to him, the fecund rays of the spirit had made all the attendant virgins pregnant.[8] And in the invention of printing, he also saw a fecundation of the spirit and "the imitation of generation." He summarized a number of his historical concepts as follows: "The Renaissance, the epoch in which nature is beginning to be reconciled with spirit, the epoch of fecundity, of maternity, the harmonious epoch begins at the moment the Virgin ends in reality through the Maid of Orléans, at the moment when, in art, we find gradually this absurd miracle of a young mother who holds her old son in her arms."[9]

Michelet's matriarchal view of Catholicism, though unorthodox, was hardly heretical in 1841; indeed, without the personal and political forces that set him on a collision course with the church in the mid-1840s, the ideas he was propagating in his draft on the Renaissance would probably not have led him to renounce Christianity. The implications for historical scholarship, however, were more radical. Inspired primarily by his relationship with Madame Dumesnil, his altered view of the role of women and natural forces in history led Michelet to an intellectual breakthrough in the conception of the Renaissance, one that preceded by a generation the more famous work of Jakob Burckhardt and laid the basis, according to Lucien Febvre, for the modern notion of the subject. Previous ideas of the Renaissance had been limited to the rebirth of individual aspects of human culture. Michelet saw it as a general phase of European history.[10]

In spite of this auspicious beginning, Michelet's passion for the Renaissance was too linked to his own rebirth through his relationship with Madame Dumesnil to survive her death. His work on the Renaissance remained in limbo until 1854. Nonetheless, the foundations had been laid for his ideas of the 1840s and 1850s. The reconciliation of nature with spirit transformed his earlier view of an eternal struggle between spiritualized liberty and natural fatality. And the feminization of nature, history, and religion allowed him to comprehend death as the basis of rebirth.

CHAPTER 5

DEATH AND
HISTORICAL RECURRENCE,
1842

Over a year of decline preceded Madame Dumesnil's death on May 31, 1842. Michelet probably knew that she was terminally ill as early as his visit to Rouen in January 1841, when he wept at viewing the old city from her terrace. As her end grew imminent in the winter and spring of 1842, Michelet, grief-stricken, undertook to harmonize the haunting approach of death with his new appreciation for the generative power of nature and to relate both his generativity and his grief to history.

By autumn 1841, Michelet was sending reports to Alfred and Monsieur Dumesnil in which the veneer of optimism about her condition became thinner and thinner.[1] On January 12, 1842, he admitted in his journal that the magnetism her doctors were using failed to assuage her violent attacks of pain. On January 30, the thought of her oncoming death (evident in a notation that her condition was steadily deteriorating) led him to contemplate the mythological and supernatural aspects of the historian's task. He recalled Caesar's dream of a weeping, beseeching army of the dead and how, when waking, the leader of Rome wrote down the names of two lost cities, Corinth and Carthage, and rebuilt them. He recalled Emperor Claudius's continuation of this work and compared that rebuilding to the labor of the historian, who also resurrected the dead: "Men of a hundred years, nations of 2000 years, infants who died while nursing, they all say that they hardly lived, that they barely began. . . . They say that if they had the time to know themselves and prepare, they might have accepted their lot; they would have ceased to wander around us, they would have gently allowed

42

their urns to be closed up, lulled by friendly hands, going back to sleep and rebinding their dreams."

The historian's task, in Michelet's view, was thus to pacify the spirits of the dead, to exorcise them by finding the meaning of their brief existences. What they needed was a soothsayer. And here Michelet quoted the passage from Virgil's *Aeneid* in which the key to the Underworld was described as the golden bough, which had to be offered to Proserpine. "Where," he asked, "should one find this golden bough? In one's own heart. It is through personal sorrows that the historian feels and reproduces the sorrows of nations; he reproduces them in order to console them. . . . As long as they have not found a soothsayer, they (the dead) will wander around their poorly closed tombs and will not rest." At the end of this journal entry he compared the historian's task of explaining the enigmatic words and actions of the dead, improperly understood in their lifetime, to the work of an Oedipus or a Prometheus.

The joint reference to the classical myths of Oedipus and Prometheus, both of which deal with the revelation of forbidden knowledge, points to a strangely productive counterpoint that soon emerged in Michelet's thought, as he mastered the grief caused by the death of the woman he loved: on one hand, an awareness and partial acceptance of incestuous impulse; on the other, his intellectual labors as artisan of past and future knowledge. His cult of Madame Dumesnil's spirit and values, particularly those linking nature, art, and work, made this creative counterpoint possible. Michelet was writing on the age of Louis XI at this time, and four days before his somber meditation, Alfred Dumesnil wrote to his friend, Eugène Noel, that the new part of the *Histoire de France* was emerging from the "entrails" of its author's personal life and that Michelet had just told him, "When you read all these manuscripts, Alfred, you will realize that both my thoughts on method and my history of France always begin with the historical moment of the night of your mother."[2]

In February, the condition of Alfred's mother deteriorated further; her personality changed and she no longer wanted to see Michelet. Soon she returned to the simplest biological relationship available to her, that with her son. On March 18, Alfred wrote to Noel: "Since Sunday I am the only person whose care she will accept; she can barely support the presence of M. Michelet, thus he rarely sees her any more. I pass the day and part of the night with her. . . . She is full of the tenderest affection for me, doesn't want me to leave her for a second. . . . she does nothing, takes nothing without asking my advice; I have to direct her in everything, she has become a child again; and it's at the moment that I have never loved her so much that I have to lose her."[3]

Even with the abbé Cœur, a former student of Michelet whom she invited to visit her frequently in her last months because of her revived religiosity, she could talk only about her illness. Although Michelet understood how she could be so estranged from those whose love was powerless to stop her agony, he felt the loss of her confidence and affection as his own death.[4]

In his misery, he asked a young disciple, Jean Yanoski, to take over his spring lectures at the Collège de France. Yanoski, however, was himself ill; in March, Michelet's superior asked him to release the younger man from a burden that might have killed him, and Michelet, his dying angel under his roof, was obliged to resume his lectures in April and May. These seven lectures, undertaken during the final agony of Madame Dumesnil, reveal a herculean effort to sublimate his private grief into universal human categories. The subject of the lectures was as broad as their point of departure was narrow: the historical relation between religion and moral philosophy, from ancient India to nineteenth-century Europe. In them appear a number of concepts that inspired his work during at least the next fifteen years, ideas on the holy spirit and the maternity of God that were to constitute his *évangile éternel.*

Michelet prepared his lecture series as usual by searching his personal history for its relevance to his scholarly work: "This morning, I decided to organize all my papers in a rigorously chronological order, in such a way that all my science entered in my life."[5] Two days later, he was mulling over the methodological and general philosophical problems of the coming lectures. His belief in intellectual creativity was already taking the shape of a private religion: "Every morning, we have to create our God, we have to prepare our daily bread, our host. The Middle Ages took a God already made." On a page of notes written for Alfred, two points stand out: the extreme subjectivity and the extreme universality of history. These were not opposed but interdependent. Thus, on the one hand: "Of what is history made, if not of me? Of what would history be remade and retold, if not of me?" On the other hand, like his subsequent admirers in the *Annales* school, he advocated viewing the subdisciplines of history in a unified framework. To explain, for example, the superiority of the domestic interiors in Flemish art over those in Italian Renaissance art, he found a knowledge of legal and social history indispensable: Flemish women had the right to inherit property, which put them in a position to impress their personalities on their households, and this led to a greater emphasis on the "interior grace" of the home in the Northern school of art. Whoever attempted to study the history of art as isolated from the broader cultural and social context would in Michelet's eyes perforce be dealing with "secondary causes or even false ones."[6]

In these weeks before the difficult resumption of his lectures, Michelet was wrestling with the problem of death: he reread Vico, whose theories emphasized the death and rebirth of cultures, and he restated several Viconian ideas, among them that humanity creates itself and, through this creation, knows itself. He also read and reacted to Pierre Leroux's *De l'humanité*. Leroux argued that, though humanity has some sort of collective spiritual existence, the individual soul dies with the body. Michelet believed stubbornly in the immortality of the soul, convinced that the very lack of consciousness of any earlier existence cited by Leroux was evidence that "only our inferior capacities are reborn," whereas "the rest goes somewhere else, with a complete memory, the profit of experience, the lively self-awareness, a total memory of all the previous lives which instruct, punish or recompense."[7] Two days after this reaction to Leroux, he admitted that he got his ideas on the immortality of the soul from Jean Reynaud, a mystical astronomer and, like Leroux, ex-Saint-Simonian, who was editing the *Encyclopédie nouvelle* with Leroux. Reynaud believed in the transmigration of reincarnated souls from one planet to another.[8]

Here, in the context of his journal polemic with Leroux and his reference to Reynaud, Michelet enters the strange illuministic world of the social romantics. Leroux published his *Revue indépendante*, as I have noted, with George Sand's help. The ideas of Leroux's colleague Reynaud, partly derived from the Lyons mystic Pierre-Simon Ballanche, were taken very seriously by such radical romantics as Alphonse Esquiros and Eugène Sue[9] and influenced the poetry of Victor Hugo.[10]

Another nineteenth-century scientist whose ideas were essential to Michelet in the last months of Madame Dumesnil was Etienne Geoffroy Saint-Hilaire, a physiologist who stressed the continuity among all living matter, from highest to lowest, and who gave Michelet a theoretical basis for overcoming his hostility to nature.[11] Michelet's ties with Geoffroy Saint-Hilaire, as well as with Reynaud, were not purely intellectual. On the day before Madame Dumesnil's death, Michelet had a long talk with Geoffroy Saint-Hilaire, and when Alfred Dumesnil and Michelet visited Quinet at Seine-Port in August 1847, they found him in a colony of like-minded intellectuals that included Jean Reynaud and the younger Geoffroy Saint-Hilaire, Isidore, who was continuing the work of his recently deceased father.[12]

Meanwhile, in April and May 1842, the months of the lectures he had wanted to avoid, Michelet's thoughts turned continually to the dying Madame Dumesnil. He posed the problem once more: "Nature, mother or stepmother? If she is a mother, why death?" He resolved this dilemma by restating his notion of death as rebirth and positing a notion of God and nature as equally maternal: "Yes, the great mystery of maternity envelops the world. What is birth? Delivery of the new-born [*accouchement*]. What is life? Delivery of the new-born. And death? Delivery of the new-born. That of birth leads to a visible fruit. One rejoices. That of death, to an invisible fruit. One weeps."[13]

Michelet saw a chain of generations, one born from the other, whose strength and perpetuity lay in knowledge of and respect for the past. Haunted by death, he confronted the young in his lectures that spring and tried to rediscover for his students the principles of immortality. These principles fused historical knowledge and religious unorthodoxy, and it was this fusion that he called his *évangile éternel,* a term he used later to describe his social philosophy in its entirety.[14] Michelet's theological arguments in these lectures, inspired by his inconsolable grief over his friend's oncoming death, his absolute need to find rebirth in that death, bordered on heresy, and it is no wonder that he was soon feuding with the Jesuits.[15]

In his lecture of April 28, Michelet discussed what he saw as a struggle between two aspects of the Christian notion of God— the Son and the Holy Spirit—that seemed to recapitulate at a theological level the antithesis of natural fatality and liberty that he had earlier postulated as the leitmotif of history. The Son now signified tradition (that is, fatality) for Michelet. The Holy Spirit, part of the Greek heritage of Christianity, could be found in the art and philosophy of Judeo-Christian culture and meant for Michelet, according to his disciple, Gabriel Monod, "liberty, movement, and love." The prophets of the coming reign of the Holy Spirit, which would succeed that of the Son, were Abelard and Heloïse, whose abbey was dedicated to the Holy Spirit, and Joachim of Fiore, who preached its imminence in *his* "évangile éternel" (which was clearly Michelet's model).

The similarity between the antithesis of "tradition" versus "liberty, movement, and love," and the opposition established in 1831 between "fatality" and "liberty" is deceptive. "Fatality," which in the earlier antithesis was the equivalent of "tradition," had been tied to nature. By the definition of love that Michelet now implied— maternal love, which he had come to identify with nature—the element of nature had shifted to the side of liberty. The only remaining step was to recognize explicitly the maternal nature of God and Providence. This he did in the following weeks. At one point he wrote in his journal that God was "a mother who had to nurse the world drop by drop." At another: "I used maternity . . . as an example of the gentle transitions of the eternal artist." At another: "The death and life of nations, the rude problem of destiny. . . . I had arrived at a God-mother, and that death is the deliverance of a new-born [*et que la mort est un accouchement*]." On May 19, 1842, the theme of his lecture was "the maternity of Providence."[16] According to Monod, it was here that Michelet offered his notion of God as "a mother who had to nurse the world drop by drop for the development of liberty."

His notations in the journal, meanwhile, made explicit the tormented personal experience that underlay his new view of history. A paragraph from his entry of May 9 reveals the connection unambiguously:

> Yesterday morning, Sunday, frightfully changed, emaciated, her face more swollen; immense, brilliant eyes, she congratulated herself with a feverish volubility on having vomited fifteen times during the night. On the other hand the two young people [her son and his daughter, who married a year later]. A frail future and the past is lost. Where is my life, where shall I refind life and warmth in this imminent coldness of old age and solitude? My life is where it always was, in what is always faithful to me, in history and the life of the world. I return to it, like Philoctetus to his isle of Lemnos. Receive me, cherished isle, where I passed so many years of solitude, so many bitter and sweet years. Receive me, receive your injured.

Michelet's reference to Philoctetus on Lemnos is revealing. The wounded Greek warrior was left on the island while his companions in arms made their way to Troy. He was brought out of his exile after ten years, when the gods made it clear that he was needed to end the siege of Troy. More interesting, however, is a different legend of the island: the belief that Lemnos was named after a title of the mother goddess Cybele and that early in its history the women of Lemnos, having been deserted by their husbands, murdered all their men and established a matriarchy. The history to which Michelet was returning had indeed also become, in a sense, matriarchal.

CHAPTER 6

GRIEF AND
INCESTUOUS LONGING

Madame Dumesnil died on May 31, 1842. After a brief sojourn in Rouen with her husband, Michelet tried to shake off his wretchedness through a five-week journey to Germany. He took with him his thirteen-year-old son, Charles, his daughter, Adèle, and Madame Dumesnil's son, Alfred: Alfred and Adèle had been secretly engaged since February.[1] During this trip, overshadowed though it was by the death of Alfred's mother, Michelet gradually regained a state of mind that enabled him to resume work. His recent shattering experiences had largely completed the transformation of his values, and it was through two of the standard experiences of European romanticism that he returned to culture: the celebration of the artisan-artist and the fantasized disintegration of the incest taboo.[2] The barrier between the living and the dead was to be overcome by the quest for harmonies that would transcend all boundaries and reconcile all differences, not only those that separated social classes but also those that normally limited the relations of sons and mothers.

In his journal entries on the trip through Germany, Michelet frequently betrayed an unconscious identification with the spirit of his lost friend. Just before departing he had begun a biography of her, the material for which he had collected on his voyage of condolence to Rouen, and had discovered, with some jealousy, her earlier friendships.[3] In Alsace, he told Alfred of his bitterness about the lost earlier years and friendships of Madame Dumesnil, about the fact that he knew her only when she was dying. When Alfred attempted to console him by reminding him of the extended family of his disciples spread throughout France, Michelet replied that they were too far away; he had refused to give them the kind of organizational center that a journal might have afforded and had wanted only to bring them the "breath" of the spirit of life,[4] thus reducing, or elevating, his influence to what Max Weber later defined as charisma. Returning to the emotional starting point—his identification with the dead mother-goddess—he then wrote: "I had the maternal genius. This maternity has its pains and an apparent sterility. A thousand children dispersed in space and time. No children whom we can embrace." Later that day, he copied three lines from the *Aeneid* about the death of Priam's daughter and recalled how he had burst into tears two days before when he thought of them in relation to Madame Dumesnil.[5]

The journal entries during Michelet's German summer of 1842[6] reveal how he gradually overcame his grief, shifting his attention slowly from the themes of death and women in the German cathedral architecture to an awareness of the forces of nature and popular culture. In the Munich museum, he particularly noticed the feminine sensuality in the paintings of Murillo and Rubens, and his comments on Rubens's paintings of his second wife, Hélène Fourment, contain phrases similar to those he would apply, soon after his return to France, to a woman with whom he subsequently became intimate, Madame Aupépin. Perhaps most important, through the patriotic and romantic poetry of Johann Ludwig Uhland and Friedrich Rückert, and through meetings with such German colleagues as F.-G. Thiersch and Johann Josef von Goerres, he also recovered a sense of social and political awareness. Crucial connections between his past historical work and his future social militancy developed out of this awareness. The last part of his journey took Michelet to Nuremberg and Frankfurt, and there, in the personality of the German artisan, he rediscovered the link between his personal history and the history of the world.

It was not the first time that Michelet betrayed a deep-seated personal identification with the artisan.[7] In book V of *Histoire de France,* he had discussed the social organization and domestic life of Flemish artisans in the fifteenth century. This earlier description was written in March 1841, midway between his visits of January and May to Madame Dumesnil in Rouen and three months before he took her into his house.[8]

Flanders, he had said in 1841, was labor, and labor was peace. Michelet saw a strongly religious element in the Flemish weaver's devotion to work and compared it to that of the *humiliati* of Lombardy and to the monks of the Order of Saint Benedict. Even more than the monks, he believed, the weavers gave themselves to God, as was evident in the terms in which he described them: "beghards," which meant those who pray, and "lollards, because of their pious complaints, the monotonous chants, like those of a woman rocking a child." Michelet called this aspect of the weaver's existence a "gentle and feminine mysticism." The numerous female weavers, the *béguines,* generally lived together in the *béguinages,* where, apart from laboring in their workshops, they ran schools and hospitals. Their vows were not strict. In an implicitly autobiographic passage, which foreshadowed his coming year's cohabitation with Madame Dumesnil, Michelet had written: "The beguine could marry. She passed, without changing her life, into the house of a pious worker. She sanctified it; the dark workshop was illuminated by a gentle ray of grace. 'Man does not need to live alone. . . .' . . . The man . . . is near his sun, his heart sings."[9]

From Alfred's record of a conversation with Michelet during the trip to Germany, it is clear that they both identified Madame Dumesnil's personality with that of the medieval weaver. Michelet recalled fondly "the great utility for her of working with her hands, the rhythmic creativity of tapestry work coinciding both with her need for activity and her profoundly reasonable genius."[10]

In Nuremberg, he came to understand—and identify with—the creative potential of the artisanal personality through the paintings of a uniquely successful master artisan, Albrecht Dürer. The invention of painting and the beginnings of wood sculpture were both attributable, he wrote, to the spare-time hobbies of the journeyman artisan. Conscience, patience, and the untranslatable *Gemüth* were the common denominators that related an artist like Dürer to the mass of skilled workers.[11]

Michelet's underlying empathy for the artisan emerged clearly a few years later in *Le Peuple.* Although this identification echoed his childhood experiences as an apprentice in his father's printing shop, he himself established the links between his new self-identification as artisan and the totality of his recent experiences and emotions in a striking piece of self-examination written on July 21, 1842, in Frankfurt.

After seeing a woman who reminded him of Madame Dumesnil, he commented that since leaving France he had actually traveled more within himself than in Germany. The high point of this introspective voyage, he wrote, had been attained on the road to Strasbourg a month earlier. He quoted the words "too late, too far," words which comprehended "the entire tragedy of the world, and which I applied to individuals as well as nations."

From the journal entry of June 24 in which he had written "too late, too far," it is clear that Michelet was viewing world history through a lens of personal sorrow. He and Alfred (with whom communication was "rapid and perfect") were thinking that "the souls that were the most analogous and the closest to loving one another were often separated by place and time." They had then applied the idea to the relations of France and Germany. Apart from the mutual hostilities caused by their separation in place, they were removed in time, since Germany was a much younger nation and the centuries of its existence did not correspond to those of France. Germany was also younger racially because it had a smaller basis in Roman civilization and young in its intuitive sentiment of infinity: "Hence, the material divorce of two nations so well made to love one another; fatal divorce, so cruel for the nations, so bitter for the individuals. . . . The name, the true name of this world, should it not be this: isolation in union and hatred in love!"

Continuing this double level of thinking, Michelet speculated on how much worse relations are when union is forced, such as with France and Algeria, "as happens, basically, in most marriages where, every day, a fortuitous rapprochement delivers the one to the other, without the consent of the heart." Having retraced his thoughts of June 24, the twin trail of personal and historical development, he recurred to the image of the family and focused on the tenderness and intensity of mother-child relations. Who mediates within the family, he asked, the mother or the child? An eternal question, the insolubility of which he compared to the theological question of whether the Son or the Holy Spirit represented love in the Trinity. And then came the solution, which in its equalization of family status suggested something Michelet probably did not consciously intend, much though he liked to compare himself to Oedipus: "The supreme goal of the family would be that between the three persons there would be neither sex nor age, that the son would be the father of his parents, the husband of his mother."

Immediately after this oblique confession of incestuous intent, he posed the question of his own future and decided that he would go on using his sorrows and his new ideas to enrich his "task of an arduous worker." The trip had brought him to understand that the worker—or rather the artisan—had developed more fully in Germany than anywhere else. At Nuremberg he had discovered how the shoemaker and the tailor had been able to become artists, and the toymaker, a sculptor in wood. He perceived four stages of development, the first of which was the isolated journeyman and the last the artist. In between were the worker as married guild master in his relation to his family and the same person as part of a grand family of compagnonnage among the masters, who met without women. The last stage, the artist, he viewed in terms of solitary devotion to an ideal.

This final stage is particularly interesting when we compare it with Michelet's journal notation fifteen months earlier on the personality of the artisan. There, too, he had described stages of development from the isolated journeyman to the enlarged family of guild master, but the last stage, superimposed on the guild, was not the artist, such as Dürer or himself, but "la grande patrie . . . la vraie centralisation . . . France." Evidently, the position of the artist in the evolutionary scheme was interchangeable with that of France, suggesting an identification of Michelet's own personality as artisan-artist with that of his nation.

In Nuremberg, Michelet cited as an example of the artist's devotion to an idea Dürer's painting of Mary Magdalen, which he had just seen in Saint Sebald's Church. His description of this work confirmed his self-identification as worker and slave to destiny: "Nature cries out at the left. Savage destiny carries the urn at the right. . . . In the center strides the Magdalen, pensive, bearing perfumes to scent the dead of the world. To scent? To resurrect? I too, artisan, laborious worker, am going to carry the urn, but not the perfumes. To make them one needs flowers, and they hardly flourish in me."[12]

Another of Michelet's idées fixes—the spirit of sacrifice—appears a bit further in this entry. A discussion of the Rothschilds leads him to ponder their enormous financial influence on European politics. There is, nevertheless, he writes, "one thing which they do not anticipate, sacrifice. They will never imagine that there are in Paris 10,000 men ready to die for an idea. They were surprised in July [1830]."

In his discussion in the *Histoire de France* of the Flemish weavers, written during the first months of his love for Alfred's mother, Michelet saw the spirit of sacrifice as an essential element of the artisan's personality.[13] Thus the artisan's character, and through it his own, was again identified with the French Revolution. These resonances received an added dimension when we see that for Michelet it was also a prime characteristic of Madame Dumesnil: a month after his return from Germany, he reflected on her desire, when already mortally ill, to accompany her son on a walking tour through the Swiss Alps, which he attributed to her "maternal passion: develop her son even at the expense of her life." It would seem that in Michelet's personal religion, there were many incarnations of the Godhead—the artisan, France, the Revolution, himself, and Madame Dumesnil.

More than anything else, the addition to the spirit of sacrifice of the "maternal passion" marked the distance Michelet had come since formulating "liberty versus fatality" as the leitmotiv of world history. When he returned to the theme of popular resistance to centralized power in his volume on France and the Burgundian realm, the new ideas were clearly in focus.

His ideas of July 21, 1842, a summum of his experiences of the preceding year, as he himself recognized, were bound by a central theme: the need to overcome the barriers between life and death, between soul and matter, between freedom and fatality, between beings that would love one another were it not for the fatal destiny separating them, beings like himself and Madame Dumesnil, like the two nations France and Germany, separated by space and time. Those brief reflections on the artisan-artist and the popular will to freedom and sacrifice in Paris pointed to Michelet's historical concern in coming months: the fifteenth-century struggle of the artisan cities of Liège and Dinant against Burgundian hegemony. A fine but essential line, however, linked his desire to overcome opposites in history with his love for Madame Dumesnil and with his newfound reverence for natural fecundity and maternal providence. This was true for the opposition France-Germany, as we have seen. It was also true for the opposition of the Walloon cities to the Burgundian realm and for the opposition of rich and poor described in *Le Peuple*. In a fundamental sense, his way of thinking had shifted since he formulated his opposition of liberty and fatality from the principle of liberation through the transcendence of nature and material determinism to the notion of a harmony between all opposites, based on love. In psychosexual terms, we might describe it as a shift from an Oedipal model of struggle to a pre-Oedipal model of mother-child symbiosis.

We might speak more accurately of a fusion of these two levels of psychosexual development. The combativeness, the commitment to action of the Oedipal phase remained, merged with an awareness of the profound original union with the mother. This awareness was expressed both through an identification with the maternal fecundity of nature and, because the Oedipal impulse had not disappeared, through a psychological squaring of the circle, a partial awareness of incestuous longing.

It was foreshadowed in the journal note Michelet had written in Frankfurt about the son becoming the husband of his mother. On September 21, 1842, midway in his writing on Liège for book XI, he noted that he was "impressed by this idea that there is only complete love between those closely related [*entre proches*]: Alfred told me that he had always been very sensitive to the physical grace of his mother. I too, in memory of my mother, have always loved women older than I, or as old."[14]

Nine days later, Michelet dreamed again of Caesar and the rebuilding of Corinth and Carthage. His first such dream, in January 1842, had led him to reflect on the historian's task as the justifier of the dead, on the need to find the golden bough, the key to the Underworld, in personal sorrows, and he had compared the interpretive, soothsayer function of the historian with that of Oedipus. This time, after dreaming of Caesar, he unraveled Oedipus's ultimate enigma. Without transition, as if hurriedly recapturing another dream sequence, he wrote: "It seemed to me that I was telling my mother of my lack of love. She said: Well now! Take here, my child."[15] Michelet, now unafraid of the maternal embrace, had returned from the "stepmother" to the "mother."

CHAPTER 7

WAR ON THE JESUITS: MOTHER-LOSS AND BROTHERHOOD

During the years between Madame Dumesnil's death and his en-counter with Athenaïs Mialaret, whom he married in 1849, Michelet became deeply engaged in contemporary events in France. In 1843 he entered a furious polemic with the Society of Jesus (*Les Jésuites* [1843]; *Le Prêtre, la femme et la famille* [1845]), and for the following decade he gave up his work on what was to become his nineteen-volume national history. His combat with the Jesuits was part of a broad resistance by July Monarchy liberals and republicans to the church's attack on the so-called *monopole universitaire,* state control of education; it led Michelet to reconsider his relation to the French nation and its revolutionary origins. This he did first in *Le Peuple* (1845) and then in his seven-volume *Histoire de la Révolution française* (1847–53).

All these works contain reflections of his new "matriarchal" and "fraternal" values. In *Le Peuple,* Michelet projected his beliefs of maternal fecundity and nature onto the French nation and de-picted the embodiment of fraternity in its common people, partic-ularly in its artisan strata. Soon after, in volume I of his history of the Revolution, he temporarily altered his concept of the nation to focus on the "masculine" value of justice, and in the parts of it dealing with the Terror (written after June 1848 and after the death of his infant son in 1850), he partially returned to the hostile view of women that had dominated his work before 1840. Nonetheless, he rediscovered his ideals of fraternity and of the maternal benefi-cence of the French nation both in the federations of 1790 and in the anticipations in 1793 of what he saw as the "social and religious age" of the Revolution.

Throughout the period 1843–48, Michelet's emotional needs

were partly sublimated into his writing and partly satisfied directly through at least three affairs. One of these, with Madame Aupèpin, seems to have held little more than carnal significance for him. The other two, with his housekeepers Marie and Victoire, appear to have been idealistically, as well as physically, motivated.[1] During the period in which he was exploring his own popular origins in *Le Peuple* and those of the French nation in his history of the Revolution, he attempted, with apparent sincerity, to educate Marie and Victoire. None of these relations, however, seems to have strongly influenced his way of viewing the world. This is not surprising if we consider that Madame Dumesnil's son, who married Michelet's daughter, Adèle, in August 1843, lived under his roof and constantly reminded him of what Madame Dumesnil had meant to him. It is, then, the values Michelet venerated in the dead mother of his son-in-law that primarily color the years before he met Athenaïs Mialaret.

Volume VI of the *Histoire de France,* the last he wrote before embarking on his more activist phase, does not reveal much of this influence, concerned as it is with a largely political narrative of the reigns of Louis XI and Charles the Bold. Nonetheless, Michelet's chapter on Charles the Bold's attacks on Liège and Dinant, written after his trip to Germany, was indirectly overshadowed by Madame Dumesnil's spirit and values. We see this in the remarkable journal entry of August 11, 1842 (in part taken over as a footnote to book XV), which he began parenthetically, "On writing about Liège." He mentioned his love for France—"so young and so reasonable, so much good sense in her eyes, so gracious and playful"—and compared the provinces of France, among which he listed Wallonia, to her daughters: "I love her, I love them and thank them for bringing back to me the adored mother, such as she was at another epoch when, younger, she was less herself. They are for me the degrees, the stations toward the supreme maternal beauty. *O sun, o sea, o rose!*"[2]

The link to his lost love, through those lines of the poet Rückert which had haunted him repeatedly on his travels through Germany, was made yet more explicit a few lines later, when he wrote: "The sorrow of the loss of France can only be compared with that of the loss of a person, of a being, of being exiled from a person."

Michelet's love for Madame Dumesnil was a jealous love. He was repeatedly embittered on the trip through Germany at the thought of her earlier friendships; even more was he hurt by the fact that in her last months she was often closed to him and seemed to confide in her confessor. Although some conflict between Michelet and the church was inevitable considering the matriarchal deity he announced in his lectures of April and May 1842, the acerbity and depth of his hostility was probably related to the personal injury he felt over the church's grip on the woman dying under his roof.[3]

Not exclusively, of course. Michelet could not have helped noticing that the real recipient of Madame Dumesnil's trust in her last months, his "competitor" for her love, was not the abbé Cœur but her son, Alfred; this, however, was a perception whose emotional implications he was obliged to repress, considering his affection for the young man and his commitment to take over the role of Alfred's mother after her death. Residues of that repressed resentment appeared from time to time in the next seven years. Meanwhile, all his conscious resentment went to the clerical enemy: both in his lectures with Edgar Quinet in spring 1843 and in his more extended work the following year, a consistent reproach was the Jesuits' control over mothers and children.[4]

Again, the conflict between historian and church hardly came out of the blue. Long before the social-romantic phase Michelet slipped into after Pauline's death and his encounter with Madame Dumesnil, the liberal circles he was educated in and which supported his career had been in a state of latent—sometimes open—conflict with the Catholic church.[5] Indeed, when revolutionaries hostile to the church's support for the Bourbon cause sacked the residence of the archbishop of Paris in 1831, Adolphe Thiers himself, then a left-leaning member of the government, was said to have been seen grinning amid the ruins.[6]

Throughout the 1830s, conflict between church and state was allayed by the appearance of a liberal Catholic group around Comte Charles-Forbes-René de Montalembert and *l'Avenir,* which did not challenge the state's right to promote secular education but merely asked for the "freedom of instruction" that had been promised in the Charter of 1815: the church was to be allowed the right to supervise the teaching of those who wanted a Catholic education. Most Catholics came to support this liberal position, and it was implemented in 1833 for elementary education. Guizot's attempt to extend the charter to secondary education in 1836 was unsuccessful, but in 1839 negotiations began again between the Ministry of Education—led successively by Michelet's old teachers Cousin and Villemain—and the church; the result was a draft project of 1841 that in the eyes of the Catholics only strengthened state control over Catholic education. It aroused a storm of protest from the clergy and defenders of the church and had to be withdrawn.

Villemain's draft law of 1841 reawakened the slumbering church-state conflict. In any case, after the repeated failures of republican uprisings in the 1830s, the revolutionary impulse seemed exhausted, and the angry reactions to the proposed legislation laid the basis for a broad Catholic challenge to the hegemony of the secular state over secondary and higher education. Incited by the violent ultramontane attacks of Louis Veuillot's *l'Univers,* as well as by the more moderate, but aroused, Montalembert, war was declared on the government's *monopole universitaire* and in particular on the liberal professors who administered it in the early 1840s: Villemain and Cousin. From the standpoint of the liberals and republicans, whose anticlerical positions were under siege, the real enemy seemed to be that bugbear of all enlightened Frenchmen since the eighteenth century, the Jesuits.[7]

In the context of this gathering conflagration, Michelet's Joachimite "évangile éternal," announced in 1842 at the Collège de France, began to attract hostile Catholic attention. The fact that comparable heresies were being advanced by Michelet's friends and colleagues, the historian Edgar Quinet and the poet Adam Mickiewicz (a disciple of the Polish mystic Andrzej Towianski) made all three excellent targets of Catholic ire, as the anonymous Jesuit pamphlet of February 1843 against the *monopole universitaire* made clear.[8]

Thus Michelet and Quinet's resolve in April 1843 to give a joint series of lectures on the Jesuits transformed the outspoken professors at the Collège de France into the prime object of attack and defense in the church-state conflict over the next few years. The "objective" merits in this controversy have long ceased to be of more than antiquarian interest. What makes Michelet's attacks on the clergy relevant for the evolution of his intellect and personality, however, is the evident mixture of rancor and personal idealism that inspired his attacks and counterattacks on the clergy. Not only did he single out for criticism the Jesuits' grip on the female sex, but in *Le Prêtre, la femme et la famille* he also included chapters on both the needs of men for nurturance by their wives and the correct maternal education of the young, and these chapters show him repeatedly using as a model Alfred Dumesnil's late, much-lamented mother.

When Michelet wrote, for example, that "the Frenchwoman, more than English and German women, is ready to second the man, and can become for him not only the partner, but the companion, the friend, the associate, the *alter ego,*" he probably had Alfred's mother in mind—the words surely do not apply to his deceased wife. Equally so when he wrote: "Modern man, victim of the division of labor, often condemned to a narrow specialization where he loses his feeling for life in general and atrophies, would need to find at home a young and serene spirit ... who would take him out of his profession and give him the feeling of harmony.... He would need a woman in the home to refresh his burning brow ...

she would reopen the lively source of the beautiful and the good, of God and nature; he would drink a moment at the eternal waters."[9]

Woman as a source of pantheist aestheticism for the overspecialized male! The significance of Madame Dumesnil's values in this apotheosis is strongly suggested by a letter she wrote to Alfred when she was becoming Michelet's close friend, in early 1841:

> If you appreciate the arts so well, it's less because you have seen many works of art than because you have lived so long in the country. It is the great book, the divine source of the beautiful and the good. When one really feels this admirable manifestation of God, one is able to perceive a painting of Raphaël and the music of Mozart. I believe that the biggest reason why men, even superior ones, are often so incomplete, is that they are content to spend all their effort on the works of man and neglect the works of God. Their spirit has reached the level of human science, but their heart has often remained cold. To the contrary, the heart ought to warm everything.[10]

Later, in *Le Prêtre, la femme et la famille,* Michelet discussed the mutual needs of mother and child; he warned strenuously against loosening prematurely the tie between the two and emphasized the active role of the mother as companion for a growing son: "When one removes him to raise him far from her . . . he cries, she cries, one proceeds further. . . . Wrongly. In these tears where one sees only weakness, there is something more serious . . . *he still needs her.* The stage of nursing is not over. Intellectual nourishment should, like the other, at the beginning [be] fluid, warm, sweet, living. Only the woman can do this."[11] And two pages further: "You fear that, left too long with a woman, he will become a woman. But it is she who would become a man if you left her with her son. Try, she will change, you'll be astonished yourself. Little walking journeys, long horse-back rides, nothing will be too much for her, believe me. She will begin the young man's exercises in good spirits, she will return to his age, will renew herself in this vita nuova."[12] Recall Michelet's praise for Madame Dumesnil's "maternal passion," exemplified in her readiness, at great danger to her own faltering health, to join her son in an Alpine climb. He himself thought, when she asked him in 1840 to suggest a suitable travel companion for Alfred, "that his best comrade is his mother."[13]

Other passages in *Le Prêtre* suggest the significance of Michelet's own mother. Thus, where he writes, "Do not chase this new man prematurely from the maternal paradise; . . . Tomorrow he will be bent at his job. . . . Today let him . . . aspire with a large heart to the vital air of liberty." Michelet himself received much of his education at his mother's side; indeed, after he started school, other children teased him to bitter tears; at age twenty-two he wrote that "mama was touched and preferred that I interrupt my studies if they made me so miserable."[14] We also feel an autobiographical note where he writes: "The idea of every mother ... is to make a hero, a man powerful in acts and fecund in works, who can desire, who is capable, and who creates";[15] further, where he says, "All superior men are the sons of their mother; they reproduce her moral imprint as well as her traits." We have seen how strong an influence his own mother was on the formation of his personality, in endowing him with the necessary character to "desire" to be "capable" and above all to be "fecund in works."

The way in which Michelet viewed his mother in the period of *Le Prêtre* must nonetheless have altered considerably for him to mix her model more or less indiscriminately with that of Madame Dumesnil. Earlier, though he had internalized his mother's hard-nosed asceticism and expressed filial piety, his underlying image of maternity, as he projected it into the suffocating natural fatality of Indian culture, produced far more anxiety than security. Now, through the model of Madame Dumesnil, motherhood and natural fecundity were no longer the born enemies of liberty but its precondition and guarantee. Clearly, his love for her had changed not merely his abstract ideas about motherhood but his perceptions and feelings about his own mother.

We have seen this in his partial awareness and acceptance of his incestuous impulses. In this connection it is perhaps noteworthy that the first mention in the journal of Madame Navailles and her son, the mother and half-brother of Pauline, whom Michelet suspected of sustaining incestuous relations, occurred less than a month after he dreamed of his own mother's obligingness.[16]

In the year after Madame Dumesnil's death, Michelet reverted painfully to his monklike, divided existence. He returned intellectually to volume VI of the *Histoire de France* and his lectures at the Collège de France. His physical needs in 1842–43 were satisfied by his affair with his housekeeper, Marie. The return to the split existences that had earlier characterized his life with Pauline, accompanied by his continued grief over Madame Dumesnil's death, depressed him, and his depression worsened when he realized that he would soon lose Adèle in marriage to Alfred.

In autumn 1842 even his work offered but a feeble outlet for his creativity, crippled as it was by the bruised state of his personality. A letter of September 7 by his thirteen-year-old son, Charles, portrayed him as barely able to work at all, complaining of pains in the heart and frequently telling his children he was going to die.

Another, from Alfred to Eugène Noel, ten days later, repeated what Charles had said about Michelet's physical condition and added, "What is more serious is that morally he seems very ill, more than I expected. . . . He struggles to work and his difficulty in producing makes him desperate. Unable to sleep, he spends nearly every night reading ancient chronicles. He sees no one."[17] Not surprisingly, the heartsick historian complained of "difficulty in breathing," probably hyperventilation.[18]

Shortly after, he was writing again, on Louis XI and Liège; but the link he had found between that city and Alfred's late mother hardly dispelled his funereal gloom. In a letter of October 13 to Alfred, then back in Rouen, he said, "I neither hope nor desire to live, feeling worse every day in body and mind. The dizziness and nausea warn me continually that I am no better in my stomach and head than in my chest."[19] As sometimes happens in extreme grief, he appears to have internalized not just the spirit of his dead friend but the physical torments of her last months as well.

On November 10, 1842, Michelet wrote with bitter irony of the meaning his study of the fifteenth century had for him: "I have perhaps taken too seriously the farce of the XVth century. One simply has to gape in astonishment at this whole comedy. . . . Gape at pleasure, at the flesh. . . . Lift yourself up, then, and take, above this nothingness here and that nothingness there, the wings of irony." And in a letter to Alfred of November 13, 1842, on the same subject: "This side of the grand irony of the world is the only one that might fit me, in my sadness which is so extreme that I dare not for a moment face myself."[20]

He seems to have touched bottom at this time. Shortly after, the approach of his new lecture series at the Collège de France forced him to focus on more general historical questions and he began to revive.[21] But the broad theoretical emphasis of his first lectures, a homage to the Swiss historian Jean Simonde de Sismondi, who had died the previous June, discussions of other contemporary and recent historians mixed with discussion of his own method, did not lead to a coherent subject matter. Ten days after completing this course, implicitly acknowledging its lack of cohesion, he reexamined his lectures of 1838 on women in the Middle Ages. In that earlier course, he now saw, he was reaching into his past for elements of integration to bind his past and present. It was, he said, simultaneously "history, voyage, and biography. It began to recompose my dispersed personality. I relived my childhood in it. . . . I found there my symbol already studied this year: *woman* . . . mediatress of the world. . . . What's more, I was introduced to the social vitality of the people which was to preoccupy me soon."[22]

Indeed, three of the subjects he had dealt with in his most

recent lectures—the legends of the people, the medieval sources of fraternity, and machinism—were joined a few years later to the reexploration of his childhood as crucial elements in *Le Peuple.*

Machinism was an immediate issue because in a few months he began his attack on the Jesuits for epitomizing it. In his first lecture of the course of December 1842 to March 1843, he used the concept to attack the formalistic rationalism of the modern age but does not seem to have mentioned the Jesuits. According to a sympathetic summary in a contemporary periodical, Michelet maintained that "a terrible formalism was invading everything. A new scholasticism, daughter of analysis and abstraction, enveloped England through the political economy of Malthus, Germany through the philosophy of Kant, and France through administration and codification. Reasoning machines, law machines, steam machines, everywhere the machine invaded the human domain."[23]

Michelet was again, as in 1831, warning against the menace to human freedom of "fatality," but, in sharp distinction to the liberal ideology he had then cherished, not nature but the machinelike world created by modern man epitomized that fatality. Nature, though he did not emphasize it here, had become for Michelet an indispensable source of freedom.

The theme of popular legends, which preoccupied him during and just after the Second Republic, appeared in his eighth lecture, "The People Made Its Legends." He used the popular legends of the saints, again according to the sympathetic account in the *Revue indépendante,* to bring to light "the thought, the desire, the popular custom incarnated there."[24] This attempt to pierce the ideological or institutional masks, to find the motives or material interests behind them, was probably what he meant by the obscure term *desymbolisation.*[25]

The most significant lecture of this series, pointing as it did to Michelet's central concerns in his coming books on the people and on the French Revolution, as well as to an important new aspect of his own personality, was the last one, on the forms of sociability in medieval France. He referred to it as "association et fraternité, confrérie et famille." Alfred, in a letter to his friend Eugène Noel, called it his "most democratic lesson, on the association of the lower classes in the middle ages," and added that the historian envisaged "fraternity in all times and places where there were people."[26]

The notion of fraternity is an ideological version of what the social psychologists mean by peer relationships.[27] In the ideology of the French Revolution, fraternity had a rather abstract character as an ideal of human brotherhood, whose apotheosis Michelet found in the *fête de la fédération,* a more or less spontaneous union in brotherhood of the French people. But in the Middle Ages—and in more recent times—popular sociability developed within the traditional economic and social forms of preindustrial societies: the associations, confraternities, and extended families, with their economic and religious functions, which Michelet discussed in his lecture of March 16.

This issue, too, marked the distance Michelet had come since his liberal beginnings. Liberal economic ideas are and were generally hostile to all traditional forms of sociability, as restraints to the free workings of the market; in this hostility they simply followed the examples of the absolute state and church of the sixteenth through eighteenth centuries, which had their own reasons for fearing popular sovereignty.[28]

The appearance during the Revolution of the ideal of fraternity, alongside those of liberty and equality, indicated the survival of traditional forms of sociability, of their importance as an organizational basis for the Revolution, and of their potential transformation, under the stress of national crisis, into the foundations of modern democratic movements.[29] Michelet did not see all of this as clearly as we now can, but he was aware that the democratic movements of the modern world did stand in some relation to the premodern popular social organizations. In fact, we can view much of his way of looking at the world in terms of his self-identification as an artisan-artist and of his research in France's past and present for social structures which supported that identification.

Yet, he was also aware of the extent to which his career as a scholar, protected and advanced by the educated liberals of the July Monarchy, had estranged him from his artisanal roots. One form of sociability in the nineteenth century , though impaired by modern development, nonetheless sometimes retained a subterranean connection with the older popular culture, even for members of the modern middle-class strata, which in all other respects were free of contamination by it. This was the youth peer group, whose late medieval form was the abbaye de jeunesse and one of whose characteristic means of expression was the charivari.[30]

Although older forms of the youth group had largely been wiped out of the European cities during the rise of the absolute state and church, they persisted in the countryside for most of the nineteenth century;[31] moreover, in spite of a lack of formal organization, close adolescent peer relations that often escaped the supervision of the bourgeois family ethic were common among young males of all classes in the nineteenth century. We know of their existence in the youths of writers, and there is no reason to think that they were uncommon outside the circles of those who would leave letters behind or describe them in autobiographies.[32]

Circles of youth that are based on such intimate sentiments

abound in the history of France and Germany at certain points.[33] In France, the romantic cenacles in the 1820s and 1830s are one example, the rowdy Bohemian Bousingots of the July Monarchy another; in Germany at the turn of the twentieth century, the *Wandervogel,* the circle of poets around Stefan George, and the expressionist groups of Munich and Berlin are others.

Michelet had never been a part of such a group. He was hostile to both the romantic and the Saint-Simonian circles of 1830, perhaps partly because of his lower-middle-class origins and liberal consciousness. In secondary school a decade and a half earlier, he had learned to fear the mockery of his peers and led a lonely existence. Indeed, for many reasons, his principal mode of relationship throughout his life was vertical, not horizontal, with parent figures or their opposites, child figures.

Yet there had been Poinsot, whom he had loved as an adolescent and for whom he had written his autobiographical *Mémorial* and, in 1820, begun his *Journal.* As Michelet matured, he abandoned some of the lonely precepts of liberal idealism. He found, and lost, his spiritual mother, Madame Dumesnil, and discovered through her the values of nature and maternal fecundity. A few years later, in *Le Peuple* (1846), he linked these values explicitly to the principles of sociability and friendship, so it is not surprising that shortly after her death he anticipated this link by a new quest for the brotherhood he had lost in 1821. As in everything else that mattered to him, he sought it simultaneously on the planes of personal life and historical existence.

PART III

FRATERNITY,
1843 – 1846

We few, we happy few, we band of brothers.

SHAKESPEARE
Henry V, IV.iii.60

CHAPTER 8

FRATERNITY, ANDROGYNY, AND REBIRTH: ORIGINS OF LE PEUPLE

The Brotherhoods of the Collège de France

On August 3, 1843, Alfred Dumesnil married Michelet's daughter, Adèle, in Rouen. The historian returned to his deserted home on Paris's rue des Postes the next day and stood, distraught and appalled, in Adèle's empty room. He invoked with acrimonious irony the "austere cares" of Providence, the "maternal cares of a stern mother who, less concerned for the happiness of her child than for his glory, severely cuts him off from everything that could retard him." The "everything" signified everything protective and feminine. "Pauline?" he asked. "No. Adèle? No. The other Adèle carried off too." (The two Adèles are his daughter and Alfred's mother, Françoise-Adèle.) To this enumeration he added a page later, "my mother," who entered the list in the place of Madame Dumesnil, and further, in a reference to the clerical offensive against him because of his anti-Catholic positions, "this great mother Church, so much the more loved by me since for a long time I loved her in liberty."[1]

When we see how Michelet regretted in the same breath the loss of the two Adèles, we wonder if he may not have augmented his conscious hostility toward the church for taking charge of Madame Dumesnil's soul with hidden rancor toward Alfred. Not only was Alfred carrying off Michelet's daughter, but he had, to his future father-in-law's distress, been the sole recipient of his mother's love and confidence during her last months.[2] Now we know from the careful and erudite Gabriel Monod that Michelet's decision to lecture on the Jesuits was sudden, taken just before he actually did so and ostensibly intended to aid his friend Quinet, who was being more sharply attacked in the Catholic press than Michelet and whose coming lectures on the sixteenth century were certain to touch on the explosive topic of the Jesuit order.[3] Further suggesting that this sudden decision was not motivated exclusively by the needs of ideological combat is the fact that midway between his last lecture of the first series, when there was no indication that he intended to lecture on the Jesuits, and the first lecture against the order forty days later, he received the formal request from Alfred's father asking his permission for Adèle to marry Alfred.[4]

If indeed he projected his bitterness over Adèle's marriage into indignation over the church that seemed to have robbed him of the other Adèle, it was a way of closing a magic circle. For whatever the objective political basis for the quarrel between Catholicism and the secular university, Michelet's perception of the church's grip on women in general and on Madame Dumesnil in particular was redolent with Oedipal envy and aggression. The Oedipal hostility, earlier objectified in his identification with liberty against fatality, had not disappeared from his psychic constitution but, on the contrary, had received a more specific object through the return to pre-Oedipal states of mind occasioned by Madame Dumesnil.[5] The need to engage in such Oedipal struggle brought with it the perspective of something like the brother band denoted by Freud in *Totem and Taboo*. Obvious allies were Michelet's colleagues Quinet and Mickiewicz. But equally if not more important was an alliance with the brother bands of the admiring students at the Collège de France. And the palpable link to those disciples was through the young student who was about to marry his daughter. All the more reason for Michelet not to react with conscious resentment to Alfred's *enlèvement* of either Adèle but to add that resentment to what he already felt about the Jesuit order.

In fact, it was Michelet's association with the younger generation of his students, not his purely peer relation to men like Quinet and Mickiewicz that was, in the long run, essential. This relation to the students may have been in part an inversion of the vertical parent-substitute relation he was accustomed to in his well-supported ascent to the Collège de France, but it was also in part a peer relation, since many of his students had become, or were becoming, his personal assistants or junior colleagues.

Although these associations with students and assistants never took the form of a fixed organization or journal, on occasion, either through his or their initiative, they seemed on the point of doing so, and the different generations of Michelet's disciples repeatedly offered him help at difficult moments. Indeed, there were so many of Michelet's students in important secondary school teaching positions and so many times when the auditors at the Collège de

France and other students and young radicals organized on his behalf that one can loosely speak of a Michelet Mafia in mid-nineteenth-century France. At a dinner party in August 1841, for
example, Madame Dumesnil enumerated among the guests of the
historian, apart from his old friends the Porets and Quinets, his
secretary Félix Ravaisson "and a half dozen young people of the
Ecole Normale, placed by M. Michelet in the provinces, all his pupils
and his friends."[6]

The older and younger generations of Michelet's students
shared a vital link that was especially visible in the case of Adolphe
Chéruel of the Collège royale in Rouen. Chéruel was one of the
master's earliest disciples at the Ecole normale, and the two journeyed to England together in the summer of 1831. Later, Chéruel
confided his most intimate problems to the older man,[7] and from
the late 1830s on he was recommending his best pupils to Michelet,
most of them coming to Paris to study law. This was how Frédéric
Baudry, at age twenty, met Michelet and accompanied him on his
travels.[8] Baudry was the school friend of the slightly younger student Gustave Flaubert and his intimate friend Alfred le Poittevin,
both of whom Chéruel also recommended around 1840,[9] but these
two did not take advantage of the opportunity, much though they
admired Chéruel's mentor. Of course, the most significant, for
Michelet, of the young men Chéruel recommended to him was
Alfred Dumesnil, who, probably because of his mother, soon
eclipsed Baudry in Michelet's affections.[10]

In spite of his ambivalence about Alfred's proximity to Adèle,
Michelet repeatedly, during the months after their return from Germany, while the bereaved son was attempting ineffectually to
straighten out his mother's estate in Rouen, urged Alfred to return
to Paris and live with him so that they could work together.[11] Then,
suddenly, there were concrete and ambitious plans for collaboration.
On December 7, recovering his energy after his prolonged depression, Michelet called in his closest assistants, Jean Yanoski, Alex
Wallon, and Charles Weiss. All three were young men of about
thirty who had studied with him at the Ecole normale; the purpose
was to organize a major collection of historical studies.[12] He called
his idea "the plan which would transform, subjugate everything"
and wrote the same day to Alfred, pleading with him to return,
informing him vaguely of the project and the role of his students
in it, and adding, "You are the person whose assistance I most
desire."[13] Three days later, he had Yanoski, Weiss, and his former
secretary, Félix Ravaisson, to dinner, noted their bickering and lack
of intelligence,[14] and apparently decided to shift course to a project
in which Alfred alone would assist him. In any case, he wrote Alfred
the following day that the young man's arrival was coming at an

important moment in his life, since he had decided "to recast this winter all of the *Histoire de France,* or rather that of modern society, and put it into one volume."[15]

Nothing came of these plans, but the impulse to unite the advantages of friendship and intellectual collaboration reappeared in April 1843, when Michelet discussed the "war on the Jesuits" with Edgar Quinet. They organized their campaign in the form of alternating lectures, which, published immediately, sold ten thousand copies before year's end. This fraternity of struggle, apart from continuing Michelet's earlier efforts to work with his students, echoed his last lecture before the "war," on the social foundations of fraternity in the Middle Ages.

The course on the Jesuits generated new sources of fraternity. More than ever, Michelet enjoyed the support of his auditors, students, and colleagues, as the clergy's attack on secular control of higher education zeroed in on the two impious professors. Supporters of the Jesuits who came to heckle brought on themselves, according to Michelet, "the indignation of the entire audience" and "were pursued by the boos of the crowd" at the end of the lectures.[16] He also reported, in his published version of the lectures, that "on Thursday, May 11, several of my colleagues and of my more illustrious French and foreign friends wanted in some way to protest by their presence against these unworthy attacks, and did me the honor of encircling my tribune."[17] Among those "foreign friends" was Leopold von Ranke.

Several times in the next months, Michelet and Quinet were approached by groups of students and younger colleagues who wanted sometimes simply to express their admiration and support, sometimes to suggest organizational forms for continuing the struggle, which Michelet found overzealous and discouraged.[18] Nonetheless, the students of the "schools" of Paris repeatedly demonstrated their support for the embattled professors. Fifty-six years after the event, a former medical student described the atmosphere to Quinet's widow: "Such days will never be seen again. We were at Clamart, we marched in groups to Sainte-Geneviève to attend these lessons; we sang all the way along the route, and once in the hall, what applause! We adored these two men, we deified them."[19]

There are signs that Quinet was more receptive to this, more willing than Michelet to join the students in a brotherhood of struggle. For though the author of the *Histoire de France* desperately needed comradeship and more and more understood the historical significance of that need as the basis of popular social organization and "fraternity," he was himself incapable of sustaining such comradeship with more than one or two people at a time. Poinsot, Poret, Madame Dumesnil, Alfred, and, of course, Quinet had been privileged intimates, irreplaceable by enthusiastic masses. Nonetheless, Michelet continued to work out on the plane of his historical studies the significance of brotherhood, fraternity, and human sociability and to integrate these notions into his new values on nature and maternal fecundity. The first major meeting place for these new concepts was *Le Peuple.*

Union of the Sexes, Union of the Classes:
Of Androgyny and the Two Nations

The joint lectures with Quinet on the Jesuits were in many senses a crucial step for Michelet, lifting him out of the depression caused by Madame Dumesnil's death, giving him a renewed feeling of dedication and of human brotherhood. The basis for this new mood as well as its object was in 1843 predominantly negative: struggle against the grip of the priesthood on women and family life. In *Le Peuple,* Michelet transcended his rancor. The central idea of the book was the harmonious reconciliation, in love of nature and of la patrie, between France's common people and upper classes, a goal Michelet shared with Saint-Simonians and humanitarian radicals of the time. Supplementing his ideal of overcoming social differences was a notion of reconciling sexual ones; this, too, expressed the age. Indeed, the psychosexual androgyny inherent in Michelet's notion of the "two sexes of the spirit," one of the most striking concepts in *Le Peuple,* places this work squarely in the mainstream of French social romanticism.

Western culture has frequently distinguished an intuitive-comprehending faculty, identified with the feminine, and a rational-analytic faculty, viewed as masculine. Where Michelet and the social romantics differed from the usual sexual stereotypes was in arguing that the two components were of equal value and that the ideal personality—*le génie* for Michelet—should combine both traits. On the one hand, as did many of his romantic contemporaries, Michelet identified the intuitive feminine faculty with the people, with nature, with children, but also with France itself. *Le peuple,* passive, young, and instinctual, became at once Michelet's child, fraternal comrade, wife, and mother—roles he transferred, after the civil catastrophe of June 1848 had shattered his faith in the French people, to his second wife, Athenaïs. On the other hand, Michelet applied the notion of the two sexes of the spirit to himself; he saw himself as being both "peuple" (feminine) and "génie" (bisexual),[20] as simultaneously bringing the message of social harmony, of mutual love, to the people and receiving from them the spirit of fraternity. In all of this his personal development merged with the social romantic mentality of the period, providing a powerful inner motor that shaped his intellectual contribution.

After the death of Pauline and the encounter with Madame Dumesnil, the secure prominence Michelet had attained permitted him the revaluation of his values concerning nature and motherhood, the evolution toward the "maternal God" we have noted. This redefinition was possible only by a more or less conscious reexamination of his personal past. *Le Peuple* was the fruit of that review, as well as of contemporary political and ideological needs.[21] Evident in the structure of the work, no less than in its direct allusions to his personal life, is Michelet's struggle to redefine his notion of history in terms of natural instinct and the fraternity of the nation by redefining himself through his rediscovery of motherhood and friendship.

The tripartite division of *Le Peuple* suggests this clearly. The first part, a class analysis of the French nation, is titled "Of Servitude and Hatred." It should be read with the more optimistic "Introduction à l'histoire universelle" of 1831 in mind, as an implicit critique of where the "freedom" of the July Monarchy, which he had extolled, had led. The second part, "Liberation through Love—Nature," reveals his discovery of the positive role played by natural instinct, particularly the mother-child tie, in laying the basis for human freedom. Here are found the most striking contrasts with the "Introduction" of 1831. Part III, "Liberation through Love—the Nation"[22] portrays the nation as the highest form of sociability, or fraternity, built on the lesser forms of local association, love, marriage, and friendship.

The bitterly critical posture Michelet revealed in calling his tableau of French society "On Servitude and Hatred" had both personal and historical sources. His own psychological development had, through the "war against the Jesuits," led him into a dialectic of sharpening conflict with secular and religious powers; this conflict merged with a struggle that had been going on since the Restoration and that became acute in the 1840s.

As Michelet made clear in his lectures of the spring of 1845, he had reached a point where his attack on the clergy had to be broadened by an appeal to the people, and, because the people lacked a sense both of their history and of what they were, his first task was to educate them.[23] What was needed above all was a new code of beliefs to inspire the people in their coming struggles. In the way he outlined the problem posed by the Revolution of 1789, we see clearly his distance from the liberal principles that had infused his early work, as well as his proximity to the social romantic critiques of the 1840s:

The people had sentimentality, sympathy, generosity, but it could formulate nothing; ... the Assembly was consumed in the impossible task of conciliating the monarchy and the Republic. It had no religious symbol; the old one has perished, the new one cannot be found, the struggle prevents it and the Assembly prevents it too, protesting that it no longer believes. There is the peril. The time of trial and sacrifice is coming, the time which will judge. When it poses the question: Do you want to die for the new principle? is it not to be feared that some will ask: "What is the new principle?" Liberty? But liberty is not a principle, it is the faculty of thinking and doing. Think what? Do what? *Equality?* Civil? Social? But a leveled people would be disharmonious and disarmed.[24]

In later lectures, Michelet spelled out his implicit critique of both liberal principles and the July Monarchy to such an extent that the press accused him of preaching revolution.[25] According to Monod, he attacked the false premises not only of the clergy and the romantics but also of the "corrupt *juste milieu,* fallen so low that it thought to support itself through the Jesuits."[26] For its lies and false hopes the center-left opposition, led by Thiers, came under his anathema no less than Guizot, the head of the juste-milieu government. The government issued from the Revolution of 1830 was, according to Michelet, "that of *the bank,* of the big proprietors and the big industrialists, that is, of a minority in this agrarian country.... To crown its weakness, it has sought support in the priestly party, that of the older branch, that of divine right." All governments of the nineteenth century, he argued, "exploited with pleasure the same thing: fear of the Revolution, this Medusa's head, which Bonaparte showed to the party of the Middle Ages, out of fear of the future; he frightens the bourgeoisie: 'Rally around us, take care. Only I can defend you. Behold the people, rising, behold the barbarians. Remember these frightful times.' Impious creed which creates two peoples." Michelet sensed a new revolution coming and saw the need for unity of the "two peoples" (bourgeois and common people), not only for the sake of internal regeneration but to assure the national defense against the hostile giants, England and Russia: "Let us try, before the crisis, to recognize ourselves, to hear ourselves, to grasp one another's hand (between two peoples). We can still do it, I beg of you, let Europe not find us divided at this solemn moment."[27]

This notion of the two peoples, which one finds at about the same time in Benjamin Disraeli's *Sybil; or The Two Nations* (1845), along with the need to unite them, was one of the central themes of the book he had pledged to write that year. Implicitly, the unity was to be the basis and the strength of the coming revolution.

Taming the Monster

Michelet wrote in his journal on January 14, 1845, that he had found his title, *Le Peuple,* and wanted to finish the book exactly one year later. We have no notion of what kind of book he then intended, except for a brief remark on January 31 that he had outlined the part of the book on the Middle Ages. Evidently he was thinking of something much more ambitious in historical terms than what he finally produced, since the book, completed on schedule, deals essentially with the present.

More than seven months passed between the first announcement of *Le Peuple* and his actually beginning to write it. There were many reasons for the delay. One was preparatory work. His lectures kept him busy that spring, and he built into them a scaffolding both of radical critique of the government and of analysis of the people's needs that would form a useful point of departure for the book. His summer trip to Cherbourg was also a preparation for *Le Peuple,* since his discussions there with local fisherfolk reappear in a chapter in part III on "Association." And he was doubtless distracted by the denouement of his and Quinet's polemic with the Jesuits: complicated negotiations by Guizot's man in Rome, Pellegrino Rossi, to barter away the professors' freedom of speech against the Jesuit order's public existence.[28]

Still, the background to *Le Peuple* is somewhat unusual. The lectures, for example, are actually much less related to the book that followed them than those that usually preceded his books, whether his volumes of the *Histoire de France* or his attacks on the Jesuits. Moreover, Michelet does not seem to have been writing anything else in the first eight months of 1845, and, judging by the rather haphazard state of his lecture notes that year, it is unlikely that the lectures filled much of his week. On August 12 in Rouen, just after his trip to Cherbourg, he wrote in his journal, "Decided on the plan of my book, drawing everything from the present." But no further progress was made during the next ten days, and on August 22 he reported disconsolately, "Every day, only at the Archives, occupied with my plan, which emerges slowly." The following day he spent in recollections of his childhood under the first empire, which he used five months later while writing the open letter to Quinet that introduced *Le Peuple.* On September 1, he noted that he had begun writing "the first part, historical," which he had apparently not yet relinquished, but that he had decided it would be better to start with the second part, "on the evil and the remedy, education, love, etc."

Suddenly there was a rapid acceleration. On September 4, he reported for the last time that he had settled on an outline—"love alone the builder of the city"—and from that point on, he wrote with what Monod describes as "feverish haste . . . having his chapters printed as he wrote them, sometimes suspending the double work to continue his research."[29] On the day before this explosion of energy began, his daughter, Adèle, now Alfred Dumesnil's wife, gave birth to a boy, Jules Etienne Félix, his and Madame Dumesnil's grandson. It was the belated fruit, once removed, of the greatest love of his life, and a number of things indicate that the long wait for this event had been blocking his energies and that its arrival released them.

Michelet had noted on Easter Sunday, March 23, that Adèle was pregnant, and although he did not again allude to the fact, he must have been anxious, since her first pregnancy had ended in miscarriage a year and a half earlier.[30] He had always been close to Adèle; his desolate loneliness after her marriage was matched by his fears for her, which had haunted him ever since he had envisaged her frailty and mortality as a child: "Adèle is throwing stones into the sea," he had written in 1831. "The child's first experience of the infinite, which it does not yet feel and which sooner or later has to swallow us up; it does not yet know this monster which devours itself to be reborn. Must you too."[31] The next day he came back to the experience: "Like Chryses, I think of my daughter. . . . I am very moved from having seen my little child pensive in the face of the sea, frail child on whom I placed my life and whom I will not be able to protect. Oh, if my name could convey you some respect, some protection after me!"[32] He recalled that first experience twice in the journal: in July 1833, when Adèle's presence with him on the tower of the cathedral at Reims so frightened him that he could not see, and in September 1839, after Pauline's death.[33]

Two weeks before his grandson's birth, the possibility of death by water was again haunting him, not in connection with Adèle but now about Eugène Noel, who was as close as Adèle to Alfred and who had become Michelet's own close friend. When news came that a cyclone had ravaged the valley in which Noel lived, Michelet wrote Noel that he had dreamed of "a great number of travelers who drowned in the Seine, a thousand dark heads that disappeared in a night shipwreck."[34] That his fear and its objects were related to his work on *Le Peuple* is suggested by his following remarks: "You, particularly, seem to me a necessary person. This bond we are seeking between the people and the bourgeois, the peasant and the urban dweller, who knows if you are not the man *destined* to give it to us." What makes the association of the birth of *Le Peuple* with the birth of his grandson yet more plausible is that in another letter to Noel, four days after the birth, his fears seem to have been overcome. If we bear in mind the terminology of Michelet's first reference to Adèle, aged six, by the sea, the metaphorical overtones are striking: "I have also suffered for some time, swimming in a sea of uncertainties and hesitations. This book is the ocean, nothing less. I think, nonetheless, that I have today finally tamed the monster. It will appear in January or I will die." Perhaps ruminating over the fate of his daughter in her coming childbirth had led him to reflect on his own infancy and childhood in the extended journal notation of August 23, 1845. And it may also have been more than a gesture that he inserted a reference to his two-month-old grandson in the most autobiographical chapter in part I of *Le Peuple,* that on the artisan.[35]

CHAPTER 9

CLASS SERVITUDE,
MACHINISM,
AND TRANSCENDENCE:
LE PEUPLE
AS AUTOBIOGRAPHY

In the first part of *Le Peuple,* Michelet confronts us with the pyramidic reality of French society. At the bottom lies the mass of small peasant proprietors. At the top sits the wealthy bourgeois with enough money not to work. In between is "the worker dependent on machines," the artisan, the small manufacturer, the merchant, and the functionary. Each description is colored by pathos; each has a characteristic form of oppression and variety of human estrangement; there is also a model of possible redemption through the potential bond of nationhood, signaled in the past by the heroic devotion of French people of all classes in the armies of the Revolution and Empire. Apart from this pathos, Michelet presents us in the compass of sixty-eight pages with an excellent analysis of the class and economic structure of the July Monarchy.

This social structure places his ideology in a specific setting. The France Michelet describes has remained overwhelmingly agrarian, and the fifteen to twenty million peasants constitute the decisive influence on French politics until after the First World War.[1] In the cities, the labor force works primarily in preindustrial occupations. "Manufactures which use machines" employ no more than 400,000 workers and most of these work in small plants, whereas the number of master artisans, small manufacturers, and merchants is more than 500,000.[2] Although Michelet gives no figure for the artisans who have neither risen to the patented master group nor been proletarianized, they probably do not comprise less than the other two categories, particularly when we consider that most of those arrested during nineteenth-century political turmoil came from the traditional artisan trades.

Apart from this statistical scaffolding, Michelet's analysis of the

French work force contains three other kinds of hard information: a briefly sketched historical background of each group, drawn mainly from his own and others' research; information about wages, the living conditions of workers, and the prices of commodities, taken from such contemporary accounts as Villermé's;[3] and information gleaned from his own experience and travels to such places as Lyons, Normandy, and Alsace. Michelet also provides information about mobility between social classes, such as that from peasantry to factory worker. Central to part I is his interpretation of the psychological condition of each class, which shades over imperceptibly into prophetic denunciations of estrangement and appeals for social regeneration through love of country.

Considering the highly personal background of *Le Peuple,* it is arguable that the more objective side of Michelet's portrayal of the French people was subordinate to his interior development, that he used the social and ideological circumstances of his day to act out a psychodrama that resembled both the perceived social reality and the psychodramas of many of his compatriots well enough for them to view his work as a contribution to political discourse. The birth of his grandson apparently triggered his creativity, allowing him to synthesize his ideals of nature, motherhood, and the heroism and fraternity of the French nation into a patriotic and social-utopian manifesto. What this meant in concrete psychological terms is that he felt strong and certain enough of himself to project intimate sentiments, both positive and negative, into historical forces, as he had earlier projected various resentments into hostility to the Catholic church.

The Peasantry: Blood, Earth, and French Glory

The fourteen-page sketch of France's peasant majority that begins *Le Peuple* emphasizes the peasant's love for the land; it contains a brief history of land ownership since the sixteenth century and a description of contemporary rural misery, attributed to government indifference. For Michelet, as for many other mid-nineteenth-century radical thinkers, the peasantry was the backbone of the nation. He demonstrated its attachment to the soil and its willingness to sacrifice to remain there, and he explained the proverbial nastiness of the peasantry as a result of its penury. All this is predictable. Less predictable is Michelet's vision of peasant military valor and the Anglophobic context of this vision: Thirty years after Waterloo, he clearly saw France's age-old rivalry with England as ongoing. In November 1845, he seriously considered cutting two-thirds of the chapter to leave this material alone. His book would then have begun: "The earth of France belongs to fifteen or twenty million peasants who cultivate it; the earth of England to an aristocracy of thirty-two thousand persons who let it be cultivated."[4] The following paragraphs make invidious comparisons of English rootlessness to French love of native soil, and the section concludes with a tribute to peasant property-holding as the guarantee of self-respect and French military valor: "Pick from the crowd at random any day-laborer with a twentieth of an acre; you won't find the feeling of a day-laborer or a mercenary. He is a landowner and a soldier (he was it before and would be tomorrow). His father was in the Grande Armée."[5] In a subsequent passage that Michelet intended to keep in this version, he decried the lack of concern for the peasant majority by the "capitalist and industrialist government,"[6] a force he had recently denounced in his lectures as "maintained by the English and the Jews."[7]

Alfred quickly convinced his father-in-law of the superiority of the longer version. That Michelet even considered such a belligerent beginning to his book nonetheless testifies to the obsessive Anglophobia and military nostalgia, rampant especially among republicans, in the France of the 1840s—a result of the renewed rivalry with the English in the Middle East and the popular opposition to Louis-Philippe's pacifism.[8] We can see, moreover, a personal root to this belligerence in Michelet's evolution during the years that led to the book's composition.

The summum of Michelet's social philosophy, *Le Peuple* was also the fruit of his new conception of his childhood and later development. The experience with Madame Dumesnil had led him to reappraise not only nature and motherhood but the meaning to him of his own mother and childhood. Indications of this reworking of childhood experiences, some with a political character, occur several times in the six months before his breakthrough in September.

Twice in these months he recurred specifically to his childhood and adolescence under the Empire.[9] Though in both cases he emphasized the personal misery he experienced at the end of the Empire, in the first instance, a rereading of his youthful *Mémorial* on April 1, he noted that he derived from that period his sympathy for those without property, whereas in the second, he remarked that the only bright spot in those years was the heroism of the army, fighting outside France. Even though the principles of the Revolution were forgotten, he argued, the great wars of the Empire derived from them. The most stubborn and dangerous opponent in these wars was, of course, England.

The first reference to his early years came ten days before his lecture at the Collège de France on the peasantry—the "sacred story ... of the marriage of the laborer with the land."[10] The second, on

August 23, preceded by roughly the same period his first draft on the subject for *Le Peuple.* Around the time of his first reimmersion in his past, Michelet rendered homage to his mother publicly in the *Revue indépendante*; while replying to his critics he eulogized her as the guiding spirit of his struggles and the basis of his broader advocacy of women: "I lost her thirty years ago (I was a child then) and nonetheless, still living, she follows me from age to age. . . . I feel myself to be profoundly the son of a woman. At every moment, in my ideas, in my words (not to mention my gestures and features), I rediscover my mother in me. The sympathy I have for past ages, this tender recollection of all those who are no more, is indeed the blood of woman."[11]

It was probably about this time that Michelet became aware that Adèle was again pregnant. A few lines after the first mention of this, in connection with the Easter Sunday service (March 23, 1845), he suggested a link between his work as a historian, his own mother living through him, and the coming motherhood of Adèle: "This chant of resurrection, so strange in the mouth of these dead ones [the clergy] what force it has from having been sung by our mothers whom we still hear, who put there the accent of their hearts, those who are renewed and brought back to life in us. It recalls them always to our ear, to our soul; they are always worshipped there."

These multiple recollections of his mother and his childhood were also linked to the Anglophobia of those early years, as was made evident during his trip to Cherbourg in August 1845, just a month before his grandson's birth and the "feverish haste" of the composition of *Le Peuple,* and shortly before his second meditation on his past. His reaction to visiting the fortifications of the port city anticipates the discarded version of the chapter on the peasantry; in his anxious obsession with the enemy across the Channel, he sounds as though he were still living in the last years of the Empire: "We are building much, we are deepening the basin and extending the dike. But good heavens! If we don't fortify the heights, nor the fort of the dike, nor the fort of the île Pelée, then one day the English, coming straight from Portsmouth, will destroy everything in a night. And then it will be twenty years before we can attack England."[12]

A peculiar orientation from which to plan a book on "Love, the constructor of the city"? Perhaps, but the pendulum swing from Anglophobia to love of the land and love of mother is comprehensible if we bear in mind the multilayered tension in Michelet's thought, the potentiality he displayed for projecting rancors and rivalries based on the love of mother figures into the social and political arena. If the beginning of *Le Peuple* was more the negative, political animosity, the work as a whole was characterized by the positive core within, the love he had associated with Madame Dumesnil and his mother. Indeed, the final version of chapter 1 replaced the Anglophobia with which he had momentarily considered starting it by a hymn to the peasant's love for his "mistress," the land.

In spite of the changes in chapter 1, the first section of *Le Peuple* remained permeated with the negative view of French society that was the point of departure for Michelet's utopian speculation on liberation by love in parts II and III. The peasants' love for their land was counterbalanced, because of their neglect by the government of bankers and industrialists, by a surly estrangement from their fellow men. Town and city dwellers, envied by the peasants for their mobility and wealth, were hardly better off. This is most evident in the next two chapters, on the factory workers and the artisans.

The Urban Workers

Factory workers lacked property and the virtues Michelet associated with its possession: sobriety and economy. Although he saw the material abundance created by the new textile industry as "a powerful agent of democratic progress," he was aware of the miserable status of the machine worker. He deplored the long, monotonous hours of silent captivity and "these pitiful faces of men, these faded young girls, these twisted and swollen children." He recurred to his antithesis of liberty versus fatality, but its meaning had changed greatly since 1831. Fatality was embodied in the machine shop, the "reign of necessity," and the reaction to it was the quest for sexual pleasure. For Michelet, this carnal intoxication was not real love but debauchery, because the rootlessness of proletarian existence also prevented fixed partnerships: "The remedy is worse than the evil; exhausted by their subjugation to their work, they are still more so by the abuse of liberty."[13]

Yet Michelet had no fear that an English-style industrial revolution—machinism—would overwhelm French artisanal production. In France, unlike in England, small property-owners outnumbered others both on the land and in the cities. And though he was aware that the factory system made needed products cheaply available to the working classes, he saw limits on its spread to France in a nonmaterial factor: the perfect uniformity of factory production contradicted the notion of individual taste and development, which was a basic value of nineteenth-century civilization. Artisanal manufacture satisfied this individuality. In fact, Michelet anticipated a harmony between the two systems: "The more basic needs will be satisfied inexpensively by machines, the more tastes will be raised above the products of machinism and will search out the products of a highly personal art."[14]

Apart from these economic perspectives, Michelet clearly valued the traditional artisanal relation to labor over that of the modern factory worker. The handloom weaver, though solitary, could dream. But "machinery will permit no daydreams.... Would you for a moment lessen the tempo," Michelet asked, "in order to quicken it later on? You cannot. Hardly is the indefatigable fly frame with its hundred spindles thrown back before it returns to you." Then comes the real critique: "The hand loom weaver works quickly or slowly even as he breathes quickly or slowly; he acts as he lives, and the work fits the man. In the factory, the man must fit the work; the being of flesh and blood, whose energy varies with the hours of the day, must adapt to the unchanging pattern of this thing of steel."[15]

Michelet's negative view of contemporary industrial society was not simply the product of his psychological needs: in 1844, both Thomas Carlyle and Karl Marx had written similarly on the estrangement and deformation of the producer that resulted from factory production, and the problem has been broadly recognized ever since. Apart from Michelet's remarks on his visits to factories in Normandy, Lyons, and Alsace, moreover, such French political economists as Villermé presented a devastating picture of factory workers' existences.[16] And the positive view of traditional artisanal labor also meshed with nineteenth-century scholarship. A few decades later, Frédéric Le Play eulogized the older forms of work and family life, and the German Karl Bücher, in *Arbeit und Rhythmus,* elaborated on one of Michelet's points about the weaver: the integration of his natural physical movements, through song, with the rhythm required by his work.[17]

There are, nonetheless, so many autobiographical elements built into Michelet's depiction of the factory worker and artisan in *Le Peuple* that they form a psychological substructure that supports, shapes, and sometimes deforms the "objective" sociological insights of these chapters. We see this autobiographical substructure beneath the surface of several aspects of the chapters on the peasantry and the factory workers and artisans. Michelet's mother came from the rural Ardennes, and she and his surviving aunts clearly represented to him the peasant virtues of sobriety, hard work, and thrift. At age twelve, Michelet moved from his mother's side in two directions: to his father's print shop, a world of machines in which artisanal and modern industrial methods were mixed, and to the schools of the Empire. Both the schools and the print shop probably signified for him the harsh discipline he described in a page on the apprenticeship of the artisan.

In chapter 2 of *Le Peuple,* in which Michelet saw the schools as a potential means of identifying with a protective and nurturing national culture, an alternative to the "English" abomination of child labor, he portrayed his own evolution from the personal model of his mother to the cultural ego-ideal impressed on him by the educational establishment: "In the absence of the mother, the child ought to find a mother in his *patrie.* She [*la patrie*] will open the school for him as a place of refuge, as a shelter and a sanctuary against the factory."[18]

More recent experiences were embedded in the themes of the machine as an agent of democratic progress and in the contrast between the Flemish weaver's and the modern proletarian's ways of life. The machine as the bearer of democratic progress, for example, enters *Le Peuple* with a reference to the year 1842, in which, Michelet pointed out, textile prices fell sufficiently to be payable by working-class women and a cotton industry with many varied colors became accessible to the masses. Michelet based this passage on a journal entry for that August 26 and 27, where he described visits to dye and textile factories in Rouen. The visits occurred three months after Madame Dumesnil's death, a month after his renewed identification with the artisanry of Nuremberg; they were, furthermore, in her home city and in the company of her son.

Between these visits to factories, Michelet discovered that Madame Dumesnil's home in Sente Bihorel, in Rouen, might have to be sold to cover her debts, hardly cheering news. In the months after he visited the factories Michelet was particularly depressed, plunged again into grief over Alfred's mother, which the trip to Germany had only temporarily assuaged. Part of his depression at this loss was probably an intensified return to his mood after Pauline's death, when he wrote with bitterness of the way he had related to her exclusively as his "moi sensuel" and wrote of his own alienation through his work: "One must live and die as a book, not a man." In any case, the relationships he undertook in the coming years with Madame Aupèpin and his housekeepers seemed to serve more the function of sexual hygiene than of the kind of love he had shared with Madame Dumesnil. This bleak prospect of having nothing more in his life than his work and an occasional carnal fling was probably projected into his conviction that the factory worker similarly found liberation from the "fatal" oppression of the machine in pure carnality.

Certainly, the personal origin is unmistakable in the way Michelet expressed the contrast between the alienated proletarian and the unalienated weaver as two forms of love. In contrast to the overheated carnality of the alienated factory worker, the medieval worker lived and worked, he thought, in an atmosphere of maternal love, just like that which he himself had enjoyed with Madame Dumesnil. Most of these points had already been written into book V of his *Histoire de France* (to which he refers the reader of *Le Peuple*) at the moment of his budding love for Alfred's mother and with her in mind. The Lollards, the Beghards, and the Beguines, apart from their place in the history of labor, were all associated with the Flemish mysticism and intense domestic life he knew to be dear to her heart. He had seen her, when she moved into his house, as one of those Beguines who "illuminated the dark workshop with a gentle ray of grace."[19]

In general, says Michelet in *Le Peuple,* the mystical religiosity of the weavers led the church to persecute them as heretics. What was held against them was their doctrine of love, which was sometimes "the exalted and subtle love for the invisible lover, for God; sometimes also vulgar love, under the forms it takes in the populous centers of industry, vulgar but still mystical, preaching a community more than fraternal which would create a sensual paradise in this world."[20] Here Michelet evokes for comparison the carnal flight of the alienated proletarian of the modern era.

One other detail of these pages recalls the circumstances of their origin during Michelet's visits to factories in Rouen, between Madame Dumesnil's death and the forced sale of her home by Alfred: When he writes about the artisan who is forced to give up domestic labor for the factory, he says, "To leave his poor home, the worm-eaten furniture of the family, so many loved things, this is hard, harder still to renounce the free possession of his soul. . . . Let us not be surprised if our weavers of Rouen . . . have resisted this necessity with all their courage, their stoic patience, preferring to fast and to die, but to die at the family hearth." Moving had been Alfred's lot in August 1842, and dying at Michelet's hearth had been the fate of the brave Beguine, Alfred's mother, just three months earlier.

The third chapter of *Le Peuple,* on the artisan, contains even stronger autobiographical resonances. As usual, Michelet gives us an objective, factual scaffolding—the social ranks the artisan climbed in the medieval guild system, the punitive authority of the master over the apprentices, the guild's monopoly over entry into the profession, working conditions and prices—but within two pages he has switched over to the family drama of the artisan. It is in large measure his own.

Michelet, contemplating the work of Dürer in Nuremberg, had fused the artist with the artisan and identified himself with both. In

Le Peuple, he shows how both the artist and the scholar develop from the artisan's child through the beneficent influence of the mother. The material in this section parallels in general terms what he had written in *Le Prêtre, la femme et la famille* about the role of the woman in the family. In both books the woman is the essential humanizing force within the artisan's family. The hardworking artisan, exhausted by the long hours at his trade, needs "a home, a hearth, a woman. . . . Once he's arrived there . . . he entrusts himself like a child to the woman. Nourished by him, she nourishes him and reanimates him."[21] It is due to the woman's many-sided domestic genius—as nurturing mother to both husband and child, as housekeeper, clothes washer, and jealous guardian of the family's meager purse—that Michelet finds nothing more morally elevated than the artisan's family.

The artisan's labor is noble and his morality sure, but the traditional trades are hard, monotonous, poorly paid, and dangerous; for these reasons the mother hopes for a different life for her child. His early talent in drawing elicits from her dreams of glory—art school, training as painter or sculptor, the coveted prix de Rome! Michelet probably modeled all this on the young Dürer, whose father was a goldsmith. But he rejects the maternal dream, perhaps because the mother portrayed in it was uncomfortably close to his own and his internal gyroscope was still set principally on the course of Madame Dumesnil. He reaches her circuitously.

The artisan's son trained as an artist in the contemporary world is without prospects, Michelet writes, because those with the money to buy art are usually themselves amateur artists. Forced back into a traditional craft, he nonetheless devotes every spare moment to learning. Although the case is not identical with the young Michelet, his criticisms of this way of life are similar to his self-reproaches five years earlier for having neglected Pauline for his career ambitions: "I pity his family, on his return, if he has a family. A man who perseveres in this struggle and is fully preoccupied by his personal progress puts the rest rather far behind. The faculty of loving diminishes in this somber life. One loves the family less, it annoys one."

The autobiographical resonances remain strong when Michelet compares positively the voluntary learning of the artisan with that of the upper classes, "which one considers superior, which in effect have everything, books and leisure, whom science comes to seek, but which leave their studies, once free of their imposed schooling, and no longer concern themselves with the truth." As against this too easy course, the historian favors the obstacle course of the worker with few books and opportunities, in whom he sees himself: "A single book that one reads and rereads, that one ruminates and digests, often develops one better than a vast and undigested reading. I lived for years from a copy of Virgil and found myself well off."

After half a page on artisan-poets, Michelet returns to Virgil, and behind the text we can trace anew his quest for Aeneas's golden bough, the key to the world of the dead. Nothing in the following page, the last in this chapter, has anything to do with its subject, the artisan. The idealistic ambitions of the worker-poets have led him to recall a line of Virgil about seeking the light, glimpsing it, and sighing. Virgil's words lead him to Goethe's on the same subject, his last: "More light." With this phrase of the dying poet, Michelet identified "the general cry of nature," an impulse found at all levels of the world of living things. Flowers turn to the light, molluscs will not live where light fails to penetrate the ocean deeps, the animals—"our companions in toil"—rejoice with light's coming and grieve with its going, and "my grandson, two months old, weeps when the day draws to a close."

The grandson, living proof of the posthumous fecundity of the mother goddess, Madame Dumesnil, played a precipitating role in the composition of *Le Peuple*. We can see in the structure of this paragraph, which moves from the death of the poet-genius to the birth of the grandson, Michelet's continued preoccupation with the dialectic of death and rebirth. There are other signs of Madame Dumesnil's presence in the last half-page of the chapter. Between two rhapsodic paragraphs about a bird in his garden who sang into the setting sun, he inserted a most striking observation: "Barbarous science, harsh pride, which so degrade animal nature and separate man so widely from his inferior brethren."[22] The spirit of his lost love breathes in these lines. Madame Dumesnil had opened Michelet completely to the significance of nature and had urged her son never to lose sight of the charms of nature with the words, "I believe that the biggest reason why men, even superior ones, are so often incomplete, is that they are content to spend all their efforts on the works of men, and neglect the works of God."

As for the scientific inspiration of Michelet's idea, the notion of a biological science that refused to distinguish artificially between lower and higher species had already appeared in his journal when he was reading Etienne Geoffroy Saint-Hilaire: to this French zoologist, he wrote, "a fish seems as beautiful as a man," and Michelet viewed Geoffroy Saint-Hilaire sympathetically as "a barbarian who invaded modern science, breaking all our classifications like vain threads." The notation was dated May 30, 1842, the day before Madame Dumesnil died, and he preceded it with the comment, "In the midst of this death, slow and without horror, I stubbornly sought new reasons to live."[23] In the chapter of *Le Peuple* on his alter ego, the artist-artisan, he was still seeking them. He closed the chapter by repeating the words of the dying Goethe and extending them to the feelings of the bird in his garden, as well as of his grandson: "Light, Lord, more light!"

At the end of October 1845, just before he wrote this conclusion, he noted that he was attending the lectures of Geoffroy Saint-Hilaire's son and successor, Isidore, in the Jardin des plantes. But before beginning that scientific communion with nature, Michelet undertook a more lyrical, personal one: he returned for nine days to the forest of Fontainebleau, which he had last visited in 1841, with Madame Dumesnil.

Interlude in Fontainebleau: Antaeus

It was a strange moment to visit Fontainebleau. His three prior visits had been during summer vacations, in July and August, and he was presumably in the midst of an extremely tight writing schedule, since he had only begun *Le Peuple* the month before and had promised himself to finish it in January. But his journal notations suggest that he had soon run out of steam after the creative explosion that followed his grandson's birth.

In fact, problems under the historian's roof, both with feeding the infant Etienne and with his son, Charles, seem to have led him to an impasse in late September, a standstill complicated by a stubborn cold. We know from Alfred's letter to Eugène Noel of September 22 that Etienne's wet nurse had run out of milk and that "we are in the painful situation of a change of wet nurse."[24] Four days later, Alfred was reporting that the new wet nurse also lacked milk and that the baby was screaming with hunger—not the ideal setting for Etienne's grandfather to write *Le Peuple,* particularly considering his emotional investment in the baby. What he did write in the last week of September 1845 seems inspired largely by thoughts of infancy and childhood. Moreover, Michelet's search at the end of September for a reliable *pension* for his fifteen-year-old son, whose inclinations for fast living were already worrying him enormously, also complicated his writing schedule and probably led him to meditate on his own adolescence.[25]

Thus, on September 23, at home with a cold, he was "extending the arguments of my book" with a meditation on the charms and rivalries of early friendships that was based on his adolescent friendship with Poinsot, which received a central place in part III. Five days later, in a house dominated by the howls of a hungry infant, he was speculating in his journal about the connection between the nursing experience of infancy and the adult's ties to the body politic: "The nation having appeared to the child as a woman (mother, wet nurse), let the man too feel the law as a mother and live in its warmth."[26] On September 30, he noted that he was busy with the Preface. And, thereafter, during nine days (for seven of which there are journal entries), not a word about the book. The visit to Fontainebleau thus has about it an air of desperation, of an Antaeus seeking strength by a return to earth.

This is probably what Michelet, consciously or unconsciously, was looking for in the old royal forest. Michelet's earth was his self-knowledge, and he had reason to associate Fontainebleau with crucial stages in this self-knowledge and above all in his conscious relation to nature. Seven years after having in 1834 described the beauty of nature at Fontainebleau as a stepmother who would intoxicate and kill,[27] he had visited it with Madame Dumesnil, who prophesied there the influence a beneficent nature would have on his work: "She is coming to you with full breasts, her hands full of flowers." In 1845, while writing what was in many respects a memorial to her influence on him, he returned with her son to the site of the prophecy.

On October 12 and 13, he revisited the parts of the forest he had seen with her on the day of her matriarchal augury: Deux-Sœurs, the obelisk, and Mont Chauvet. The first of these appears to have been the site not only of that augury but of the historian's matriphobic comment seven years earlier about nature as stepmother. Arrived at Deux-Sœurs, he remarked in the journal on its melancholic charm and, in a self-censored text (it is followed by three dots),[28] then referred to that earlier experience alone: "Vivid recollection of 1834, which recurs with unexpected force and keeps me serious." Perhaps because the more recent memory was so painful, he could not bring himself to mention it. But it is inconceivable, particularly since he was in Alfred's company, that he should have forgotten it.

In any case, on October 14 he noted, "All night, meditated on my book," the first time he had mentioned it in two weeks. Although he was dissatisfied with his first day's work after returning to Paris,[29] the next day he was writing on a central theme of the transitional chapter between parts I and II ("se passer d'amour"), and on the two days after that he was writing on instinct, the subject of part II. In the two weeks between October 29 and November 12, he revised the first three chapters of part I and wrote the other four on the manufacturer, the merchant, the official, and the wealthy bourgeois. He seems to have been meditating about the last of these on October 14 in Fontainebleau,[30] and here above all he picked up the autobiographical thread he had woven into the first three chapters and used it to extend the tapestry of his vision.

Bourgeois and Students

Michelet gave chapter 7 of *Le Peuple* the title "Servitudes of the Rich and the Bourgeois." He called the bourgeoisie without further ado "the governing class" and described it as in decline. After its glorious role as architect of the "Revolution" of the fourteenth century, he wrote, much of the early bourgeoisie found its way into the nobility, to become an object of ridicule for the older aristocratic culture. Although revitalized by the industrial class that, according to Michelet, led the July Revolution, the bourgeoisie had had the weakness to succumb to a mortal fear of the common people, assiduously cultivated by military and other governments which held up to the wealthy class the Medusa's heads of the Terror and Communism. As a result, France divided into two nations. All this was taken from his lectures of the previous spring.[31]

Though he identified primarily with the bourgeoisie, Michelet was conscious of his popular origins, and in keeping with his social-romantic ambiance and his values, he desired above all else a reconciliation of the classes. Communism, he argued, was not a doctrine anyone should take seriously in France, with its twenty-five million small property-holders. The bourgeois, estranged from the people by a wall of fear and class privilege, saw in every crude gesture or loud voice on the street the sign of a violent disposition, but in fact working-class organizations responded, he contended, with courageous moderation to government persecution. And the "terrorists" of 1793, he reminded his readers, "were not at all men of the people but bourgeois, nobles: bizarre and subtle cultivated minds."

Michelet saw the moral qualities of the social classes as inversely proportional to their elevation. The class climber declined ethically: "As a peasant he had the severe morals of sobriety and saving. As a small industrialist, he was active and energetic; he had his industrial patriotism, which strove against foreign industry. All this he has left behind and nothing has taken its place; his house is full, his coffers are full, but his soul is empty."[32] The frightened egoists of the wealthy class, moreover, thought only of allying themselves with ephemeral governments and "the capitalists, who on the day of the revolution will take their funds and cross the Channel." Obviously Michelet was distinguishing here between the English-oriented capitalists in the seat of power and the landholding class of the wealthy bourgeois; he appealed to the latter, for their own self-interest, to ally with the people: "Proprietors, do you know who is not going to budge, no more than the land itself? . . . It is the people. Ally with it."

Thus the "salvation of France," as well as of the wealthy, lay in the alliance of bourgeois and people, in the rich man's overcoming his fears and ignoring the fables about the lower orders. "You must understand one another, open your mouths and your ears as well and speak to one another as men."[33] Only through such an alliance with "men of instinct, of inspiration, without culture or from other cultures" could the further degeneration and decline of the French elites be avoided, a regeneration of France be achieved.

Michelet little expected that the wealthy would heed his warning—the spiritual rot had gone too far. But he clearly conferred a different statute of possibility on the sons of the wealthy, the students, and from them he hoped for a renewal of the grand alliance of 1789. "These young people," he wrote, "have always greeted every word in favor of the people with a warm heart. May they join with them quickly in an alliance for a common regeneration." The literal revitalization of France and of the bourgeois itself was Michelet's goal: "These rich youths are exhausted from birth, and, young as they are, they need to grow younger by breathing the popular spirit. Their strength lies in their still being close to the people, their root, whence they have sprung. Ah! May they return there with all their heart and sympathy and regain a little of the vitality which has been the genius, the wealth, and the strength of France since 1789."[34]

A confession followed this appeal to the students. Those who had crossed class lines like himself, he wrote, who in spite of their trials had preserved the "fecund instinct of the people," had nonetheless lost too much of their strength in the struggles along the way. Not only this exhaustion prevented Michelet from being the historian of the people. Though he saw in them "my past, my true country, my hearth, and my heart," he was incapable of taking over their "most fecund element"; the abstract culture he had been given had long desiccated his spirit. "I needed many years to efface the sophist they had made of me. I only arrived at myself by letting go of this alien accessory; I only discovered myself by a negative path."[35]

Salvation—a new warmth, the revitalization of the world, of life, and of science—could come only from the young and the workers. This invocation of the worker-student alliance, that political utopia of 1968, thus appears two years before its last incarnation in nineteenth-century France, the barricades of February 1848. It was, of course, a realistic variant on the class alliance of the French revolutionary epoch between bourgeois and people. But Michelet's formulation of it harbored an important subtheme, ambiguously stated, which suggests again a deeply personal note: writing history of the people and for the people.

He writes that "from the people will emerge the historian of the people," which seems to exclude anyone of bourgeois origin. Yet he had already characterized the strength of the sons of the wealthy in their proximity, as students, "to the people, their root." Which leaves open the possibility—inherent in his metaphors— that the appeal which closes this chapter was addressed not to some hitherto undiscovered artisan's son but to his intimate disciple, his son-in-law, Alfred:

> To you, young man, to you will come all the gifts I have lacked. Son of the people, being less distant from them, you will come all at once upon the field of their history with their colossal strength and inexhaustible vitality. My streams will come of their own accord to lose themselves in your torrents. I give you all that I have done. You will give me oblivion. May my imperfect history be swallowed up in a worthier mon- ument, where learning and inspiration blend in better harmony, where among vast and penetrating research we feel every- where the breath of immense crowds and the fecund soul of the people.[36]

Michelet's "streams [that] will come to lose themselves in your torrents," the repeated invocations of "fecundity," the confession of his own "loss of strength," and the appeal to his successor to bring new life—we might view all this as no more than the rhetoric of the time if we did not know the crucial role that Alfred's literal "fecundity," the birth of Michelet's grandson, had played in the composition of *Le Peuple,* if we had not seen that chapter 7, on the bourgeois, was the first he had begun to think about after visiting, with Alfred, the sites of his earlier visit to Fontainebleau with Ma- dame Dumesnil.

Machinism as Metaphor

The conclusion of the first part of *Le Peuple* is also the introduction to the second. Its three points together summarize the negative conclusions of the preceding chapters about the human condition in contemporary France and point the way to the solutions offered in the second and third parts.

The first argument takes the form of a geological metaphor. The higher one rises in the social ladder, the colder, the more un- sociable becomes the human environment. Human warmth and love of country are found among peasants, artisans, and factory workers. Merchants and small industrialists tend toward selfishness but are restrained from total egoism by national rivalry with the English. The bourgeois inhabit a world of snow and ice: "a sudden frost of selfishness and fear." One step higher, to the very rich, and Michelet feels he is in a glacier where fear gives way to "the pure egotism of the calculator who has no fatherland. . . . The cold is too great for me there and I cannot breathe"—lines the young Marx may have had in his head when he wrote two years later, in the *Communist Manifesto,* of "the icy water of egotistical calculation."

Michelet's second point concerns machinism, which he locates in the failure of Christian love to build the world it had promised. The medieval order had preached love but had consecrated inequality, injustice, and hatred. The Renaissance had attempted to bring the concept of love back to its roots in nature but succeeded only in destroying the old order. Thus, the world, needing order, created it without love, Michelet argued, and the result was the administrative machinery, bureaucratic and military, of the seventeenth and eighteenth centuries, in which men were forced to work together systematically.

Modern machinism extended these principles to the sphere of production and threatened to subjugate even the worlds of artistic imagination and philosophical speculation to mechanical principles. Michelet attacked with sarcasm the liberal school of political economy he had been close to in the early 1830s: "The English economists have dreamed of an ideal industrial world with one single machine and one single man to set it going. How much finer is the triumph of Machinism to have mechanized the winged world of fantasy and imagination. . . . We have the state without the sentiment of the nation;[37] industry and literature without art; philosophy without inquiry and humanity without man. Why are we surprised if the world shakes and suffocates under this pneumatic machine? It has found a way to do without its soul, its life; I mean love."[38]

"Doing without love"—*se passer d'amour*—was Michelet's theme two days after his return from Fontainebleau. The principled juxtaposition of machinism versus love was central to the book, for the result of machinism was "society actively working to become unsociable." This machine-caused social estrangement encouraged the mutual ignorance and enmity between the educated and unlettered classes that kept them, and France, disunited and impotent. In a lament that anticipated Albert Camus's critique of bureaucratic alienation, Michelet wrote: "A thousand mechanical ways of acting without the soul allow us to avoid knowing what a man is and to avoid seeing him as something besides a force or a number. Being numbers and abstractions ourselves, relieved of vital action through the aid of machinism, we feel ourselves declining every day and sinking to zero."[39]

The result was a populace with no comprehension of "the powers of study and persevering reflection" and with an inchoate desire to humiliate the wealthy and powerful, in contrast to an educated, wealthy elite that had no understanding of "instinct, inspiration, and the energy which makes heroes" and that thought it would strengthen society by reimposing on the poor a religion dead for two centuries. This mutual incomprehension and scorn between the powers of instinct and reflection constituted the main feature of the modern world. Michelet viewed the bridging of this chasm as the task of the educated, since their limitations were insignificant compared with the "fatality of ignorance . . . the suffering that closes and dries up the heart" of the people.[40]

The historian proposed to start this task of national reconciliation by explaining the meaning of instinct, the motor of popular action, as the basis of civic morality. In a striking conclusion to part I, he wrote, "The political city will not understand itself, its evils, and its remedies until it has seen itself in the mirror of the moral city."[41] If the phraseology is Rousseauistic, the strong emphasis on instinct as the basis of civic morality gives the next third of the book a surprisingly modern ring. But what he works out in part II is as much an expression of his personal mythology as an anticipation of Freud. The thesis that the sentiments of fraternity, the indispensable framework of the political community, grow out of the instinctual reality of maternal nurturance echoes the way his own rediscovery of fraternity grew out of his conversion, through Madame Dumesnil, to a quasi-pantheistic, matriarchal view of nature and society.

CHAPTER 10

LE PEUPLE, *PART II:*
POPULAR INSTINCTS AND
LIBERATION

Michelet's exploration of the "instinct" of the people—part II of *Le Peuple*—is one of the least commented on and understood parts of his social-philosophical oeuvre. And for good reason. These nine chapters, in the middle of a work that seeks both to define and to regenerate the French people, purport to deal with their subject in terms of natural science; the science then turns out to have a transparently religious significance; and both frameworks are comprehensible primarily through their resonances in the author's recent life. Much more than the first part of *Le Peuple,* the second part is autobiographical.

The subject made it almost inevitable that Michelet's personal needs and vision would be systematically projected into these chapters. His previous work had been shaped largely by the demands of historical description. Part I, though more defined by autobiographical motifs, was also restricted by the need for a factual description of social classes. But when Michelet turned to popular "instincts," his work escaped factual limitations, and his writing took on the character of an exercise in projection, an elaborate, intellectualized Rohrschach test.[1]

The first three chapters of part II, which in good measure continue the effort of part I to describe the people as they were, also carry the negative tone of that first part. Michelet attacked economists and criminologists, as well as romantic novelists, for creating folkloric stereotypes about the lower orders as criminal and violent.[2] Apart from genuine, isolated folk societies—to which he attributed "the wisdom of a forgotten world"—he viewed the popular culture of French cities and villages in his own day as impotent. It lacked the virtues of both civilization and savagery, and where it aspired to poetry it was so overawed by elite culture that it had lost its ability to express itself directly and naively and simply aped upper-class models. Michelet was convinced, however, that behind this cultural impotence the people's instinctive core, its capacity to live through action rather than reflection, remained healthy.

Before exploring the meaning of this "instinct," the historian acidly criticized—as "bastard classes"—those of the lower orders who tried to rise into the class of merchants and small manufacturers. The autobiographic impulse shaped this part (chapter 3) much as it did the chapter on the artisan. He considered such social ascension as corruptingly materialistic, depriving the man of the people of his "true nobility, the power of sacrifice." Workers who stayed where they were retained "the large instinct of the masses, the courage of the spirit." Yet another sort of social mobility had his enthusiastic support; in fact, it reflected his own. Artisans who remained in their class of origin were sometimes compensated by having their sons rise to the rank of artists. That just this sort of social ascension now appeared possible to him, whereas he had suggested its impossibility in the chapter on the artisan, indicates a shift in his perspective from part I; perhaps it is because his example was the painter of Madame Dumesnil's deathbed portrait, Thomas Couture,[3] perhaps because this section was so based on the values he had developed under the second mothership of Madame Dumesnil that the uncomfortable resonances of the artist's mother with Michelet's own were no longer shaping his attitude.

Chapters 4 through 6 bring us to the core of *Le Peuple*: the sources of popular instinct and the relation of successive civilizations to the natural world. The organization of the putative subject is so riddled with digressions, however, that only by recourse to the "personal myth" under the surface of the narrative can we make sense of the whole. Chapter 4 (*Des simples. L'Enfant interprète du peuple*) recapitulates the contrast at the end of part I between the abstract analytic way of thinking of the educated and the instinctual grasp of the man of the people. Michelet compared the naïveté and grace of this innate mode of thought with the instincts of the child, whom he presented as "the people itself, in its native truth, before it is deformed, the people without vulgarity, rudeness, or envy, inspiring neither distrust nor repulsion."[4] From here until the end of part II, his train of thought locked onto other, only dimly related subjects. In the rest of chapter 4 he discussed the thought that obsessed him during Madame Dumesnil's last months: the dialectical interrelation of death and life, the unity of nature. In chapter 5 he attacked the dogma of original sin. Realizing that his attack seemed unrelated to his subject, he warned the reader in a note that it was essential nonetheless. It was, but only in relation to the religious speculations of chapter 6, which Michelet freely admitted to be a digression. Ostensibly on the instincts of animals, chapter 6 returned to the intellectual problem he was grappling with at the moment of Madame Dumesnil's death: a new theological notion of the relation between man and nature. Chapters 7 and 8 came closer to his subject, but, instead of taking it up directly, he presented as the incarnation of the spirit of the people—the man of genius. In spite of the vagaries of part II, Michelet showed in his conclusion the relevance of it all for his point of departure: the necessary reconciliation between elites and lower orders, the creation of a new social harmony.

Michelet's spiritual and personal hegira begins, then, in chapter 4. After describing the prelogical child from birth to age four as a "petit dieu" who "lived on the large fund of instincts and swam in a sea of milk ... this sea obscure and fecund,"[5] he compared, as though it were an obvious equation, early childhood and death. Both were "moments when the infinite radiates through man, grace in both the artistic and theological sense."[6] A half-page later, he had returned to his personal experience of death and resurrection at the bedside of Madame Dumesnil: "I especially recall a long winter day which I passed between the bed of a dying woman and the reading of Isaiah."[7] The text that follows is clearly based on his journal entry for April 4, 1842. One cardinal point emerges from a comparison of this passage in *Le Peuple* with the text of the journal entry. It has to do with Michelet's religious conceptions, in particular with the place of generations to come in that scheme. Recalling "the uncertainty between two worlds," Michelet wrote in *Le Peuple*: "The witness of this great struggle, who shared this ebb and flow and all the anxieties, clung as in a shipwreck to the firm belief that the soul returning to our primitive instincts ... could not be going on to annihilation. Rather, everything suggested that she [the soul] was about to endow with this double instinct some young existence that would resume more happily the work of life, and express the dreams, the developing ideas and mute desire which the departing soul had failed to realize."[8] In a note he then denied that he believed in the "transmission of souls" but said that he was nonetheless "tempted to believe that our first instincts are the thoughts of ancestors which the young voyager bears with him as provisions for the journey."[9]

This passage represents the end result of Michelet's wrestling, in the week of March 28–April 4, 1842, with several philosophical and religious ideas about the soul's fate after death. Against Leroux's notion that only the collective soul of mankind survives individual death, he opposed a poorly argued belief in the immortality of Madame Dumesnil's soul, clearly about to be separated from her moribund body. His intellectual support for this belief was an article by his friend Eugène Burnouf on Indian religion, which Michelet had presented in his *Origines du droit français* of 1837. What then had been an unimportant remark in an intellectual exploration of folk beliefs became a permanent part of his private religion, his évangile éternel, in April 1842.

In keeping with his conviction that birth was the answer to death, Michelet had scattered several passages on "the veritable dialectic from one generation to another" into the remarkable entry of April 4. The most striking was an invocation to the young that fits the central role he was to give his students and that ends where the composition of *Le Peuple* was to begin: "Grow, oh youth; the world is yours. Make haste to grasp it. Our hope is that ... you will further the embellishment and advancement of the ages. *The grandfather says, at the cradle of his grandson: Here you are born again, oh my soul.*"[10]

Michelet's tormented speculation on rebirth as the answer to death during these April days was clearly provoked by the oncoming death of the woman he loved—if the death was hers, the reborn soul had also to be hers. It may have been wishful thinking in 1842, this grandfather who envisaged the rebirth of a soul dear to him in his grandchild, but for the Michelet of 1845 the idea had taken on a special reality, and that is probably why he integrated it with a slight disguise ("aïeul" and "enfant" for "grandpère" and "petit-fils") into the same footnote of *Le Peuple* that dealt with the inheritance by the young of their ancestors' thoughts.[11]

Through the birth of Alfred's son, in other words, the death of Madame Dumesnil had become part of a harmonious chain of generations; her soul had been reborn. The personal chain that went from Michelet to his daughter and his "fils adoptif," Alfred, and from there to the joint grandchild of himself and Madame Dumesnil, was a particular, if essential, example of a metaphysical chain that joined the generations in a harmony of death and rebirth. Similarly, man and nature, elites and people were to be reconciled and harmonized in subsequent chapters of *Le Peuple*. Indeed, the first chain of reconciliation, which at a less personal level seems to lack any relation to the historian's subject, was a psychological precondition for his belief in the other reconciliations. Harmony had to prevail in his private life before he could project it into nature and society. The metaphysical excursus of chapter 4 suggests that Michelet obtained that inner peace through the birth of his grandson.

The path back from this quintessential basis to his book's main theme of social reconciliation led Michelet through a definitive formulation of the revaluation of values that had been underway since the encounter with Madame Dumesnil. He justified that revaluation with then current ideas of biological science and built on it a new interpretation of human culture and religion. His first concern was to protect the child, the embodiment of the instinctual character of the people, from the forces of antinature—that is, the church and its dogma of original sin. In chapter 5 he thus attacked the church for damning nature and natural instinct—a complete turnabout from the "Introduction à l'histoire universelle" of 1831, in which he had praised Christianity for its immolation, in the name of the spirit, of "life, nature, matter, and fatality" and condemned pre-Christian religions for their "obscene" message of life and generation.[12]

This attack on Christian doctrine cleared the way for the "digression" of chapter 6, on the history of the West's attitude toward animals. Behind the veil of a mystical pathos, Michelet was grappling with three closely related insights. One concerned the concept of fraternity, later a major principle of his work on the French Revolution. A second anticipated the idea advanced by Mikhail Bakhtin and by more recent historians of popular religion and culture, such as Emmanuel Le Roy Ladurie and Carlo Ginzburg, on the very different relations between human beings and the natural world in premodern peasant societies.[13] The third was a notion, most interesting for psychohistorians, on the roots of human sociability in the mother-infant relationship.

These insights emerge through Michelet's review of attitudes toward nature from ancient India to the modern world, which, as one might expect, implicitly refuted what he had written on the subject in 1831. His vision of nature in *Le Peuple* was infused with his thinly concealed belief in reincarnation: "Naturalists have remarked that the young animal, more intelligent at birth, seemed then close to the child. As the animal grows, it becomes a brutish beast. It seems that its poor soul succumbs under the weight of the body and submits to the fascination of nature and the magic of the great Circé. . . . Would you not say they are children whose development some evil fairy has prevented . . . or perhaps are chastised and humiliated souls under some passing curse."[14]

The Orient, he wrote, never departed from these beliefs. The maternal fecundity of Indian civilization, which he had earlier feared as a mortal peril to human freedom, had in *Le Peuple* become "an admirable gift," the basis of "universal fraternity." He pleaded with those fatigued by the contentiousness of the Occident to "return to your mother, this majestic antiquity, so noble and tender." India's attitude toward nature is reflected in its "gentle consideration for the inferior creature," which insures that "a river of milk flows forever for this blessed land."[15]

Greek and Roman culture broke with such harmony. "A world of pride, [it] scorned nature. . . . Everything that appeared base and ignoble disappeared from sight; the animals perished as well as the slaves. The Roman Empire, disembarrassed of the one and the other, entered the majesty of the desert." Christianity continued the Roman tradition of hostility to nature, which it inherited from its Jewish origins: "Judea knew herself, was afraid to love too much this sister of man, and fled from her with curses. Christianity, faithful to these fears, kept animal nature at an infinite distance from man and debased it."[16]

In the Middle Ages, peasant culture, and especially its children, rehabilitated the animal world. Michelet found evidence to support this notion in the manifold presence of domestic animals in popular legends of the saints and in representations of animals in popular legends of the Nativity. He also attributed to this rehabilitation the revival of agriculture after the decline of Rome: "The animal, as soon as it was loved, endured and multiplied. The earth became fertile again, and the world that seemed at an end grew rich and strong again."[17] The maternity of nature became explicit through the legend of Geneviève of Brabant: Suspected of infidelity by her husband, she fled to the forest, where she and her child were nursed for six years by a beneficent doe.

The popular restoration of the animal species to their rightful place in the Creation had no influence on Christian theology or on philosophy, which followed the theologians in denying that animals had souls. Michelet insisted, however, that modern scientific insights supported popular notions of the union of the human and natural worlds. Ineluctably, his obsessive recollections of Madame Dumesnil's last months had moved him from one moment in his intellectual wrestling with the angel of death during her agony—the Indian doctrine of rebirth—to another: Geoffroy Saint-Hilaire's rehabilitation of the animal world, his demonstrations of man's unity with lesser forms of life: "Our age will have one great glory," he wrote. "It has produced a philosopher with a human heart. He loved the child and the animal. Previously the unborn child had excited interest only as an outline, as a preparation for life; but he loved it in itself, followed it patiently in its little obscure life, and discovered in its changes the faithful reproduction of animal development. Thus in the bosom of woman, in the true sanctuary of nature, the mystery of universal brotherhood has been discovered. Thanks be to God!"[18]

In his chapter on the artisan, Michelet had already used the knowledge gleaned from Geoffroy Saint-Hilaire to dismiss as barbarous a science that artificially separated man from the natural world. Now he went further and deduced far-reaching political and psychological consequences from the biologist's doctrine: universal fraternity, the inner force and goal of the French Revolution, had its origin in man's relatedness to other forms of life and was born in the mother's womb. This derivation of fraternity from the child's bond to the mother was one of the essential notions of Michelet's social vision, which he would restate more fully in part III of *Le Peuple*.

Before he began part III, he wrote two chapters on the relations between the people and the genius that further connect the ideological and autobiographical motifs of *Le Peuple*. Much of this book appears to harmonize apparent opposites: birth and death, animals and people, wisdom and instinct, lower and upper classes. This is above all true for Michelet's view of the character of the genius. In these chapters, the man of genius is shown to be the epitome of the people. Both possess the instinctive character of childhood. Like the people and the child, the genius has little taste for analysis: "If genius, through all the fictitious divisions and subdivisions of knowledge, always preserves within itself a *simple* being who never agrees to unalterable division and always tends to unity . . . it is because the characteristic of genius is the love of life itself—the love that causes life to be preserved and the love that produces it."[19] In fact, Michelet confessed, the ideal potentiality of the people was to be found only in the "harmonious and fecund" man of genius. To explain his "inventive and generating power," he used the metaphor of androgyny I have mentioned: the genius "combines what may be called the two sexes of the mind—the instinct of the simple and the reflection of the wise. In a way he is man and woman, child and adult, barbarian and civilized, people and aristocracy."[20]

Michelet probably viewed his own character in these terms. He certainly saw himself as someone who combined, through his social ascent, the qualities of the barbarian and the educated, and he clearly identified with what he saw as the instinctive idealism of children. As to the union of man and woman, less than a year earlier he literally described himself as pregnant with history: he saw his role vis-à-vis the unfinished elements of the past as "a living asylum in which they vegetate slowly while waiting until they burst out and make your future. . . . You are the fecund womb that bears them and carries them, the mother from which they want to achieve their being."[21] He might have been thinking of the twice-begun but never completed French Revolution, on which he wrote a magnum opus immediately after *Le Peuple,* as those unfinished elements he bore within him. The identification with woman is in any case unambiguous.

These chapters on the man of genius as the incarnation of the people lead to a more general historical problem that would underlie Michelet's study of the French Revolution: the role of great men in history. A journal entry of February 1845 contains a remarkable discussion of Mickiewicz's celebration of Napoléon in which Michelet clearly set out the basic issues. Both he and Mickiewicz saw a certain interrelationship between leader and people. The Polish poet denied, however, that the collectivity could be a source of action and sought "a man who will carry everyone with him by a mystical authority," whereas the French historian saw history as proceeding "from low to high." "Life," he wrote, "ascends from the people to the great man, up to the great force in general, individual or collective, that realizes the divine idea." The last hero of modern times was thus not Napoléon but the Revolution itself, "an idea that did without great men, heroes, false gods, idols. It was—much more than Kant—the critique of pure reason." As for the emperor, Michelet's judgment was merciless: "Able and fortunate in deeds, original in words, sterile in ideas, this man rediapers the Revolution in the old rags of the Middle Ages which it has cast off and squeezes it, a living mummy, into the funeral bandages recaptured from the exhumed corpses. Today we continue to be hurt by him, both by his false resurrection of the past and by the worship of force we have inherited from him. . . . Mystical unity in an individual man (successive messiahs) is the return of materiality and fatality."[22]

Thus, the chapters on the man of genius in *Le Peuple* could lead to the idea that Michelet ascribed a greater political role to those individuals who so perfectly expressed the character of the people than he actually did. In fact, these chapters have a twofold function. They are an indirect admission that his definition of the people lacked reality; to locate that reality, Michelet had to move outside the lower orders to isolated individuals who combined the qualities of these classes with those of the educated culture. In addition, these individuals who possessed the "two sexes of the spirit" were perhaps the only means of bridging and uniting the "two nations" he had earlier discussed.

Nonetheless, the shade of Napoléon, whose ashes had, amid great funereal pomp, only recently been returned to the Invalides, hovers obscurely over the conclusion of part II. More significant than a specific reference to Bonaparte as the reconciler of Europe and Africa was Michelet's narration of the dream of Caesar—recounted by Plutarch but taken up in the storehouse of his own dreams—when sailing along the African coast: "He saw a vast army weeping and stretching their hands to him. On awaking, he wrote down upon his tablets Corinth and Carthage, and he rebuilt those cities."[23] Michelet made it clear that he saw his task in the intellectual and spiritual realm as exactly analogous to Caesar's in the political realm (which, we note, was also identical to the role he had ascribed to Napoléon a page earlier). When he dreamed Caesar's dream, he understood on his own terms the tears of the suffering masses; he, too, saw them as a plea to be restored to the city, but it was above all the "City of Right from which they have been excluded until now."

Through his book, then, Michelet meant to give a voice to the common people, to "all those who groan or suffer in silence, all who are aspiring and struggling toward life." These suffering masses were intended, through his work, to find a home in the city of social justice. "Let all," he wrote, "without class distinction . . . weak or strong, simple or wise, bring here their wisdom or their instinct. Those weak and incapable ones, those miserable persons who can do nothing for themselves, can do much for us. They have in them a mystery of unknown power, a hidden fecundity of living springs in the depths of their nature. In summoning them, the city calls the life which alone can renew it."[24]

Michelet's just society is infused with the principles that had characterized the main themes of *Le Peuple* thus far—reconciliation both with one's fellow man and with nature—and a markedly matriarchal imagery: the "protective City," which nurtures the "hidden fecundity" of the people, "stretches from heaven to the abyss, vast as the bosom of God!"[25]

The conclusion to part II prepares the way for part III, on the social bases of the city of social justice, but it also points toward two shadows that hang over the composition of the entire work. One was the inescapable comparison with imperial imagery in the French romantic and republican traditions of the first half of the century. The other was more personal. The passage on Caesar's dream constitutes another palimpsest manuscript behind which we can trace the shadow of Michelet's rediscovery of himself just before and after Madame Dumesnil's death.

Caesar's dream entered Michelet's journal twice before *Le Peuple,* both in the year of her death. On January 30, 1842, he wrote an extended meditation on it, just after noting that her condition was deteriorating steadily. Only four days earlier he had told Alfred that "my thought on method and my History of France always begin in the historic moment of the night of your mother."[26] That more was involved in the descent to the Underworld implicit in the report of Caesar's dream becomes obvious if we recall the text of its second mention; on September 30, 1842, a few months after the night of Alfred's mother had become eternal, a recurrence of Michelet's dream of Caesar was followed by one of incest with his own mother, dead since 1815.

Excursus: The Sociology of Alienation

Focus on the recurrent intrusion of Michelet's "mythe personnel" into the text of *Le Peuple,* though necessary to grasp its hidden meanings, holds the danger of a loss of perspective. The work was, after all, apart from being a landmark in the development of France's most celebrated romantic historian, an important example of nineteenth-century social thought. Before examining part III, which purports to return to the political—to reintegrate the people into la patrie—it may be useful to take a long view of the place of this little book in the history of ideas.

What Michelet does in *Le Peuple* can best be understood in the framework of a broad speculative questioning by European intellectuals of the early to mid-nineteenth century of the character of the new society and the new man then emerging in England, France, and Germany after political and religious absolutism had disintegrated. Although this process of deterioration had begun in England more than a century before it did in the other two countries, it was largely the double shock to established ways of looking at humanity caused by the Industrial Revolution in England and the French Revolution on the Continent that precipitated a wave of critical thought about progress and estrangement reflected in the thought of Schiller, such German romantics as Heinrich von Kleist and Friedrich Hölderlin, Marx and the young Hegelians, Carlyle in Britain, and in France, the utopian socialists, the social romantics—and Michelet. Marx's ideas on estrangement, in his *Economic-Philosophical Manuscripts of 1844,* reveal the main lines of this critique in distinguishing sharply the alienation of the producer in the new mode of production from his own biological impulses, from the process of production, and from his fellow man.

Although subsequent Marxists (and even the later Marx, to a certain extent) tended to trivialize the problem of alienation by making it contingent on lack of ownership of the means of production, the sociological and psychoanalytic thought of the past century has grappled more seriously with it. Sociologists have generally focused more on the problem of social alienation. Some, like Max Weber, have considered both social and instinctual alienation as the unavoidable price of a progress in personal security and welfare that could be administered only by an extensive bureaucratization of economic and political existence. Others, like Emile Durkheim, looked more optimistically to new forms of social organization to overcome the rampant normlessness—*anomie*—that stood in the way of feelings of solidarity.

The question of estrangement from the nonrational bases of personality—variously seen in terms of instinct, drives, and will—has been the subject of psychoanalytic thought and existential philosophy since Kierkegaard, Nietzsche, and Freud. If the first two emphasized the necessity to cultivate an autonomous morality, a will freed from the impersonal and dehumanizing collectivities of the modern world, Freud explored through psychoanalysis the world of unconscious impulse and spontaneous emotion and sought a means to restore the bonds with that world which rational consciousness, in its quest for mastery over nature but at the price of mutilating its own inner nature, had cut. A radical wing of the psychoanalytic movement merged with a Marxist-influenced sociological current in the Frankfurt School to combine elements of a Marxian, Weberian, and Freudian critique of modern institutions: in the work of Max Horkheimer, Theodor Adorno, Herbert Marcuse, and Erich Fromm, we find attempts to analyze the phenomenon of estrangement at the level of both instinctual character and social organization without losing either the humanitarianism of the young Marx or the realism of a Weberian analysis of bureaucratic domination.

What Michelet accomplished in *Le Peuple* may have been rooted in personal suffering and conditioned by social-romantic and nationalist ideologies born of the French Revolution, but, in a broader framework, it can be comprehended in terms of that critique of alienation that runs from the first half of the nineteenth to the end of the twentieth century, more specifically from the young Marx to Freud and his followers. In parts I and II of *Le Peuple,* Michelet has presented the social facts of alienation, from oneself and from one's fellows, in the strata of the French people. His interpretation of the problem differs fundamentally from Marx's insofar as Michelet traces its source not primarily to the new mode of production (which had made little headway in France before mid-century) but to a machinism that derives from the increasing dominance of bureaucratic, religious, military, and political structures. His solution, outlined at the end of part I and throughout part II, is at two levels: a rediscovery of the biological nature that rational humanity shares with the rest of the animal kingdom, and a social reconciliation of the educated upper class with the "instinctual" lower orders. He considered this reconciliation necessary both because each of the "two nations" had attributes the other needed to be complete and because national strength and social harmony required the transcendence of mutual estrangement. Reconciliation was also possible, he thought, because the social divisions were mediated by a large stratum of small property-holders—a blessing of France's slow economic development, we might add, which also insured that similar class coalitions could spark revolutions in 1789, 1830, and 1848.

We have seen how Michelet's numerous references to the tragic events of his own recent history recur in and behind the text of *Le Peuple* and how the rhetoric of the period combines with the evident rethinking of his autobiography to lead him consistently to couch his argument in terms of family relations; we stumble frequently over the metaphoric mothers, wives, mistresses, and brothers he projected onto the social and historical world. In part III he merges and resolves the critique of alienation and the solutions to it he has already advanced into the ideology of the nation-state as protector and liberator—an idea that did not palpably influence either Marx or Freud but that was critical for the republican currents of nineteenth-century French thought. Michelet's pathos on this question anticipates not only the patriotic republicanism of the Third Republic but the more systematic ideas of the Solidarists and Durkheim in the fin de siècle.[27] But again, what is remarkable in Michelet's passionate nationalism is not simply the wealth of the intellectual currents visible in it—the critique of estrangement, the surprisingly modern historical, psychological, and sociological insights, the use of natural science, the rejection of Christianity combined with the assertion of a new religion based on the French Revolution—but also the powerful autobiographic elements that tangibly underlie and integrate all these.

CHAPTER 11

LE PEUPLE, *PART III: THE NATION AS LIBERATOR FROM ESTRANGEMENT*

Michelet presents his own view of the "City" of man in the last part of *Le Peuple,* proceeding from lesser forms of sociability to higher: from simple friendship to love and marriage, to associations, to the fraternity of the French nation (chapters 1–5). In chapters 6–9 he considers the religious foundations of French nationalism in terms of the universal education promised, but not given, by the Revolution and in terms of the spirit of sacrifice.

The way the nation emerges in Michelet's thought suggests a triadic dialectic, the first two elements of which were (1) the foundation of sociability in the biological tie to the mother and (2) all the lesser forms of sociability—friendship, marriage, and association—which in the modern world appeared as limited and doomed. Only (3), a restoration of the nurturant role of the beneficent mother, at the ideal level of the nationstate, could restore the fraternity, the sociability that had everywhere disappeared from social existence and that it was the unfulfilled task of the French Revolution to deliver. This revolution, point of origin of French national consciousness, thus has the same relation to the social bond in Michelet's republican theory as the Industrial Revolution has in Marx's political economy. The same force whose immediate effect is to destroy all the old solidarities lays the basis for new, transcendent ones. This potential new social harmony of the nation is presented briefly at the beginning of chapter 1 of part III as the summum of the lesser forms of sociability ("The nation is indeed the great friendship [*amitié*] that contains all the others"), and there are occasional references to it throughout the first three chapters of part III, but in general these chapters show the insufficiencies of the inferior social ties. Michelet suggests the problem that underlies these insufficiencies and its resolution when he pinpoints the mother-child bond as the origin of sociability. Rejecting the Hobbesian notion that man is by nature unsocial and that this unsociability justifies the artificial social cohesion imposed by modern machinism, he points out that man was at birth a "social being" who loved society before opening his eyes and wept when left alone. What, he asks, was surprising in this: "On the day we call his first day, he leaves a society already quite old, and so pleasant! There he began, and now nine months old he must forsake it, experience loneliness, and grope about in search of a shadow of the dear union he had but lost. He loves his nurse and his mother, and hardly distinguishes them from himself."[1]

This view, which anticipates the emphasis of post-Freudian psychoanalysis on the importance for personality development of early "symbiosis" or "mirroring," to use Lacan's term, between mother and child,[2] is the basis of Michelet's mystique of the nation as a nurturant collective. Indeed, birth itself signifies for him the loss of union. What has been lost by the act of birth can be found again only within the French nation, which thereby signifies the rebirth—re-naissance—of fraternity.

We have seen how the idea of maternal nurturance as a positive force in history emerged in Michelet's work only after his encounter with Madame Dumesnil and how her death provoked within him a reconstruction of his personality and a reassessment of his personal history. As did the earlier sections of *Le Peuple,* part III reveals important traces of this reassessment in his political and social philosophy.

The chapter on friendship, for example, is based principally on his recollections of Paul Poinsot, likely reawakened by his comradeships of the mid-1840s. After noting that the very young child barely distinguishes his mother and nurse from himself, he wrote of the "rapture" of the child's first experience of "an other, a child of his age who is himself and not himself. . . . The family, the nurse, even for a time the mother, give way to the comrade, who has made him forget the rest."[3] Inequality in capacity or cultural background does not inhibit these spontaneous friendships, he maintained, but rather spurs them on; the weaker learns eagerly from the stronger.

What destroyed the Edenic friendships of young males, Michelet said, was the school system, which by its harshness aroused their spirit of rivalry—a clear reflection of his experience in the Lycée Charlemagne. In a passage that recalls Rousseau, he wrote, "Man, in this respect, is born generous and heroic. He must be taught envy, for he does not know it by himself." The lack of envy and rivalry in "natural" relationships, even when unequal, Michelet saw as rooted in the pattern of love within the family, where the stronger protected and developed the weaker and calculations based on the assumption of equality had no place. His democratic political ideal was founded on this family relationship; it was "the adoption of the weak by the strong—inequality but for the advantage of the weak." He excluded from this ideal, as artificial and conducive of servility, the feudal system of patronage. But even more representative of the natural relations between men than the family, he argued, more suitable as a model for the city of the future, were boyhood friendships, such as his with Poinsot; it was to this adolescent friendship that he recurred, seeing "the sacred bond of the city" in this "innocent disinterested friendship." An invocation at the end of this chapter to the selfless friendships among the generals of the French Revolution clearly reflected the early tie with Poinsot and the militant friendship with Quinet and Mickiewicz which echoed that tie.[4]

The next chapter, on association, bears only a superficial relation to Michelet's own experience but is of interest both for historical sociology and for Michelet's view of the French Revolution. His principal example of a workers' association was the traditional organization of Normandy fisherfolk encountered in his travels the previous summer. He viewed this kind of association in terms that Ferdinand Toennies would characterize a half-century later as *Gemeinschaft* (community) and that more recent sociologists would define as a primary group. It formed a link between the "natural association" of the family and the "grand association . . . of the nation." Michelet described a number of agricultural communities in which property was held in common and families were linked, as in the case of the Cherbourg fisherfolk. But these communities were, he argued, irrevocably doomed by the spread of modern economic forces, especially by the power of the banks. As a result the predominant and growing mentality in the working population had become one of mutual estrangement. A small producer in Lyons, for example, reported to him that the ultimate evil of modern times, quite apart from unfavorable government policies, was that "we are unsociable."

Michelet was too sensitive to the liberal economic doctrines of his time to believe in either the possibility or the desirability of a return to the guild system. Indeed, he saw in the still surviving compagnonnages and confréries of nineteenth-century France the remnants of a barbarous medieval system built not on the mutual love he sought but on self-interest and economic necessity. Yet, his liberalism was by 1845 subordinated to his social romanticism, which in turn was highly nationalistic. He could endorse new workers' associations motivated by positive ties rather than by self-interest, but he could only envisage them in the framework of a religion of sacrifice based on the French Revolution as an act of Divine Revelation. "People seldom sacrifice themselves," he wrote, "for anything but . . . a God in whom men recognize themselves. . . . We have lost our Gods! . . . It was necessary that God should have a second period and appear upon earth in his incarnation of 1789. He then gave to association its broadest and truest form, which alone can still unite us, and through us the world. Oh glorious mother France! You who are not only our own, but who are destined to carry liberty to every nation, teach us to love one another in you."[5]

Relationships of men with women seem to have been even more problematic for Michelet than those among men. In the chapter on love and marriage, his view of the other sex is in good measure fearful, even hostile. Although Michelet's anxieties on this score probably cannot be dissociated either from ideas of the time or from a surviving fear of his dominant mother, an added source of concern was probably his predicament at the time of writing—three and a half years after Madame Dumesnil's death. Between the lines one can read an explanation of his commitment to bachelor-hood directed at the women with whom he was then maintaining relationships.

Two conjugal possibilities were open to Michelet. One was a marriage to a woman below him socially—his housekeeper Victoire. The other was to marry the wealthy widow of a doctor friend who had treated Pauline—Madame Aupèpin. The possibility of marrying his housekeeper was real. Pauline had filled that function before their marriage. But from the paragraph in which he wrote of knowing "all the inconveniences of choosing a woman of inferior condition and education," we can assume that he had learned his lesson. The result of such marriages was, he found, social isolation and an unpleasant exposure to the crudeness of the woman's family. As to endeavors to educate the woman involved—efforts he had omitted with Pauline but quite earnestly attempted with Victoire— "these tardy educations that we try to give to the strong races of the people, who are harder and less malleable, seldom make any impression on them."[6]

Marriage to a woman of wealth and breeding was even less advisable. French women of this background, he argued, had been taught to insist on eternal amusement, one reason for the bourgeoisie's exhaustion. Michelet's annoyance at the potential claim on his time of such a marriage is transparent: "In this age of work when time is of incalculable value, serious productive men who want results cannot accept so enormous an expenditure of life as a condition of marriage. The night spent in promenading a woman prematurely destroys the next day."[7]

Michelet did endorse the working-class marriage, in which the weary laborer found rest, respect, and a wife who sacrificed every waking moment to his well-being. The traditional role division, which Michelet emphasized only in this proletarian setting, is striking. When the man comes home,

> The table is set, and the mother and children are watching for him. If that man is worth much at all, she will center her vanity on him and admire and revere him. And how careful she is! I see her keeping the smaller portion of their scanty meal for herself. She is reserving for the husband, who works harder, the wholesome food that will recruit his strength. He retires to sleep and she puts the children to bed. Then she works far into the night. Early in the morning, long before he opens his eyes she is up. Soon everything is ready—the warm food he eats at home and that which he takes with him. He goes off with his heart satisfied after kissing his wife and sleeping children, with no worries about what he is leaving.[8]

We note that in this domestic paradise, the man does nothing, the woman everything. One wonders what unconscious fantasies underlay such an idyllic portrait of female enslavement. Michelet was probably recalling childhood experiences transfigured by the sieve of memory. All his childhood tensions, the fearsome irritability of his mother and the manifold insecurities of his father's life, became invisible in a glaze of retrospective idealism. The husband merged with the child in this vision, not only through his total dependence on the loving nurturance of the mother but in his sleep pattern as well.

If indeed the transfigured imagery is less that of the faithful spouse than that of the all-giving mother, an interesting possibility is opened: that behind the denigrating portrayal of the frivolous upper-class wife, exhausting her husband by her demands for "amusements and pleasures," there lies the residue of what was omitted from the good mother image, the projection of all those aspects of his own mother that the infant Jules, like other infants, had learned to fear and repress: the image, in psychoanalytic terms, of the "bad mother"—the menacing figure whose symbolic manifestations in the natural world he had earlier labeled "stepmother."[9]

We have seen that Michelet viewed all existing forms of sociability—friendship, marriage, and association—as corrupted by the perversity of modern social institutions and that he sought salvation in an ideal French nation with the attributes of a nurturing mother. The obverse of this projection of the good mother into his patriotic idealism appears where he shows the depravity that would result from a loss of national identity. This, too, is a palimpsest passage—one that must be read with the lines from the journal on which it is based. In the book, Michelet said he once had a hallucinatory daydream in Dublin along the banks of the river near a bridge. He suddenly realized that it reminded him of the Seine and of Paris, minus the expensive shops, the Tuileries, and the Louvre:

> A few poorly dressed persons were coming down from the bridge, not in the blouses we wear but in old stained coats. They were arguing violently in a harsh, guttural, and very barbarous tone with a dreadful, ragged humpbacked man whom I still see before my eyes. Other persons were passing along, miserable and deformed. As I looked at them, a strange idea took possession of me and terrified me—that all of those figures were Frenchmen. It was Paris; it was France—a France grown ugly, brutal, and savage. . . . I said to myself that another 1815 must have happened, but long, long ago; that centuries of misery had oppressed my irrevocably doomed country; and that I had returned to take my share in that world of suffering.[10]

The specific notions that underlay this passage can be read only out of the original journal notation, from which Michelet excised certain details that had perhaps a too personal significance. This is the paragraph of the journal (I have italicized the parts omitted in *Le Peuple*):

> Although these quais are more regular and the river less broad, I find them similar to our own. What is missing is the Louvre, the Tuileries, the Champs Elysées, the Invalides, in other words, the force, the nationality. In the population too I recognized France, but made ugly, brutish, savage. *Sensuality and drunkenness were on every face. At almost every door a sad and moronic woman was holding in her arms one or two children.* The better class of people are vulgarly English. At the stairs of a bridge which could easily be compared to the staircase of the Saint-Michel bridge toward the Palace of Justice, a man and *a woman properly dressed* were quarreling with a horrible old small hunchback in rags; the shouts were so hoarse, so savage, that one would have thought they were going to cut each other's throat, but they separated rather peacefully.[11]

The journal text, with its sensuality and drunkenness and feebleminded women, was written in 1834, within five weeks of Michelet's first anguished tirade against "stepmother" nature, the "incestuous mother" who "caresses us, makes us drunk, and kills us." The "incestuous mother" brings to mind the mother of Michelet's wife, Pauline, whom he suspected of fornicating with her son, and suggests that perhaps the other qualities associated with the wicked mothers of Fontainebleau and Dublin—sensuality and drunkenness—were equally close to home. Two months later, Pauline's husband wrote for the first time with open annoyance of her "sensuality, return to wine,"[12] apparently an old problem that bothered him increasingly in the years before her death.

In the passage from *Le Peuple,* this hint that the difference between a people living in the grace of national existence and a nation deprived of that grace roughly equaled the difference between a good mother and a bad one, was supported by the addition of 1815 as the year that marked the turn from salvation to damnation. It was the year not only of Waterloo but of the death of Michelet's mother.

All this does not, of course, mean that everything remained the same in Michelet's value scheme between the appearance of the "stepmother" theme in the early 1830s and its restatement in the mid-1840s. In the earlier period, his hostility to sensuality and drunkenness—omitted from the recapitulation of his Dublin vision in *Le Peuple*—was part of a total rejection of the world of nature, in which attributes of femininity and maternity were blasted, together with all other manifestations of instinct, by the universal curse of the wicked mother, the marâtre. The puritan model that then guided Michelet's view of the world led him to see nature and political despotism as part of a world of material fatality against which only the free (and presumably masculine) spirit of human will and intellect could prevail. In the later period, he came to see nature and the instinctive behavior grounded in it as the indispensable bases of freedom and human brotherhood. Fatality remained in this view, but it was largely removed from the natural world to become embodied in the reified social and political machinery of state bureaucracies, armies, large factories, and the church. Against this "machinism" Michelet wanted to reconstitute the "natural" social ties of early childhood—between mother and child and between friends—through a new social harmony of the French nation, which would combine maternal nurturance with the highest form of brotherhood.

The vision of the wicked mother, or stepmother, if radically revised, had nonetheless not been eliminated from the realm of nature. The good mother infused only those parts of nature and the social order that conformed to the teleological scheme leading from the mother's womb to la patrie. Those that did not, as Michelet made clear both in his recapitulation of his Dublin vision, which simply equated denationalization and degeneration, and in his paranoid fears of women who did not conform to the sacred laws of nurturance, remained as blasted by the curse of the wicked mother as the machine world his patriotic idealism was intended to end. This Manichaean dualism was modified during the first decade of his second marriage, which served as a refuge, following the civil strife and the imperial denouement of the Second Republic, for the shattered remnants of his political idealism.

The concluding part of *Le Peuple* showers the reader with rhapsodies of political exaltation that are nevertheless specific enough to touch on most of the essential matters of patriotic faith in the period before the Revolution of 1848. The religious elements of the national tradition, the educational accomplishments and omissions of the French Revolution, the concepts of sacrifice, justice, and fraternity—all were intended to show readers the path from the Revolution of 1789 to the one Michelet sensed looming ahead.

The course Michelet himself was on had a somewhat shorter trajectory. It had begun in 1841 with the revalidation of nature, a result of his encounter with Madame Dumesnil. Its other end was the religio-nationalist exaltation of February 1848 and the first two volumes on the French Revolution. *Le Peuple* was the initial formulation of his popular nationalist credo, and its continual recurrence to his reawakened sense for the maternal shows that book's direct connection with the love that, five years earlier, had reawakened his feelings and reorganized his notion of his own past. In the work on the French Revolution, the connection to Madame Dumesnil, though still active, is attenuated, and what one might call a more masculine spirit, a stronger focus on justice rather than nature as the dominant value, betrays Michelet's return to the male world of political engagement.

PART IV

MICHELET'S FRENCH REVOLUTION: BASTILLE TO FEDERATION, 1846–1847

In describing Marat, M. Michelet has given his portrait un-justifiable proportions. Instead of limiting himself to pre-senting Marat on the stage of politics, he has written on this strange man a veritable biographical sketch. He takes the trouble to narrate his first years, his education, to analyse his scientific work as if Marat had his place between Lagrange and Laplace. . . . History is a too severe genre to lend itself to all these distractions. Episodes that are not directly relevant to the principal subject ought to be rejected without mercy, and M. Michelet has too often forgotten it. The new historian of the French Revolution has thus failed in his mission. . . . M. Michelet does not seem to comprehend properly the duties of the historian.

GUSTAVE PLANCHE
Nouveaux portraits littéraires

Let them reproach me, if they like, for what they call a digres-sion; it is in fact the heart of the matter, the core of the core. The first condition of history is truth. Moreover, I am not sure if the severely geometrical construction affected by mod-ern writers is always reconcilable with the profound demands of living nature; in everything organic, nature proceeds by curves. I also see that my masters, the oldest sons of nature, the great historians of antiquity, instead of slavishly follow-ing the straight geometric path of the indifferent traveler who had no other goal than to arrive, instead of racing along the arid surface, stop sometimes, if need be even turn around, so as to make powerful and productive openings into the heart of the earth.

MICHELET
Histoire de la Révolution française

CHAPTER 12

THE BOOK OF
THE FATHER,
1789 AND 1846

In February 1846, *Le Peuple* behind him, Michelet began in earnest to prepare for what was to become his seven-volume *Histoire de la Révolution française*.[1] Three years after he had interrupted the *Histoire de France* to wage war on the Jesuits, years in which his publications had been more tracts for the times than scholarly studies, he no doubt relished the prospect of resuming his labors as a historian, with the cataclysmic birth of modern France as his subject.

Michelet's perspectives had altered significantly in those three years, and more changed in the year it took him to write the first volume. The links between his approach to the Revolution and his preceding writings are many. Certainly *Le Peuple,* which concluded with the salvation of the people through la patrie, pointed Michelet toward the emergence of patriotic idealism in the Revolution. The first sentence of his new work—"The convocation of the Estates General of 1789 is the true epoch of the birth of the people"— suggested not only the book's innovative emphasis on the popular collectivity as the principal actor of the Revolution but also the role of that upheaval as the political "mother" of le peuple. Yet the line of continuity between volume I on the Revolution and Michelet's work and thought of 1843–45 is not that clear, and for good reason. Before he had finished that volume, his assumptions and values were shaken to the core by yet another personal disaster. Equally important, the political-social climate changed radically in these three years.

Take, for example, the issue that first led Michelet from erudition to contemporary politics: the conflict between liberals and Catholics over the control of higher education. The Jesuit order was in 1843 legally forbidden but openly organized and challenging the secular monopoly on higher education. When Michelet and Edgar Quinet began to attack the Jesuits, they had reason to think that the government, whose position they were supporting, would back them. They had no idea what a hornet's nest they were stirring up. The center-liberal government did not, of course, want to hand the educational establishment over to the church, but neither did it desire the political polarization that the attacks of the left-liberal professors at the Collège de France threatened: such a split could only diminish the electoral base of the regime while increasing that of the opposition Left and the Bourbon-Catholic Right.[2]

Guizot handled the matter by negotiating with the pope through the French-Italian emissary Pellegrino Rossi. Apparently Gregory XVI also feared the results of polarization; he agreed to a public acceptance of the ban on the Jesuits but obtained the tacit agreement that behind this ban the order would be able quietly to continue most of its activities under other names.[3] Correspondingly, in what seems to have been a gentleman's agreement,[4] the government of Louis-Philippe undertook to silence Michelet and Quinet, either by intimidation or by forcing them out of the Collège de France by mobilizing their opponents within the university. Quinet was suspended in April 1846, Michelet, after numerous warnings, twenty months later, in January 1848. Both suspensions sparked student demonstrations that were subsequently seen as premonitory signs of the Revolution of 1848.[5]

Apart from the polarization in religion and education, in 1846 the July Monarchy was approaching its demise politically, socially, and economically in ways that could not have been imagined three years earlier. Its liberal cadres, who possessed an electoral base only marginally broader than that of the Restoration, had changed little in a decade and a half and were proving incapable of averting a new revolution. In the years 1846–47, a rash of scandals shook a government that had already failed to react quickly and imaginatively to the crop failure of 1845–46 and the ensuing financial collapse. The kind of incidents reported in the press and picked up in Regnault's *Histoire de huit ans*[6]—grain riots, hunger, widespread beggary—were appearing in letters to Michelet and to his son-in-law from their close friend Eugène Noel, who noted carefully the signs of social collapse in the Norman countryside in which he lived.[7]

The university purge, crop failure and famine, financial malaise, increasing turmoil in rural areas, and lethargy of the government were reigniting the revolutionary temperament in 1846, and Michelet saw his history of 1789–94 as a means of clarifying the issues that were, with a new revolution, certain to occupy the center of the political stage once more. In September 1846, when the spirit did not move his pen fast enough, when he felt hobbled by recent illness and insufficient knowledge, Michelet wrote to Noel, "This delay is serious, not only for me but for the public too, which I see wretchedly split by these questions of the past, which will perhaps be those of the future, the near future."[8] He nonetheless began that day to write his history, and the following night his sense of urgency invaded his dreams: in his sleep he organized "a meeting of Lamennais, George Sand, Béranger, Quinet, Eugène Sue"—a general staff of the romantic revolution with which he had come to identify.[9]

The weight of the times inspired others besides Michelet to reformulate on their own terms the lessons of the first revolution. Louis Blanc, a radical journalist who played a major role in the early months of the February Revolution, also began his *Révolution française* at this time; the poet Alphonse de Lamartine, who figured prominently in the provisional government of February 1848, had had the foresight to begin his *Histoire des Girondins* in 1843 and published all eight volumes in 1847. Lamartine's work, celebrating with equal fervor Girondins, Dantonists, and Robespierrists, lacked the sharp edge of clear-cut political choice.[10] Perhaps for that very reason it did not interrupt the cordial relations between Lamartine and Michelet, even though it sold better than its competitors.[11] Michelet and Louis Blanc, however, began a major historiographical quarrel over the significance of Maximilien Robespierre and the Terror.[12] Since Blanc was inspiring many of the students becoming radicalized in the late 1840s to view Robespierre as their model of political heroism, Michelet believed that a realistic appraisal of the head of the Jacobins was urgent.

Accordingly, he attacked Robespierre and his faction, first, for systematically purging or destroying every competing revolutionary group by using the danger of foreign intervention as an excuse. The Terror eliminated two essential elements of the revolutionary camp: the leadership of the revolutionary peuple of Paris in the Commune (Pierre-Gaspard Chaumette, Anacharsis Cloots, and Jacques Roux), as well as in the sansculottes section cadres; and those who wanted a more humanitarian, less bloodthirsty revolution (men like Georges-Jacques Danton, Camille Desmoulins, the marquis de Condorcet, and some of the Girondins purged in 1793 were held in high regard by the common people). Popular democracy, as well as simple humanity, vanished in the two years of increasing terror between Louis XVI's imprisonment and Robespierre's fall in summer 1794. It was for good reason, Michelet argued, that the Thermidorian reaction produced no popular uprising, and even the purge of the Girondins from the Convention in June 1793, he contended, was provoked by only a fraction of the popular insurrectionists who had attacked the royal palace, the Tuileries, less than a year earlier.

Second, and this is the broader theoretical import of his work, Michelet attacked Robespierre and his nineteenth-century apostles for undermining the principled antagonism between the Revolution and Christianity. The Catholic Robespierrists, Buchez and Roux, in their popular and massive *Histoire parlementaire de la Révolution française* (1834–38), had, with extensive documentation, presented the message of the Revolution as an extension of Christianity, as the realization of the doctrine preached in the Gospels. For Michelet, the basis of the Revolution lay in the ideas of justice propagated during the Enlightenment by Voltaire and Rousseau, whereas the essence of Christianity and of the Old Regime it legitimated was the notion of arbitrary Grace.

The narrative of Michelet's work, though based more on documentary research than any previous study of the Revolution, is shaped throughout by these criticisms of Robespierre and the Terror. Yet other, deeper-lying attitudes and embedded values mediate among his personal evolution, his book, and the political storms of 1847–53. This mediation is particularly evident in his depiction of certain aspects of the Revolution that seem at first sight to be peripheral but that cast a penetrating light on the changing mentalities that infused the behavior of masses and individuals during its course: the festivals of federation in 1790, the decreasing popular enthusiasm of 1792–94, the roles of Madame Roland and Madame de Condorcet, the ruin of figures with whom Michelet identified, such as Condorcet, Philippe Fabre d'Eglantine, and above all Danton. On the whole, however, the narrative of these five years of French history, though permeated with Michelet's choices, demanded of him a more rigorous attention to questions of fact and chronology than had his essays of the years 1843–45; he had considerably less opportunity than in *Le Peuple* to use his writing as an arena for working out his personal dilemmas.

Where we do find texts comparable to *Le Peuple*, in their mixture of social philosophy and personal values, is in the Preface and Introduction to book I, written after a full year of research and writing on the first six months of the Revolution. These essays are like Michelet's periodic summations of his thought in his journal or lectures. They reveal that, behind a superficial appearance of ideological continuity with the last part of *Le Peuple*, Michelet's values were developing in a new direction. From having identified la patrie with a metaphoric nurturant mother, and after having rooted fraternity in mother-child symbiosis, Michelet was reevaluating the significance of paternal imagery, for the French people and for himself. Let us examine these texts, then, for their Rousseauistic selfrevelation, as well as for their historical content.

Preface: The Bullet from the Bastille

At the beginning of the brief Preface to the *History of the French Revolution,* Michelet projects himself into the close of his year's lecture series: "Every year, when I descend from my lectern after the last lecture, when I see the crowd of auditors disperse—another generation I shall see no more—my thought turns inward."[13] The key words are *descend, generation,* and *inward.* Descent and generation move from metaphor to biology before the Preface ends. Inwardness of thought also obtains a physical framework; in the first two pages of the text it interweaves and interreacts with Michelet's material environment.

Moving back and forth between the barren spaces of Paris, which echo the lost grandeur of the Revolution, and a desolate inner space, where the spirit of the Revolution is lodged within him, Michelet presents in these eight pages the tragic question of the failure of the Revolution, which can, he argues, be explained only in terms of a moral failure by the people and its leaders to comprehend their own principles: "the triumph of Right, the Resurrection of Justice, and the belated reaction of the idea against brute force." Gradually the revolutionaries substituted the ideals of force and success for these principles, and it was with this perversion of the revolutionary tradition, still dominant in his own day, that Michelet felt obliged to enter combat. "Do not ask why this people declines, weakens ... the evil is within. That an insidious tyranny could corrupt it was possible because it had lost sight of the idea that alone sustained it ... the sun of Justice and Revolution."

The targets of his anger were the unprincipled compromises that both the Center and the Left seemed willing to make with French Catholicism, in his eyes inherently antirevolutionary. Apparently addressing the entire liberal-left spectrum as "the party of liberty," he first attacked the "inner disease" of his former liberal friends. Faced with an offer of support from the Catholic party— "a perfidious, odious hand, the hand of death"—the liberals, unsure of their political base, accepted it, erroneously believing "that the enemies of religious liberty could become the friends of political liberty." Michelet condemned this belief as "a vain scholastic distinction ... Liberty is liberty."

Here Michelet introduced another of those family metaphors that frequently held a deeper significance for him than for his readers. To please the enemy, the party of liberty denied its friend:

"What I am saying: its own father, the great XVIIIth century! It forgot that this century founded liberty on the liberation of the spirit, until then bound by the flesh, by the material principal of the double incarnation, theological and political, sacred and royal. This century, that of the spirit, abolished the gods of the flesh, in the State and in Religion, so that there was no longer any idol and there was no other god but God." The reason for this unholy alliance with "the party of religious tyranny" was the feared numerical weakness of the party of liberty. Again he invoked their ancestors: "Our fathers did not act that way. They never counted their number." Both Voltaire and Rousseau, he contended, carried on their struggles for spiritual liberty in isolation—and won.

Michelet then turned his fire toward the Left, attacking what he viewed as the source of the numerical decline of the party of liberty, the dogmatic, sectarian intolerance of the orthodox. He repeatedly invoked the abused ancestors, the "fathers" of the Revolution, the Enlightenment thinkers who laid the basis for the revolutionary ideals of justice and liberty. Picking up the catchword of revolutionary France, he insisted: "Fraternity! fraternity! Repeating the word is not enough. If the world is to come to us as it once did, it has to see in us a fraternal heart. It is the fraternity of love that will win it over, not that of the guillotine . . . 'Fraternity *or death,*' said the Terror. Another fraternity of slaves. Why join to it by an atrocious irony the sacred name of liberty?" For: "Liberty alone, established in the last century, rendered fraternity possible. Philosophy found mankind without law . . . and it said, 'Let us create man, let him be, by liberty.' No sooner was he created than he loved."

Michelet's emphasis on love returns us temporarily to the matriarchally tinted notion of *Le Peuple,* of love as the constructor of the City. Indeed, the link he is postulating between liberty and fraternity is to be institutionalized in the state educational system of the future, where it will be based on a reformulated "two sexes of the spirit": "a constant exchange between the spontaneous intelligence of the crowd, based on inspiration and faith, and the considered intelligence of the thinkers, based on science and reflection."[14] The Preface contains other echoes of his revived maternal object relation. It is the metaphor of birth that posits "French liberty" as the "nouveau-né." More to the point, "the people," he tells us, was "the principal actor" of the Revolution, the people that "in general was worth much more than its leaders"; he reduces the leaders to "ambitious marionettes" whose strings are pulled by the plebs. And to underscore the link between his new work and the little book he had finished a year earlier, he uses the same geological metaphor to locate the beneficence of the common folk: "The more

I dug, the more I found that the better people were underneath, in the obscure depths."[15] Michelet's resurrection of this heroic populace is doubly symbolic of midwifery: he is assisting in the decade-long, painful birth of the French people (announced in the first sentence of book I) and—to the extent that he has rediscovered his popular roots—assisting at his own birth.

In spite of these bows to the matriarchally oriented political theory of *Le Peuple*, Michelet now focuses primarily on what he sees as the masculine aspects of his social thought. His derivation of the French revolutionary ideals of liberty and fraternity from the "fathers" of the Enlightenment is one sign of this. The location of the social bond in the mother-child symbiosis of the womb, that essential insight of *Le Peuple*, is here forgotten. Indeed, he later described the ideal of Justice, the cornerstone of his anti-Christian, revolutionary ideology, as brought to the child by the father.[16]

In the climax of book I, the physical assault on the Old Regime's most concrete embodiment of paternal despotism, the Bastille, the people of Paris were translating into material reality what the philosophes had accomplished in the realm of ideas. We could say that the common folk were attacking the false, despotic fathers of the flesh in the name of a purified idealism—*liberté*—of the fathers of the spirit.

At the end of the Preface, after a tremulous evocation of the "marvelous unity" of this first period of the Revolution—"the unanimous epoch, the holy epoch in which the entire nation, without any party division, without any (or very few) class oppositions, marched under one fraternal banner"—Michelet moved suddenly from unity and exaltation to disunity and heartbreak, from the political to the personal:

> And as everything in life is mixed, while I had so much happiness in renewing the tradition of France, my own broke forever. I lost him who so often recounted the Revolution to me, who was for me the image and the venerable witness of that great century, the XVIIIth. I lost my father, with whom I had lived my entire life, forty-eight years. When this happened I was elsewhere, I was realizing, in haste, this work I had so long dreamt of. I was at the foot of the Bastille, I was raising on its tower the immortal flag. This blow came to me, unexpected, like a bullet from the Bastille.

The death of his father—here recalling the allusion to Madame Dumesnil's death in *Le Peuple*[17]—led Michelet to an insight into his personal reaction that had a broader significance: He was reaffirming his faith through his losses and his hopes, he said, "pushing myself, to the extent that my own family was breaking up, into the family of the nation."

Michelet had been alluding to this kind of family disintegration in his work ever since his autobiographic lament of 1841 over the breakup of the Flemish weaver's hearth.[18] He was, however, also touching on a historical phenomenon of utmost importance for the shift from a traditional to a modern social consciousness: the evolution of a sense of national identity as a surrogate for the ruptured ties of preindustrial social and family organization.

Michelet lacked the social-historical awareness, now common among historians of mentalities, to realize the larger dimensions of this problem, the discrepancy between the culture of the prerevolutionary popular strata and the ideas of 1789, the enormous jump that national revolutions impose on group and individual consciousness. Most of the ancien régime's rural inhabitants lived in small villages, insulated geographically, culturally, and economically from any coherent national sentiment. Their customs, beliefs, and habits of thought were light-years away from those of the tiny minority of intellectuals who prepared the Revolution. Both the church and the juridical and taxing arms of the royal state had for centuries been attempting to curb aspects of the local cultures that were incompatible with their hegemony.[19] The revolutionaries, using cultural standards derived from the enlightened bourgeois minority, tried to do something similar, in the name of ideals that Michelet generally saw as legitimate, but at the same time they relied on the brute force of these premodern masses to overcome the military resistance of the Old Regime.

As an intellectual born into the popular classes but educated by the liberal inheritors of Enlightenment thought and revolutionary action, Michelet understood and supported the historic birth of French nationality; he perceived in it a revolutionary force to disarm the arbitrary and unjust Old Regime. The heroism of this world-historic role, needed to achieve justice and liberty, was inseparable from the unity between common people and bourgeois elites that he so admired in the first period of the Revolution. And the imperative of revolutionary unity demanded in turn a mystical nationalism—an ideological position that Michelet felt it his historical responsibility to incarnate. Yet the tragedy of every revolutionary epiphany, a tragedy perceived with bitter anguish by this artisan's son become professor, was that breakdown and reaction always seemed to follow. The Revolution once gained, bourgeois and plebs looked at one another under their fraternal banner and discovered the enemy.[20]

Michelet clearly sought to supersede the social conflict of upper and lower orders by a political union in the name of higher ideals.

But his closing line suggests something else: a dawning awareness that the breakup of traditional solidarities—in his own case, of his immediate family, in many others, of the ageless local communities of village, guild, or neighborhood, all fractured and partly dissolved by the spread of a centralized bourgeois society and economy— could be made good at the political level, through the sense, the fantasy, the mystique of membership in the great "family of the nation," founded on a common language, common pedagogy, and common idealism.

Introduction: The Death of Furcy Michelet and the Birth of Revolutionary Justice

As in his previous work, Michelet's most penetrating insights, as well as his most exalted intuition of historical moments, were being steered by his family novel. The terms on which the new family of the French nation was to be established were set by the hidden guilt felt within the decaying biological family. Such guilt arose in Michelet's case—and in those of other radical bourgeois—in part from the squeeze between Deist convictions and the pressures and lures of an overwhelmingly Catholic environment. The clearest echoes of this appear where Michelet castigates the "party of liberty" for its blindness to "the idea that alone sustained it"—justice and revolution—for its denial of "its own father, the great XVIIIth century." This echoes a bitter self-reproach that Michelet expressed in his journal two months earlier, on the day of his father's funeral.

He had been extremely close to Furcy Michelet, had left no record of a quarrel with him, had as a married man brought him into his house, had never lived apart from him. In summarizing Furcy's life, Michelet noted that his father's best years had been between Thermidor (1794) and the birth of his son, Jules (1798). Then followed the slow death of the printing trade, under the repression of the Napoleonic era, and bankruptcy. Yet this aging failure never lost his serenity. In a passage charged with insight into his father's character and with guilt about his own, Michelet wrote:

> He belonged essentially to the XVIIIth century, to the century of Voltaire and Rousseau. Whatever he had of opinions or ways of thinking he kept from this period and hardly departed from them. An almost indifferent witness of what happened afterward, he let the world go its way. The most terrible catastrophes, private and public, even his own personal ruin, did not change his serenity. People were often astonished at this.

No one guessed its cause. It was that he didn't live any more in himself, nor in the present, but in the future, in me.

Yes, he always kept me in view, in my preparation for life, agitated, swimming in the tide of the times and its opinions. Emerging from the XVIIIth century, I left it sometimes briefly, yet always came back. Always I refound my father, that is, the true France of Voltaire and Rousseau. My strange whims never worried him. He looked on them with indulgence; the son in whom he had faith could not be separate from him since he bore him within himself.

This indulgence, this easy hope in my future wisdom, broke twice, in two circumstances that I ought to mention at the expense of my own amour-propre. The first time, at age eighteen, my heart softened during this period of love and imagination; I suffered from not being associated with the great Christian association, the only, alas, that still exists. . . .

With this oblique reference to his conversion to Christianity in 1816, and the pain it caused his father, he broke off the entry. Later that day, however, he returned in his journal to the subject of Christianity. Although it professed scorn for the body, it had become materialistic, allying itself with tyranny: the Napoleonic Empire, the Restoration, and now the bankers. And then Michelet reproached himself again, presumably the second time his father's faith in him had shattered. Referring to the first volumes of the *Histoire de France,* he wrote: "What was I doing when I embellished the ideal of the Middle Ages, hid the reality? I worked against myself, against the progress of the world. How essential it is that I live to weaken the tragic prejudices I supported without realizing it."[21]

A constant theme in Michelet, this intertwining of personal and social commitment. In the autobiography he began in 1820 for his friend Poinsot, one of the motives, no doubt inspired by the insurrectionary mood of the moment, was to "improve the future by the past." In 1846, though, the commitment was heightened by a bad conscience.

At the end of a chapter in book II, written between his father's death and the composition of the Preface and Introduction, Michelet veiled only slightly the guilt that underlay his commitment to the Revolution: "How tardy you were, o glorious day! How many times our fathers awaited you, dreamed of you . . . The hope that their sons would finally see you was alone capable of supporting them; otherwise they would not have wanted to live, they would have died of their afflictions . . . And I, their companion, laboring alongside of them in the furrow of history, drinking of their bitter cup, what was it that allowed me to resurrect the sorrowful middle ages and yet not die of it, was it not you, o splendid day, first day of deliverance? . . . I lived in order to relate your history."[22]

Through this projection of his family drama into a drama of his nation's history, the reality of Michelet's motives appears, transfigured but not concealed by the haze of idealism. Michelet's father, too, lived by his faith in his son's character and future, but his pains and sorrows were post- and not prerevolutionary. Michelet had indeed worked alongside his father, sharing his "bitter cup," but in his father's print shop, not in the fields. Most important, the guilt he had felt at his father's death, about his earlier celebration of medieval Christianity, was here transmuted into his pride in recreating the social tragedies of the Middle Ages,[23] a recreation made possible only by the Revolution itself. In fact, the sense of social responsibility he derived from being blessed with insight through the Revolution ("I lived in order to relate your history") was inseparable from the guilt he had expressed after his father's death ("How essential that I live to weaken the tragic prejudices I supported").

There is, of course, a social dimension to the guilt he felt about his earlier celebration of Catholicism. Educational matters aside, the church did its utmost to pressure anticlerical Christians in all sorts of ways, particularly at their deathbeds. The abbé Cœur's attention to Madame Dumesnil when she lay dying was not merely a personal incident. The death in 1850 of Charles Levavasseur, a close friend of Alfred and a republican club leader in Rouen, as well as that of Michelet's friend Lamennais in 1854 and of his daughter, Adèle, in 1855, were accompanied by determined if unsuccessful efforts by the clergy to obtain final obedience to the church, arousing the anger and militancy of surviving friends and relatives. At the death of Michelet's father, two nuns showed up to ask with mocking disbelief and cruel hope, "Is it not M. Michelet?" The historian asked himself if this was a spontaneous act of hatred or if they came at the behest of their superiors. This incident, discussed angrily in his journal, undoubtedly contributed to his guilt vis-à-vis his progenitor for his earlier bows to the church and to his desire to purge himself of it by interpreting the Revolution as essentially anti-Christian.

In any case, after having written books I and II of the *Révolution* in four months, punctuated in the middle by the death of his father, Michelet turned to questions of basic principles only in January 1847, in his introductory chapters. The anti-Christian slant of the Preface became the overriding theme of the Introduction. He presented the Revolution, incarnating the ideal of justice, as the historical antagonist of Christianity, whose basic principle was arbitrary grace. In fact, a draft Introduction of October 1846—a month before Furcy Michelet died—does not, according to a sketch of it in the journal, seem to have dealt with the principled conflict of Christianity and the Revolution but only with the misery of the people toward the end of the ancien régime, which strengthens the impression that Furcy's death decisively altered Michelet's perspective. Indeed, the terms of this perspective as expressed in the Introduction suggest that Michelet's guilt about his earlier celebration of the Christian faith was leading him to rewrite his earlier antithesis of liberté and fatalité: liberté and justice became in 1847 uniquely linked to the Revolution, fatalité and corrupt, material nature, to the Christian church. In this way the son's expiation erased his earlier praise for Christianity as the torchbearer of liberté.[24]

Michelet's attack on Christianity thus has a double line of descent in the history of his ideas and psyche. It continues his attack on the church, begun in *Les Jésuites,* as a conspiracy of false fathers who have infamously gotten the women and children in their grip. Yet, the challenge to that grip is clearly based not on the biological tie to the mother, which in *Le Peuple* was the source of filial fraternity, but on the purely spiritual principles of justice and right, the legacy of the good fathers of the Enlightenment. The "material, carnal principle," associated in the earlier work with the beneficent maternal womb, source of fraternity, now receives connotations of evil, similar to those in the "Introduction à l'histoire universelle" of 1831. This carnal principle, basis of the dogma of original sin, "puts justice and injustice in blood ... makes them circulate ... from one generation to another [and] contradicts violently the spiritual notion of justice which is the basis of the human soul ... Justice is completely in the soul; the body has nothing to do with it."[25]

The "good mother" of the natural world glimpsed in *Le Peuple* here seems to be completely eclipsed by the "bad mother" of church dogma. Resistance of the sons (fraternity) against it can no longer be founded on the natural ties of mother-son symbiosis, which are implicitly grouped with the corrupt "material, carnal principle," but can be based only on the abstract principle of justice of the Enlightenment fathers: "The body has nothing to do with it."

Nor, one might think, has nature, or its human representative, the mother, anything to do with justice. Michelet sustains this position throughout the first ten pages of the Introduction, a self-contained section on the conflict of grace and justice, ending it as it began: "The Revolution is nothing but the tardy reaction of Justice against the government of favoritism and the religion of Grace."

Only in the following chapter does Michelet begin to integrate into the icy purity of this notion of justice something of the recently evoked natural warmth of the people. He does this by depicting a volcanic explosion, a metaphor for social revolution:

What were then the subterranean revolutions of the earth, what incalculable forces struggled in its bosom so that this mass, lifting up mountains, piercing rocks, splitting layers of marble, could pour to the surface ... Nature too clearly reminded me of history. This chaos of piled up rock oppressed me with the same weight that during the Middle Ages pressed on the heart of man; in this desolate peak which the earth, from the depth of its entrails, had launched against the sky, I rediscovered the despairing cry of the human race.[26]

Such powerful chthonic imagery signals a return of Michelet's populist identification of nature, folk, and motherhood. The echoes of this identification become clearer a page later, when he discusses the plight of the common people during the Middle Ages, confronted by a social system void of liberty and justice and a church in which only the privileged could enjoy the blessings of grace. As in *Le Peuple,* Michelet believed that what sustained the common people in their long torment were their half-pagan, half-Christian local cults: "From this broken heart escaped a living spring of loving and tender fantasy, a flood of popular religion against the dryness of the other kind ... the arid Byzantine metaphysics and the theology of death."[27]

Michelet soon reintroduced, in a more exotic historical context, the "good fathers" of the Enlightenment. His metaphor now employed slaves in the Colosseum, whose lives depended on their carrying eggs past the wild beasts of the arena up to the altar. In the ridiculed, trembling victims Michelet recognized his "fathers" and "brothers," Voltaire, Molière, and Rabelais. To Michelet's imagination, they answered that they were unconcerned at the danger and the ridicule, since their egg was really the treasure and the salvation of mankind—"Liberty, Justice, Truth, Reason." Unfortunately, Michelet observed, the altar to which they were bringing this treasure, the sanctuary to which the philosophes looked for protection from the intolerance of the church, was royal authority.

In this passage, more than in any other in the Introduction, Michelet rewrote his own history to cancel out an earlier, pro-Catholic position. The most striking example of this position, in the "Introduction à l'histoire universelle," also featured the Colosseum. Michelet had then (1831) written a lyrical celebration of Christian asceticism: "In good faith I kissed the wooden cross that triumphantly dominated the Colosseum. How the young Christian faith must have embraced it when it appeared in this arena between the lions and the leopards. Even now, whatever the future may bring, is not this ever more solitary cross the unique asylum of the religiously inspired?"

In 1847 others have taken the place of the cross amid the lions and leopards of the secular power—those trembling slaves, the spiritual "fathers" of modern France: Rabelais, Molière, and Voltaire. Michelet had offended his own father's Voltaireanism in 1831 by his appearance of Christian devotion. Now, less than two months after the old man's death, he had returned to the Colosseum and had put the fathers of human enlightenment in place of the cross.

The meditation on the Colosseum led Michelet to the second major section of the Introduction, in which he dealt with the old French monarchy, the philosophes' imagined sanctuary. Here, too, his metaphors reveal a struggle to synthesize the naturalist, "maternal" values of *Le Peuple* with the more abstract "paternal" ones he was returning to after his father's death. Since he intended in his new work to establish the common people rather than the Jacobin chiefs as the dominant force of the Revolution, he had to integrate the plebeian second sex into the abstract idea of revolutionary justice exalted in his opening pages. This integration emerged from a complicated reformulation of his family drama.

Essentially, he implied that under the Old Regime a false maternalism and paternalism pervaded church as well as state power. False maternalism: "The *religion of Grace,* partial to the elect, the *government* of Grace, in the hands of the privileged, are completely analogous." False paternalism: "Two paternal powers: ecclesiastical paternity, characterized by the Inquisition; monarchical paternity . . . by the Bastille."[28]

At a certain point in his narrative, Michelet presented the good fathers of the Enlightenment, who had sought to protect the spiritual goods of justice and reason in the sanctuary of the Bourbons, as actually replacing those paternal despots. This occurred, he argued, after an economic and social crisis at mid-century led to an abrupt popular rejection of the monarchy: "The king, this god, this idol, becomes an object of horror . . . And in his place arises the royalty of the spirit. Montesquieu, Buffon, Voltaire publish in this brief interval [1744–54] their great works; Rousseau begins on his."

In parallel fashion, the people take the place, in his implicit social-psychological framework, of the false mother aspect of the Old Regime. The people had earlier believed in the false gods of church and state, and their liberation from these idols in the eighteenth century was the precondition of all change.

The key to Michelet's notion of the people is his conception of nature, which is always portrayed as a maternal force. In part II, chapter 2, of the Introduction, nature appears to be strangling and starving the peasantry during the centuries of royal absolutism. As if sensing the need to correct his perception of nature as a cruel stepmother, a vision close to his views of 1831 but no longer useful,

Michelet made it clear at the end of this chapter that nature no less than humans required liberty to thrive—in other words, that the increasing misery of the peasantry before the Revolution was caused by social and political, not natural, forces. Chapter 3 begins, "Never say that nature has become a stepmother ... This earth is always the good mother, the wet nurse who only wants to help mankind; sterile and ungrateful superficially, she really loves it." And, he adds, this love would emerge when the people, no longer blinded by their credulous devotion to those who claimed to protect them, cease to look to priests, nobles, and kings for salvation. "Poor man, save yourself," is his advice.

Michelet was convinced that this withdrawal of belief occurred in the mid-eighteenth century and that from then on the two sexes of the spirit—plebs and intellectuals, female nature and male rationality—found each other. Even the metaphors he used to portray the people and the philosophes became complementary, symbiotic. The image of the volcano returns, now for the intellectuals: "From the bosom of Nature—glowing, boiling, as when Etna awakes—flames forth an immense volcano. Every science and every art bursts forth. The eruption over, a mass remains—an enormous mass of mingled dross and gold: the *Encyclopédie.*"[29]

Similarly, once new ideals of justice have replaced the false gods of the Old Regime, nature is no longer sterile. Here, too, a comparison with *Le Peuple* is instructive. There Michelet viewed the "natural" forms of sociability—friendship, marriage, and professional association—as failing to elevate mankind from shallow egotism as long as the highest level of sociability—the nation, la patrie, incarnation of the good mother—remained unattained. In this Introduction, the masculine ideal of justice, essence of the Revolution, is necessary to make nature fruitful: "There is a prolific force in the Justice of God. Every time it touches the earth, the latter is happy and gives birth. Sun and dew are insufficient, justice is needed. Let it come and the harvests will come." A few pages later, he presents this abstract justice, from which the earth itself would bear fruits, as becoming concretized in the writings of Rousseau.[31]

Yet, just as nature required justice, the message of the philosophes would become effective only when the natural force of the people acted on it. Michelet symbolized the injustice of the Old Regime by citing the fate of an innocent man, Latude, trapped in the Bastille. Latude was liberated in 1784 by the indefatigable efforts of a disinterested woman of the people, Madame Legros. Linking this incident, just a few years before the the Old Regime disintegrated, with the contemporary fears of intellectuals that the Revolution would never come, Michelet made evident most of the connections I have been discussing—the equation of women, the people, and nature and the impotence of reason, liberty, and justice unless merged with the plebs:

> Men of little faith, do you not see that as long as it [the Revolution] remained among you—philosophers, orators, sophists—it could do nothing? Thanks to God, here it is everywhere, in the people and in women.—Here is someone who by her persevering unconquerable will opens the prisons of the state, has taken the Bastille in advance. The day when liberty and reason emerge from abstract principles and descend into nature, into the heart (and the heart of hearts is woman), all is over. Everything artificial is destroyed. Rousseau, we understand you, you were right to say, "Return to nature."

Thus, with the exception of a quiet transposition from a maternal to a paternal ideal, all the elements of *Le Peuple* seem to be in place. This subtle change is nonetheless crucial. Shortly before he began the Introduction, Michelet had ended the Preface by writing that his father died while he himself was resurrecting the assault on the Bastille. The shade of Furcy Michelet no doubt hovered over the tale of Madame Legros, the woman who, as the incarnation of nature, the people, and revolutionary justice, had "taken the Bastille" in 1784. In *Le Peuple*, which was built on the matriarchal ideals that inspired Michelet after Madame Dumesnil's death, salvation of the French people was to be obtained by its union in love of la mère-patrie. At the conclusion of this Introduction, love and even grace return, but only as epitomized in the revolutionary principle of justice, repeatedly identified with the fathers.

The spirit of the ex-printer was indeed haunting his son. A page after Madame Legros had vanquished the Bastille, Michelet was addressing justice in terms that—put next to the conclusion of the Preface and his journal notations after Furcy Michelet's death— read like a masked plea to his father for forgiveness and understanding for earlier moments of religious weakness:

> Pardon me, oh Justice, I thought you to be austere and hard and I did not see that you were the same thing as Love and Grace . . . And this is why I had a weak spot for the Middle Ages, which repeated this word of Love without performing the offices of Love. Today, returned to myself, my heart more ardent than ever, I ask your forgiveness, heavenly Justice of God. For you are truly Love and identical with Grace. And since you are Justice, you will support me in this book, where my path has been marked out by my heart and never by self-interest. You will be just to me and I will be so towards all. For whom have I written this if not for you, eternal Justice.[32]

This plea reinforces the notion that, at the end of 1846, Michelet was subordinating the matriarchal values of *Le Peuple* to the more austere masculine ones of his "Introduction" of 1831. It seems as though the experience of rebirth and rediscovering his mother that resulted from his encounter with Madame Dumesnil had run their course, replaced by the need, after the shock of his father's death, to establish a "masculine" image of revolution. The reflections of this change, apparent in the subsequent text despite occasional reappearances of "good mother" figures, were renewed images of woman as evil, as vampire, as the wicked mother; these would play a more important role in his vision of the Revolution than they had in his work of the previous six years.

In the context of this return of Michelet's earlier fears of "stepmothers," his formulation regarding his father's death—"pushing myself, to the extent that my own family was breaking up, into the family of the nation"—may contain a hidden dimension. Evidence suggests that his reaction to such family losses was not unambiguously desolate, that a part of him may actually have desired them: more than once in the early 1830s, he saw historical benefits in the disintegration or decline of the natural family. In the "Introduction à l'histoire universelle," Michelet wrote admiringly about the Italian genius that replaced "the natural world of the family" with "the artificial world of the city."[33] This coincided with the ideological emphasis in that work on the "progress of mankind toward freedom from subordination to nature and natural ties." At a more personal level, in an autobiographic note of 1834 he wrote: "Could not the progress of the author's life be aligned, up to a certain point, with the march of individual and general events? Thus every loss he would undergo would be a step beyond his individuality. He would thus grow in stature at the same time as the public spirit during the Restoration. His powers would burst out like those of France after the July Revolution. It is the epoch in which he began his abundant production. Finally, detached little by little from every local tie, he would begin a European life."[34]

Although Michelet wept bitter tears after the loss of those dear to him—his mother, Poinsot, Madame Fourcy, Pauline, Madame Dumesnil, his father—he seems to have been prepared to see benefits in such losses. This ambivalence may have been rooted in secret aggressions against those close to him: In 1821, he admitted that the sorrow he experienced after his mother's death six years earlier had been followed by a "cruel happiness," a feeling of "a freedom unknown until then, gentler, and less worried."[35] Such ambivalence was certainly shaped and encouraged by the social conditions of his rise to eminence. Michelet's impoverished lower middle-class family background gave him little prospect for cultural immortality, in spite of the examples, in his mother's family, of sacrificing for a proper education. What did move him rapidly up the social and professional ladder was the public educational system, represented in his models Villemain and Cousin, and later by Guizot, Thiers, and others who identified and helped him develop his unusual talent. These teachers and friends were part of the liberal establishment, which was unthinkable without the revolutionary upheaval and the Napoleonic reforms. It was for good reason that, just after invoking "Justice my mother, Law my father," Michelet wrote: "Whom else can I invoke, I, one of the crowd, one of those who were born ten million strong and who never would have been born without our revolution."[36]

At the threshold of what he hoped would be the final reenactment of the Revolution, the historian's emotions at the death of Furcy Michelet must have been powerfully mixed: genuine grief at the loss of a father whose quiet confidence and love had accompanied him all his life, and yet a tinge of guilty relief at being able to take one more "step beyond individuality," to separate himself from one more of the "natural" bonds that hindered his union with the nation whose fate he was simultaneously trying to describe and determine.

Perhaps it was this extra, inadmissible guilt that simmered under his obsessive consciousness that he had fifteen years earlier offended both his father and the revolutionary cause in his adoration for the Christian Middle Ages.

CHAPTER 13

FEDERATION AND EPIPHANY, 1790 AND 1847

Nostalgia and Fraternity in Two Generations: Michelet and Flaubert

Though Michelet disdained romantic novelists for distorting social reality, he respected and liked Gustave Flaubert, sentiments Flaubert reciprocated. The two artists, in spite of differences in aesthetic and political values, valued friendship and fraternity above all else and shared a nostalgia for an earlier human warmth and closeness. Yet key expressions of their nostalgia, in Flaubert's *Sentimental Education* (1869) and in book III of Michelet's *History of the French Revolution* (1847), though strikingly similar in phrasing, reveal sharply contrasting social visions, probably arising out of different generational positions (Michelet was twenty-three years older than Flaubert).

At the conclusion of Flaubert's novel, Frédéric Moreau and the closest friend of his youth, both of them aging failures, review the ambitions, and the loves, that drove them from adolescence to adulthood. They recall a common adventure in a rural brothel, when they were about sixteen. Frédéric, carrying a bouquet of flowers from his mother's garden, fled the premises at the threshold, and his friend, who was dependent on Frédéric's pocketbook, had to leave with him. The novel ends with their nostalgic sigh, "It was then that we had it best." Flaubert clearly shared this nostalgia for the picaresque intimacy of youth.

Michelet, discussing the federations of 1790, cited a similar phrase in a report from a village committee about its local festival of federation: "So passed the finest moment of our lives." He added, "These words which the fédérés of a village wrote on the evening of the festival at the end of their report—I was close to writing them myself on finishing this chapter. It is over, and nothing like it will come back for me. I leave with it an irreplaceable moment of my life, a part of myself, I feel, which will remain there and will not follow me. I depart impoverished and diminished."[1]

Michelet's confession signaled the generational gulf between him and the novelists. Though we can assume that Flaubert felt the same nostalgia and loss on concluding his work, he could never have discussed it outside a personal letter. Michelet's intimate comment, characteristically romantic in its assumption of a larger community between the writer and his readers, was always eschewed in the published novels of his young friend, whose motto—"cache-toi"—forbade public expression of private feeling.

Other differences are tied to this one. For Flaubert, closeness, the sense of human fraternity, was personal and exclusive. He detested politics and was a Nietzsche *avant la lettre* in his cynical distrust of idealism. For Michelet, personal closeness and the fraternity of the nation were dialectically interdependent. This difference characterized not just the two men but their generations. Flaubert epitomized the social disillusion and cynicism of the postromantic generation; it was no accident that his mature work was written after the Revolution of 1848 had failed. Michelet, nearly a quarter of a century older than Flaubert, became the prophet of French national consciousness in the wake of the Revolution of 1830 and promulgated the social and religious revolution in the years preceding 1848. As more than one scholar has noted, this was the golden age of social prophecy.

Throughout his career, Michelet joined a powerful identification with his country's destiny to his sharp insights into historical processes. This identification sprang ideologically, from the radical nationalism that saw the French Revolution as the dawn of a new age of humanity, and psychologically, from his awareness that he owed his social identity to the educational system established in the revolutionary period. If, in his seven years of work on the Revolution, his most exalted moment, the "best day" of his life, was his apotheosis of the federation movement of 1790, it will be useful to find out why.

To comprehend what this movement and his work on it meant to Michelet, we have to take into account both its significance for his total view of the Revolution and his personal and political situation at the time he was writing on it—his father's death and the oncoming revolution. Moreover, we have to continue our effort to comprehend theoretically the link between the historian and his subject, in this case perhaps focusing on the anthropological and psychological significance of the epochal events that so fascinated him as a key to what was occurring within him.

Federation, Fraternity, and the Transcendence of Particularism

The federation movement was for Michelet a first, largely spontaneous step toward a patriotic, revolutionary, and national consciousness in France. The anarchic rural uprisings in the summer of 1789, the burning of the feudal charters that had given the aristocracy control over peasant land and labor, had begun a process that gradually led the peasantry from a limited village consciousness to an exalted identification with la patrie: it was this identification that Michelet viewed as the necessary basis of the new revolutionary religion.

French historians have recently explored in depth the prerevolutionary rural mentality. Dominated by a secular or ecclesiastical lord, the village was the normal framework of everyday experience. Peasants and others who worked locally rarely left it, normally produced only for local markets, and usually spoke not French but a local patois, which made them impervious to the national literature (most were, in any case, illiterate). In matters of property rights and morals, local custom was all-important, provincial or national legislation insignificant. A complex web of norms and values determined how one ate, dressed, married, worked, raised children, treated parents, inherited wealth, and worshiped. Youth groups prepared the village festival days, half-Christian and half-pagan, and meted out punishment, normally some form of public humiliation, to those who transgressed local mores. Outside the village, the world was largely unknown and assumed to be hostile. Even a nearby village with almost the same customs could be an object of fear and scorn; battles between the youths of neighboring villages were as common as between working-class adolescents of adjoining neighborhoods in this century.[2]

Scholars attentive to the policies of the first and third French republics have argued that the integration of rural life and consciousness into an awareness of French nationhood after 1789 was contingent on the imposition of a common language that replaced the patois and was taught in a national school system; the schools, in turn, depended on political events to create the need for a social and cultural identification with the nation.[3] Now Michelet combined these sociological insights with a normative political ethic; for him, such an identification had to be founded on a religious awareness of the significance of la patrie, not in Christian terms but in revolutionary nationalist ones inspired by principles of social justice.

The federations were so important to him because they made the transition to the new identification from below: they seemed to convey the spontaneous aspiration of the entire French people for such a revolutionary nationalist brotherhood in the framework of la patrie.

In the summer of 1789, traditional local structures began to disintegrate in response to the combination of agrarian crises and revolution in Paris. The collective terror that arose from this collapse and from the various threats to peasant security gradually gave way to a broader pattern of identification, first with the region and then with the nation. The assault on the Bastille inspired innumerable peasant villages to undertake their own attacks on traditional authority, and the response of August 4 to these assaults—the voluntary surrender of local aristocratic privileges—gave a national seal of approval to the peasantry's burning of feudal charters: rural fears and rebellions abated temporarily. Nonetheless, political and economic events, such as the grain shortage and the royal insistence on veto power over new laws, motivated a new popular action on October 6, when thousands of Parisian working-class women, accompanied by the National Guard, marched on Versailles and brought Louis XVI back to the Tuileries.

The return of this symbol of national unity to the protective embrace of the capital seems, for both psychological and ideological reasons, to have accelerated local movements of alliance and federation throughout the country. Psychologically, the "capture" of Louis XVI liberated the rural movements from deep-seated fears—*la grande peur*—of retribution for peasant audacity in burning manorial records. This liberation enabled them to look toward the nation as the framework of their new sense of brotherhood and freedom. Ideologically, the successful march on Versailles marked a turning point in the significance for the common people of the concept of fraternity. As Marcel David has pointed out, the initial uses of this concept in 1789 were antirevolutionary: in May, Louis XVI appealed to the Third Estate in the name of "fraternité" to cooperate peacefully with the aristocracy and the clergy in the Estates General.[4] All through the summer of 1789, exchanges between representatives of the Third Estate and those of the traditional powers demonstrated that fraternité was viewed as an ideological trap by the plebs, a weapon of the counterrevolution. It was only to be cleansed of this taint, to be integrated into the revolutionary lexicon and made usable for the new revolutionary élan, after Louis XVI's humiliating return to Paris, which signified the decisive neutralization of royal power.

The federation movements had begun in the summer as a limited village response to the fear of brigands. After the march on

Versailles, the movements gained in intensity and scope, expanding first to the level of the province and then quickly taking on a national character as peasants and townspeople of adjoining provinces pledged federation and mutual aid at the banks of the rivers that separated them.

The climax of the movement was the national festival of federation, presided over by Talleyrand and the marquis de Lafayette on the champs de Mars in Paris on July 14, 1790, in commemoration of the assault on the Bastille. The Assemblée decided this, after long hesitation, in June, as a fitting crown to the federations at the village, provincial, and city level. With barely a month to organize, the Paris fête—the first of the major revolutionary festival days—required and received a great deal of spontaneous improvisation. The result was a well-orchestrated oath of allegiance and fraternity by the 400,000 spectators and 100,000 National Guardsmen—in good measure from the provinces—followed by an enormous banquet. Descriptions of the event suggest a controlled celebration of the new constitutional monarchy. But both the transportation of tens of thousands of provincial militiamen over the poor roads that linked villages and towns throughout the country and their reception in Paris were possible only through the inspired support and cooperation of local groups in all parts of France, as well as in the capital. And the source of the federation movement seems to have been a genuinely spontaneous popular phenomenon, rooted in rural mentalities and folklore.[5]

Approaching a Book through Its Author: Michelet's Value-Conflicts in 1847 and the Joachimite Aspects of the Federation Movement

If in the France of 1790 the federations had reconciled local mentalities and national consciousness, in Michelet's fascination for them in 1847 we can glimpse the tensions of the value-conflicts his father's death had awakened in him. Those tensions, implicit in his concept of the "two sexes of the spirit," were resolved at a practical level in his vision of the federations: an integration of the naturalist, intuitive, folkloric, "feminine" peuple with the elevated "masculine" idealism he had recently outlined in the Introduction to his book. But at a more theoretical level, the tensions between the two value-systems persisted.

Michelet always retained a fundamental commitment to a transcendental rational ethic that made freedom the antithesis of nature. In *Le Peuple,* the genius was portrayed as uniting both freedom and nature, and France, incorporating the maternal principle, was the fructifying force that brought both sexes of the spirit to that harmonious social unity so dear to the social romantics. The *Histoire de la Révolution française* shows the continuation of Michelet's struggle to harmonize these competing systems of value. After his father's death, the highest ethical value, la patrie, no longer had the exclusively maternal quality it had had in *Le Peuple* but had become dominated in Michelet's ideological code by the abstract paternal significance of la justice. Although he continued to value the natural roots of popular culture, the ideal that he considered necessary to fecundate the culture of the people had become a thoroughly masculine abstraction: the social idealism of the "fathers" of the Enlightenment. His homage to these fathers was a way of exculpating himself to the shade of his own father for his earlier celebration of that Voltairean bête noire, the Catholic Middle Ages.

We can see in book III the continued need to atone for this celebration. To begin with, its main theme, the evolution of the festivals of federation, is depicted as a struggle for the realization of the new revolutionary religion, which Michelet sees as the necessary and inevitable replacement of Christianity. He explicitly rejects the notion that he had earlier maintained in the *Histoire de France* of a possible transformation, renewal, or reform of Christianity in the modern world.[6] The federation movement, then, has the same function in book III as the trembling philosopher "fathers" in the Roman arena had in the Introduction: it takes the place of the old religion. The language is inspirational, particularly where Michelet compares the federations to those two previous fusions of civic and religious devotion, Jerusalem and the Crusades: "Everybody is in motion and all march forth as in the time of the crusades. Whither are they all marching thus in groups of cities, villages, and provinces? What Jerusalem attracts thus a whole nation, attracting it not abroad, but uniting it, concentrating it within itself? ... It is one more potent than that of Judea, it is the Jerusalem of hearts, the holy unity of Fraternity, the great living city, made of men. It was built in less than a year and since then it has been called *patrie.*"[7]

The inseparability of Michelet's revolutionary religion of fraternity from the guilt inspired in him by his father's death appears clearly in his journal on certain key dates. July 14, 1789, the day of French liberty, of the attack on the stone symbol of paternal despotism, was bound in his memory to his father's death on November 18, 1846, and his attendant grief and guilt. Thus on July 14, 1847, while on vacation in Germany and the Low Countries, Michelet reiterated his guilt over having celebrated the Gothic church of the Middle Ages, which he had recently, in his lecture notes, labeled as a "harsh wet nurse, terrible mother."[8] Equally important, in the light of his tendency since Furcy Michelet's demise to finish once and for all with Christianity, was the link he forged on that July 14 between the new morality he was seeking and the Joachimite évangile: "Let a higher morality flourish, as Joachim of Fiore says, 'from this tomb of scriptures.' Let the imagination, stigmatized by the two systems of the banks and the bigots, reflourish on a better basis: the heart. No longer just the individual paradise, salvation, but the common paradise, found in fraternity."[9]

Michelet's enthusiasm for the Joachimite évangile had been evident since his lecture of April 28, 1842. In *Les Jésuites* (1843), he had cited approvingly the prophetic eschatology that linked the doctrine of liberty to that of a "third age" of friendship and childlike innocence.[10] But in 1843 he still hoped for a rejuvenation of the church.[11] In 1847, the évangile éternel of Joachim had become a prophecy of the new revolutionary religion, based on justice and fraternity[12] and intended to replace a moribund Christianity.

Just as Michelet was attentive to the connection between the federation movement and July 14, he was also sensitive to the relation between his work on that subject and the date of his father's death. A similar relationship ties his summary chapter to books III and IV, "On the Method and the Spirit of this Book," to the first anniversary of that loss. He suggests the bond between this summary and his life in a journal notation of November 12, full of nostalgia for those who had loved him and died:

Yesterday, 11 November, I finished the writing, today, the 12th, the correcting of Volume II. My book completely made me forget my life. [The previous journal entry was a month earlier.] I only recall that with Adèle's return, two weeks ago, I began a four-page note that grew to fifty: On the method and the spirit of this book (end of the second volume) where I struggled physically with the clergy and the Terror.

This morning, in my bed, I offered this act to God and to those I loved [who] . . . left me en route. How, where, when do we rejoin one another? I glided all year in my book as in a bark, like a man with a wounded foot who is afraid to land. Thus I lived outside myself, in a perhaps higher self, but . . . Now, for the past hour, disoriented. It's really November, the cold rain entering the earth where soon our bones will rest. In any case, I say: Thank you. I've done something human.

We need a popular abridgement of the method and spirit of this book to circulate widely and so reply to Cabet, Buchez.[13]

A journal entry of November 19 refers explicitly to the anniversary of his father's death, and an entry of the twentieth reveals the sharp rebukes his conscience dealt him on the days before and after that anniversary. These complaints suggest the increasing hold on him, after his father's death, of a punitive superego, which expressed itself through an idealism of republican patriotism and self-sacrifice and condemned sensual pleasures.

This republican patriotism emerged sharply in a letter, also of November 20, to a young radical lawyer, in which Michelet argued that his recent writings were "the strongest manifesto for republican institutions since Camille Desmoulin's La France Libre" and summarized his new work as an effort "to found the idea of the Republic on its true stoical base."[14] In his journal entry of the same day, Michelet applied the severity of the Republic's "true stoical base" to himself. He rebuked himself for being "an egoistic artist, closed off in his study," for having "a soft, lazy soul," too fond of the pleasures of hearth, sensuality, and women, too forgetful of the character of Pauline, modest, self-sacrificing, and faithful: "You should rise, in love, to a higher level, beyond sensuality. On spiritual humility: live humbly, near the poor. You will become a man; you will be less a book, less a scribe, less an amputee, less dreamy, less vain, less subtle. You will be cured perhaps of this soft artistry which Dante admits to so sadly. You will be less sensitive to dreams, to woman this living dream. Your sensitivity will become force and courage (to suffer with the world that suffers)."[15]

The work he had just completed, in which he acknowledged having played the part of "the veritable priest, who celebrated ... the holy of holies on the altar of the Federations," was, he felt, simultaneously his glory as an "artist" and his failure as a man, since he was aware of using his work to escape direct human responsibilities. In two areas in particular he felt remiss: in his human obligations to those around him, both his family and the poor, to whom he felt lacking in charity and fraternity; and in the cause of educating the people. This last was what he was trying to do throughout books III and IV and especially in the note on method and spirit; it was the realization that he had probably failed in this popular instruction that led him to desire a "popular abridgment" of the note on method.

Perhaps Michelet's fear that he could not write simply enough to educate the people was based on some awareness that behind the popular beliefs on the Revolution that he had tried to summarize in his note on method lay all the complexities of his larger historical perspective. Although the ideal he invoked was national unity, he felt repeatedly the need to explain the lack of unity of the quarreling revolutionary factions. And when he did so, his underlying explanatory principle remained the "two sexes of the spirit," which in 1847 could not help but reflect the ambivalence of his tormented conscience.

The basic message of the Revolution, according to the note on method, was the supreme religious value of France as a mystical entity, as the bearer of enlightenment and social justice, and as the protector of the peasants, the poor, and the oppressed. The federations, as the embodiment of a nascent national consciousness, were for him the most important mass religious movement since the Crusades. Because he fervently believed that the only threats to this new national order came from an aristocracy and a Catholic church dependent on foreign powers, he categorically denied the main tenets of contemporary socialists: that there was a class struggle within the Revolution between rich capitalists and poor industrial workers, that the Terror was in these terms both justifiable and necessary, and that the Jacobins, friends of the poor, followed in the Catholic tradition.

Michelet, committed to the notion that the Revolution was the new manifestation of the Godhead and the incarnation of justice, saw it as the absolute antagonist of Christianity and the Old Regime, both based on the principle of arbitrary grace. As to the struggles of industrial workers, he argued that the industrial class was only born after the Revolution and that the bulk of the French people in 1789 and of the revolutionaries were small property-holders who sought liberation from the burdens imposed on them by the privileged elites. Essential in Michelet's opinion was the education of the people in the Enlightenment values of justice and reason as an antidote to the obsolete values of Christianity.

Thus, in opposition to the Jacobin historians who viewed such figures as Rabelais, Molière, and Voltaire as mere "agents of an egoistic individualism of the bourgeois classes," Michelet saw in them "the people, the true and powerful expression of the French spirit, such as we earlier found it in the *fabliaux,* fables, stories, and popular poetry of every age, form, and species." The Terror came from a failure to grasp the new ideal of justice, from the persistence of obsolete Christian political assumptions about "salut public" (public safety), which one was entitled to protect with fire and sword. As such, it was in the tradition of Torquemada and the Inquisition, of the fourteenth-century royal legate Nogaret and *raison d'état*: "Marat, in sharpening the blade of the guillotine, only creates royalists and prepares the Reaction."[16]

In Michelet's view, the Girondins, who impeded the progress of the Revolution, did so not because they were bourgeois—as he notes, so were the Jacobins—but because they were lawyers and scribes with a fatuous sense of superiority over the common people. Again the historian appealed to the "two sexes of the spirit." In criticizing the Girondin Brissot for comparing the distance between a "philosophe patriot" and an "ordinary patriot" with that between a free man and a slave, he wrote: "Brissot does not realize that instinct and reflection, inspiration and meditation, are impotent without each other; that the philosophe who does not continually consult the instincts of the people remains in a vain and sterile scholasticism; that no science, no government is serious without this exchange of illuminations [*lumières*]."[17]

It was the glory of the federations that they incarnated this mutual fecundation of popular instinct and enlightened principle. In his lecture at the Collège de France of May 6, 1847, a summary of his just-completed chapter on the federation movement, Michelet made it clear that the spirit of the federations was carried over into the new revolutionary armies.[18] Elsewhere in his book, he suggested that the club movement, especially the Jacobins and the Cordeliers, inherited the spirit of the federations. Yet the club movement was a response to the *divisions* within France, whereas the federations, for a few brief months, signified the transcendence of all division. In fact, the federations, culminating in the Paris festival on July 14, were a high point of popular unity and enthusiasm in Michelet's vision of the Revolution. During its first year, they organized a nascent national consciousness and unity that overshadowed and made impotent the machinations of church and aristocracy. Within months after they had heralded the "Jerusalem of hearts," new divisions appeared, and the club movement, especially the hundreds of local Jacobin societies, arose to defend the Revolution against them, institutionalizing the sacred moment of the federations.

Yet, for Michelet, something essential was lost in this institutionalization. In the first chapter of book IV, called "Why the New Religion Could Not Be Formulated," he explained what it was. In the postfederation mood, enormous moral resources were at the disposal of the revolutionary regime. Not only was there a popular spirit of sacrifice available to the revolutionaries, France possessed, at the moment of the Paris federation, a young generation of powerful and genial personalities who were between twenty and twenty-five. He then—nonpartisanly—named Bonaparte, Cuvier, Chateaubriand, Saint-Simon, the "two Fouriers" (the utopian socialist and the mathematician), Madame de Staël, Chénier, Maistre, Bonald, Geoffroy Saint-Hilaire, and Ampère, and added: "What a crown for the France of the Federation . . . these magic diamonds that sparkled in the shadow."[19]

The problem was that these figures, for all their genius, lacked nurturant warmth and fecundity. Most were "men of action, of invention, of calculation, predominantly in the physical and mechanical sciences [who] pushed violently toward results. An immense force, but too often arid . . . None of them had this flowing heart, this spring of fresh water at which the nations sate their thirst."[20] Clearly it was the vital warmth of the people, its intuitive wisdom, which was lacking in the genial figures of the revolutionary decade. In renewed accents of Joachimite prophecy, Michelet then described "the immense soul of the Revolution, under its two forms and its two ages":

> In the first age, which was a reparation for the long insults to the human race, an impulse of justice, the Revolution formulated into laws the philosophy of the XVIIIth century. In the second age, which will come sooner or later, it will emerge from these formulations, find its religious faith (on which all political law is founded) and in this divine liberty which only excellence of heart can give, it will bear an unknown fruit of goodness, of fraternity. Here is the moral infinity that germinated in this people ... when, on July 14 at midday, it raised its hand. On this day, everything was possible. All divisiveness had ceased; there was neither nobility, nor bourgeoisie, nor people. The future was present ... That is, time stopped ... A lightning bolt and eternity. There was nothing, it seemed, to prevent the social and religious age of the Revolution, which still recedes before us, from being realized. If the heroic goodness of this moment could have been maintained, the human race would have gained a century or more. It would, with one step, have passed beyond a world of sorrows.[21]

Of course, the sublime moment was not sustained, which meant a postponement of the "social and religious age of the Revolution" to the future, under the conditions of 1847, hoped Michelet, to the imminent future. In his populist vision of the revolutionary message, the codification of justice and liberty was only a prelude to the "second age" of social and religious fraternity—an echo of Joachim's "third age" of friendship and innocence. Indeed, his chapter on the Dantonist Club des Cordeliers, the political association of 1790 that, much more than the lawyerish Club des Jacobins, included the common people and anticipated the Commune of 1793, connects that club explicitly with Joachim's *évangile éternel* through the mystical order of monks that occupied the club's building in the fourteenth century.[22] Michelet's use of chthonic imagery in describing Danton and the Club des Cordeliers, similar to his evocation of the plebeian "chaleur en bas" in the Introduction, underlines the connection of the Cordeliers with the spirit of the federations. Both are rooted in natural popular forces, though the Cordeliers and Danton betray more the revolutionary force of volcanic eruption than the redemptive quest for harmony and fraternity that characterized the federations: "We have to see them [the Cordeliers] assembled in their night sessions, bubbling and fermenting together at the base of their Etna ... What an awesome face this Danton has! A cyclops? A god of the underworld? This face frightfully marked by the pox with its small obscure eyes, seems like a shadowy volcano ... Nonetheless this monster is sublime—This almost eyeless face seems a volcano without a crater—volcano of mud and fire, within whose closed forge one hears the combats of nature."[23]

Michelet's return to the ascetic, paternally oriented values of heroic sacrifice and justice that surfaced after his father's death and flowed out of his guilt, had suffused the Introduction to his work. The presence of these values in book III, as well as in the journal notations of 1847, suggest their continued preeminence in his perspective on the Revolution. Yet, these values—the values of eighteenth-century philosophy, of justice and labor—were relativized in the note on method as those of the "first age" of the Revolution. It was the second, Joachimite, age of fraternity, "the social and religious age of the Revolution," represented briefly in the federations, abortively continued in Danton and the Cordeliers, that he clearly yearned for as the realization of the visionary dream of 1790, the "Jerusalem of hearts." In many of the connections Michelet made between the federations and other revolutionary phenomena we can see the traces of what the "second age" of the revolution was supposed to signify in relation to the "first age": the return of the nurturant, maternal principle that had prevailed in *Le Peuple*. We see this return in the spontaneous popular component of the federations and their rootedness in folklore; we see it in their connection with the spirit of the Commune of 1793, nurturant and protective of the poor; we see it in the link, through the Joachimite évangile, with the Club des Cordeliers, where Michelet used the same kind of chthonic imagery that had earlier served (in the Introduction) to signify the—implicitly matriarchal—bond between people and nature.

To gauge the relative importance of these two value emphases, both plausible centers for Michelet's personality in 1847, it is useful to approach the federations in terms of recent anthropological and psychoanalytic theory, to elucidate any underlying meaning he may have intuited in them. Here an objection is in order: Why discuss the inner psychological meaning of an aspect of the Revolution that Michelet was in any case obliged, by his politically motivated choice of subject, to deal with? The decision to focus book III on the federations, however, was hardly imposed on him. He was in fact the first historian of the Revolution to see the federations as important and the only one to see them as central in the year following the attack on the Bastille.[24] Thus the question of what Michelet may have intuited in his enthusiastic perception of the federations, without necessarily being able to articulate it theoretically or even being altogether conscious of it, can be of capital importance in assessing the valence of his personality just before the mid-century watershed, the Revolution of February 1848.

Approaching an Author through His Book: Theoretical Approaches to the Federations and Their Significance for Michelet

My point of departure is the work of Mona Ozouf, who in her *Fête revolutionaire* opens Freudian and Durkheimian perspectives for this inquiry.[25] Like Michelet, she stresses the religious aspect of the federations. According to Durkheim, she says, festivals are collective communal events that solidify social ties by engendering exaltation. For Freud, the festive event has a different meaning, she argues: exaltation occurs only through the violation of taboos, by the excess authorized by the festivity. Freud, of course, saw the violation of taboos in terms of an archaic tribal rebellion of sons against paternal despotism in prehistoric times, a model that might be applied to the peasant attack on seigneurial rights.

If we examine Michelet's description of the federation movement in terms of the theories advanced by Ozouf, it is clear that the Freudian interpretation—the breaking of taboos—could be relevant only to the folkloric beginnings of the movement, whereas the Durkheimian interpretation becomes increasingly applicable as the festivals come under the control of the new bourgeois power. Now there is no question that the folkloric aspects, stressed by Ozouf, play a large role in Michelet's account.[26] Michelet repeatedly mentions the enormous farandoles and banquets that united the participants, and he also mentions the "mai sauvage," the trees planted ritually by insurgent peasants, decorated by the wind vanes of the châteaus and other plundered symbols of aristocratic privilege.[27] If we remain with Ozouf's "Freudian" interpretation of these events simply in terms of the violation of taboos, signifying some archaic rebellion of sons against fathers, then the principal meaning of the rural federations would be consonant with the "Oedipal" character of Michelet's interpretation of the attack on the Bastille, which coincided with the death of Furcy Michelet: revolt against the false fathers of the flesh in the name of the enlightened fathers of the spirit. At their culmination in Paris, the federations appear as an instrument for consecrating the Revolution's "modernizing" national dimension, its Durkheimian aspect.

Superficially attractive, the totem and taboo interpretation has limited value. For one thing, in 1790 neither the king nor most of the aristocrats were killed. Louis XVI presided over the Paris festival, though not with excessive enthusiasm. For another, the sexual side of the brother band's activities, the appropriation of the despot's women, is conspicuously absent. Rumors of peasant rape of aristocratic women (as in Arthur Young's *Travels in France*) proved groundless. Furthermore, in the case of Michelet, the father was the reverse of a paternal despot; he depended completely on his famous son and in earlier days usually played second fiddle to the historian's tough-minded mother.

Other theories, however, can be applied more fruitfully to the federations described by Michelet and Ozouf—for example, the ideas of Victor Turner on liminality, communitas, and anti-structure. Originally intended to explain African tribal rituals of passage from one status to another, they have, Turner argues, a universal significance for marginal groups or boundary periods in history.

Liminality is a concept Turner borrowed from the ethnographer Arnold Van Gennep's work on *rites de passages*. As the condition of temporarily being between two statuses, it implies that one is free from the customary demands and expectations associated with either status.[28] Liminality, dissolving the normal structures of everyday existence, that web of customs and rituals that surrounds every act of life in premodern societies, thus coincides with a condition of anti-structure, which is the negative pole of a shared sentiment of communitas among those in the liminal status: "In liminality, communitas tends to characterize relationships between those jointly undergoing ritual transition. The bonds of communitas are antistructural in the sense that they are undifferentiated, equalitarian, direct, extant, non-rational, I-Thou (in Feuerbach's and Buber's sense) relationships. Communitas is spontaneous, immediate, concrete—it is not shaped by norms, it is not institutionalized, it is not abstract."[29]

Turner views the principles of liminality, communitas, and antistructure as engaged throughout history in a dialectical interaction of conflict and accommodation with the normal structures of social life. Marginal groups—initiates, bohemians, pilgrims, crusaders, adherents of millenarian movements—are usually characterized by liminality and communitas and for this reason are opposed by established social structures.

Two applications of Turner's theory are relevant to Michelet's celebration of the federation movement. One is Turner's extensive discussion of pilgrimages as scenes of liminality and communitas. The other is his singling out for special discussion, among the many millenarian movements that embodied these principles, the early Franciscans.[30] As the anthropologist notes, the Spiritual Franciscans were strongly influenced by Joachim of Flora, whose *évangile éter-*

nel seems to have been the foundation of Michelet's notion of the revolutionary faith.

Indeed, the festivals of federation that Michelet immortalized were suffused with the symbolism of liminality, communitas, and anti-structure. Consider their origins: in the summer and autumn of 1789 peasants experienced a multiple disintegration of traditional structures. Vagabonds tried to blackmail them and then plundered or burned their fields. In their angry and anxious reaction, the village peasantry broke into the neighboring châteaus to arm themselves and, while there, burned the parchments that had legitimized centuries of servitude. National Guardsman were sent out from the cities to restore peace to the countryside but in most cases only heightened the peasants' anxiety, inducing the grande peur of aristocratic brigands. Much of the traditional rural structure of subordination and legitimation lay in ruins in the summer of 1789, as did, in faraway Paris, royal authority.

The first act of the peasantry—banding together to break into the nearby château—was simultaneously an act of communitas and a transposition to liminality. Planting the "mai" and decorating it with the symbol of aristocratic privilege, the *girouette* (castle windvane), and burning church benches (thus the destruction of another symbol of social differentiation) were further declarations of war on the old structure of inequality, further movements into an unknown realm of communitas and marginality. As the elements of the older structures crumbled, peasants reached out to one another, using the archaic anti-structural symbolism of the planting of the mai and of the altars at the great rivers that connect the French provinces. The movement of federation, the spontaneous association of villages and towns, was a rejection of all the old social, political, and geographical divisions of France. Given that the framework for the disintegration of the old order was national (the attack on the Bastille, the night of August 4, the forced return of the king to Paris on October 6), it was only logical that the framework of the new communitas would be the fraternity of all French people. What Michelet was seeing, as he pored over those yellowed documents in the Archives de France, was the enormous jump from a premodern, traditional consciousness to a modern, national one, mediated by sentiments of communitas associated with archaic rites de passages.

In the void between the breakdown of royal authority and the establishment of an infrastructure for the Revolution—such as the club movement, the National Guard, and the representatives of the revolutionary regime "on mission" were to form after 1790—it was no wonder that the principles of liminality, anti-structure, and communitas prevailed in the federation movement. Michelet compared the federations to the Crusades, one of Turner's examples of a pilgrimage movement. In fact, the dancing, the communal banquets, and the disappearance of social distinctions were typical features of the pilgrimages of communitas-based religious movements in Turner's account.[31] The exalted chiliasm of so many of the participants in the federation movement, the sense of "mystic nationalism," of being en route to the "Jerusalem of hearts, the sacred fraternal unity," are all characteristic of what Turner has called "existential communitas," and it is perhaps relevant that Michelet began writing on the federations between Palm Sunday and Easter Sunday, 1847: although he then viewed Christianity as a moribund cult, he was open to the symbolic implications of the death and resurrection of a God; certainly his évangile éternel was a gospel of resurrection.

Of course, the organization of the festival in Paris, though built on the same enthusiasm, was of a different character—a belated concession by the moderate bourgeoisie in the government to the existential mood of the federationists, at most an example of what Turner calls "normative communitas," which is its institutionalization in the name of social control. Nonetheless, even at the construction site on the champ de Mars the exalted Parisian volunteers who worked around the clock in the last fevered week of preparations sang continually the *ça ira* of 1790, the revolutionary song whose leveling refrain repeated: "Celui qui s'élève on l'abaissera / Et qui s'abaisse on l'élèvera."[32] This, apart from being borrowed from the Christian Gospels, is part of Turner's definition of liminality: "that he who is high must experience what it is like to be low." And the millenarian, Joachimite language used by Michelet in looking forward to a return of the federation spirit in the "social and religious revolution" of the future—the rejection of "formulas," the celebration of "religious faith . . . divine liberty . . . excellence of heart . . . fraternity"—this is clearly the language of existential communitas.

How does this Turnerian interpretation of the federations cohere with the depth-psychological perspectives I have been applying to Michelet's life and thought? Clearly an Oedipal, "Totem and Taboo" interpretation of the federations has major shortcomings. But another side of psychoanalytic theory—no stranger to these pages—does fit very well with the liminality-communitas aspect of the federations: the pre-Oedipal child-mother connection. We have seen how Michelet was primed by his own sense of rebirth after 1840 to be sensitive to such phenomena. Behind the communitarian aspect of the federations is that echo of the early feeling of symbiosis with the mother that Freud presented as the "oceanic feeling" and that for Lacan was the basis of the mirror phase of child development. (Lacan saw the father as the source of symbolic thought and social differentiation.)[33] Turner's description of the stripping away of social distinctions, of the euphoric feeling of communitas among neophytes, strongly suggests a return to a pre-Oedipal condition. His terminology indicates it repeatedly: "passive humility, near-nakedness—in a symbolic milieu that represented both a grave and a womb."[34] And at another point: "Liminality is frequently likened to death, to being in the womb, to invisibility, to darkness, to bisexuality, to the wilderness, and to an eclipse of the sun or moon ... Secular distinctions of rank and status disappear or are homogenized." And at yet another: "We are presented, in such rites, with a 'moment in and out of time' and in and out of secular social structure, which reveals ... a generalized social bond that has ceased to be and has simultaneously yet to be fragmented into a multiplicity of structural ties."[35]

In his essay on pilgrimages and communitas, the connection of pilgrimages such as the federation movement with pre-Oedipal symbiosis is also implicit. Pilgrimages are, according to Turner, "the ordered antistructure of patrimonial feudal systems" and as such, the successors to the rites de passage that accompany puberty in tribal societies.[36] The shrines to which pilgrimages are conducted generally have their origins in earth and fertility cults that one can reasonably associate with earlier mother goddesses.[37] Interestingly, these universalistic shrines that presumably were based on such archaic matriarchal cults were all found outside the cities and towns, whereas the urban cults represented exclusive specific interests and powers. The festival of federation occurred in the champs de Mars, now enclosed by Paris but in 1790 an open field used to train soldiers just to the west of the city.

It may seem strange to view the federations in this light. They were begun by armed and anxious peasants and they climaxed with a military demonstration in Paris. Yet Michelet saw the exaltation and the liminality of the months in between in terms of what Turner calls communitas and antistructure. All the old local structures that separated village from village, province from province, that impeded the free movement of persons and goods, came tumbling down when confronted with the communitarian warmth of the federation movement.[38] The most striking expressions of unity are the farandole, the folk dance of southern France, and the banquet. Michelet writes of the "great farandoles of the Midi ... the immense farandole of the southeast, continually linking up and forming new circles, advances to Dijon, which is connected to Paris." In one village, the sight of the fraternal embrace, at the altar of federation, of an aged aristocratic officer of the National Guard and an even older farm laborer so moved the people to hopes of universal reconciliation that "they threw themselves into each other's arms and took each other's hands; an immense farandole swept up everyone, without exception. It wound through the town, into the fields, towards the mountains of the Ardèche and the prairies of the Rhone: wine flowed in the streets, tables were prepared for a communal feast. In the evening the entire people ate together this ceremonial banquet [*agape*] while blessing God."[39]

Michelet's insistence on this communal banquet as a central feature of the federation movement[40] is one of the strongest indications of its underlying nurturant, maternal function. Indeed, reciprocal love and nurturance is a recurrent theme in his discussion of the federations.[41] In his lecture notes of May 1847 he summarized what he had just written in his book: "Simple festivities? No. Defend one another mutually. Nourish one another mutually. Love one another . . . peaceful fraternity in the idea of the patrie."[42]

This mutually nurturant character of the federation experience, in Michelet's vision sometimes approximating the mythical oral paradise of the pays de Cocaigne, together with the remarkable chain of unity created by the farandole, is the most striking symbolism of the federation movement. It is as if every individual, through the warmth of this collective experience, truly a time out of time, refound in the others of the group that "shadow of the precious unity that he had, that he lost"[43] in the prenatal tie to the mother.

Michelet's intuitive grasp of the federation experience reveals as much about the strength of the social romantic mentality of 1847 as about his faculty, since 1841, to perceive the matriarchal elements of history. His view of the Revolution was shaped initially by his father's death, which led him to break with the harmonious vision of the world he had developed at Madame Dumesnil's side and to return to the harsh antinomies of his early work. But that harmonious vision—of reconciliation between humanity and nature, man and woman, elite and plebs—had been nurtured not only by his lost love but by the social romantic climate of his age, and it was a testimony to the hold of this climate on his way of thinking that, only six months after his father's death, he returned to it in his chapters on the federations.

There is another, more durable, significance of Michelet's description of the federations that also takes us beyond the personal source of his vision. Nearly a century after he wrote these chapters, the symbolism of unity and brotherhood he had discerned in them maintained its potency in the shadow of France's most crushing defeat since the Hundred Years' War. Under the guns of the Nazi occupiers, Jean Guéhenno, author of a biography of Michelet,[44] appealed in July 1940 to the Festival of Federation as the touchstone of national fraternity, when everyone "had come to this conviction that for man and country, freedom is the source of daring, the means to greatness."[45] And the historian Marc Bloch, executed a few years later by a German firing squad for his role in the French resistance, wrote:

> There are two categories of Frenchmen who will never under-
> stand the history of France: those who cannot resonate to the
> memory of the [coronation] rites of Rheims; and those who
> read without emotion the account of the Festival of Federation.
> Their present political orientation is irrelevant. Their imperme-
> ability to the beautiful upwellings of collective enthusiasm suf-
> fices to condemn them. In the Front Populaire—the real one,
> of the crowds, not of the politicians—something revived of the
> atmosphere of the Champ de Mars, in the grand sun of July
> 14, 1790.[46]

Bloch, who as much as any twentieth-century historian incarnated Michelet's spirit, then involuntarily repeated his predecessor's plea: "Donnez-nous des fêtes!" "It is not accidental," wrote Bloch, "if our régime, purportedly democratic, has never been able to give festivals to the nation that were truly meant for everyone."

In the wake of the student explosions of the late 1960s, echoes of archaic festivities, more elementary, perhaps, than those invoked by Michelet and Bloch, mocked and shook the rigid partitions sep-arating the worlds of politics, scholarship, and popular emotion. Mona Ozouf's *La Fête révolutionaire* was paralleled in 1974 by an impressive colloque—*Les Fêtes de la révolution*; intellectuals and scholars began seriously to consider the social implications of the fête; and a number of historical works on the mentalities behind popular festivities in the pre- and postrevolutionary periods ap-peared.[47] The prototype of these works, Bakhtin's marvelous book on Rabelais, even began with a generous quotation from Michelet, who saw the author of Pantagruel as a "golden bough" to the underground of popular culture and festivities. Michelet's passion for the federations and for the democratic fêtes he so ardently sought as a bond between French republicanism and popular cul-ture, as the rites of a new social religion, thus refracts like a gem under water into the twentieth century's dreams of an alternative existence.

CHAPTER 14

NOEL, THE STUDENTS, AND THE RETURN TO REVOLUTION, 1847–1848

The new revolution year of 1848 followed Michelet's year of the federations. To his emotional life and to his complex ideological reactions, it brought exaltation, devastating disappointment, and finally retreat to the consolations offered by the love of a twenty-two-year-old woman who early in 1849 became his second wife. Mixed with this turmoil were the development of Michelet's views on the meaning of the Revolution, his appeal to and interaction with his youthful disciples, his sharpening awareness of the need for a popular republican propaganda capable of imbuing the unlettered masses with revolutionary ideals. For months, he was too absorbed by the turmoil to focus clearly on the theoretical problems he had been grappling.

Just before the revolution, in the Collège de France lectures that he began in December 1847, Michelet was still struggling to reconcile the two value-systems that had informed the first volumes of the *History of the French Revolution.* More prominent in these lectures, however, was the immediate problem of overcoming the gulf between rich and poor, between educated and uneducated, to lay the cultural and social foundations for the Republic. His chosen agent for resolving this dilemma was the idealism of the young people attending his lectures, to which he appealed repeatedly. Michelet's lectures were suspended by ministerial decree on January 1, on the alleged grounds that radical students were denouncing the government before the enthusiastic crowds that attended them. Fortunately, Michelet had already decided, on the prodding of his son-in-law, to publish his lectures every week as separate brochures, so that their contents, since republished as *L'Etudiant,* are accessible. These remarkable pages constitute a clear link between Michelet and the tumultuous end to a millennium of monarchy that followed only a few days after their last installment. Their impact, and that of the memorable chapters on the federations that had preceded them, can be gauged by the epistolary reactions of Alfred Dumesnil and his closest friend, Eugène Noel, then thirty years old. Noel had for some years been becoming Michelet's intimate as well; by 1847–48, this intimacy had superseded all others for Michelet, including both Dumesnil and Quinet.

Noel's letters, unlike those of the verbose and repressed Dumesnil, were earthy, witty, and genial. Though educated, Noel was, like Michelet, the son of an artisan who had set up his own business—a mill for dyeing wood products in the countryside north of Rouen. Noel was skeptical about intellectuals and anticlerical from experience rather than ideology (his father, a part-time rural church deacon—*marguiller*—was frequently at odds with the church hierarchy). He could write lengthy critiques of Fourier and Blanc, village utopias about what he would do as mayor or minister of education, was sensitive to the joys and perils of human sociability in his circle of intimates, and always had his ear close to the ground, picking up the litanies of misery of the impoverished, the aged, the despairing victims of economic crisis in the last years of the July Monarchy, relaying them to his friend in Paris and through him to Michelet, his friend's father-in-law, landlord, and teacher. And he corresponded with the historian directly.

Michelet saw in Noel, more than in Dumesnil, an incarnation of the bond between bourgeois and plebs that he viewed as the foundation of the coming revolution and appealed to his students to recognize in themselves.[1] In turn, Michelet's model for this reconciliation of upper and lower classes, the federation movement of 1790, became for Noel and Dumesnil the ideological goal, the ultimate meaning of their friendship. It adds an extra dimension to Michelet's ideas on these subjects to see how they were both spurred on and mirrored in the exchanges between Dumesnil and Noel on the subjects of friendship, fraternity, and revolution. And in the letters from Noel to Michelet in response to Michelet's work in 1846–47 we see a fragment of intellectual reception at its most productive in its reinforcement of the historian's impulses.

Indeed, Michelet's *History of the French Revolution,* intended to guide intellectuals toward an imminent next stage, had a special impact on the small circle of his admirers in Rouen, an impact surely echoed in other circles elsewhere.[2] Michelet's letter accompanying his gift of volume I to Noel is striking for its warmth and for its confidence in Noel's ability to speak to the people:

> My very dear friend, you should know that there is no one on earth that this book is more meant for than for you—for Alfred

and for you, it's the same thing. All your letters touch me deeply ... Pursue your education of the people; you are on the right path. Your conditions for this are better than those of any man of letters. You have the rare thing they all lack: the sense of the people and its character. On rereading what I've sent you, I feel I'm missing a lot in this area. My poetry is sometimes obscure, inaccessible to the multitude.[3]

Noel reacted twice to this homage, in letters to Dumesnil and to the author himself. To Michelet, he replied immediately, in a letter invoking the impassioned "vision" of 1789 induced in him by volume I and stressing their common origin in the revolutionary spirit.[4] To his best friend, Noel wrote tenderly that Michelet's history offered the key to their friendship and the promise of an imminent translation of their ties into the fraternal civic bonds of a new revolution: "This history is for me nothing else than the explication of the long dream we have dreamt together. The question now for us is to know if we want to continue to dream or if we are not finally going to awaken, to act ... Day has come, dear Alfred, let us rise, the day will be beautiful, perhaps a bit stormy, but after this rain we will dry ourselves in the lovely sun among the flowers."[5]

The letters of Noel and Dumesnil in the twelve months preceding the February Revolution are replete with such allusions to the transcendent social significance of their friendship, a significance illuminated by the dawn of the coming upheaval. Shortly after Noel's letter to him, Dumesnil replied: "I will be everywhere and always your companion ... We shall not be two authors ... but two brothers ... The problem of association, this quest of fraternity that everyone thinks they can find in formulas and systems, we shall offer a simpler prescription in our work *of friendship*. All this is not a utopia."[6]

When the second part of Michelet's magnum opus appeared, with its moving chapters on the federation movement of 1790, Noel grasped immediately its potential significance for the revolution to come, reported on its extraordinary effect on their friends in Rouen (Levavasseur "wept like a child"),[7] and reflected on the prophetic significance of the depiction of the federations:

We are a society of invalids who have been trying for 4000 years to cure ourselves. The world has only felt well at very rare intervals, and its best days were assuredly those of the beautiful federations. Here is the true remedy, it is that everyone sings, loves, and embraces. We will only suffer from feeling separated from one another ... I will only feel healthy, I

assure you dear Alfred, when I will have seen this great spec-
tacle of fraternity, when I will have seen all the children of
God hold each other's hands, recognize one another, and joy-
ously dance the great farandole. Believe me, my friend, we will
see again these immortal scenes and still better ones, for in '90
it was France and this time it will be all of Europe.[8]

Noel seems in turn to have inspired Michelet in 1847 at several
important points in his work on the Revolution. That the chapters
on the federations should have so moved Noel may be related to
the fact that at the moment Michelet began them—March 28—he
had Noel in mind. On March 29, Dumesnil wrote Noel that his
father-in-law had said, the day before, "that you have perhaps more
than anyone in France today the genius of the future revolution."
Michelet went on, "He will be able to talk to everyone. We are all
aristocrats here, he said, looking at me and Delaunay. There is only
one plebeian in France, it's Noel, and I'm not exaggerating; it's the
profound sentiment of the revolution I'm studying that makes me
say this."[9]

Michelet repeated this praise for Noel's "marvelous secret of
speaking to all" at the end of the year and, according to Dumesnil,
supported his views by citing Noel's letter to Alfred on the federations.[10] The essay "On the Spirit and Method of This Book," especially toward its end, was also, Alfred wrote his friend, written
with Noel in mind.

The heavily attended course that Michelet began on December
16, 1847,[11] presented many of the themes already discussed in *Le
Peuple* and in the first volumes on the French Revolution: he referred
to Poinsot, to the "great . . . national family" of the people, to the
two sexes of the spirit, to the plebeian family life of his childhood,
to the spirit of the federations, and there are reflections of the "maternal" and "paternal" value-systems between which he had been
wavering. Most interesting from the standpoint of Michelet's interaction with his immediate environment in these crucial months before the February Revolution are the resonances of Noel.[12]

Michelet made his most direct reference to Noel in his lecture
of December 30, which, without naming him, began with a handsome tribute to a letter-writer from the country, "a young man, a
friend who sometimes discusses our moral situation with me in
writing. No one has a more exact eye because no one has a healthier
soul. He lives there gay and strong, all alone, in a profoundly spiritual culture, an original culture, popular and scholarly, between the
books and the peasants, a peasant himself, speaking to all the language and the ideas of all, learning with all, crossing the countryside
in wooden boots, Molière in his pocket, or Rabelais." The place of

this homage to his young friend is significant. The previous lecture was supposed to have been on "how the young man could be the mediator, the pacifier of the city,"[13] but lack of time forced Michelet to adjourn it to the next lesson. In his closing paragraph he had invoked the two sexes of the spirit and denounced the education that sustained social division by creating half-men: "Such an artificial education that refines our minds at the expense of our active faculties makes of each of us the half of a man, the speculative half which, to create a whole man, must await the other half of instinct and action. The social divorce that makes two nations out of one and renders both of them sterile appears no less strikingly in the impotence of every soul and every mind."

The description of Noel that began the next lecture was tacked onto a cryptic quote from his most recent letter—"Nothing is needed but a grand character."[14] In defining this character, Michelet resumed his quest for the two sexes of the spirit, for "the man in equilibrium between science and experience, instinct and reflection, speculation and action." He reached this ideal personality after an attack on contemporary intellectual and educational ideals that in part echoed critiques expressed in Noel's letters to Dumesnil. In February 1847, for example, Noel referred Alfred to a conversation they had had at the Dumesnils' house in Sente-Bihorel—in the room used by Michelet—

> on the need of young people for a life of movement, adventures, of danger . . . Condemning the young to lead the life of old men is to lose the feeling for human nature . . . From the age of 7, when we have so much need to run, so much need of air and games, they force the unfortunate child to sit on a schoolbench; he will stay there for 10 years! Then, as a young man full of ardor, he will be sent to sit anew in an office or on another schoolbench, and at the age that his passions are building up, he is presented with the chair of a junior administrator, followed 2 or 3 years later by an administrator's position and there he is (from age 25) seated for eternity. Untold numbers of Frenchmen (the entire bourgeoisie) stagnate in the same way that France itself, administered and represented by them, seems to languish in the infirmity of a premature old age.[15]

Compare Michelet's lecture of December 23:

> Who suffers most from this state of abstraction, aridity, isolation? . . . I will tell you, but you know it already: the young man. What does young mean? It means active, living, concrete, the opposite of abstract . . . The worst for the young man is

that . . . from the moment his eyes are open, he is given gram-
mars and catechisms . . . an Arabian Desert of tables of contents
fit only to sterilize the mind . . . I could cite schools where two
hours of study are followed by two hours of class, in all, four
hours of uninterrupted immobility. I say that if we consider
the mobility of this age, the need of movement imposed on it
by nature, this is beyond all the torments imposed on the child
of the poor by the perpetual movement of manufacturing.[16]

The main lines of Michelet's analysis of the situation of the
students and of his appeal to them were of course drawn up independently of Noel. On the one hand, there was the critique of the
age: the notion of a France split into two nations, contradicting the
French Revolution's promise of national union; the suffocation of
this promise by bourgeois egotism, by Catholic intolerance, and by
a school system that perpetuated the vast difference between rich
and poor. On the other hand, there was the proposed remedy in
the idealism and the social position of student youth. Coming from
the wealthy classes, their living conditions in the poorer quarters
and their temporary lack of integration into their parents' social
milieu opened them to the situation of the impoverished, illiterate
majority and made of them the ideal bearers of revolution and
enlightenment to both rich and poor. The ideological accent on class
conciliation and fraternity, the repeated celebration of the child, the
woman, and the people, the identification with the *barbare*—all res-
onated to the social romantic values of the age as well as to Michelet's inner quest for harmony.[17] Yet how much of the tone of these
lectures and how many of the details mirrored the letters of Noel!
In two important themes in particular we glimpse the traces
of Noel's influence on Michelet. One was Michelet's critique of the
church as the agent of a civilizing offensive and his celebration of
a plebeian response to it in Rabelais, Molière, and popular culture.
Though more sophisticated than Noel, Michelet was completely in
accord with what the Norman "peasant" wrote him in a letter of
October 12, 1847: "Ah! monsieur, if I had a chair in the Collège de
France, I would use it to show in detail what the Council of Trent
really was (the veritable prohibition of all justice and truth). But
God did not abandon the world; he spoke again in the solitude to
sincere souls and our Rabelais (a simple village priest) answered
each session of the Council with a book of Pantagruel."
The second theme, broached at both the beginning and the end
of these lectures, was dear to Noel's heart: the people's need of
instruction and culture, of festivities, theater, and literature. Noel
repeatedly cried out in his letters to Dumesnil for free popular
theater and for festivities,[18] and in posing the question of writing

books for the common people Michelet singled out Noel as the only person capable of speaking the popular language.

The lectures began with this problem. Michelet cited a conversation with a "man of genius"—probably P. J. de Béranger—in which he pleaded the necessity of overcoming the barriers between rich and poor and of reestablishing the social bond and was told to let the poor find their own enlightenment, to abandon the "aristocratic privilege" of instructing the people. Dissatisfied with this response, he nonetheless had to admit that the mass of working people was in no position, "because of the fatality of time and work," to study abstract ideas. Was the press an answer? No, for only 5 percent of the population read daily papers, and the cheap offprints circulated by peddlers (*colportage*) were either pornography or religious propaganda or works of erudition far above the capacity of the common people to understand them. In the novels, feuilletons, and theater pieces of high literature he found on one hand an audience restricted to the wealthy and a few skilled workers and on the other the mores of a corrupt bourgeoisie.

Certain that France had reached its nadir in the scandals and social misery of the preceding year, Michelet apparently believed more in the power of the spoken than of the printed word to resurrect patriotic idealism. He pinned his hopes on a future theater of national renovation, "a theater immensely popular . . . responding to the popular ideal, which would circulate through the smallest villages." Apart from this, a new social literature was on the way whose themes he would outline in his course, as was a huge social movement of national reconciliation, "a crusade of men in search of men." Michelet's immediate goal was "to characterize the role of the young man as mediator in the city and as principal agent of the social renewal we shall soon see"—a role he viewed Noel as uniquely equipped to fulfill.

Noel's ability to mediate between elite and plebs seems to have impressed Michelet on a third occasion: when he cited Desmoulins's exalted comparison of the Parisians of the Revolution with the citizenry of Periclean Athens: "We are all Athenians." Noel had used the phrase, linking classical culture with revolutionary populism, in a letter to Dumesnil about an after-dinner walk through the Norman countryside during the crisis months of 1847. Michelet, who was shown all such letters from Noel, was no doubt struck by the closeness to his own position of Noel's evocation of the popular spirit. Indeed, the report of Noel's nocturnal excursion signified as much the handwriting on the wall for the July Monarchy as anything in Michelet's subsequent lectures.

In this letter, Noel first described conversations with a mason about the apple harvest and with an unemployed woman who was gathering plants for oil. Then he wrote:

> Further on I found Benoît-le-cochon, the maker of pottery clay: he was cutting down a large pine tree.—What, I said, you have abandoned your trade in pottery clay?—It's my trade that has abandoned me, he replied. Sales have stopped dead. And I can't eat my pottery clay. I've begun to work by the day. M. Noel, the times are really hard! Then, laying down his axe and crossing his arms: Do you think, he said, that all this will lead us to a new revolution?—It could, I answered.—Ah! he cried, it takes a disorder to restore order, and he spoke scornfully of the king. I told him, good citizen that I am, that the king was a thief and recounted the ... cutting down of the state forests.—And his children don't say anything to him? said Benoît. And there he is, philosophizing about it. But all Benoît's philosophy, derived from the cabaret, is pure patriotism. He talked about taxes ... the small businessmen that were being ruined. After having talked for a long time with the maker of pottery clay, I returned to Tôt by a large dark road.

Underneath his quiet irony, Noel was glimpsing another 1789. He concluded his report: "Decidedly, I resemble Camille Desmoulins a little, and I shouted as he did: they are all Athenians ... It's at the street corners, by the hedges, in the cabins that the word is fecund. The academies, the scholarly and aristocratic gatherings, are often only sand and stone. Jesus sowed the gospel along the pathways of Judea and only preached to the poor devils of his time. He might have made an apostle of Benoît-le-cochon, but our big village gentlemen scorn him because he is a drunkard, because he is a poacher, and because he doesn't remove his hat when they pass."[19]

This letter was sent on October 13, 1847, a few months before the revolution Noel's luckless friend had asked him about. Michelet's last lecture of 1847–48, echoing brilliantly Noel's gentle subversion, bore the date February 17, 1848. Noel, who had descended on the capital a month earlier to visit his Paris friends and who had assisted Michelet in preparing the printed versions of his lectures, had left on February 12, prophesying that "in three months, the streets of Paris will be red with blood."[20] The insurrection erupted on February 22, led by students whose disaffection had grown through the suspension of Michelet's course and by republican artisans protesting the prohibition of a political banquet in Paris. It made no difference that Michelet had been gagged since January 1; his lectures circulated as brochures and the questions implicit in them were settled, temporarily at least, on the barricades. Louis-Philippe's children had indeed failed to warn him of Benoît-le-Cochon's discontent.

PART V

SECOND REPUBLIC, SECOND MARRIAGE, 1848–1851

The city is rent by lightning, and spits under the teeth of fire, great blocks of a gaping ripped city sinking with the horror of obscenity, and falling into the sea with the hiss of the eternally damned. No cry of horror from Lot and his daughter but from the city in flames, from an unquenchable desire of father and daughter, of brother and sister, mother and son.

ANAÏS NIN
The House of Incest

CHAPTER 15

MICHELET'S POLITICAL ENGAGEMENT AND DISAFFECTION, 1848–1851

Expectations that Michelet would play an important role in the provisional government established after the February Revolution remained unfulfilled, even though his name appeared on at least one of the first printed lists of government ministers.[1] On February 25, son-in-law Alfred explained to Eugène Noel how it came about that Michelet did not join the government:

> In the first list posted throughout our district, M. Michelet was named in the provisional government. I led him to the Hôtel de Ville, but the crowd was so dense that he could not reach the assembly to find out about his nomination. In the official list, which appeared this morning, he was absent, not having appeared in the Hôtel de Ville. Anyway, he's better off staying in his study. No one has more moral authority in this country and will be able to render greater services, provided he abstains from taking a too active part in affairs of the moment, which would take up most of his time.

In fact, apart from writing an occasional letter to an acquaintance like Lamartine, a leading figure in the new government, or backing the candidacies of his "adopted children," Noel and Dumesnil, in the April elections, Michelet played no role in the events of the revolution—except perhaps that of victim. He wrote almost nothing for the proliferating radical press, his history of the Revolution of 1789—intended to prevent the repetition of its errors in 1848—stagnated until after June, and ideas for brief, popular books explaining the ideals of the revolution began to bear fruit only toward the end of the Second Republic, when the Left was largely

165

crushed and the Bonapartist coup was being prepared. Even Michelet's lectures, whose striking radicality and massive attendance had helped prepare young intellectuals for the revolution, lost both influence and audience in the spring of 1848. And little wonder: In May, when radicals were invading the National Assembly to demand support for the Polish Revolution, and in June, when Bonapartist demonstrations distracted public opinion from the fact that haves and have-nots were about to massacre one another over the national workshops, Michelet was lecturing to minuscule audiences about the religions of ancient India, Persia, and Judea.

This sounds as though he was a stereotypical woolly-headed intellectual, without the slightest sense for practical politics. He was not, as every reader of his *History of the French Revolution* knows. He had a sharp sense of political tactics, of the ways in which men—like Robespierre—could exercise enormous political influence without holding office. In his own life, he proved a master at the politics of intellectual life, which is not so different from that of party strife: he had come close to maneuvering into a Collège de France "chair" when he was only thirty-two and did so when barely forty. If, then, Michelet played no role of significance in 1848, if he spent the crucial months before the June rising lecturing to an empty hall on esoteric subjects, this was not due to incompetence but choice.

A glance at the place of those lectures in Michelet's intellectual-political perspective explains why. They were an attempt to excavate the foundations on which the new religion of the Revolution was to be built—a religion he saw as implicit both in the credo of revolutionary justice and in the fraternal epiphany of the federations. For the Revolution to succeed, Christianity had to be replaced, and Michelet allotted to himself the prophetic—and inevitably lonely—task of announcing the new religion of humanity.

He had every reason to doubt the chances of the February Revolution. The seeds of the June civil war were visible in the political banquets that the legal opposition organized to push electoral reform in the last six months of the monarchy. Noel described to Dumesnil the elitist contempt for the common people at the Rouen banquet, and Dumesnil wrote back that Michelet had heard the same criticism from Béranger. Michelet carefully noted all the signs of discord and reaction in his journal, from the demonstration of right-wing National Guardsmen on March 16 to the Bonapartist demonstrations of June. From Rouen he had heard through Noel about the hopeless situation of the radical democratic group around his friend Lefèvre and the unchallengeable machine of the conservative republican oligarchy led by lawyer Marie-Antoine-Jules Senard.[2] Rouen, with a considerable population of textile workers, was, like Limoges, an early scene of class hatred in 1848;[3] a violent explosion following the April elections anticipated the June uprising by almost two months in its eradication of the last hopes for revolutionary fraternity.

Parisian artisans had fought the February Revolution, but they triumphed only because many bourgeois had also felt excluded from the July Monarchy.[4] It was the press of middle-class reformers that exposed government scandals and incited middle-class idealists in the National Guard, the Sorbonne, and the Ecole polytechnique to side with rioting artisans in the February days, and this massive public support undermined the effectiveness of the army in opposing the uprising.

Through the press and the political parties, however, middle-class opinion mobilized after the revolution to take advantage of the new situation in a way that the hitherto disenfranchised artisans and peasants could not. One of the first acts of the provisional government was to write out elections for a new assembly, based on universal manhood suffrage, for April; whatever the intent of the ministers, the influence and experience of the notables and the peasants' ancient habits of deference insured an overwhelming majority of seats for conservative republicans. A new left-wing republican movement did challenge the program of the conservatives, which was antisocialist and more or less stopped with demands for clean government and an expanded suffrage. Inspired by such July Monarchy socialists as Louis Blanc and Etienne Cabet and such social romantics as Pierre Leroux and Eugène Sue, radicals used the left-wing press and scattered organizations of artisans to demand a social republic—a serious effort to remedy the unemployment, illiteracy, insecurity, and despair of the masses. But these new, previously disenfranchised groups had no time to organize and circulate their message before the elections took place. The countryside, where most voters lived, was practically untouched. Post-election outbursts in provincial cities, a feeling of frustration among radical democrats, and the June explosion in Paris resulted. The conservative republicans consolidated power everywhere. Dumesnil's friend Delaunay, who, in spite of his reverence for Michelet, sided with the conservatives, wrote Noel that it was only after the workers' revolts had been suppressed that the Rouen elite could embrace the republican cause.[5]

As the cacophony of class warfare approached its climax in mid-June, Michelet, distracted and irritated by the Bonapartist demonstrations in Paris, worked out a plan for republican propaganda for the unlettered masses, which he thought the government should undertake, especially in the countryside, to prevent a Bonapartist takeover.[6] Though he failed to see the immediate danger to his ideals from the government's imminent dissolution of the national workshops, his long-run perspective was perfectly accurate: through a dearth of the republican propaganda he was urging, Louis Bonaparte gained election to the presidency on December 10, 1848, with 80 percent of the vote. Three years later, his political machine used the army to mop up the remnants of the Second Republic in a coup d'état.

This is not to say that the fate of the Second Republic was sealed with the June days, as an older historiography—and Michelet's own reactions-might lead us to believe.[7] Indeed, that the coup-d'état was necessary—for a president elected by such a one-sided majority—suggests that the democratic opposition had by 1851 jeopardized this majority, as indeed it had. Although throughout the forty-six months of the Republic, the Left faced continual decimation and repression, although its leaders were repeatedly jailed or exiled, by late 1848 a loose coalition of democratic socialists had begun working the rural and provincial electorate with all the means of mass propaganda that Michelet had advocated. Unable to stop the Bonapartist steamroller in December 1848, they so penetrated the electorate five months later that they elected 25 percent of the representatives to the National Assembly,[8] far from a majority, but equally far from the derisory results of the first legislative election a year earlier. In spite of a new wave of repression following the June 1849 demonstrations against French military intervention to crush antipapal revolutionaries in Rome, in spite of the suffrage restriction that disenfranchised 30 percent of the voters, democratic socialist influence and propaganda spread through the provinces between 1849 and 1851, laying the basis for the massive armed resistance to the Bonapartist coup of December 1851.

Michelet was largely impervious to these successes. After June, he seems to have abandoned hope in the revolution in France. He did retain a vague commitment to his Joachimite ideal of the "social and religious revolution," a concept he attempted to work out in the early years of the Second Empire in the unfinished *Le Banquet*; he also continued, for a time, to ponder the ancient foundations of a religion of humanity, his obsession in the month before the June uprising, which a decade and a half later became his *Bible de l'humanité*. But for the most part he gave up on the revolution he saw crumbling around him, pinning his political faith on the rising of oppressed nationalities elsewhere in Europe (Italy, Hungary) and seeking a new sense of self in the love of a woman to replace what he had lost in revolutionary pride.

This tendency is evident in his writing after June on the history of the first French Revolution. In book V, which preoccupied him between July and the "coup de foudre" of November, when he met the governess he married three months later, what stands out are the brilliantly sympathetic portraits of two revolutionary heroines, Madame Roland and Madame de Condorcet. Book VI, which he reluctantly completed under the prodding of Noel and his bride-to-be a few weeks before the wedding, deals with the background of the assault on the Tuileries in August 1792, which led to the incarceration of the king and the establishment of the First Republic. Although this was the sublime moment of the revolutionary "peuple," the hero of Michelet's vision, he chose to close this book with the moving personal testimony of Lucie Desmoulins, the wife of Danton's friend, expressing her fears and those of Danton's wife for the fates of their husbands, and ending with the lines, revelatory of Michelet's state of mind fifty-seven years later: "What will become of us, oh my poor Camille? I have lost the strength to breathe ... My god! If it is true you exist, then save the men who are worthy of you ... We want to be free; oh God, what it costs!"[9]

The dual direction of Michelet's thought and life appeared transparently in October 1849 when he indicated his decision, in his writing on the Revolution, "to interrupt the negative labors that were consuming me (*the Vendée, finances, debates of the Convention*) and to reimmerse myself in love (*Campaign of '92, Europe giving itself to France*)."[10] The details of the Revolution within France, both in 1792 and in 1849, had become too unpleasant to focus on; instead, Michelet chose "love," which apart from his young wife, Athenaïs, signified in his *History of the French Revolution* the love of neighboring peoples for the French revolutionary armies that were liberating them from ancient despotisms. And in a corollary reflex he centered his political attention on the extension of the Revolution of 1848 among the peoples of eastern and southern Europe. France itself was a lost cause. This resolute discouragement about the prospects of revolution in France raises a central question: why was Michelet so impervious to the spread of democratic socialist influence, which was largely based on the very methods he had been propagating in June 1848? He was certainly not out of touch with the Left. As late as April 1850, the worker poet Dupont and other leaders of the Paris democratic socialists pleaded with him to be their candidate against Emile de Girardin, the opportunist editor of *La Presse*.[11] Nor is it likely that the success of radical democratic propaganda in the countryside escaped him, since his friend Noel was delightedly announcing it to Alfred Dumesnil in April 1849.[12]

There are three good reasons for Michelet's lack of sensitivity to the advance of democratic radicalism: his geographic isolation, the Jacobinism of many democratic socialists, and the popular Catholicism they compromised with. The isolation was, to begin with, that of Paris, where, after the effervescence of the club movement in spring 1848, the social conflicts were most sharply felt and the repression most visibly decimated the leadership of the left.[13] Tied in with the Parisian orientation was a North French one: Michelet's parentage gave him close ties to the Ardennes and Picardy, his son-in-law and Madame Dumesnil to Rouen. Athenaïs grew up in Montauban, a city of the southwest, but her background gave him no reason to look to that area as a bastion of enlightenment: she had turned to his writings to escape the grip of an omnipresent church. Ange Guèpin, the friend with whom he found refuge after the Bonapartist coup, lived in Nantes, in darkest Brittany. Now the most striking democratic socialist successes during the Second Republic were in southern France: all sixteen departments where they secured a majority in the legislative elections of May 1849 were south of the Loire, as were thirteen of the seventeen regions where they obtained 40 to 50 percent of the vote.[14] Moreover, the massive armed resistance to the coup, possible only in areas with a powerful democratic socialist infrastructure, was concentrated in the southeast.

Social historians of the Second Republic have explained this greater radicalization of the southern French countryside in terms of the stronger interdependence and cohesion in southern France between peasant and artisan economies. Northern agriculture largely produced food staples; northern industry found its materials as well as its markets largely outside the region. Southern rural areas were much more integrated with the raw material needs of local artisans. As a result, northern peasants and artisans were rarely affected by the same economic climate, whereas southern ones often were: radicalization of one group by crisis was furthered by radicalization of the other. Peasant and artisan discontent fed on each other in the south, leading to stronger and faster politicization than was possible in the north. Interacting with this economic factor were the dense networks of sociability the radicals had at their disposal in the southeast: the informal male clubs characteristic of the Mediterranean, the Chambrées.[15] But Michelet, with his antennae oriented largely north of Paris, probably did not pick up the democratic socialist radicalization south of the Loire.

Even if he had, however, his enthusiasm would inevitably have been tempered. For the democratic socialist leadership included two groups that Michelet had never been happy with: Jacobin politicians like Louis Blanc, whom he saw as whitewashing Robespierre and the Terror, and adherents of the socialist system-makers of the July Monarchy, such as Etienne Cabet, whose ideas he derided as impossible.[16]

The third reason for Michelet's insensitivity to the new radi-

calism was probably the democratic socialists' softness on Christianity, their acceptance of peasant versions of Catholic teachings
and promulgation of a populist Gospel. That some left-wing interpretations of the Revolution—in particular Buchez and Roux's *Histoire parlementaire*—had long attempted to argue the underlying
affinities between Catholicism and the French Revolution had an-
gered and disgusted Michelet, as it subsequently did Flaubert.[17]

In fact, even in Michelet's and Dumesnil's friend Noel appreciation of the new peasant radicalism went hand in hand with Christian populism. Shortly before the elections of May 1849, Noel wrote
to Dumesnil of "the invincible current" of peasant radicalism:
"There is not a cabin here that is not miraculously inundated by
the pamphlets of *Joigneaux* (representative of the people) and the
villager *understands,* and he is no longer in the elections to come—
as he was last year—a passive instrument in the hands of the lords
and the bourgeois." The reason for this social earthquake, Noel
said, should be clear to his "brothers in religion": "It is because
Christ has shaken off the old Catholic mantle. Christ has moved,
he is marching, he has emerged from his old home to build a new
one with us where all will be admitted next to him for we are all
his brothers. The old doorman of the old house, seeing its walls
cracked, has fled. The rats which inhabited it have spread out here
and there, and it is to the assistance of the Vatican that the ministry
Barrot, Faucher, Falloux has sent our army."[18]

Michelet's isolation and ineffectiveness during the Second Republic is thus largely explicable in ideological terms. He had been
too radical for the liberals before February 1848. Afterward, in spite
of his social romantic values and his quest for the social and religious revolution, his hostility to authoritarian Jacobinism and to
Christianity alienated him from his democratic socialist friends. In
fact, apart from his revolutionary mystique, his anticlericalism, as
well as his democratic inclinations and his desire to export the Revolution to the oppressed nationalities of Europe, could be viewed
as characteristic of the more militant wing of 1830s Orleanism ("the
movement") against the conservative one ("the resistance").[19] It
was only briefly, in *Le Peuple,* that he seemed to be breaking sharply
with the essentially liberal and ascetic premises of his "Introduction" of 1831. These earlier premises returned two years later, after
his father's death, in the "Introduction" to his *Histoire de la Révolution
française,* and from that point on, the heroic voluntarism of his earlier
view was continually in tension with the quasi-matriarchal views
of *Le Peuple.* He reconciled these two systems by ranging then in a
first—Voltairean, voluntarist—revolutionary period, characterized
by the demand for justice, and a second—Joachimite, harmonious,

nurturant—phase characterized by fraternity. But his anticlericalism, transformed after church attacks on him into anti-Christianism, retained for him both a kinship with the Voltairean liberals whose cause he had embraced two decades earlier and an estrangement from the populist Catholicism of the democratic socialists.

CHAPTER 16

1848:
FRATERNITY TO
FRATRICIDE—THE
WOMEN OF THE
REVOLUTION

Michelet's ideological posture largely explains his rapid withdrawal from political engagement, particularly after June. Nonetheless, like so many of his compatriots, he was initially dazzled by the Revolution. That the revolutionaries demanded, among more remote goals, the restoration of his, Quinet's, and Mickiewicz's chairs in the Collège de France gave him a personal stake in the outcome. Beyond that, he saw in the upheaval the fulfillment of his notion of social harmony: "Appearance of fraternity," he wrote on the second day of the uprising, "National Guard, students, and people ... people and army salute one another."[1] Whatever the outcome, he saw a new era of fraternity beginning, sparked by student youth, which "has the time and the heart and is itself still proletarian."

For about six weeks Michelet felt engaged, hoping the Revolution might bring about the social harmony so integral to his social romantic faith. Indeed, the immediate consequence of the February days was not only the hypocritical enthusiasm for the Republic among archbishops, legitimists, and aristocrats derided by Flaubert in the *Education sentimentale* but also a more genuine union of July Monarchy socialists, democrats, and republicans. In early March, two principal papers of the Left opposition, the semisocialist *La Réforme* of Ledru-Rollin and the more moderate *Le National,* established a "Central Committee for the General Elections to the National Assembly." The committee's letterhead listed Michelet in a group of fifteen that included three artisans associated with the communist monthly *La Fraternité de 1845.*[2] An editor of *La Fraternité,* Pierre Vincard, was among the thirty-four candidates Michelet voted for in the April elections; he also gave his suffrage to Agricol Perdiguier, Béranger, Félicité de Lamennais, and Leroux.[3]

Another sign of Michelet's sympathies was his letter to the new minister of public education, Hippolyte Carnot, on February 28, in which he recommended expanding the Academy of Moral and Political Sciences beyond thirty members. Apart from Jean Reynaud, Carnot's principal assistant in the ministry, and Reynaud's friend Leroux, Michelet suggested his friends Quinet, Mickiewicz, Béranger, and Lamennais, his rival Louis Blanc, plus Lamartine, Arago, and Félix Ravaisson. He added a special plea for the nomination of George Sand, "The foremost socialist writer who in her last two works has just created a new literature, immense hope of the future."[4] A few days later, he wrote to two friends in the provisional government to plead the urgency of enlightening the peasantry, to whom local curés were feeding horror stories about the revolution, by means of daily bulletins to be read in churches and posted in town halls. Alfred Dumesnil asked Eugène Noel, whose writing Michelet praised as comprehensible to the plebs, to send a sample bulletin to support Michelet's case, which Noel obligingly did, in a little homily describing Paris as tranquil, hopeful, and joyous and advising peasants to obey their hearts rather than local notables in the coming elections.[5]

Michelet reported in his diary on April 4, with "joy and sadness," his decision to withdraw from political involvement and to focus on his history of 1791.[6] We can only guess at his reasons, because there are no journal notations for the preceding two weeks, but he probably felt that his position would be adequately represented by Dumesnil and Noel, both of whom, with his blessing, were running for the National Assembly,[7] and he was undoubtedly already disheartened by the rift emerging between the leftist minister of the interior, Ledru-Rollin, and Lamartine, the government's leading moderate. Ledru-Rollin's *La Réforme* had chosen Michelet for its electoral committee; while Michelet supported Lamartine in his stand against postponing the election, he seems to have supported Ledru-Rollin's effort to democratize the National Guard.[8]

In any case, four days later he modified his decision, complaining that the exclusive focus on 1791 "isolated me from the movement." He would join to his work on the first revolution two tasks: preparations for his spring lectures on the religious revolution and a popular republican *History of France* for use in the schools.

And until the June Days, Michelet reacted to the accumulating bad news—the invasion of the Assembly by the Left on May 15, the Bonapartist agitation in June—either by entrenching himself in plans for his esoteric, long-run *Bible de peuple*[9] or by formulating brilliant but premature proposals for reaching the peasants with republican propaganda, such as his school history or the populist almanach Noel was working on.[10] One such proposal, of mid-June, ran:

> For those who can read: schools for adults, papers, very short bulletins, posters for two *liards,* circulating libraries ... For those who cannot read: picturesque poster press, songs sung and posted in different dialects, clubs for public readings; further, for the cities, giant concerts. Act through the schoolmaster: send him copies of every act and circular sent to the mayor. Act through the married priest and nullify all legislation contrary to the marriage of priests. Act through the peddler by giving him facilities for restocking in every prefecture: give him 100%, sell him the bulletin for a liard, let him sell it for two, use the singers as hawkers, send them to the fairs, at St.-Jean and St.-Michel ... Above all ... reach those who cannot read, create a central republican book trade, supported by purchases for city halls and schools, which would be the equivalent of a national workshop for the artist, a headquarter for the book and song peddling.[11]

He sent a version of this plan to his friend Béranger, with whose backing he hoped to approach the government, on June 17, but the aging poet, who thought popular propaganda should come from the people, saw little merit in it. The day before the June rising began, however, Michelet had worked out a plan for a series of publications, most of them popular, enough to make of him a one-man ministry of republican propaganda. Two days later, his only recorded reaction to the outbreak of war between rich and poor was four words of Latin: "Excidat illa dies aevo!"—roughly, wipe out this day! On June 24, he reported what a painter friend had seen in the popular faubourg Saint-Antoine, "a cataract of blood pouring from a window where the troops had beheaded everyone in the house," a cruelty he attributed to lies about the insurgents in the press. That day the army stormed the barricades on the Left Bank, near Michelet's house.[12] Shortly after, Noel informs us, Michelet was visited by another friend, sculptor Auguste Préault, who found the historian pacing desolately in his garden, a barricade still standing in front of the house. Apparently when someone had informed the street fighters that their barricade was exposing the residence of the renowned professor to grapeshot, their reply was, "Who is Michelet?" Saddened, Michelet told his friend that he could no longer write *Le Peuple.*[13] Nonetheless, on June 27, when the dust began to settle over a tortured city, he wrote only that he "felt the urgency of the education of the people," and in the following month, while visiting Noel in Normandy, he tried, and failed, to write one of those short, popular books he had been envisaging just before the uprising.

Michelet's withdrawal from active political involvement in 1848 was accompanied by an inner loneliness and desolation that only love—not for mankind but for one person—could remedy. It is arguable, however, that this need for personal love was not merely the result of his political disaffection but perhaps a more profound condition, one that led him to reject the political because it could not satisfy his underlying needs. Michelet's notes for his lecture of May 12 suggest that this longing hid beneath the surface of his most abstract labors. Temporarily leaving his examination of ancient religions to criticize the ideologies (of Cabet and Proudhon) and the egoistic spirit of the times, he sketchily defined the social ideals of his populist republicanism through the familiar values of family, land, and labor, and he defined the state—modeled on the federations—in terms of its maternal functions, "as a fraternal banquet where the cup is passed around, where all serve all."[14]

Following on this utopian view of politics as a ritual of mutual love and nurturance, Michelet tried to define the new religion, for which he found the times favorable. In this context, he suddenly skipped from a celebration of the cosmic unity of human culture to a dream of the resurrection of Paul Poinsot:

> My delight when from the abstract diversity I glimpsed the living unity . . . of science and languages of law . . . of religions. Grand communion of the world . . . my brothers revived, all returned in the family.

> Dream in which I saw Poinsot again:—What! We had buried you . . . you are very pale . . . but it really is you! . . . Oh! you will never die, I have refound you . . . a part of you kept the right to live, the unrealized part, by which you were to exist again.
>
> In the same way, the holy religions of the past living again, via India, infinite tenderness for nature—charity extended to animals; Judea, sublime expectation of the future, so superior to the principle of imitation . . . Greece, heroic education.[15]

Apparently he felt he had introduced his dream of Poinsot too abruptly, and he indicated in the margins of his sketch that this analogy between personal and religious resurrection should follow a less personal reference to digging up the dead. After criticizing the cruel efforts of Christianity to prove the death of all other religions and asserting their eternal value as children of the human heart, he wrote: "Here one must dig . . . the stone of the sepulcher is raised, the shroud is removed . . . appear then at last oh adored body!—Let me see once more this eternal Inès de Castro. [On a new line:] Here the dream. . . ."

Placing the dream of the resurrection of Paul Poinsot next to the legendary one of Inès de Castro, Michelet revealed the layers of personal need that accompanied his desire to infuse the revolutionary creed with the love of nature evident in Indian religion. With the love of a dead princess being equated to Michelet's undying love for his deceased comrade, and with what we have seen of the long-lasting influence on the historian of his love for the moribund Madame Dumesnil, it is comprehensible that the theme of death and the maiden should increasingly have haunted his imagination and tempted his resurrectionist talents, as the futility of revolution and the impossibility of fraternity became oppressively evident to him.

At the peak of Bonapartist agitation before the June Days, Michelet even abandoned the revolutionary faith of his introduction, that justice as the religious principle of the Revolution was replacing the Christian notion of grace. In a journal entry of June 17, he seemed to merge Bonapartist idolatry with Christian messianism and doubted that the Revolution could lead to more than a new form of hero-worship. This skepticism born of experience no doubt underlay his subsequent critique of the Jacobin idol Robespierre, whose affinity with Catholicism he was going to stress in his history of the Revolution, but it left little more of his earlier political idealism than a handful of dust.

Michelet returned, late that summer, after so many fruitless efforts to make himself useful to the Second Republic, to his history of the Revolution. Volume III (books V and VI) was to cover the period from the king's capture at Varennes in June 1791 to the assault on the Tuileries on August 10, 1792—the gestation of the First Republic. Louis's attempted flight proved the long-term impossibility of the constitutional monarchy, but it took another year and the menace of royal complicity with foreign invasion to goad the sansculottes into direct action against the monarchy. In all of this there was an exciting political story—of the maneuvers within the Jacobin and Cordelier clubs, of the evolution of the revolutionary leadership and the sea-change in popular opinion. Michelet narrated it with his customary verve and insight.

Nonetheless, what gives volume III its inner structure is not the politics of this period but its women. Michelet closed this volume with the moving passage from Lucie Desmoulin's memoirs I have cited. If we look here for a chapter that sets the tone, such as the introduction of volume I or the note on method in Volume II, the obvious choice is "La Société en '91—Le Salon de Condorcet."

Michelet defended himself in the text against the possible reproach that this chapter was a digression: for him it was "the heart of the matter." He resorted to a definition of historical truth that revealed much of what separated him from both pre- and postromantic mentalities. Against the "geometrical" construction of reality, he upheld the "exigencies of living nature," which "proceeds by curves in everything organic." Although he invoked the historians of the ancient world in support of his case, he was clearly defending a nineteenth-century romantic view of reality, based on the new biological sciences, against an eighteenth-century Newtonian one.

He then recurred briefly to the conflict of two religions, now defined as the Clerico-Royalist and the Republican. There are other, more substantial changes in his summary description: he no longer defines the old religion by the principle of arbitrary grace but—following his anxiety over the Bonapartist rage—by material incarnation, "idols of the flesh." And he defines the revolutionary one not by "justice" but by "the cult of the pure idea; no more idols, no other religion than the ideal, *la patrie,* liberty." One justification for concentrating on the women of the Revolution is that they are more clear, more advanced than the men in expressing these religious principles. Another flows out of a highly personal comparison between the revolution Michelet was experiencing in 1848 and the one he was writing about. In spite of the heroic sacrifices of the present era, he found more warmth in the first revolution. Shifting his scholarly focus from the realm of politics and parties to the level of individual biographies was for him essential to explain this difference in emotional climate:

> *One loved.* Interest and ambition, man's eternal passions, were engaged, as now; but the stronger part was that of love. Take this word in all its meanings, love of the idea, love of woman, love of la patrie, and of the human race ... Women reign, in '91, by feeling, by passion, by the superiority, it must be said, of their initiative. Never, before or after, did they have such influence. In the XVIIIth century under the encyclopedists, intelligence dominated in society; later it will be action, murderous, and terrible action. In '91, feeling dominates and therefore women.[16]

Everywhere Michelet looked, in the first years of the Revolution, he found the influence of women, private passions merging with and shaping public emotions. In the next twenty pages he celebrates the Revolution's most virtuous and idealistic heroines, focusing particularly on two remarkable women: Madame Roland, wife of the prominent Girondin and herself active politically, and Madame de Condorcet, spouse of the last surviving philosophe.[17] These women displayed qualities that enabled them to function well as fantasy embodiments of the fifty-year-old historian's need for feminine companionship: they were both more than twenty years younger than their husbands, both the inspiring muses of brilliant salons, and both active as writers and thinkers, and thus able to be spiritual as well as physical partners for their husbands, a trait Michelet had sorely missed in Pauline and deeply regretted he had lost in Madame Dumesnil.[18]

When he later wrote of the proscription and death of Condorcet, the philosophe's loyal, young widow became the more important of the two women for Michelet. In the summer of 1848, though, he was equally drawn to Madame Roland, whose character as he depicted it probably made romantic projections onto her irresistible.[19] Himself a printer's son who learned typesetting in his father's shop, Michelet wrote that Madame Roland, like himself of plebeian origins, "had an engraver for a father and she herself engraved in the paternal house." Her relation to her older economist husband was exemplary: "Without being bored by the dryness of his subjects, she copied, translated, compiled for him . . . with no other distraction than the birth and breastfeeding of her only child. Closely associated with the work and ideas of her husband, she had for him a sort of filial cult."[20]

About six weeks after writing this, in an autobiographical note of October 16, 1848, Michelet was frank about his inner desolation: "Too many wounds: June, my father, and so many other losses which resurface. I can hardly walk in this apartment without knocking my heart against these memories"—by which, apart from his father, he meant above all those of Madame Dumesnil, who had also died under his roof. Then, noticing Pauline's maiden name in a document of 1791, his mind locked into a peculiar relationship between Madame de Condorcet, his first wife, and the revolutionary turning points he had been describing. His wife, he remarked, was conceived during the year of the festivals of federation, whereas Madame de Condorcet conceived her child at the time of the assault on the Bastille. The wheel of memory had taken Michelet from the death of fraternity in the June uprising to that of his father, which had occurred while he was describing the assault on the Bastille, to his wife's conception in the year fraternity was born in the federations, and to Madame de Condorcet's pregnancy during the actual storming of the Bastille. From the pit of his misery, the translator of Vico seems to have been invoking a personal *ricorso,* and three weeks later historical recurrence indeed came full cycle for him. On November 8, 1848, the resurrected spirit of Madame de Condorcet knocked on his door in the person of a twenty-two-year-old governess, Athenaïs Mialaret.

.

CHAPTER 17

EROS AND DISCORD

There is a long prehistory to Michelet's instant infatuation with Athenaïs at the end of 1848. I have already described part of this: the inner loneliness that underlay his prophetic role in 1847–48, the shattering impact of the June rising, the molding of book V of his history of the Revolution around a hidden quest for feminine companionship. There is more.

In the context of Michelet's psychosocial development, Athenaïs closes a cycle of personal evolution that began with his love for Madame Dumesnil. From the reawakening of his suppressed need for mothering, accompanied by the rediscovery of forgotten, early ties to his own mother, Michelet had drawn a new cosmological map of God and humanity. God became a woman; nature was transformed from destructive stepmother to nurturance personified; finally, in *Le Peuple,* France, too, became a beneficent mother. The legacy of Madame Dumesnil to Michelet, apart from this transformation of his cosmos, was her son, Alfred, who after informal adoption became his legal son-in-law. Alfred, overcome with gratitude and love for the man he seemed more than content to adopt reciprocally as father, could not have realized that he was a pawn in Michelet's largely unconscious striving to liberate himself from his biological family. Michelet's real son, Charles, whose place Alfred took, may possibly have been more aware of the situation: shortly after his supercession, Charles began to take on the Cain-like attributes that seemed the only ones still possible for him. He gambled, lied, whored, refused to study, and, by the time of his father's second marriage, had contracted a venereal disease that made him anathema to the family of a girl he was in love with.[1]

In spite of this high cost of Alfred's surrogate son-ship, which the unhappy father paid without any insight into the double-entry bookkeeping of his emotional life, the transformation of his existence through the adoption of Alfred was only partial. For one thing, he must gradually have become aware that Alfred, though reverent, adoring, and the fruit of Madame Dumesnil's love and beneficence, could be extremely dull, as well as morose and clinging. For another, given Michelet's inner need to escape the clutch of his biological family, and given the ideologically proffered opportunity to romanticize that escape, it is reasonable that he would have looked further than Alfred, that he would have sought a female companion with whom he could combine the psychological functions of fatherhood with the biological ones of lover and husband. Those mixed needs were the raison d'être of his relationships—pedagogical and sexual—with his housekeepers Marie and Victoire in the seven years after Madame Dumesnil's death. Yet he seems to have had to dismiss Marie in 1844 after her jealousy for his still active cult for Madame Dumesnil led her to attack that lady's portraits.[2] And Victoire, though more stable, never became the educated idea-mate he had hoped for. There was another woman in those years, the wife and then widow of a doctor who had treated Pauline, Madame Aupèpin, but Michelet fended off her desire, after her husband's death, to legalize their relationship by marriage; he cut himself off from her in 1847 to devote all his energies to his *Histoire de la Révolution français* and to the coming political crisis.

Madame Aupèpin soon remarried, and in June 1848, just a week before the June troubles, Michelet noted in his journal that Victoire was going to marry a greengrocer. The candidacy of Athenaïs Mialaret as the successor to these varied daughter and mother symbols was as yet incorporeal, but its traces are visible in Michelet's correspondence and they were to continue until the dramatic encounter of November.

Athenaïs Unseen

Athenaïs first wrote to Michelet on October 23, 1847, about a year before they actually met. It was a long, autobiographic, remarkable first letter, considering that the writer was a twenty-one-year-old governess in Vienna, of respectable but not overly distinguished background, and the recipient was France's most famous historian.[3] The young lady recounted her adolescent infatuation with "the world of the Church" and attributed her subsequent distance from it to the historian's book on the priest and the family. She concluded with a passage that might have been written for her by some sly and omniscient goddess of love:

The world does not admit that a young girl can seek a guide outside of the priest. If you deny it to her, what will remain of her?

For six months I have been coming back to your book without being able to emerge from a labyrinth that is quite differently inextricable than that of the mountains where I began it. The Frenchman who obtained it for me was one of your auditors at the Collège de France. He told me you were married and the father of a family. If you have a daughter, monsieur, you will be so much the more touched by my situation.

I am like an orphan in this country so far from my own. I lost my father at fourteen. If I still had him, I would have no need of a director; even at a distance, he who knew all my thoughts would have been my surest guide. Since he is no longer with me and since you have been the occasion of my difficulties, allow me to ask you to take his place just this once, briefly, to speak to me as you do to your child and to help me, for I know that I shall never refind myself as I was before reading you.

I need a new orientation. If you will give it to me, I will be infinitely grateful to you and will bless you.[4]

Michelet's reply was so cautious that it raises the possibility he may have feared a Jesuit plot. Though touched by her "filial confidence," he invoked the deity to preserve him from shaking her faith, urged prayer and spiritually edifying literature to overcome her difficulties, and predicted she would have no trouble in finding "an aged and pious priest who will completely reassure you and will perform, without inconvenience, these communications in which you have until now found support"—a wordy advice to return to the confessional. From his "paternal heart" he advised her to abandon polemical works like his own and to seek peace in reading the Bible, Plutarch, Dante, Shakespeare, and Cervantes— "all full of God." Of his own works, he recommended only his essay on Joan of Arc in his *Histoire de France,* not, he added modestly, for his own narrative but for the texts of Joan herself. Then, after urging her to read above all in the book of life, of practical experience, his reserve crumbled and he accepted wholeheartedly the style and substance of her plea to him:

I have a daughter, mademoiselle, and even a grandchild. Nonetheless, I am not far enough from your age to have forgotten your moral situation, which was mine. I can see you young, sad, isolated without even having the sad joys of solitude. You will only raise yourself above this difficult condition, full of danger, in one way: *do not be a girl*, expand and fortify your soul; *be a mother in spirit*, for your pupils, for the unfortunate. There is no remedy for a woman's heart outside of the maternal sentiment, thus elevated and enlarged.[5]

Examined in context, Michelet's first letter to his future bride links his nascent relationship to her with the main line of development of his ideology and values in the 1840s. This line was partly broken after the February Revolution, but I have established the competing "paternal" and "maternal" principles that inspired him before then and that he had integrated in the notion of a first, political stage of the Revolution, built on justice and sacrifice, and a second, social-religious stage, built on mutual love and nurturance. This chronological program appears initially in the summary chapter of volume II of his *History of the French Revolution*: "On the Method and the Spirit of This Book."

Now this chapter on method was completed, according to the journal, on November 12, 1847. Before that date, there is a one-month gap in the journal. When Michelet picked it up again he wrote that his book had made him forget his life. He also wrote that he had begun the note on method only on the return of his daughter, Adèle, two weeks earlier, suggesting that this gave him the energy to write the crucial chapter on "method." Adèle's return, probably from her husband's estate in Normandy, must have been about October 28, a date roughly coinciding with the letter from the aspirant daughter in Vienna.[6] Neither that letter's arrival nor Michelet's reply of the thirtieth are mentioned in the journal. In other words, the reference in the journal to Adèle's arrival covers the tracks of the first appearance of her future rival and replacement. In spite of Michelet's cautious reserve, it could well have been the *cri de cœur* of this aspirant surrogate for liberation from the clerical embrace that galvanized his imagination into formulating the important summary chapter, which he himself characterized as a physical struggle with the clergy and the Terror.[7] In any case, his answer to Athenaïs clearly linked her to his preoccupation with the nurturant, maternal principle that he had located historically in the federations and theoretically in the Joachimite Gospel.

Michelet's injunction to this professed daughter substitute to become a mother in spirit thus connects Athenaïs to most of the main events of his life and work in the 1840s: to Madame Dumesnil and to the sublime echoes of her significance in his anticlerical work *Le Prêtre*, in *Le Peuple*, and in his chapters on the federations, but above all to the important theoretical essay he was beginning when Athenaïs's letter arrived. Concomitantly, it also suggests the possibility that all these echoes of Madame Dumesnil's influence could subsequently be channeled into the unseen frame of the young governess, infusing her filial ambitions with a significance for Michelet far beyond her dreams and laying the basis for the *coup de foudre* a year later.

Of the five subsequent letters that her unseen friend wrote to Athenaïs before meeting her, the last two also correlate interestingly with major events in his life. But all evidenced this strange and increasing intimacy with a very young woman he had never met. His reply in January 1848 to a letter of thanks for his first reply that she had sent at the end of 1847 began with a vague reference to the suspension of his course and to his faith in a better future for humanity. Apparently she had let him know she was depressed and asked him if he had known similar states, which he—not very honestly—denied. He then addressed her own unhappiness. His tone was stoical, but after begging her to avoid tears and despair, he hinted clearly that he was struggling against an involvement that was deeper than he wished: "We should not," he wrote, "become too moved by our sadnesses—nor by those of persons who interest us; this is an advice I have to address to myself while reading you. No one more than myself needs serenity and force, in the midst of this unhappy, destroyed world on whose ruins I obstinately continue to hope." In closing, he urged serenity and work as remedies and offered "the confidence, the support that is given, even from afar, by a serious and solid friendship."[8]

Athenaïs's reply showed little regard for Michelet's advice to abandon his book on the priest and the family. She had picked it up again and commented on it at length in her letter of February 9. She also told him of her daily routine as governess in the household of Princess Cantacuzène of Rumania, who had come from Bucharest to Vienna to obtain medical treatment for her ill, half-mad husband. She closed by thanking him, "profoundly," for the "serious and solid friendship" he had offered, and she promised to try to be worthy of it.[9]

Two weeks later, Paris was gripped by the February Revolution and Michelet became briefly involved in its aftermath. In mid-March, uprisings shattered the monarchies of central Europe, including the Austrian one, and Athenaïs's concerned friend, who had not yet answered her letter of February, sent her a brief note requesting assurance that she was unharmed (she was, after all, part of an aristocratic household). He was quickly answered by a long letter in which she described the outbreak of revolution in Vienna, emphasizing the importance of the ten thousand students—come from all corners of the empire—and her own role during the funeral cortege for the three students who had died in the uprising.

Absorbed by the darkening political horizon and by his lectures at the Collège de France, Michelet seems to have replied only on June 9, briefly, to his Viennese admirer.[10] She, in turn, replied on June 22, about a week after receiving his letter. It was just before the workshop issue exploded into civil war: apparently Louis-Napoléon's letter of June 14 to the president of the National Assembly, amid the Bonapartist demonstrations, induced fears in Vienna of the imminent death of the French Republic, to be followed by a return of imperial authority in Austria.[11] Athenaïs was now as concerned about Paris as Michelet had been about Vienna in March.

By the time this letter reached the French capital, the incident that had occasioned her fears had paled next to the bloody civil war of June 23–26. Shocked, obsessed by the need for popular education, Michelet nonetheless failed, during a visit with Noel, in his effort to compose a short republican history for the masses. His resolve to write once more to Athenaïs, several weeks after receiving her anxious letter, coincided with his return to Paris and to his *History of the French Revolution*. His reference, on the day he wrote her, to his resumption of this work as "touchant ma terre nourrice," is a hint of the growing tie between Athenaïs and the "maternal principle" in his work.[12] There are others. In ensuing weeks, the meagerness of his epistolary contact with Athenaïs, as yet invisible, was compensated by meeting her old friends from Montauban, Mathilde Gronlier and her brother, for whom he attempted to find employment. On July 26, he noted that the Gronliers were visiting and wanted to borrow Adèle's piano. The only other journal entry for the twenty-sixth reads: "Prepared chapter III: Mme Condorcet, Mme Roland."

On September 29, the putative reincarnation of those ladies announced her determination to return to Paris. The prince's days were numbered, the princess was about to return him to his native Rumanian soil to let him expire in familiar surroundings, and Athenaïs, whose health was being undermined by "an insidious little fever," decided that rather than increase her own danger—and thereby add to the princess's worries—by a journey into the rude winter climate of Bucharest, she would seek employment in Paris. She timidly requested her new friend's counsel and assistance for her return.

Clearly perplexed, Michelet delayed answering this urgent plea for help for two weeks. When he finally responded on October 16, his letter betrayed an underlying sympathy and engagement, diluted by ambivalence and veiled by evasion. He began, to explain the tardiness of his reply, by referring to his difficulty in deciphering her "pretty and expressive handwriting," then told her her letter had saddened him, had "merged with the vexations of the times and with the universal renewal of all my sadness, which, of ancient origins, have become recent." He then excused himself from answering directly but implied that the condition of Paris was such that she would be wise not to look for employment there. The city seemed "poor and depopulated." The student pensions where she might have obtained tutoring work were largely closed because of the parents' fear of continuing turmoil. As for himself, he said he had been working for three months on a volume of his "Revolution" (which was true) and then, with an utter lack of candor, further excused his delay in replying to her by saying that during those three months he had neither visited anyone nor written a single letter:[13] he gave her the flattering but false impression, after overtly discouraging her from coming to Paris, that she was important enough to him to break out of a prolonged monklike immersion in his work. His ending further undercut his negativity: "What you tell me about your health much afflicts me. So young, so spiritual, and so courageous, you have within you a powerful liqueur, which ought to keep on fortifying and reanimating you. If the sincere affection of a friend, the interest of a paternal heart can also be an alleviation, please accept it mademoiselle, and believe that I am your devoted J. Michelet." A postscript expressed a more immediate concern: "Today's papers, which lead us to fear the bombardment of Vienna, oppress my heart. Can I not know if you are out of danger."[14]

Just how Athenaïs's illness merged for him "with the vexations of the times and with the universal renewal of all my sadness" was spelled out in the journal entry for the day he wrote to her. The wounding memories he kept knocking against that day included explicitly the June rising and his father's death and implicitly Athenaïs's predecessor as romantic attachment, Madame Dumesnil. And it must now be clear that the references to the births of Pauline and of Madame de Condorcet, in the context of these vexations and the ones raised by the governess's poor health, were far from incidental. At the moment he invoked the ricorso, the possibility of an imminent meeting with Athenaïs was much on his mind.

Athenaïs in Paris

The immediate background of Athenaïs's arrival in Paris on November 8, 1848, as well as the details of Michelet's private life in November and December, are obscured by the absence of his journal for this period.[15] The two letters Athenaïs says she wrote on October 21 and November 1 only feebly illuminate her circumstances and motives at the time of her return. The first of these, which she admits to having delivered personally to her friend in

November rather than posting, was a twenty-five-page account of the final phase of the Viennese revolution and the military attack on the city in October 1848. Though dated October 21, in Linz, where the Cantacuzène household had then taken refuge, it refers to the siege and capture of the city by the army of Windischgraetz, which occurred between October 20 and November 1.[16] This letter was probably written simply as a chronicle to be shown to the famous historian (and her other friends) in Paris. Amid a sympathetic account of the student rebels' last stand against the imperial army, during which the frail governess, wearing a tricolor sash and assisted by the princess's chambermaid, says she helped build barricades, there is a striking indication of the international influence of her friend. The chaplain of the academic legion, the theologian Anton Füster,[17] is described as publicly reading to the revolutionaries from Michelet's chapters on the federations of 1790. The pages were, according to Athenaïs, particularly moving since the multiethnic students "were themselves a federation of nations tightly bound together to serve the holy cause of liberty."

Athenaïs's "letter," though almost certainly written during the two weeks after she received his of October 16, refers neither to his warning about the conditions of Paris nor to anything else he mentioned to her. But on November 1 she does seem to have replied to his letter of the sixteenth, to explain why, in spite of the lack of prospects in the French capital, she was nonetheless returning to it. To begin with, she had been told unequivocally by the Cantacuzènes' doctor that her health was not up to another German winter. Why Paris, where tutoring work was unavailable, rather than her native Montauban? Apparently, the unstable situation in central Europe had discouraged the princess from going back to Rumania with her moribund spouse, and she had determined to seek medical treatment for him in Paris. Athenaïs was therefore to precede the Cantacuzènes in France, to visit her family briefly in Montauban and then return to the capital "to prepare everything in advance." This included visiting Michelet, whom she was to consult on medical matters for her employers, as well as to express her gratitude for his "paternal assistance."

The situation was clearly more complicated than this. Once in Paris, Athenaïs made no effort to visit her family—even resisted an order from her mother to return to Montauban. Moreover, a fragment of one of Michelet's subsequent letters to her raises the possibility that she left the service of the Cantacuzènes to avoid her mistress's sexual advances.[18] In any case, Athenaïs's stated reason for coming to Paris was at most a fraction of the truth. She was determined to acquire a new father, just as her avuncular friend was to find a daughter-partner.

Athenaïs left Linz on November 4, arrived at the gare du Nord in Paris during the night of November 7–8, and took a room in a hotel near the *bourse*.[19] At 10 A.M., she knocked on the door of the house on the rue des Postes. The proprietor, however, had given strict orders that his morning work was not to be interrupted. Victoire, his housekeeper and mistress, asked the pale visitor to return at 4 P.M., which she did. Michelet quickly perceived a number of details about her situation that awakened both pity and indignation and set the creaky machinery of Eros in unstoppable motion: she was ill, very young, and pale, and she had been tracked by his archenemies, the Jesuits. He later said he was "touched" and "saddened" at this first meeting: "She wanted a position, but she seemed so afflicted. She admitted she vomited blood. I promised her benevolently I would look for something for her and the easiest possible. But I was desolate at the thought of how difficult it would be."[20]

Athenaïs, who had apparently been prepared, on the basis of his polemic against the priesthood, to find a choleric, violent type, subsequently told him of her pleasant surprise in his study; his formulation of her impressions gives us one of the few descriptions of the historian's lair: "Decorated exclusively with books, large, half-lit, unornamented except for the portrait of my father and an engraving of Albrecht Dürer's *Melancholy,* [it] made a rather gentle impression on her. My cat, sleeping on my papers, recalled childhood memories of her father's taste for cats. This faithful guardian of the hearth, sleeping so perfectly, seemed an image of peace."[21]

If she so clearly identified him with her father—who, incidentally, had also tutored a sovereign's children, in Port-au-Prince—he in turn had the physical evidence to view her as his child. When he helped her with her coat, she received it, "with the grace of a child rather than a girl ... with a smile, a thank you, a charming little bow." Touched, he became aware of her body: "Her young bosom, not very marked and seemingly that of a fifteen-year-old, was well shaped. Very delicate above, below she was stronger and well poised on her loins ... From which she appeared shorter, quite young, having kept something of a child whose growth had been stopped. Sensual charm or not, the heart was still more captivated." Masking the confused turmoil of senses and spirit produced in the fifty-year-old by this adolescent apparition was an overwhelming compassion and an instant assumption of responsibility: "To see her, this child all alone and so little supported, launched into an unknown life and subjected to the harsh labor for which she was so poorly equipped! It saddened me. She recurred to me all night. I said to myself: What can I do for her?"[22]

On the same day that she visited Michelet, Athenaïs moved to a hotel on the rue Saint-André des Arts, to be close to her friends from Montauban, the Gronliers. Michelet, worried that his "paternal" interest was becoming an amorous one and apprehensive of rejection because of the twenty-eight-year difference in their ages, allowed five days to pass before reminding her of his existence: on the thirteenth, unable "to continue an appearance of coldness and negligence that was in no way in my heart," he left with her concierge a copy of book V of his history of the French Revolution, which contained the chapters on Madame Roland and Madame de Condorcet.[23]

The example of these revolutionary heroines, both married to much older men of letters, was immediately useful. Within two days, Athenaïs, who was bedridden, received a letter from her mother ordering her to enter a Catholic institution—school or convent—if she had not yet found a position. Strengthened in her refusal by Michelet's sign of continued interest, she visited him again, with the Gronliers, on November 15 to thank him.[24] She did not, however, inform him of her difficulties with her mother until about a week later. Still plagued by ambivalence, he meanwhile limited himself to one brief note to her, whose formal mode of address was undermined by implications of future intimacy: "I beg Mademoiselle to glance at the chapter indicated [he had sent her *Le Peuple*] . . . An idea has occurred to me which I would communicate to her and which would change many things. I would have had the honor of going to explain it to her if I had not feared troubling the arrangement of her day."[25]

In this eighteenth-century dance they were performing, the rules of the game apparently required Athenaïs to respond to his cautious step toward her with little steps both backward and forward. She immediately replied that, with all respect for his "paternal interest," she would have felt less worthy of it if she did not try to take care of her future herself, so as to diminish his preoccupations with it. And, reminding him of their respective positions, she begged him: "Do not take my reserve for coldness. It is so natural for me not to forget the great distance that God has put between us." Reversing ground, she then added: "You really want to call me your child, to tell me that I will count from now on in your destiny. Regard me then as a second daughter. I shall serve you with a heart more capable of devotion by the tests it has undergone."[26] What Michelet could not have realized was that the combined forces of clerical reaction and family propriety had been struggling, in the preceding week, to put that "great distance" between Athenaïs and the entire male sex by shutting her up in a convent.

Athenaïs's mother had backed up her initial demand by sending the abbé Caulery, a friend of the family attached to the church in

Paris, to implement it. Liberated through Michelet's polemics and her experience in Vienna from unthinking obedience to the church, Athenaïs was fertile in arguing against these pressures. The same abbé, she countered, had told her in Montauban she was unsuited to the cloister. If she went to her mother's house, did not the abbé know there would be no room for her because of the birth of her sister's baby? How could they demand another long trip of someone as ill as she was? Moreover, she was twenty-two, no longer a minor subject to parental authority. And the princess would soon be coming to Paris and would give her her old position back (just as much a pretext here as in her letter to Michelet of November 1).[27]

When her distinguished protector finally resolved to visit her in her room on the rue Saint-André des Arts on November 22, she had won her little skirmish with the Jesuits but was nonetheless on the point of giving up the battle against maternal authority and returning to Montauban.[28] Forewarned by the Gronliers about the clerical pressure on her, Michelet reacted to her decision to return to Montauban, if she could not find a position in Paris, by telling her he knew of her duel with the abbé. At which point she asked him directly if she should resist her mother's order.

They were now approaching the first critical hurdle in their relationship. She told him the details of her upbringing: a father who loved and protected her but died when she was fourteen, a mother partial to her sons, guilty of "excessive severities" toward her daughters.[29] He told her that she had refound her father, that whether or not she secured a position, he would look after her, and that, considering her poor health, she should delay resuming work. As to her scruples about resisting "l'ordre maternel," he simply told her: "Stay. You are not alone."

In the brief "Mémoires" he wrote in 1861, Michelet admitted that with this advice and commitment he was breaking a longstanding policy of never accepting "these dangerous tutelages of young girls," of never counseling them to stay in Paris. He had done it this time, he said, because if he had failed to defend Athenaïs's freedom, he would have been giving the lie to his entire life and principles. He was fully aware of the gravity of his decision, a gravity he then saw not in terms of marriage—they had not yet reached that point—but in terms of his five-year-old war with the order of Jesuits: "I knew perfectly that with such a counsel, defending a young and charming person, I was making myself a target for the [Jesuit] party, . . . that even the indifferent would reproach me for making her disobey, for substituting my authority for that of the family."[30]

This last was of course the heart of the matter. Later that night, while a violent storm battered the shutters of his house, he reflected on the unequal contest he had entered with church and family over Athenaïs. He subsequently wrote, "I heard the struggle of the devil and the angels over this soul. I said, 'I will take her from him. Whatever happens to me, no matter!' And I adopted her in my heart."[31]

With this singular act of adoption, Michelet consummated the liberation of Athenaïs both from clerical power and from her natural mother, establishing his moral authority over her as spiritual father and mother; he also consecrated his own emancipation from the biological destiny that had given him a daughter through Pauline. He did not realize it, but Adèle, who had always lived under his roof, did. Within a month, she would be telling him that she hated the intruder in their lives. Within two, he would be negotiating a move with his future bride to the northwest edge of Paris: Adèle and Alfred, shattered, would move to a new address not far from the rue des Postes. On November 22, Michelet had little notion of what the future would hold. He was in love, he knew it, but beyond the paternal responsibility for Athenaïs, which she clearly accepted, he little hoped that she could reciprocate his feelings. A week later, bursting with these emotions he had so far kept to himself, convinced that Alfred and Adèle would have to be informed, he wrote a long, extraordinary letter to Eugène Noel, with a request that he gently inform Alfred (he admitted that he feared wounding his son-in-law too much to tell him himself, had noticed that Alfred was not "disinterested" on the subject of his father-in-law's possible remarriage). The letter to Noel contained, in abbreviated but rapturous form, much of what I have recounted, but it also included a valuable account of Michelet's state of mind, which was anything but optimistic.[32]

He professed a state of utter hopelessness and suffering: "Will she leave? I will suffer again. And even if my age, less advanced, were to permit me to marry her, I would suffer without doubt, accusing myself of burying her young destiny in the tomb of an old man." Perhaps, he thought, considering her sickly condition, nature "will cut this knot more barbarously . . . I feel her dying, and myself with her." Yet his sudden encounter with Eros was generating new sources of creativity, the fruits of which he wanted to share with Noel: "The more I feel myself sinking under destiny, dear friend, the more I feel growing within me a . . . new and fecund soul, determined to produce, to revenge itself on fate by the expression of its force. You are going to receive the second half of the volume [volume III of *History of the French Revolution*] written with three lightning bolts. All the knots I had in my spirit have melted at the flame. I am marching strong and rapid like an untiring giant with shoes of iron."[33]

On December 1, 1848, during one of their promenades through Paris, the historian proposed to Athenaïs.[34] Her letter of acceptance conveys to us her hesitations and the ambivalence of their relationship.[35]

Monsieur, friend,

I remain troubled to the bottom of my soul by our promenade. You have let me see too much of your wound for me still to have the right to be silent.

My whole heart nearly escaped me when you said, in this profound accent that is yours alone, "I will await from your decision what will be life or death for me." Oh, mercy! Above all, live! He who has led us toward one another does not wish you to die. So many souls expect their lives from your own.

You can only help them, and heal them of their afflictions, by keeping the liberty of your genius.

Your compassion for my suffering creates a mirage for you, you see me as your heart would like to.

I have a duty to be courageous, to recall you to a feeling for reality. At the physical level, by my health, I am perhaps in danger. You yourself are frightened to see me, "so white, so pale!" In spirit, I am still the child in quest of herself, I have nothing to give but an immense good will.

You tell me that's already too much, that with me you will be stronger, more powerful, more fecund; that you will find in a life together, always sought in vain, a rejuvenation of your action on the world.

But if all this were only an illusion of your tenderness? If the day after, too late, you were to find yourself alone again?— I promised to see you tomorrow, with my friends of the rue de Savoie [the Gronliers]; I shall keep my promise. Before witnesses, we shall be strong against ourselves.

The more serious the moment, the more I feel the need to put God between us. It is not without having prayed to him on my knees that I write this.

Whatever happens, I shall remain *yours*. I shall follow you in liberty and in fatality.—Do not speak to me again of the age difference between us. Those who cannot die remain young eternally, time for them, is without duration.

As I see you today, I would see you in a thousand years, always crowned with a divine halo.

Serious as we are at the entry to this new world, it is our souls which move toward each other. Down here, I shall be for you what, in my desire for independence, I have been for no one. I will be *yours,* so completely that I will no longer find myself back."[37]

A remarkable acceptance! The warnings at the beginning of the letter about her health and about her childlike lack of clear identity are imbedded in her fear that he has created of her "an illusion of . . . tenderness." Nonetheless, she twice pronounced herself "*yours.*" The first time this was accompanied by the—for Michelet—nearly mystical phrase, "I shall follow you in liberty and in fatality," the second, by an obscure promise that she would be for him "down here [*ici-bas*], what, in my desire for independence, I have been for no one." This last, following on her conviction that their souls were about to merge, suggests that she was referring to a more carnal, and for her unprecedented, level of approach. It was an obscure forewarning of the sexual problem that was to plague their marriage, particularly in its first six months.

Ecstatic at a positive reply, Michelet threw off the veil of caution: he wrote to Noel on the day he received this letter, "It's an adoption, my friend. *Consummatum est.*" And he said he found the question of whether she was his wife or his daughter to be of secondary importance.[37] To Athenaïs, who had visited him as she promised on December 2, he wrote at 5 A.M. on the third that he had received her letter in the evening after she left and had stayed up the entire night reading and rereading it, "not daring to believe my eyes." Adèle, he wrote, told him that he looked transfigured. What the sensitive Adèle actually thought of her father's intoxication with a woman her own age remains unrecorded.

Indeed, with Michelet preparing to take on permanently the role of Athenaïs's father, mother, and husband, he must have exuded the "violent happiness" he mentioned in his letter to Athenaïs, but the cost was an escalating alienation from his own daughter and son-in-law, whose places Athenaïs was taking. Although he had not yet informed his children of the changes in his life—before December 2, he had no idea of what the future would hold—they were hardly blind to what was going on, as Adèle's comment showed. A few days later, after Noel, at Michelet's instructions, had informed Alfred of the earthquake about to disrupt his existence, his son-in-law wrote him that, "without having read the letters, he had seen everything, *felt* everything."[38] Alfred's missive, written from one wing of the house on the rue des Postes to another, was in its very form an unmistakable sign of estrangement, handwriting on the wall in several senses, but his father-in-law, lost in his euphoria, did not see it. He even wrote Noel of a sort of *ménage à quatre* of those who intuited one another without words—presumably himself, Noel, Alfred, and Athenaïs, which conveniently left out Adèle.

Michelet was counting on Noel to maintain the link between himself and Alfred, to mediate between them in this difficult moment. Noel, meanwhile, was completely torn between his two allegiances. The letters between the three men have largely been preserved[39] and show Noel walking a tightrope between Michelet's joy and the catastrophic pain this joy was about to bring to the lives of those closest to him: Alfred and Adèle were not only losing the father they depended on but their home as well. In early December, this father's emotions were invested elsewhere—first in whether his lady would have him at all, then in her health, about which he had great, as it turned out, unwarranted, fears (she died, as he did, in her seventies). Noel, who possessed in Michelet's view "the most divine of divine gifts, heroic gaiety,"[40] would explain it all to Alfred and ensure his enthusiastic support.

As Alfred's misery grew and his collision with his father-in-law became unmistakable, Noel's letters in fact became simply schizophrenic. Since he loved them both, he felt bound to support them both—even when Alfred wrote to Athenaïs on December 13 asking her to withdraw from his father-in-law's life[41] and Michelet charged Alfred with betrayal at the dinner table.[42] In any case, midway between his confident assurance that Noel's heroic gaiety would reassure Alfred and his icy attack on his son-in-law as a traitor a week later, Michelet admitted to Noel that he was deeply troubled by Alfred's malaise.[43]

It was not the only shadow on his existence. He also found, about this time, that he was losing interest in his work: he complained bitterly that the effect of his continued effort to write his history of the Revolution was "to separate me from my interior life of philosophy and love."[44] The "matriarchal" values he had projected into his work since 1842 were now being invested in Athenaïs. If in July he had written Noel that his return to writing the history of the Revolution was a return to his *terre nourrice* (literally, wet nurse earth), he now applied that metaphor to his contact with Athenaïs: "She is to my spirit what the lovable and fecund earth was to the giant in the fable; it sufficed for him to touch it to regain his strength." Another refraction of his maternal principle, praise of the Indian reverence for nature that had characterized the second part of *Le Peuple*, also was applied to Athenaïs, in the journal entry of December 9: "Oh, how much better she lets me understand the religions of nature! How much, since I know her, have I reoriented my heart toward the gentle, the profound, the mysterious Orient! ... I feel myself all Indian, full of devotion and fervor, before these gleams of God embodied in woman."

Inspired by this Indian religion of harmony in nature, Michelet oriented his lectures at the Collège de France that winter toward

the reconciliation of all human differences toward the overcoming of all barriers between religions, nations, and classes.
Leveling the barriers that the pale governess's arrival had erected
in his intimate family would prove more difficult—in fact, impossible.

Shadows over Eros

Alfred's clumsy letter of December 13 was intended to persuade
Athenaïs to stand down in favor of the French nation. His reasoning—already identified by his father-in-law as lacking the necessary
"disinterestedness"—was that Michelet's marriage to anyone would
be a disservice to humanity, which needed its "men of genius"
untrammeled by "individual ties." The missive contained a postscript requesting her not to show it to "anyone."[45]

It was this more than the letter itself that triggered Michelet's
wrath after Athenaïs, obeying Alfred's request, paraphrased it to
him. At dinner on December 14, hearing his father-in-law cite and
rather pointedly translate an Italian verse that warned against the
perfidy of intimates, Alfred felt his heart sink. "For a moment," he
wrote Noel, "I thought I was dreaming, not hearing right, but the
pain I felt assured me of the reality."[46] He left the table and wrote
a brief letter to his father-in-law, defending his motives and complaining bitterly of the wounding lack of faith in him. And he enclosed a copy of the letter he had sent to Athenaïs.

Michelet spent the entire night composing responses and finally settled on a long, impassioned one in which he accused Alfred
of meddling in his personal life behind his back, when he had neither
the right to do so nor the necessary insight into the character of
the person to whom he had addressed his extraordinary plea. The
root of his bitter anger lay in a double fear: that Athenaïs might
indeed have silently left him after receiving Alfred's letter and that
his new love was estranging his children from him to the point that
they were capable of desperate acts of betrayal to keep him single.
After explaining the harsh words at the dinner table, he devoted the
rest of his letter to appealing to Alfred's better nature while trying
to convince him that Athenaïs would only enhance and could not
possibly compromise his life as a historian:

> The greatest [misfortune] without any doubt would be sepa-
> ration from a person with whom I have this profound relation
> of spirit, of life, and of art, she with whom I have been able
> to communicate not only by the word but, what is very rare,
> by the written word. You are enough of an artist to feel the
> importance of this. Art for us is not only in the form but in

the essence, in life. The supposition that such a hard-working and sedentary person, in delicate health and already leading a writer's life, could radically change my own, would be inadmissible.

Why this estrangement from she who is one of us, who alone has our ideas, who feels them enough to express them with eloquence, with delicacy, with force? I would not recognize here your great heart ... I say, love those close to me—by doing so, they become yours as well. Be for me a principle of peace and union. At the end of a life devoted to others, I do have a right to happiness, at least a right to seek it according to my heart ... Who will say: I am the only wise one—is it you who will say this?

When I unburdened myself before you (without saying completely, it's true, to what point I am committed) I thought that, as always, you would smooth my path. It did not occur to me for a moment that it would be you who would roughen it, that you alone would be against me, and that you would darken the last place in the sun that I would want in this world.[47]

The angry defensiveness at the end undermined the conciliatory tone of the previous paragraphs, and the quarrel intensified. As a result, both Alfred and Michelet agreed to honor the hapless Noel with the dignity of "judge." Alfred made clear to Noel both his skepticism about his friend's enthusiasm for Michelet's new love and his own animosity toward her: "You wrote me that it was necessary to accept it all with a divine heart, without *bitterness*; in your letters to M. Michelet ... you sang hosannah for this new friendship; and I was already glimpsing the sad reality, that this new person was perhaps not what you thought and what I wished, that she was cold, simulating, egoistic, insidious."[48]

Alfred added that he thought "nothing will be able to cure this wound," and it was perhaps the only thing he saw accurately in those difficult days. Noel could not, of course, sit in judgment over his two closest friends, but he did, in reply to the above, give Alfred some good advice about Michelet's desire for a new life: "That you should have tried to hold him back was right; but at the departure, my dear Alfred, what is our duty, our solace, except to embrace him and to nourish the hope in his heart for this difficult navigation."

On the nineteenth, Noel asked Michelet what kind of trial this was, in which everyone wanted his happiness. He then gave his own standpoint: "When I see in your letters the smallest spark of joy, I bolt to the heavens to thank the good Lord: but other times you write that you are going to die, and then I receive tearful letters from Alfred, to such an extent, dear sir, that there was a day when I could only wander in the bare woods softly chanting the *dies irae* ... Your letter to Alfred was severe, so much the more since, in writing to Mlle M. he had followed the inspiration of conscience and had done so with a heroic openness."

Michelet answered Noel by conceding that both sides had been carried away by passion. But for the rest, he indicated that the conflict was sharpening. Adèle had told her that she hated Athenaïs, which provoked the bitter comment: "At age twenty-five, she finally remembers me, to whom she never confided the least of her feelings. The first that is revealed is that of hating the one I love."[49] As to Alfred's avowals of love and friendship, he had his own ideas on the subject: "I had conceived, I admit, another idea of friendship ... When they asked Blosius, at the point of dying with his friend C. Gracchus: If he had said to you: burn the capitol, what would you have done?—I would have burned it."

Such unthinking fidelity was in short supply in Michelet's household. Alfred rejected the idea that he should encourage this love for an unknown woman simply because Michelet willed it: "It would be to love you as a slave," he wrote his father-in-law, "and I shall never do that." Moreover, Adèle was not the only woman in her father's entourage to reject the intruder. Alfred, who had earlier been the indignant witness to the housekeeper Marie's defacing of his mother's portraits, now reported approvingly on the resistance of Victoire (still unwed) to the young woman who had taken over her employer's heart.

> Victoire, who for several nights has been drinking poppy seed tea to calm her tears and insomnias, asked Adèle, whom she saw in tears the day before yesterday: "Madame, is it really true? Monsieur is going to be married?" Adèle, who was revolted by her father's reproaches, answered, "Maybe nothing is decided, but it is after all possible." Then Victoire, with the intrepidity of a quite naive soul, said, "I will prevent it." And when M. Mt. returned, she told him with a heart-rending fervor, "No monsieur, you will not do it."
>
> In a transport of fury, M. Mt. came immediately to us to accuse me of having set up Victoire. I was totally ignorant of what had passed between Victoire and Adèle. Moreover, there was nothing to teach Victoire. M. Mt. has initiated her until now in his entire life, and she must have been astonished to see him completely change his habits in the last two weeks, to see him leave at the break of day and only return for dinner—moreover, she hears all our table talk.

Two days before Christmas, Alfred wrote Noel that Michelet was determined to wed immediately after completing volume III, that the rupture was now irreparable and his heart broken for good. Alfred seemed most affected at this point by the pain felt by Adèle: "It's not by this marriage ... that she is so hurt, it's by having been so misunderstood, by having been so easily displaced from an affection in which she felt secure. Every morning, every evening she asks me: Is it really true? Isn't it a bad dream? And when she's with her father, she feels an uneasiness that's painful to see. M. Mt. has really been hard on her. He said to her and repeated to me that he could never tell if she loved him ... What kind of love is this new passion, which renders him so unjust?"[50] Indeed, a few days later, Michelet informed Noel of Adèle's decision "to separate herself in the most radical way possible" and professed total incomprehension.

No one seems to have been sleeping much during these tense days on the rue des Postes. Not Michelet, not Victoire, probably not Adèle, and certainly not Alfred, whose insomnia was accompanied by neuralgia, eye problems, and a urinary tract infection.[51] Alfred's father-in-law, trapped between the rival claims on his feelings, could—apart from frequent communications with Athenaïs—only express his new love to the eternally sympathetic Noel. At one moment, after singing Athenaïs's praises ("infinitely tender, intelligent, discreet"), he sighed that she was "in so many respects *Alfred as a woman.*"[52] More accurately, it was the ghost of Alfred's mother that haunted him in Athenaïs, willed into her pale frame in a moment of great need and tenaciously held in place by a love that had wandered too long without satisfaction.[53] But it was also his quest for a daughter to replace the one Pauline had given him, whose love he seems never to have accepted, that bedeviled his existence and devastated Adèle's.

The second half of December 1848 was, then, a most difficult period for Michelet, in which he was daily confronted with the emotional price he had to pay for his joyous acceptance of Athenaïs's surrogate daughtership. Athenaïs had, in fact, briefly considered giving him up after receiving Alfred's letter on the fourteenth.[54] And the lovers' letters are often shrouded by the melancholy of her future husband. On December 18, Athenaïs alluded to "your broken internal harmony" to remind him of the real cause of that melancholy, the war of nerves in his family. Between Christmas and New Year's Day, Michelet made the decision to leave the rue des Postes after his marriage, and in January he sought and found a home for Athenaïs and himself in the northwest outskirts of Paris.[55]

Other shadows darkened the couple's existence. Athenaïs's poor health, aggravated by her exhausting trip from Vienna to Paris, preoccupied her fiancé to such an extent that he called in his private physician, Dr. Rostan, to examine her and, alarmed by the doctor's apprehensiveness, wrote to the doctor who had treated her in Vienna. Though reassured by the Austrian that her illness was not mortal—he seems to have found her lungs delicate but not tubercular—Michelet remained so concerned that he spent half of the letter he wrote a few days later to her mother, asking permission to marry her, in discussing her health.[56]

A larger problem was the darkening political climate. On December 10, Louis-Napoléon was elected president of the French Republic. Four days later, Jean-Antoine Letronne, Michelet's superior at both the Collège de France and the National Archives, died. Michelet became interim head at the archives and hoped to be appointed permanently there, but the conservatives in the ruling Party of Order mistrusted him and appointed instead a bureaucratic confidant of Louis-Napoléon, Chabrier, whom Michelet saw as an enemy. At the Collège de France, Jules Barthélemy Saint-Hilaire was installed as his chief, a disciple of Cousin whose "narrow police-agent spirit," Michelet wrote, "played the game of the Reaction."[57]

Early in January 1849, he felt obliged to discuss these matters with Athenaïs, and the young governess, who had twice written him in December that she would be his in liberty and in fatality, assured him again that it was her duty "to associate myself in advance with the trials, with the reverses of fortune that you seem to predict."[58] She suggested, quite practically, that they forego from that moment on any unnecessary expenses, adding that she hated jewelry and that her happiness did not depend on expensive cashmeres. Nonetheless, she retained a clear preference not to live in the same house as Alfred and Adèle. She had, she said, only one desire: the solitude of a small house with trees and flowers, a "petite maison de berger," about which she had often dreamed. For the rest, Athenaïs was clearly worried about his difficulty in working during these feverish days and suggested that once he had moved away from the rue des Postes, his work would come easier, the grief of Alfred and Adèle would be less afflicting, and his life would regain an inner harmony.[59]

Michelet's reply to this oath of fidelity in hard times is the first statement from his hand on his somber career perspectives: "Yes, you have linked yourself to the destinies of a poor man, who will be persecuted. The brutal and barbarous period we shall have to go through will be hostile to thinkers. All this would be somber for me if I did not know your heroic heart, which, if I am not deceived, will be all the more attached to me as my misfortunes increase." For the rest, he fell back on lessons of austerity absorbed in his impoverished youth and undoubtedly followed in his marriage with Pauline: "The whole secret [of economic habits] is to keep track of the *small daily* expenses; for the heavy expenses, the sum itself warns you, you naturally look closely, and besides, they are rare."[60]

It would be three years before the end of the Second Republic compelled Michelet and his wife to implement these lessons. Meanwhile, other problems, connected with Athenaïs's physical constitution, posed a more serious threat to their happiness than even the estrangement of Alfred and Adèle. On January 12, unable to sleep, Michelet got out of bed at 3 A.M. to condense to a few lines an eight page letter about Athenaïs to Dr. Rostan. He and Athenaïs had an appointment with the physician that morning and he resolved to ask him, he wrote his fiancée, "if complete union is possible for us without too much inconvenience for you." He added that the situation was killing him ("je meurs") and that his work on the Revolution was blocked: "Here I am for hours at my desk without writing or thinking." He promised, as her friend, to be "careful . . . to restrain a part of my ardors. I will only show them to the extent that habit and familiarity will have diminished your emotions and that I will be sure of touching without breaking." He complained of their being so near and so far from each other at the same time and of being "devoured and consumed" by a recurrent struggle. As to her own persistent complaints of "langor," he clearly suspected that they had a sexual basis: "Where does it come from? From having given or from having as yet given little? . . . Oh, I beg of you, let us not struggle to destroy ourselves."[61]

Jeanne Calo, aided by medical monographs, has deduced that Athenaïs was suffering from vaginismus—a tendency of the vagina to contract rigidly on approach, thus preventing intercourse—probably caused by traumatic enemas and suppositories for chronic constipation as a child. The studies Calo cites argue plausibly that reflexes of resistance to painful and feared insertion of objects in the anus leads in children to the spread of such defensive reflexes to the neighboring genital and urinary tracts.[62] Michelet himself wrote in his "Mémoires" about Athenaïs's extreme constipation in Austria, which at one point led to a two-week-long rocklike barricade in her bowels, and about her "lively repugnance" to the proposed treatment. A complication of her condition, he added, was that the rigid encumbrance "repressed the neighboring organ, sealed it hermetically, and she had the horrible torture, rather rare in a woman, of being unable to urinate."[63] The journal of the 1850s and 1860s shows an intense attention to Athenaïs's bowel movements. So the assumption that it was a lifelong problem and that it indeed crippled her capacity for sexual intercourse is anything but far-fetched.

Evidence from Michelet's journal suggests that his torment over Athenaïs's revulsion to sexual contact was more than a passing problem. It was not simply an irrationally tenacious virginity he was confronting, nor was it any flaw in her love for him, which, the letters make evident, was abundant at a nonphysical level.[64] Michelet's erotic impulse, however, was powerful; he could neither envisage nor accept a mature love for a woman without a genital outcome. If he had made an exception for Madame Dumesnil—and it is by no means certain that he had—it was because that mother goddess was dying of cancer. So the months before and after his wedding to Athenaïs must, as the letter of January 12 and numerous journal entries suggest, have been filled with sexual frustration. His first noteworthy genital contact with his young wife seems to have been in September, nearly five months after their marriage.[65]

Though willing and able to sublimate Eros into spiritual substance, Michelet clearly hoped for something less incorporeal. A letter written at 6 A.M. on New Year's Day, 1849, began with a triple lament about his work, about his "domestic tragedy," and about "every night a world of dreams, desire, impossibilities" and then focused on the reciprocity between his love for her and his creativity:

> Love in me will be a movement, a progress, a renewal, a fecundation of every hour. Every hour, I shall take the spark from your lips, from your charming discourse—and, once received, I shall render it into creations of the spirit. I shall unceasingly plumb the infinity in your eyes and I will transform it into eternal language. Yes, I say the *infinite*; you give me much more than I can return to you. Hence the painful plenitude in which I now live. But then, happier, I shall extinguish in you the excess of flame you have poured into me.
>
> Extinguish? No. Bring back the spark to the hearth from which it departed. The spark, obscured for an instant in the burning shadows of union, will be reborn, luminous, from a word or a look ... Thus continually fecundated and relit, created every hour by your breath, I will go creating myself, producing without strain. And I shall render perhaps to the human race, to God, what God gives me through you. If the spectacle of your power, of the good that you can do will make you happy, oh my dearest, you will be so.[66]

A week later, on January 7, he explained to her how each important book since 1844 brought him closer to her. *Le Prêtre* was "often a very tender book"; *Le Peuple*: "full of love"; the second volume of the *Revolution* contained "the tenderest thing I ever wrote:

the Federations." So, he apostrophized his fiancée, "from book to book I was on my way to *the living book* . . . you."[67]

The "living book" that was to be the final repository of Michelet's love for humanity, Athenaïs, could not, alas, be touched without breaking. Michelet's tortured letter of January 12 reveals his shocked discovery that "the burning shadows of union" he had referred to on New Year's Day, in which he would return to her the unsublimatable part of her gift of Eros, were not to be his for some time. Being practical as well as much in love, he redirected his energies to his work. Significantly, with the exception of brief notes on January 13 and 28, there is a sudden three-week hiatus between his pained letter of January 12 and the next long love letter on February 2.[68] He reports regular meetings with her in the journal, but the almost daily rhythm of their written communications was broken. During this period, Michelet completed volume III of the *Révolution,* with Lucie Desmoulin's despairing cry over the fate of her husband at the end, and prepared for the lectures he was supposed to begin at the end of January. It was above all through these preparations that he resumed the connection, ruptured since February 1848, with the main line of his intellectual development.

The Winter Lectures of 1849 and Michelet's Marriage

One basis of the new lecture series was clearly personal: the barriers of mutual enmity divided not only nations, classes, and religions but, aroused by his new love, his family as well. That love, moreover, turned out to have the built-in barriers of Athenaïs's vaginismus. Yet, however tempting it may be to attribute the prophetic voice of social harmony, in his winter lectures of 1849, to the intractability of the obstacles to his personal happiness, it would be myopic to see this as more than a partial explanation. Another, highly important, part was his return, stimulated by his new love, to the social romantic ideal of harmony in humanity and nature that had been central to his work since his encounter with Madame Dumesnil. In the bitter atmosphere of social tension after the June Days, Michelet undoubtedly felt the need to reassert the "Jerusalem of hearts" he had exalted in the federations of 1790, but it was only after meeting Athenaïs that he felt able to do so.[69]

The bond between his restored idealism and his new passion is evident in a summary of January 21, addressed to Athenaïs, of the lectures he was to begin on the twenty-fifth. The poetic tone of this "idea of the course" resonates to a whole century of erotically tinged social prophecy, from the mystical lyricism of William Blake to the Promethean prose of the Saint-Simonians and Walt Whitman:

Oh my fiancée, I shall make you a marvelous bouquet of flowers, such as woman has never received from the hand of man.

Every flower is a new hope of love for the human race. Tomorrow I shall break the barriers that suppress the religions, I shall reconcile the gods and, joining their hands, I shall lead them to the same altar.

Later, I shall break down the barriers that are in the cities and the classes of cities. I shall reveal to rich and poor their community of interests, I shall give to them an immense, inexhaustible source of riches to divide in reconciliation, the fraternal association.

Later, I shall penetrate to the profound, mysterious world of the individual soul and, finding in a soul the barriers and divisions that divided the cities, perceiving in one and the same person factions, civil wars, tyrannies, I shall undertake to reconcile this person with himself; I shall pray him to found in himself a wise and strong republic. And this prayer, my friend, I address to myself. May my poor soul, too saddened, weakened, be strengthened by the very cause of its weakness. If you knew this cause, you would tell me, my friend. Who would know it if not you?

Then, when I have pacified the religions, the cities and the individual souls, then, my friend, I shall also try to pacify what seems to be peace itself: I shall pacify love.[70]

The "idea of the course" became increasingly personal. After granting the mutual goodwill of souls in love and their desire to merge, he admitted that they were sometimes in a state of war caused by "mysterious obstacles, invisible threads woven by jealous powers . . . infinite demands, appropriate to infinite desire."

Approaching these questions "trembling and with a very troubled soul," he addressed to his fiancée the hope "that your young heart . . . constricted until now by the injustice of the world, by the harshness of fate, armed for resistance . . . will disarm, return to nature, soften at the affectionate breath of a heart . . . which loves you with all the love of the world at the same time (love of a lover, mother, wet nurse, and nurse . . .)." In the passage that followed, Michelet revealed an understanding of a phenomenon not formulated theoretically until Wilhelm Reich's notion of character armor: the relation between emotional defenses and muscular rigidity. He may have been referring to Athenaïs's vaginismus. In any case his solution to her rigidity was the one he had learned for his own, at the moment of Madame Dumesnil: acceptance of maternal love.

I hope that the painful contraction that was in you for such a long time will dissolve in the embrace of a friendship so tender that you will increasingly say: "What need do I have to be armed. The world is no longer at war. The world is my friend in whom I am enveloped. His heart is for me like a wet nurse's cradle. I feel everywhere around me the gentleness, the friendly warmth. I renounce everything I had of effort and virile defense and I relax. I achieve peacefully my nature as a girl and a woman. I really want it, since in him I have a mother. I want to become a child again."[71]

Just before his first lecture on January 25, Michelet invoked the barriers his love was to dissolve: "hatreds of race, hatreds of peoples, hatreds of class, hatreds of family," following this litany, "alas," with "this absurd and cruel word, sharper than death: hatreds of lovers, hatreds of love."[72] At one point, he even equated "the fury of class war, which we have just seen with horror in June," with "imperious violence or bitterness in the family." On the twenty-third, retreating from his total absorption in her person to his old sense of social mission, he pleaded with Athenaïs to give him the power to expand his love for her from its unique origins to the world whose wounds cried out for it: "Let it ['this force of love'] . . . efface the hatreds, let it commence on this poor bleeding earth a great sea of love and consolation, the fecund mother of milk from which India assures the birth of the young worlds, the best gods and the gentlest of men!"

The return to the image of India as the "fecund mother" of the world is the clearest indication of the direction of Michelet's thought under Athenaïs's influence. In spite of his quarrels with her and his fears about the physical side of their marriage, in spite of the rupture with his daughter and son-in-law and the darkening political horizon, his love for her induced a hopefulness that would allow his "matriarchal" ideal of harmony to shape his ideas for the next year and a half. This changed after their infant son died in August 1850. But until then, a politics of hope—adapted to the dwindling perspectives of the Second Republic, but hope nonetheless—inspired him.

A letter to Noel on the day after his first lecture revealed the fruits of this optimism. It gave Michelet the hope of reconciling the terrible rift in his family. Noel, who could be heard "gliding above our troubles down here like the consolatory violin of the great curé of Meudon [Rabelais]" was not to conclude that conciliation was impossible, for "one morning we shall become reconciled, we shall throw ourselves in each others arms." In addition, his new love served as an extra bond with his young audience, he told Noel. After addressing his faithful auditors, whom not even the cannon of civil war could keep away from his lectures,[73] after invoking "the living tradition of the Collège de France . . . this rare originality of illuminating the crowd with the mysterious light of intimate affections," he had spoken directly to his fiancée: "I see here young hearts, born yesterday to the new faith, who have told me: We shall follow you always and despite everything, both in your doctrines and in your destiny, at the onset of a barbaric age, hostile to free thinkers. We *shall follow you in liberty and fatality.*"[74]

The reference to "liberty" and "fatality" does not signify a return to the harsh antagonisms of Michelet's earlier period.[75] The underlined words were Athenaïs's, written first in her acceptance of his marriage proposal and repeated in the letter she wrote him after Alfred's missive requesting her disappearance from his life: she was unaware that her future husband's work was less than a seamless web. In fact, just before his lecture of February 15, in acknowledging the dependence on her of his new intellectual work, Michelet suggested by his metaphors that imbeddedness in nature was no abhorrent fatality, as in his "Introduction" of 1831, but the condition of creativity. Apostrophizing his fiancée as the "dear tyrant of my thought," he explained: "Your innocent tyranny . . . is the tyranny of the earth over the plant, without which it would have no place to take root, the tyranny of the light without whose gentle rays it would die. Tyranny? No, rather: the gentle empire of nature. You are now my nature and in you I live. You are still more, a nature superior at several points, luminous, whole, and young, looked up to by my own, from the inferior and rough path of work and production on which I am marching."[76]

That this nearly symbiotic absorption in Athenaïs's higher nature brought back other aspects of the strange natural philosophy he had learned at Madame Dumesnil's deathbed is shown by a letter from this period to a bereaved doctor whose fiancée had just died. Moved to tears by the letter of the unknown physician, a disciple of his through his books, Michelet confided in him his serene trust in nature and divine providence:

> Do not think, I beg you, that death dissolves individuality . . . We are visibly mere beginnings here, fetuses of the life to come. Everything shows that we are on our way there. If the fetus could reason in the womb, it would say: "I have organs that are useless here . . . Therefore, I shall go elsewhere, I do not belong here. Therefore this rough and sad passage which makes me fall so cruelly from my gentle, warm home into the cold, into life, is not an end but a beginning." . . . Yes, Monsieur, your fiancée lives elsewhere, I insist on believing . . . Nature would be too barbarous if it exhausted its forces by bringing its masterpiece to life and then breaking it.[77]

Michelet's optimistic Deism, mixed with the biology of the romantic age, makes this a most revelatory letter. It reminds us both of the strange thoughts Jean Reynaud's article "The Heavens" had inspired in him at Madame Dumesnil's deathbed and of the belief in reincarnation he had expressed in *Le Peuple*. He supplemented these notions interestingly in his journal on the day he sent the letter. After outlining the principle that life proceeds from molluscs to men to "higher life—angels, if you like," and that this is a process of individuation leading, through the brief transition of death, to ever more distinctive, effective, creative, and "divine" characters, he wrote:

> Every time we climb to a higher degree, by tearing ourselves from the soft nature in which we were imbedded, there is something like parturition [*accouchement*], the moment of the sword, of hate, or of death, in relation to the earlier condition ... The sublimity of this progressive march ... is that to the extent that we attain—at the price of a moment of death, hate, war, or criticism—a higher stage in life, to the extent that we become more powerfully original ... we become nonetheless more easily sympathetic, more capable of heartfelt solidarity with other existences; we are free of them through the vigor and originality that distinguish us, and are tied to them by the gentle and free servitude of pity, of benevolence.[78]

The notion of accouchement appeared in Michelet's journal at the time of Madame Dumesnil's death. Derived from Ballanche, it telescoped to one process the notions of birth and death. Tied in with the notion of reincarnation, this philosophic spiritualism echoed widespread beliefs of European popular cultures which saw—just as the Indian text cited by Michelet in *Le Peuple*—children being born with the souls of deceased grandparents.[79]

It is nonetheless fascinating to see the twist Michelet gave this notion, his implicit application of it to less drastic situations than literal death and rebirth. For the idea in the last sentence, that the attainment of a more elevated condition of life—"at the price of a moment of death, hate, war, or criticism"—leads to more powerful originality, as well as to "the gentle and free servitude of pity, of benevolence," certainly could be applied to his relation to Athenaïs, to his feeling of new creativity, and to his painful rupture with Alfred and Adèle. It suggests his more general inclination noted above[80] to view liberation from his formal and biological ties as the precondition of his creative freedom and individuality. To the ambivalence that accompanied his farewells to his mother, first wife, and father, we have now to add his painful departure from Adèle and Alfred, some six years before his daughter's actual death.

The renewed intellectual vigor that accompanied this liberating negativity included a return to another of the ideas he had broached in *Le Peuple,* the right to freedom of the nationalities oppressed by the European powers. On February 5, he sketched "the secret idea of the next lecture," which was "to intervene in favor of races purported to be barbaric, which still exist and which European barbarism makes disappear every day." Apart from fitting into the scheme of his lectures, this emphasis on oppressed nationalities signaled Michelet's turn from the domestic political scene, which he had come to view as hopeless, toward the struggles for independence of the subject peoples in the Habsburg and czarist empires. On the day before he married the young woman for whose love and companionship he was prepared to surrender so much of his past, he wrote a reflective journal entry on the pieces of his life he was leaving behind in which this shift is discernible.

Michelet wrote this lyrical farewell to his twelve years at the rue des Postes shortly before he left it on the morning of March 11. After evoking hurriedly the books he had written there and his memories of his wife, father, daughter, and son, of the brief passage of Madame Dumesnil, and of the adoption of Alfred, he said he had been uprooted by two hurricanes. One was the June uprising and the social hatreds that followed, which revealed the impotence of the university-bound idealism he represented. The other, apparently the alternative to his moribund populism, was falling in love with Athenaïs, which he described as "the natural effort to renew life, the impulse of my heart toward my new child ... so suffering." While healing her, he wrote, he healed himself.[81]

Toward the end of this valedictory, he naively signaled a second alternative to the hopelessness of civil discord in France by reporting the visit of a giant young Polish nationalist Mickiewicz had sent to him, a "good augury." The young man symbolized the "sister nations," in which Michelet, inspired by his new love, would subsequently invest his social hopes: "If only I can live and work again! I shall perhaps have the happiness of doing something for you, of meriting, for her and for me, your benedictions."

Before reaching this herculean symbol of the oppressed nations, Michelet continued the metaphor of meteorological violence with which he had introduced the poisons of social strife and their remedy, Athenaïs. In three paragraphs of unusual intensity, he expressed his inner turmoil through his perceptions on his last walk home from the right bank of the Seine and the resolution of this turmoil in the fire of his new love:

The setting sun yesterday was a striking red, splendid, and mysterious. It was on the heights of Passy, seen from the Pont de la Concorde, not the effect of an aureole, as often happens, but of a furnace over which a vaporous and fantastic cylindrical cloud hovered. All this setting sun burned, but burned in vapor, in cloud, and dream.

All this had disappeared when I arrived opposite my Pantheon, cold, austere, more than ever under the glacial wind of March. It looked at me again. And me, I saluted it. Farewell my serious friend, farewell, without rancor. If I were of stone and marble like you, if I had your solidity, I would be content to be strong and fixed to the same place. I am a man and I have a heart. This heart, so often wounded, both by history and by itself, let it be. Let it beat on, let it associate its youth, obstinate with sentiment and ideas, to the youth of the times that is in this new flower, noble too, fecund too, though more fragile than you. Stone is no longer enough for me. Let her be my temple and my altar.

And tomorrow I shall sacrifice at it. Let my flame, plunged in her flame, augmented by her young and mysterious powers, be a conflagration! Stormy, no matter, like the one I saw last night, in the sky of the setting sun. May this great flame of love, if it does not devour me, bring life to this languishing world and warm the nations.

He concluded his valedictory to the rue des Postes by evoking the echo of his footsteps in the courtyard, which tomorrow would be silent, the empty rooms, the extinguished lights—and his cat: "My cat came up to me, visibly disquieted by this move that is depriving it of the furniture it loves and as if saying:—*What does all this mean? And us, what is to become of us?* I answered in myself and without talking.—*We shall become new and young; with this young mistress, so wise and so tender, what is there to fear? Let us enter with confidence this vita nuova.*" The celebration of a vita nuova was whistling in the dark, and Michelet knew it. The same morning, Victoire heard him, distraught and alone in his study, repeating, "Ah! c'est cruel!"[82]

The marriage, witnessed by Béranger, Quinet, Mickiewicz, Lamennais, and Michelet's lifelong friend Hector Poret, took place on March 12, 1849.[83]

CHAPTER 18

TOWARD THE COUP,
1849 – 1851

Echoes of a Marriage: The Matriarchal Principle
Returns in Michelet's Historical Vision

Michelet's life in the nearly three years between his marriage to
Athenaïs and the Bonapartist coup of December 2, 1851, was punctuated in the summer of 1850 by the birth and death of his infant
son, Yves-Jean-Lazare. In the period before the baby's birth, though
it was filled with difficult moments, Michelet developed further the
ideology of social harmony that accompanied his courtship and
marriage, a return to the "matriarchal" openness to nature that had
dominated his historical vision between 1841 and 1846. The death
of his infant son hardened his mood—primed him for the coup and
the personal privations to come. But the eighteen months before
that death were a prolonged honeymoon in which even his political
perspective was hopeful. Inasmuch as neither the France of the First
Republic, in which he was immersed by his writing, nor that of the
Second, in which he lived, gave him grounds for optimism, he was
inclined in both cases to shift his vision over the borders to the rest
of Europe, where the love of liberty was stronger, he felt, and the
principles of revolutionary fraternity were maintained.

Michelet's optimism, however was no longer focused on the
political revolution but on the social and religious one he had begun
to propagate in his note on method. If his father's death had temporarily obscured for him the "matriarchal" naturalism he had
learned through Madame Dumesnil, if the June fratricide had battered his social idealism, his love for Athenaïs restored much of the
conviction of an imminent social harmony that had permeated *Le
Peuple* and his chapter on the federations. More than ever the social

prophet, he continued in spring 1849 the lectures on ancient religions begun in May 1848. Just before his marriage, he had been preaching anew the doctrine of harmony that had inspired his course on the students a year before. He began a course on the education and social role of women in December 1849, and in the spring of 1850 his subject was the need to transform human personality to avoid the moral bankruptcy that had afflicted all previous revolutions.

Even the leaden disappointments of this year and a half could become, through the alchemy of his new love, sources of creativity. Shortly after marrying Athenaïs, he was notified that the new head of the Collège de France, from whom he had anticipated trouble, had submitted an unfavorable report on his teaching to the Ministry of Public Instruction: he lectured too infrequently and his course was being used for political demonstrations.[1] Though inclined to restrain his anger for fear of hurting his son-in-law's career—Alfred replaced Edgar Quinet in the collège after Quinet was elected to the National Assembly—Michelet nonetheless answered the administrator's implicit reprimand by writing a polemical piece, "History of the Collège de France to 1849." He modified this draft in the following weeks into a plan for a work on the means and ends of education, which, though he put it on the shelf at the end of March, twenty years later became his philosophy and history of pedagogy, *Nos fils*.[2] His teaching in the year and a half before his child's death similarly served as the basis for three other books he wrote during the Second Empire. His lectures on ancient religions became the framework, in 1864, of his *Bible de l'humanité*, and his courses on overcoming social barriers to mutual love and on the upbringing and character of women, became the respective bases for *L'Amour* (1858) and *La Femme* (1859).[3]

The impression of a return to "matriarchalist" principles in this period is reinforced by a comparison of a journal entry of March 28, 1849, with his notes of two years earlier for a Collège de France lecture. In both places he used the images of a geometric reorganization of reality with ruler and compass and of Judea as the mother of Christianity, but the values associated with these symbols were reversed.

In the lecture notes of 1847, written a few months after his father's death, Michelet's theme was the need to cut loose from history and all the positive imagery was paternal. He invoked "our fathers" of the Revolution, whose great achievement on the night of August 4 was not the abolition of feudal privilege but the replacement of the age-old provincial organization of France by the new departmental one. Although necessary for national unity, dismemberment of the old provinces, to which the revolutionists were sentimentally attached, was seen by them as impossible. Nonetheless, "The priest Sieyès coldly takes a compass, a ruler, and makes the departments—the legist Thouret executes.—Cut one's father in pieces! . . . wait, he's going to revive, *whole* and young. This dismembering is the path of unity. *History killed,* history begins. The *provinces killed,* France is born."[4]

In this metaphoric view of dissecting the old provinces, the patricidal means serves the resurrectionist end. The father, France, was ill, and the son's surgery, cutting him to pieces, had the miraculous effect of restoring him, "whole and young"—another example of *accouchement.* As a similar case of a necessary break with history, Michelet cited Jesus' rejection of his mother, identified with the Jewish nation. This rejection heralded no subsequent resurrection of the mother but rather the—presumably comparable—abandonment of the Catholic church as a marâtre: "A Jew says to Judea, which comes to arrest him at the Temple in the shape of his mother: What have I to do with you?—a profoundly revolutionary word . . . What, this great Jewish history will not hold him back? What, this tender and venerable mother! . . . Well! What he says to his mother Judea, we say to the Middle Ages our nurse, our mother . . . harsh nurse, terrible mother! *What have I to do with you?*"[5]

In his journal of March 1849, Michelet repeated both the geometric image and the reference to Judea as mother, but he reversed the value signs. He ascribed the manipulation of "ruler and compass" to "philosophes" and "utopians," whose "infantile" effort to determine future growth "would make circles, square, and regular geometric shapes which life never produces, apart from minerals and certain inferior classes of animals." In contrast to these pathetic efforts, he argued, "nature, all-powerful Circé . . . would throw out millions of profoundly organized beings, admirably varied, of men and women, of fruits and flowers, a prodigious rainbow of energetic and charming lives, lives of individuals and of peoples." The celebration of natural fecundity, keynote of Michelet's refound romanticism, thus replaces the "infantile" geometric efforts to reorder the world of those he had earlier called "our fathers."

A following paragraph, "Contre le chrétien," bears comparison with his earlier depiction of Jesus' rupture with Judea. Here, too, he presented Judea as Christianity's mother, but now he emphasized the naturalness of her maternity, her fecundity, rather than her quality as "harsh nurse, terrible mother." Attacking Christianity for its pretended uniqueness, he questioned the Christian's scornful dismissal of other religions as "inferior brothers" and asked, "What if, going further back, you discover that your brothers are your fathers! Are you sure that Judea produced you unaided?"

The celebration of "all-powerful Circé" had its limits, however, particularly in view of the remoteness of Athenaïs's "fecundity" during the first six months of their marriage.[6] On March 25, curiously anticipating Freudian ideas on repression and sublimation, Michelet distinguished three approaches to "the passions." One was to suppress them, to "castrate nature"—the method of Christianity. A second was to use the passions directly, as in the system of Fourier. Both approaches were unacceptable: "By addressing the enemy, the flesh, directly, they cultivate and strengthen it, exaggerating its importance." The third approach, clearly his own, was what Freud was to call sublimation, the silencing of the passions "by the energetic employment of force and life."[7] In a passage that shows his proximity to the Promethean, productivist ethos both of the Saint-Simonians and of many idealistic liberals and democrats in the nineteenth century, he argued that the flesh "was weak in the heroic age when man conquered the earth. Let it be weak in the new heroic age, when it is a matter of conquering the earth more profoundly and converting it for mankind! In the heroic age, it is neither amputated nor suffered. It is silent."[8]

Thus, alongside the invocation of natural forces, Michelet appealed to his creative powers to sublimate—and silence—his carnal impulses, a reasonable solution to the literal barrier, in Athenaïs's physical condition, to their expression. The character of his scholarly work on the French Revolution put an additional claim on those creative powers. Having always prided himself on the link between his life and his work, he now had to contend with the discrepancy between them. "My contradiction," he wrote on June 2, 1849, "Spiritual condition completely Oriental, gentle and religious, pacifist (I couldn't watch a caterpillar get killed)—and I am obliged to describe the battle of '92."[9]

His artistry was indeed now being put to the test, for in books VII and VIII, which he wrote in the first year of his marriage, there seemed little basis in his current life for empathy or projection. Covering the tumultuous events between August and November 1792, he had to discuss everything from the attack on the Tuileries and the subsequent jailing of the king to the rupture, shortly before Louis's trial, that split Danton from the Girondins: the frenetic fear of invasion that plagued the revolutionaries after the sacking of the Tuileries, the September massacres of aristocrats and priests in the prisons of Paris, the beginning of civil war in the Vendée, and the first military victories of the Revolution at Valmy and Jemmappes. Yet, even in his "oriental" cast of mind, Michelet could find both in his personal condition during 1849 and in his political environment sources of inspiration for much of his labor on the Revolution.

Some of these were negative. There can be little doubt that the continued Catholic piety of his chaste bride, the uncertainty she expressed, nearly two years after having read his book on the priest, over the violence of his attacks on the Jesuits,[10] contributed to the acid portrayal of the priest-woman connection as the key to the revolt in the Vendée.[11] And his concern about the lesbian inclinations of aristocratic women, first brought home to him by Athenaïs's account of Princess Cantacuzène, resonates in the passage on the September massacres, where he describes the crowd's "obscene and ferocious curiosity mixed with hatred" for the imprisoned Madame de Lamballe, former counselor, confidante, and "something more" of Marie-Antoinette.[12]

Michelet's interpretation of the September massacres also reflects his political perspective at the moment he wrote about them: June 1849. The repression of a left-wing revolt against Louis-Napoléon's military support for the pontiff in that month deeply impressed him. From then on, he tended to shift his revolutionary hopes to the risings of the Italians and other oppressed peoples. Both his political writing in the latter part of the Second Republic and his scholarly work on the Revolution reflect this shift.

Michelet seemed largely unaware of the rapid spread of socialist influence in 1849 and 1850. More attuned to the Revolution's defeats than to its successes, he referred several times in his journal to young disciples who were imprisoned either for literary incitements to revolt or for their part in the abortive rising against French intervention in Rome.[13] Another of his young friends, part Rumanian and married to a Hungarian, who died of tuberculosis after participating in the Hungarian resistance to the Austrians, was memorialized in the *History of the French Revolution* as an example of the international support for French ideals.[14]

Indeed, the European echo of the February Revolution increasingly became the repository of Michelet's politics of hope as his faith in the durability of the Second Republic crumbled. His political convictions during the four years of the republic took on book form only once, in spite of numerous plans and false starts: about half of what in 1854 would be his *Légendes démocratiques du Nord,* the part dealing with Poland and Russia, was published in 1851.[15]

Before his interest had reached this intensity, we can trace in his history of the Revolution both his domestic disillusion and his interest in revolutions elsewhere. I have mentioned his turning, in autumn 1849, from the bleak negativity of the France of the Vendée and the parliamentary quarreling of 1792 to the "love" that inspired both the revolutionary armies and the enthusiasm that greeted them abroad. How closely he modeled this love on that which Athenaïs inspired in him is evident in the chapter "The World Gives Itself to France." Just as Michelet took on a consciously maternal role in caring for his sickly young bride,[16] what decided France to liberate and protect the French-speaking peoples of Belgium and Savoy "was the salvation of these peoples themselves. Young, mere children in liberty, they could only preserve their freedom through the aid of the great nation. To leave them to themselves was to let them perish . . . France must at any cost open her bosom." Rebellion against the nation was tantamount to matricide. The Vendée was "so bizarrely misled that it [took] up arms against the Revolution, its mother."

The coupling of the maternal principle with the religious concept of salvation (*salut*) represents the positive inspiration he drew from his life in 1849 for his chapters on the Revolution. The death of his father had led him to begin his magnum opus with a radicalization of his anti-Christianism, a refusal of reconciliation between the Revolutionary religion of justice and the Christian one of arbitrary grace. When in September 1849, after a long estrangement from his subject, he decided to focus on those aspects of it that harmonized with his love for Athenaïs, he injected into the beginning of book VIII references to Christianity that seem like an unconscious revision of the harsh antinomy of 1847. Perhaps through an impulse to compete directly with the Christian faith still professed by Athenaïs, perhaps as an echo of the "romantic heresy" of the period,[17] in which the people were given the redemptionist role of the suffering Christ, he repeatedly described the mission of France among the people in 1792 in terms borrowed from the Gospels: "For three years, she [France] had made into laws the wisdom of the ages; she had already suffered for these laws, earned with her blood . . . and tears. These laws, this blood and tears, she gave to all, saying 'It is my blood, drink.'"[18] And: "The world of the poor and the slaves, the people of those who weep, shook at this great sign; they read there distinctly what Constantine had earlier read: 'In this sign, you shall conquer.'"[19]

Within France, the Revolution took over the salvationist role. Instead of a carpenter, Michelet incarnated the savior in a simple tailor, Leperdit, the republican mayor of Rennes who had saved his city from both the Vendée and the Terror and who answered the furious crowd that stoned him during a famine: "I cannot change stones into bread . . . But if my blood can nourish you, it is yours to the last drop." At which, Michelet assures us, his assailants fell to their knees. Extrapolating from Leperdit's example and rejecting the reproach that the Revolution was not Christian, Michelet presented it as the savior incarnate: "From what has the world lived, if not from the blood of France?" In a passage that recalled the heroic terms of his Introduction of 1831 but undercut the antithesis established in 1847 in the first volume of his work, between Christianity and the Revolution as rival religions, he now argued that the Revolution "was ultra-Christian; she performed the acts that Christianity should have done." The priest, by contrast, had become anti-Christian: "Through the peasant, he waged the ultra-pagan war which would have reestablished the feudality, the domination of the earth over man and of matter over spirit."

Although the general tenor of Michelet's thought between his marriage and the birth of Lazare was a return to the naturalism of *Le Peuple,* his emphasis on sublimation as the answer to his blocked libido led him in this passage to condemn again the dominion "of matter over spirit": an apparent echo of his antinaturalism of 1831. Yet in many respects, he had grown beyond the stark simplicity of this early statement. The ideal of nurturant maternity reappeared at the end of this chapter in the image of a France indeed able to "change stones into bread," to feed an ever larger population.[20] And the joyous fraternity of the federations, whose maternalist overtones of mutual nurturance and love I have noted, appears transfigured in the brotherhood of the untrained but victorious revolutionary armies of 1792: "The federations of '90 had foreshadowed this. When one saw a whole canton, sometimes a whole department in arms, around the altar, it was not difficult to predict the immortal demi-brigades of the Republic. And when one saw the immense federations which united several departments at once, and these grand corps of fédérés, who, increasing continually, held hands and formed across France the choruses and farandoles of the new friendship, one could comprehend that these men in '92 . . . would constitute our great military federations."[21]

Revolution and Christianity Reconciled

Michelet's discussion of the period from the September massacres of 1792 to Thermidor (July 1794) contained only one bright spot: the heroism of the Revolutionary armies and their young generals. All the important domestic events—the trial and execution of Louis XVI, the Robespierrist purges, and finally Thermidor—he portrayed with the solemn majesty of a Greek tragedy, moving the protagonists, Robespierre and Danton, inexorably to their deaths.

Multiple layers of interpretation, explicit and implicit, political and psychological, collective and individual, are contained in Michelet's narrative. The political explanation for the bankruptcy of revolutionary ideals is explicit: at the individual level, a failure of decision-making, and at the collective one, the disappearance of the Revolution's popular base—the mass participation that pushed the Robespierrist faction of the Jacobins into power in 1792–93. Psychologically, in his focus on the moral decadence that accompanied and supported the Terror, he suggests a collective psychodrama of guilt and projection behind the accelerating malignancy of the purges; he also provides a fascinating and revelatory interpretation, at the individual level, of the political failure and death of the Jacobin tribune Georges Danton, with whom he identified.

Michelet's ability to draw on his troubled personal and political experience for his interpretations was often a source of strength rather than weakness. To establish the framework for the decomposition of the heroic Revolutionary idealism of 1789–90 into the Terror and collective apathy of 1793–94, for example, he redefined, midway through his book, the revolutionary ideal of justice to contain, rather than oppose, the ideal of Grace.[22] Significantly, the generous notion of a harmony between these antagonists arose during the optimistic period of his finally consummated love for Athenaïs and his anticipation of her giving birth, and it received its most elaborate formulation during the brief life of his infant son.

Eleven days before the baby's sudden death, he was planning his *Bible du peuple* (later the *Bible de l'humanité*). In preliminary reflections on the difficulty he had in writing "popular" books, he commented insightfully on the relation between his life and his work in the preceding year. "Love, spurred on by privations, always at the edge of a happiness which I rarely touched, made me very productive. Repelled by envious nature, perhaps by Providence, I extended my love into the chant of my thought. One thing, however, was lacking ... It was the gentleness, the calm and the grace, this dew of God, which perhaps alone makes books truly popular."

Presumably reflecting his newfound "calm and grace," his *Bible of the People* was to trace a double development of human history: toward individuality and toward fraternity. Reformulating his notion of the two sexes of the spirit, he saw these two goals as being accomplished by religions he characterized as male and female: "Male religions, heroic, which organize individuality ... through law"; and "female religions, which organize sociability, prepare fraternity ... by grace."[23] An introductory part, showing the two religions at the end of the ancient world, was to discuss "its male genius: Rome and the law, and its female genius: Christianity and grace." A section on the prerevolutionary history of the French nation would show the struggle between "law and grace, individuality and sociability, without fraternity yet emerging." And a section on France since 1789 would demonstrate "how the Revolution is working to reconcile law and grace in a true marriage of the two principles which have alternated and fought until now."

Michelet had earlier sketched an integration of the "paternal" and "maternal" principles that inspired his historical vision. In the "note on the method,"[24] a first, heroic-individualist phase of the

Revolution, political and built around the ideal of justice, had to be followed by a second, nurturant-fraternal phase, social and religious in character and built on the principle of mutual love. But in the passage I have cited, written in the euphoria of Lazare's fleeting existence, he went further and in a world-historical framework for the two phases of the Revolution actually accepted his old enemy, Christianity, with its principle of Grace, as a legitimate expression of the "female genius" and a worthy precursor of the revolutionary religion of fraternity. The sketch of August 13 also makes it evident that he himself viewed the fraternal epiphany of the federations in terms of "female religions" of sociability and grace.[25] In the second half of the *History of the French Revolution,* this restated ideal illuminates brilliantly the ensuing night of revolutionary Terror and human failure.

The Revolution slowly collapsed, Michelet thought, because it could not sustain its original ideals of liberty in law and fraternity in mutual nurturance. He attributed this failure in part to the lack of an educational, spiritual, and psychological infrastructure to carry these ideals to fruition, in part to the terrible pressure of the first revolutionary wars against the European powers, and in part to the political and human failure of those who best incarnated the ideals of the Revolution: the Girondins, the proto-socialists of the Commune, and Danton and Desmoulins.

Proposals for free secular education—Condorcet's and Lepeletier's—were intended to replace the antipatriotic and authoritarian church schools by a republican school system, but these proposals were too little and too late. The entire educated class had been brought up by the church, which meant that even the Jacobin leadership of the Revolution, especially Robespierre, took on priestlike, authoritarian attributes and became increasingly susceptible to traditional Catholic influence.[26] In his discussions of the Festivals of Reason and the Supreme Being, Michelet traced the gradual return, alongside the new cults celebrated by the revolutionaries, of the older religion. If a few, such as the humanitarian Deists of the Commune and the strongly anticlerical Danton and Desmoulins, were more resistant to such a restoration of church power, time would reveal even here certain fatal weaknesses. Much depended on the steadfastness of Danton and Desmoulins, in Michelet's view. As against the growing irrationality of the Terror, these and a few others were the very incarnation of the "Revolution of clemency," which he saw as indispensable for the fulfillment of the revolutionary notion of justice and for opening the path to the religious and social transformation he saw as the necessary next step of the Revolution.[27]

Michelet showed a shrewd practical grasp of political tactics in his depiction of the protagonists of the revolutionary drama and their maneuvers. The focus on individuals, though it detracts from the role of the anonymous masses, presumably the true hero of his tale, does serve as a lesson in the meaning of power. Sending up trial balloons through others, choosing the right moment to say nothing or be absent, was often more useful to someone like Robespierre than the oratorical talents of a Danton. By his scrupulous analysis of motives, moreover, Michelet brought home to his readers the complexity of human character and avoided simple good-versus-evil dichotomies: even Robespierre and Saint-Just, whom he generally disliked, emerged as quite human.[28]

Overshadowing the personalities, tricks, and rhetoric of the parliamentarians nonetheless remains the larger question of the role of the revolutionary masses. Michelet pursued this in detail, analyzing both the participation in the "journées" of the Revolution, like the storming of the Bastille and the Tuileries, and the forms of popular organization: the clubs, the sections, and the Commune. He concluded that the last more or less spontaneous and massive involvement in the Revolution by the people of Paris was the attack on the Tuileries of August 10, 1792, when sansculottes radicals, convinced that Louis was betraying the Revolution to the Austrians, forced the National Assembly to imprison the monarch. Thereafter, exhaustion from the war and the prolonged subsistence crisis, combined with the Robespierrist purging of the popular leadership, brought about a serious erosion of enthusiasm and participation. If the Robespierrists were in May–June 1793 still able to manipulate an apparently spontaneous mass action to push their incorruptible leader into supreme power, a year later these masses were so apathetic that Robespierre's friends in the Commune and the section were unable to prevent his arrest and execution at Thermidor.[29]

Paralleling the declining energies of the revolutionary mass base in 1793 was an atmosphere of sensuality and corruption, Michelet showed.[30] The heart of this decadence was the complex of cafés, gambling dens, and prostitution around the palatial Paris residence of the duc d'Orléans, the Palais-Royal.[31] In the accents of the lower-middle-class Puritanism of his youth, Michelet asked, "This Palais-Royal, so alive, dazzling with light, luxury, and gold, with beautiful women who came up to you, begged you to be happy, to live, what was it in reality if not the house of death?"[32]

Seat of the dissident, reformist branch of the ruling dynasty, the Palais-Royal had had a totally different meaning in the first years of the Revolution: It was in the Café Foy that the journalist Camille Desmoulins had openly preached rebellion after the sacking of the reformist finance minister Jacques Necker in July 1789—the rebellion that became the assault on the Bastille. Revolutionary men of letters, many of them in the employ of the duke, regularly met in the Palais-Royal in 1789–92. But by 1793, it had become "the dirty, infected, obscure domain of shameful pleasures, where a crowd of men, some counterrevolutionary, others without a party, disgusted, bored, broken by events, void of spirit and idea, had taken refuge." The shameful pleasures were gambling and women, and Michelet reconstructed a Dantean world of feminine evil to explain them. Above a pit of prostitution and debauchery was a demimonde of actresses and *femmes de lettres.* At the top, most dangerous of all, were the salons of young upper-class ladies, who seduced the men of the Gironde by their need and weakness: "They influence by their graces, often still more by the touching interest they inspire, by their fears that one wants to calm, by the happiness they really have in reassuring themselves next to you."

Those best armed to resist the seductions of beauty were helpless. "How do you defend yourself against a woman who is afraid and who says it, who takes your hands, who presses against you: 'Oh, monsieur! Oh, my friend! You can still save us. Speak for us, I beg you; reassure me, see this person, talk to that one . . . You will not do it for others, I know, but you will do it for me . . . See how my heart is beating!'" The cleverness of these needful ladies was diabolical. Idealistic young Girondins from the provinces initially were introduced only to decent, moderate republicans in their salons. At a second visit they would meet supporters of the constitutional monarchy, feuillants, and friends of Lafayette. Only when their hostess had fully gained their confidence would they discover the urbane gentlemen who were their hostess's oldest friends, on whose behalf she was working: royalist spies, intriguers working for the enemy. Thus was the nerve, the political will of the Girondin party broken.

If the imagined dialogue Michelet conveyed in this passage bore a passing resemblance to his own seduction by the weakness and need of Athenaïs, it was for good reason. Though there is no doubt that his republican stoicism had been in combat with his sensuality for decades, nor that his indignation was being fed politically by sentiments that the Second Republic was going to rack and ruin for lack of moral fiber, at the personal level he was profoundly troubled, during the weeks he was working out this chapter, by a notable dearth of physical warmth in his pregnant spouse.[33]

There was a warning of this problem three days after he started writing on "the morals of the Terror," when he praised Athenaïs's "patience and goodness" during intercourse. She "suffered," he wrote, "everything with sweetness . . . looked at the portrait of her father and wept while embracing me."[34] That his acid depiction of feminine weakness as a trap in 1793 coincided with a sudden bitter awareness of the imperfections of his marriage emerges from a journal entry of April 7:

> All these recent days, I have worked relentlessly on the second chapter (Palais-Royal . . .). I completely lost sight of the high regions of love. In this interval I had only one very intense moment. I stumbled on some papers that recalled the violent agitation of my darling in other periods. I contemplated this a while. All this is calmed down? There she is, established in nature? But am I in nature? Am I sufficient to her heart? The barriers which her health placed between us also sometimes filled me with melancholy. Then I dived back, so much the more bitterly, into my Jacobins.[35]

Politically, the spring of 1850 gave Michelet much less reason for personal bitterness than his private life. He was solicited on three occasions between April 5 and 10 to accept the democratic-socialist candidacy in the Paris parliamentary by-elections later that month.[36] As it turned out, Eugène Sue received the candidacy and won. The turning point in the fortunes of the Left, the elimination of the poorest third of the electorate from the voting lists on May 31, was partly the result of conservative fear and vindictiveness after Sue's victory.[37]

Michelet's popularity—and the Left's militancy—apparently had no influence on his pessimistic bent. In the midst of being urged to run, he indicated in his journal a fundamental revision of his conviction that the masses were the driving force behind the Revolution. These, he now felt, had been secondary to "the great and supreme movement from above: conquest of the liberties of the peasant and of the national domains, conquest of the liberties of Europe." Yet the period of Athenaïs's pregnancy and of the brief life of his son Lazare also saw the high point, in his visionary reconciliation of Christianity and the Revolution, of his effort to integrate the antagonistic principles that had earlier shaped his thinking. With the death of Lazare, everything changed radically.

Lazare, Danton, the Hidden Enemy

Michelet invested great hopes in his posterity. His beliefs in the harmony of birth, death, and rebirth, in the divinity of Nature, and in motherhood as the source of social fraternity were all in part contingent on his biological succession: it was no accident that the birth of his grandson had triggered the writing of *Le Peuple*. If the course of the Revolution of 1848 had dented those beliefs, he still retained most of them, along with a vague faith in the common people, in the first half of 1850. When Lazare died, probably through the insufficiency of his nurse's milk, something snapped; Michelet's journal reveals an abandonment of his popular origins and orientation, a sudden fear of plebeian treachery. "To the extent that the social war becomes more acute," he wrote on the day after the baby's death, "there is danger in trusting a wet nurse. It means delivering oneself to the enemy. The wet nurse as well as the domestic servant become impossible."[38]

Compounding the pain caused by the loss of the infant was Athenaïs's insistence on having him baptized before he died. Michelet knew all about Athenaïs's Catholic upbringing and had had more than once to explain his anticlericalism to her. Yet how humiliating it must have been for this freethinker who had long denounced the dogma of original sin and its application to children[39] to be confronted with it in his own most intimate environment. And he had no choice but to submit! He saw the "execrable dogma that damned the innocent" as a returned terror of Athenaïs's childhood that, if defied, would haunt the rest of her life. Though opposed ideologically, humanly he had to give way:

> For myself, at the unanticipated moment that I saw my enemy, the old system, rising from this ambush to take me from the side where I least expected it, I had not a moment's hesitation. In the scales of justice, the mother weighs so much more than the father, she has so much more authority over the creature that has made her suffer (and will make her suffer so much, alas, by regret and memory) that I decided quickly, frankly, against myself. I threw myself with a savage avidity on this bitter chalice, readily filling sorrow with sorrow.

Accepting this "maternal Right," he conceded that others might ridicule his inconsistency and that his moral authority might be damaged. But: "My real value has been augmented."

Michelet's admitted bitterness over abandoning his ideals apparently obscured his feelings about Lazare's death, but amid further justifications of his concession and reformulations of his anti-Christian principles, he briefly broke through to them. Summarizing his thoughts on the long day he spent looking at "the gentle and solemn face" of his dead infant, he wrote, "I felt there so well the grace of the ineffable and holy moment that gave him life, the charm of such a profound moment. I felt there the perfect decency, the loyalty, the purity of his mother. I felt there his future progress, alas, all the germs of the great qualities he will never develop." This last he qualified by restating his beliefs in the immortality and rebirth of the soul, following which he returned to his attack on the dogma of original sin.

After Lazare's death, Michelet took a two-week leave from the National Archives and journeyed with his grief-stricken wife to the forest of Fontainebleau, where he had often sought peace with himself at difficult moments. Much of what he recorded of his thoughts and impressions confirm the notion that the baby's death was a turning point for him. He saw the social crisis of the Second Republic[41] as equivalent to that of the later Roman Empire, when the culture of classical antiquity was being forgotten and the world seemed mesmerized by the new faith of Christianity. He also compared his times "to the period of Shakespeare's death, when the old England, *merry England,* was disappearing for a moment before the somber Puritans." The result of Puritan Christianity was "no more nature; the idée fixe dominates."

In these circumstances, Michelet saw his task as an essentially conservative one, of retaining the link with the cultural genius that prevailed before the rise of Christian asceticism: "The partisans of the idée fixe, of the Christian legend, were ignorant that there were certain things in old Virgil that went beyond Christianity and that were only heard by Dante. The English of Milton's day, partisans of the idée fixe, were ignorant that there was in the old Shakespeare a prophetic gleam that went beyond Puritanism and which has been properly understood only by us, men of the Revolution." Against the new ascetic idée fixe that was about to invade the world, he intended to stay at his post, "to protest in the name of history and of nature, the eternal nature that will return tomorrow." His right to do so, he wrote, came from "my impartial sympathy for the times and for the ideas, the great heart I have for all, the most sacred right, love."[42]

Toward the end of this week in Fontainebleau, he returned, dissatisfied, to his prophetic task. He seems to have been brooding on his frustrated aspiration to popularize his style, to become a Danton of the pen.[43] The message of "human fraternity . . . the law of God," whose explication and propagation he saw as his role, was beyond him, and he now attributed his shortcoming to the two captivities of his spirit: his love for Athenaïs and his profession as historian-artist. His paragraphs on this problem point obscurely to his suppressed resentment of Athenaïs, who could only awaken but not fulfill his desires; to his renewed hostility to her Christian faith; to the Bonapartism that would snuff out the Second Republic fifteen months later; and to his presentiment of what Marx, Nietzsche, Weber, and Georg Simmel have analyzed as reification, the transformation of cultural or spiritual means into ends in themselves:

My spirit is languishing, twice captive, twice bound by carnality, by incarnation. First of all this woman, young and already perfect, who is both my queen and my child, where my being would like to be altogether hidden. And this other mistress, history, its tragic poetry, art and its temptations which charm and enervate. Here are our human conditions, happy and unhappy: we only climb to God by ladders. But these ladders (art and love for example) which elevate and support us, also hold us back; it seems as though our feet are glued to them . . . The need to materialize and incarnate the spirit is the fatality of this world.[44]

Being "enclosed in art and love," he was prevented, he thought, from "climbing," from "enlarging my heart to comprehend the universal love"—that is, from reaching the masses. But even if he could, he feared that the "formulas" and "legends" worshiped by those masses—Napoléon for the men, Jesus for the women—would make them inaccessible to the real message of fraternity.

Michelet was reverting to his idea of the two incarnations, which he had broached just before the June Days, when the enthusiastic Bonapartist demonstrations first shook his revolutionary faith. He had then considered replacing his idealistic vision of the Revolution as the incarnation of Justice with the notion that it led inexorably to the new church, the idolatry of Napoléon instead of Jesus.[45] In the two years since, Athenaïs had entered his life, propping up his shaky faith in the Revolution, restoring its "maternal" components. Only three weeks earlier he had outlined his reconciliation of male religions of individuality and law (such as in ancient Rome) with female religions of sociability and grace (such as in Christianity) through the achievement of true fraternity in the Revolution. But at this point he believed that incarnation and idolatry made fraternity unattainable. The ideals of Rome and Christianity recurred, but as examples of reifications based on human weakness: "Men, little united by the sentiment of fraternity, have had the need to group themselves artificially, either around a social idea (Rome, Athens, the city-Gods) or around a great individuality (man-Gods: Alexander, Caesar, Jesus, Napoléon . . .)."

The death of Lazare, though the catalyst of this new and somber vision, was clearly but one of the forces that energized it. Michelet's physical difficulties with Athenaïs remained a source of concern: her determination to have Lazare baptized nurtured a pessimistic conviction of the ineradicable credulity of the masses and, as is evident through its reflections in his work, caused enormous subterranean disturbances and hidden rancors. And, of course, the steady advance of Bonapartism and Reaction also fed his pessimism. Suffrage had been limited, the Left was in full retreat, the death blow of December 2 was but fifteen months away.

The darkness shrouding Michelet's political and personal hopes in the fall of 1850 was not alleviated by the subjects he had to deal with in his history of the Revolution. Shortly before Lazare's death, he had finished book IX, in which he discussed the trial and execution of Louis XVI. From that point on, the juggernaut of the Terror was in motion. As though the September massacres and the king's execution had concentrated too heavy a burden of patricidal guilt in the revolutionaries, Michelet depicted the events of 1793 and 1794 increasingly as a fatal destiny of fratricide and betrayal. Lazare's death closed off an epoch in his life, as did Louis's in the course of the Revolution. In an eerie homage to the event that had initiated this epoch, the death of his father, he twice had Furcy Michelet exhumed in the weeks after he lost the child, on August 31 and September 11.[46] As part of his broader explanation for the king's execution, Michelet had cited the belief of the Romans that they would endow their capitol with eternal life by burying in its foundations the bloody head of a monarch.[47] Apparently he wanted, at this critical juncture, to reexamine the foundations of his personal republic.

Echoes of these events, feelings, and resentments can be heard in Michelet's narrative of the Revolution. In the first chapter he wrote after Lazare's death, he depicted the assassination of Lepeletier, architect of the Revolution's educational system, by royalist fanatics just hours after the announcement that Louis was to be executed. This gave him the opportunity to insert a violent denunciation of the traditional Catholic view of children and their education: "Barbarous beliefs that slander nature, that suppose the infant guilty at birth of the sin it has not committed . . . this theoretical enormity of believing that a creature so visibly innocent is born a criminal [leads to] this practical barbarism of subjecting it from birth, fatally miserable, to hunger and beatings. Education in the Middle Ages is called . . . chastisement . . . It is nature which is chastised, the work of God, God in his most touching creation. Do you hear the blows, the cries, the tears of these poor innocents? . . . It is a school, the Hell of this world."[48] So much for Athenaïs's Catholic upbringing and beliefs in the month after she had persuaded him to baptize their dying child.

In Michelet's description of Lepeletier's funeral, we see the alternative to this abomination: the slain revolutionary's orphaned daughter would be brought up by the nation, the protective family of all the French. The child of the murdered patriot walked behind his coffin as "the daughter of the Republic, solemnly adopted by France." The "grande Mère," the Republic, further insured that the orphan would be accompanied by other children "in such a way that the adopted one, in these young brothers and sisters that were given to her on this day to replace her father, felt the consolation and the embrace of La Patrie." One can wonder, in this idyllic vision of protected orphanhood, about Michelet's projections. Did he see in the reception of the orphaned child an inverted image of his dead Lazare, rescued from Catholic bigotry by the revolutionary patrie? Did he identify with Lepeletier, the slain revolutionary educator? Or did Lepeletier signify Furcy Michelet, and did Michelet identify himself with the orphaned child, liberated from biological bonds into the great family of the nation? In the unconscious, where contradictions do not disturb, all possibilities were present.

In any case, the clearest projections into his work of Michelet's suppressed rancor about Lazare's baptism occurred only two years later, after the Bonapartist coup, in his description of Danton's end. Even though Danton was not an intellectual but a man of action, tribune of the Revolution, Michelet clearly felt at one with him in his losing struggle against Robespierre, the high priest of revolutionary virtue.[49]

What happened to Danton in the year before his death was, according to Michelet, symptomatic of the weakness of the revolutionaries in general when confronted with the rigid puritanism of Robespierre and the sanguinary fugue of the Terror: "At the point that public business became private business, a matter of life and death, they say: 'Business can wait.' They entrench themselves where they live, take refuge in the family hearth, in life and nature. Nature is a good mother. It will take them back soon, absorb them into its bosom."

The bitter sarcasm we sense behind the last two sentences surfaces in the following paragraph on the death of Danton's first wife. A week after her death, "lost and raging with sorrow, he reopened the earth to embrace in the horror of the funeral shroud, she who had been his youth, his happiness, and his fortune. What did he see, what did he crush in his arms (at the end of seven days!)? What is certain is that she carried him with her."[50]

Michelet's necrophilia, his own distraught digging up of the corpse of his first wife (indeed of everyone he loved who had the temerity to leave this world before him), is well established.[51] Striking in this context is the symbolic character of Danton's despair and the shadow of the legend of the Bride of Corinth—the fatal embrace of the corpse of the beloved—with which Michelet ten years later was to begin *La Sorcière*. There, it was to symbolize the death of nature through the triumph of Christianity. But here, it confirmed the notion that the return to nature effectuated by the tired revolutionaries of 1793 was a return to the womb, to oblivion, to death—a standpoint perfectly compatible with the antinaturalist Michelet of 1831 but hardly of a piece with the reverence for nature that Michelet had since then expressed in *Le Peuple*. What had happened?

The rest of the chapter on Danton's second marriage gives the key. While dying, Danton's Catholic and royalist first wife steered her husband in the direction of a sixteen-year-old girl as reactionary as she herself. Danton was already infatuated with the girl and they married four months after his wife died. The girl insisted, however, that the marriage be performed by a nonjuring priest and that Danton first confess to this priest. Danton, "this serf of nature," more beholden to "the tyranny of blind desire" than to the Revolution whose spirit he bore, went down on his knees in the attic before the priest, "profaning in a single act," wrote Michelet, "two religions at once: ours and that of the past." Then comes the lesson: "Here it is, the new force that is to reign omnipotently in the sanguinary epoch we shall recount: a soft force, a terrible force that dissolves and breaks from within the nerve of the Revolution. Under the apparent austerity of republican morés, amid terror and the tragedies of the scaffold, woman and physical love are the kings of '93. Condemned men were seen on the executioner's cart, uncaring, with roses in their mouths. That's the true image of the period. They lead men to their death, those bloodstained roses . . . Love in '93 appeared as what it is: the brother of death."[52]

In Michelet's description of Danton's immobility in his last months and his consequent impotence in the face of the Robespierrist juggernaut, it was above all the retreat to his second marriage that paralyzed this man of action.[53] His neighbors in the village of Arcis "saw him standing in his night bonnet for hours at his window, dreaming. The fields, nature, love, these were his supports. His young wife of sixteen was pregnant. The soul of Danton was there, absent elsewhere."[54]

The pages devoted to the betrayal of the revolutionary religion in Danton's second marriage, where Michelet focuses on the moral collapse of the great tribune, contain a striking allusion to Desmoulins. Deploring Danton's acceptance of Catholic ritual, Michelet wrote: "Where is it, the altar of the Revolution, where the good Camille, the friend of Danton, had brought his new-born son, giving the first example for generations to come?"[55] If Desmoulins's civic rectitude put to shame Danton's laxity, it also contrasted implicitly with an acceptance of infant baptism by Robespierre discussed later in the book and thus linked Danton's spinelessness not only to an action of his antagonist but to a comparable one of the historian. Michelet, aware of the personal significance of his examples, castigated Robespierre's willingness to be godfather at the baptism of a Catholic Jacobin's child in terms that were far from disinterested: "A serious act, because he was free. In the family, *the mother*, sovereign mistress of a fruit that emerged from her with so much pain, *often forces the philosopher father* to have the child baptized. But here, who forced him?"[56]

Although this is the clearest reference to the baptism of Lazare, it alerts us to the significance, for Lazare's father, of Danton's earlier genuflection, to satisfy his young spouse, before the power of the counterrevolutionary church. Michelet identified with the revolutionary tribune as the incarnation and indispensable stimulus of the popular spirit. His great disappointment, expressed again during the period of mourning for Lazare, was his inability to write for the masses as Danton had spoken for them. Michelet's depiction of Danton's love as the hidden poison that killed the tribune's revolutionary nerve and presaged his death must be seen, then, as a refraction of his fear, after Athenaïs had forced *him* to go on his knees before the clerical enemy, that the absorption of his spirit by "this woman, young and already perfect," was a principal reason for the failure of his role as prophet of fraternity and universal love during the Second Republic. It is in the account of Danton's fatal love in 1793 that we find the real expression of Michelet's suppressed rancor in September 1850, the hidden meaning behind his words: "The need to materialize and incarnate the spirit is the fatality of this world . . . I am enclosed in art and love; and I have difficulty in climbing, in extending love, in enlarging my heart to comprehend the universal love."

PART VI

REVOLUTION UNDER THE EMPIRE

1852 – 1854

The prophet, this hunted, detested man, this pallbearer of Empires, who inters them at their place in the infernal cone excavated by Ezekiel, is so much the more odious since, if one strikes him, the blow will be prophetic and, if one kills him, his death will symbolize the death of a kingdom. One must flee this man-sign, this living menace, or force him into the desert.

MICHELET
Journal

CHAPTER 19

DISMISSAL AND RIOT: ROBESPIERRE

Meanwhile, a world had crumbled.

Michelet formulated his bitter projections into the doomed Danton in 1852, after his own execution as historian by Louis-Napoléon's bureaucrats, after the coup d'état, during his voluntary exile in Nantes.[1] His two dismissals—from the Collège de France and from his position at the National Archives—were representative of the remorseless advance of reaction in the period before and after the Bonapartist coup. His awareness of this helped him, paradoxically, to retie a bond to the social world that had been getting looser since the June rising. It did not happen immediately. The suspension that preceded the first dismissal was echoed instantly in riotous student protests, which the historian disavowed. Nonetheless, this turbulence was a sign of the claim he had on the hearts of his young followers, a claim that in less militant forms he accepted and reciprocated. His reaction to these riots casts an interesting light on his political personality, as well as on his subsequent interpretation of Thermidor.

Michelet's troubles became evident in February 1851, when his student supporters discovered dubious-looking fellows, assumed to be Jesuits or government agents, making word-for-word records of his lectures. Since 1843, his lectures had been subject to disruption by clerical opponents. Old liberal friends protected him in the mid-1840s, and when they failed, more radical elements took up his cause. It was January 1848 before his enemies were able to force his suspension, only to see him triumphantly reinstated a week after the February Revolution had toppled the regime. By 1851, however, Michelet's radicalism and the weakening of the humanitarian leftists he had supported during the Second Republic had again made him an exposed target. Police spies[2] and Jesuits were building a case for an administrative purge, and the defensive reactions of Michelet's student supporters only strengthened their hands.

The students did everything possible to hinder their professor's foes: his disheveled supporters—led by two future left-wing journalists and spokesmen for the Paris Commune, Jules Vallès and Charles-Louis Chassin[3]—arrived en masse an hour before each lecture so as to force their suspiciously well-dressed peers to sit in the back of the hall, where it was difficult to hear.[4] Michelet's jealous guardians were prepared to hurl the Jesuitical-looking, the sarcastic, or even the unenthusiastic out of the hall's (ground-floor) windows. In the last weeks before the suspension, after the right-wing and Catholic press had published distorted summaries of Michelet's lectures,[5] the students were particularly mistrustful: one of the bespectacled fellows they assumed, because of his copious notes and his long black coat, to be a Jesuit agent turned out to be no other than Michelet's ardently republican young friend Emile Ollivier.[6]

The government had several reasons for wanting to purge Michelet. His anti-Catholic vehemence, especially after the death of Lazare, infuriated clerical allies of the ruling party of order. He was, moreover, a symbol of outspoken republican resistance among educators, at a moment when more than a thousand "Montagnard" republicans were being fired from teaching posts throughout the country.[7] Finally, Michelet's courses had become, as at the end of the Orleanist monarchy, a center of student opposition to the regime.[8] Earlier attackers had been unable to find the necessary majority within the self-governing Collège de France to remove Michelet, but by March 1851, so many of his former supporters were cowed by the Reaction that the well-coordinated administrative purge encountered little resistance.

On February 25, Michelet read in the papers about demands for his suspension.[9] On the twenty-seventh, Barthélemy Saint-Hilaire, chief administrator of the collège, attended his lecture, a denunciation of what the historian called the "Byzantine habits" of French public life, and, as if to prove Michelet's point, had a stenographic record made of the lecture.[10] On this basis, the administrator called a meeting of the professors for March 9. Michelet boycotted the purge meeting; he labeled the stenographic record "a grotesque parody of my course" and urged his colleagues to read it and judge for themselves if it conveyed either the style or the tenor of his instruction.[11] Though intimidated, they refused to act in his absence and invited him to attend another meeting two days later. At this assembly, a majority of his colleagues rejected his defense, and he was censured for lending his course "to passion and polemic." On March 13, a ministerial decree suspended his course indefinitely.[12]

Michelet's journal entry that day reported laconically: "Suspension. Burial. I encounter the young people." Seven words that conveyed the bureaucratic execution of France's most important historian of the Revolution, his fleeting encounter with future spokesmen of the Paris Commune—in March 1851 his ardent, if undesired, defenders—and the death of a friend.[13] This is what happened.

The day of the suspension was a Thursday, Michelet's regular lecture day. When Chassin arrived at the entrance to the hall, as usual more than an hour before the 1 P.M. lecture, to weed out *agents provocateurs,* he was confronted by a small handwritten sign: "The course of M. Michelet is suspended until further order."[14] Chassin and company repaired to Vallès's café, where those two militants worked out the text of a petition to the National Assembly, protesting the suspension as a violation of freedom of thought. They signed it, wrote out numerous copies, then returned quickly to the Collège de France to pick up signatures from the angry throng milling at its gates.

Ordered by the police to remove themselves from the street, Chassin, Vallès, and their friends retreated noisily to the courtyard of the Sorbonne and sent out emissaries to collect signatures from the medical and law schools, canvassing the libraries, reading rooms, hotels, and cafés. They then reassembled in the interior court of the Sorbonne, fifteen hundred strong, according to Chassin, to march to the National Assembly.[15] It was raining heavily and the police escort was clearly intended for the protection of the state rather than of the students, who, under their umbrellas, maintained a disciplined, if anxious, silence. After delivering their damp petitions to two left-wing deputies just outside the assembly, the demonstrators marched in ranks of three around the adjacent Palais-Bourbon, where the legislative offices were located. About a third of the participants then walked through the rain over the pont de la Concorde to the right bank headquarters of the republican papers, intending afterward to reunite and march to the home of the purged professor, to bear witness to their solidarity.

At that point, Chassin wrote, "As we were passing the Madeleine and entering the Boulevards, we encountered Michelet in person. He begged us to disperse, otherwise we would compromise everything: ourselves, him, our cause." And their master jumped into a passing coach. Undaunted by this rejection and abrupt disappearance, the dwindling band of disciples shouted, "Long live Michelet! Down with the Jesuits."[16]

By then, only a core group of a hundred remained, and, in spite of Vallès's desire to continue the demonstration at Michelet's house, the others, fearing ridicule, decided to split into delegations that would carry the story to the five most republican newspapers of Paris. Chassin was greeted warmly at *L'Evènement,* run by Victor Hugo's sons and friends and politically sympathetic to the purged historian. Invited to write an account of the protest in the paper's office, young Chassin turned out his first newspaper article, on the revered professor's dismissal.[17]

The results of all this activity were nil. The *chambre* debate that ensued upheld the suspension; according to Chassin, their grounds were that the controversial lectures had become a center for the political excitation of youthful zealots, and that "the celebrated historian, by transforming himself into a tribune, was compromising the dignity and the dearest interests of the Collège de France."[18] The head of the pension where Chassin tutored, seeing Chassin's name on the article in *L'Evènement,* cashiered him on the spot. A student committee, after deciding to support the proscribed professor by a rally at his home, received a letter from him urging them to stop demonstrating and telling them categorically that he would not be home on the day they planned to come.

The committee nonetheless decided to go ahead with the rally, and on the following Thursday, March 20, a band of five hundred gathered in front of the Panthéon, observed by the police and heckled by clerical opponents. At the last minute, accommodating to Michelet's total lack of enthusiasm for their enterprise, they agreed to restrict the visit to Michelet to Chassin and two comrades and to hold the mass rally at the nearby home of Edgar Quinet, known for his greater militancy.[19]

Just as the discouraged students were debating whether to delegate this visit as well to a small committee and to go home, the police began to make arrests, the clerical hecklers began applauding, and a free-for-all broke out among police, students, and hecklers. The attempted march to Quinet's residence that followed disintegrated in the course of repeated clashes with the police. Chassin, having fought his way out of police encirclement and still bearing the letters to Michelet and Quinet, hurried to his friends at *L'Evènement* to flex his literary muscles a second time; he denounced the police, the Jesuits, and Louis-Napoléon, went home to bed, and was arrested at midnight.[20]

Michelet himself, whose martyrdom had originated this insurrectionary skirmish, limited himself on March 20 to the lapidary comment: "La manifestation, malgré mes avis," and four days later asked himself if he should not, after all, have responded more positively to his young friends, have intervened for them. The answer was no: "To all this external movement there is a correspondingly great physical agitation, which I felt in my entrails. Nothing makes one more doubtful of oneself." On March 31, he accepted a personal visit from one of the briefly jailed students, probably Chassin.[21]

Michelet never returned to his chair in the Collège de France. Adèle, dining with him on May 2, told him of the decision to cut off his salary.[22] Barely a month before the coup, Barthélemy Saint-Hilaire informed him he was to be put back on half-salary, a measure he categorically rejected "as long as my chair has not been reopened."[23] It was not.

The purge, together with the reactions to it of the victim and his supporters, cast a long shadow over Michelet for the the rest of his life. From the standpoint of the government, genuinely concerned about his influence on his students,[24] his dismissal may have had the character of an exorcism. Michelet, however, had long ceased to believe in the efficacy of preaching to idealistic but socially powerless young bourgeois, and from the beginning of 1851, he was sending signals to those close to him that the loss of his chair would not be the worst thing that could happen. Noel had received a most revealing letter from him that January: "We are being stupefied by aristocratic entourages or, which is worse, by bourgeois ones. How I would like to take off my shoes and put on boots . . . My book and my course are consuming me . . . for nothing. We don't reach the masses. I aspire violently to descend. For I believe it is to rise. My wife is capable of every sacrifice—both for me and because she loves greatness. We shall ponder the means of becoming great while descending."[25]

Michelet's abrupt rejection of his student's actions had, then, a broader foundation than a simple dislike of extraparliamentary action: he looked forward to being relieved of the obligations of his status—book, courses, entourage—in order to write directly for the masses. That was the theme of one of his last lectures, on popular books as confessions of faith by their authors, and on the day he gave it, Emile Ollivier cited him as having said: "Our present propaganda . . . resembled strongly that which might be made by a man enclosed in a crystal glass. He finds his voice to be resounding and very strong: that's because it breaks against the inner surface. But those who are outside, the men of the people, hear nothing."[26] His plans, immediately after his dismissal, for a series of short popular "legends" on heroes of the revolution in Europe[27] solidified these desires to break the glass, to "rise" by "descent"; at the same time they were an effort to resolve the material problem caused by the loss of one of his two salaries.[28]

We must, then, not be blinded by Michelet's rejection of the students' protest methods. If he no longer had faith in them, it was because he had ceased to believe that they represented the link he sought between bourgeois and plebs. As his letter to Noel makes clear, Michelet felt increasingly that such an alliance was no longer in the offing; rather than preach brotherly love to a bourgeoisie he saw as looking ever more fervently toward the authoritarian "messianism" of Louis-Napoléon, he was inclined to cut loose from the bourgeois world altogether and seek "la chaleur en bas"[29]—the warmth below of the common people—which had been his point of origin.

Nonetheless, there was probably more to Michelet's rejection of the students' protests than a mere refusal to see in his disciples what he had earlier perceived. Much though he may have celebrated the mass attacks of 1789 and 1792 on the Bastille and the Tuileries, in his own lifetime there is not a single example of Michelet actively supporting popular insurrections. When only twenty-two, he was enthusiastic about the student riots protesting the repression after the assassination of the duc de Berry, but his hopes for a revolution excluded the common people ("un terrible auxiliaire"), and he looked to the army for salvation.[30] Journal entries are absent for July 1830 and June 1832, though we know he was happy enough with the *results* of the 1830 Revolution. In 1848 he eagerly greeted the Revolution as the dawn of a new era of liberty and fraternity, but his only direct reaction to street demonstrations, on February 22, was fear that the demonstrators would be annihilated by the army, and in the reflex of one notable appealing to another, he wrote Lamartine, begging him to move the chamber to send in the reform-minded National Guard to save the demonstrators.[31] He viewed the popular invasion of the assembly on May 15, a protest in support of the Polish revolution, as an abomination,[32] and in the weeks before June, though he anticipated nothing of the coming explosion, was so upset by the Bonapartist demonstrations that he began, even before the bloody rising of the poor, to dismantle his ideal of revolutionary justice.[33] The June insurrection was, of course, the bitter end.

There is a peculiar echo to Michelet's association of republican morality with the repudiation of popular violence in his account of Robespierre's exit at Thermidor. In general, when one of Michelet's villains was at the point of death, he metamorphosed into a hero. The case of Robespierre is a noteworthy example both of this metamorphosis and of how spectacularly wrong guesses about historical evidence can be based on the values and projections of historians.

Thermidor—the end of the Terror and of the Robespierrists,

who were at that end its only moving force—occurred for two reasons. First, the wars that had begun at the time of the king's imprisonment in 1792, on the borders and against the counterrevolution in the Vendée, had ended with victories for the French Republic. The summary justice of the Terror was based on the fear that opponents of the revolutionary regime as well as corrupt politicians constituted what we now would call a fifth column in aid of the enemy. The end of the military menace ended this fear. Second, after directing the Terror primarily against left-radicals and Dantonists, Robespierre seemed on the point, in July 1794, of broadening his purges to undefined sections of the Montagne and perhaps even to moderate rightists who had been cowed into accepting the Terror for more than a year. This is what provoked the conspiracy to arrest Robespierre on the floor of the Convention.[34]

Historians generally agree that the results of the plot of 9 and 10 Thermidor to purge the Robespierrists were confused in the extreme. Robespierre was first imprisoned by the Convention late in the afternoon of 9 Thermidor (July 27, 1794), but he was liberated in the evening, after one failed effort, by a delegation from the Commune—controlled by his followers—and brought to the Hôtel de Ville. Apparently, Robespierre opposed his liberation and went only reluctantly to the city hall of Paris. He stayed there for four or five hours, rejoined by his closest associates, who had likewise been liberated from captivity, before an armed force of the Convention invaded the Hôtel de Ville in the early morning hours and recaptured him. Wounded during the recapture, Robespierre was guillotined the next day.[35] On these bare facts, there is a consensus.

Michelet's animus against Robespierre as cold, authoritarian, and priestlike, actually open to a Catholic revival, has been decried by all the supporters of the Incorruptible from Ernest Hamel to Albert Mathiez. Yet even Hamel, worshipful author of the first major biography of Robespierre, saw in Michelet's treatment of his hero's end a "poignant beauty."[36] Michelet squared a circle in describing Robespierre's stoic acceptance of his fate.

According to Michelet, as the armed force of the Convention approached the city hall in the early hours of 10 Thermidor to recapture the errant dictator, he and his inner circle were at odds over what to do. His close followers saw as the only means of escaping execution an appeal to the common people to rise in his defense:

> Saint-Just, Couthon, Coffinhal, nearly all, wanted to act.
>   Robespierre wanted to wait. And whatever one may have said, he had a few reasons on his side. To change roles, to

begin a war against the Law, was it not at this moment to deny his entire life, to erase with his own hand the idea from which he had lived, which constituted all his power? ... On the other hand, after having written to Couthon to come, to have involved so many friends in this peril! ... "So we have nothing left but to die?" said Couthon.

This seemed to shake him for a moment. He took a sheet of paper with the stamp of the Commune on which an appeal to insurrection was already written, and, in a slow, careful handwriting, he wrote three letters that one can still see: Rob ... Having come that far, his conscience revolted and he threw the pen down.

"So write," they said to him.—*"But in the name of what?"*

It is by this word that he assured his doom. But also his salvation in history, in the future.

He died a great citizen.[37]

Seventy-one years after Michelet wrote these stirring lines, Albert Mathiez investigated Robespierre's end.[38] He discovered that indeed a document had been signed with the first two (not three) letters of Robespierre's name. It was, however, not an appeal to insurrection but a hortatory address to the "patriots" of the section of "piques" (Robespierre's own), informing them that Robespierre and his friends were liberated and in the Commune (that is, the Hôtel de Ville), which would henceforth be the seat of "the Committee of Execution that has been created to save la patrie."[39] Judging by the text, and the fact that it was found among the papers of the section to which it was addressed, this exhortation had been sent earlier in the evening, soon after Robespierre arrived at the city hall, and—since it *was* sent—his first two letters were deemed a sufficient signature.

This was, however, not an appeal to insurrection. Mathiez did find reference to such an appeal being drafted in the final moments before the attack on the city hall and, in connection with it, to Robespierre's questioning in whose name it might be issued. In two depositions, one by a pair of gendarmes present during the discussions in the Hôtel de Ville, another by an agent of the Committee of Public Safety, accidentally present, it appears that the "Committee of Execution" had drafted appeals to the people and the army advising them to recognize no other authority than its own and to arrest the Thermidorians behind the purge. When the agent of the Committee of Public Safety entered the meeting room, he heard Couthon say, "We should write immediately to the armies." Robespierre then asked: "In whose name?" Couthon answered: "Why in the name of the Convention. Isn't that where we still are? The rest are just handful of rebels which our armed force is going to take care of." At this point, the deposition went on, Robespierre was thoughtful, and spoke briefly with his younger brother. Finally he said, "My opinion is that we should write in the name of the French people."[40] Thus, no question in the evidence discovered by Mathiez but that the Incorruptible was prepared to invoke the furies of civil war to triumph. Exit the "great citizen."

In Mathiez's analysis of Robespierre's behavior, he agrees with Michelet that Robespierre was initially reluctant to undertake any illegal act and even opposed his own liberation. It was not, however, because of Republic legality, said Mathiez, but because he saw no sign that the Commune had any serious popular support; further, he had hopes of being able to sway the revolutionary Tribunal the next day to turn on his accusers, as Marat had done a year earlier. After some hours in the Hôtel de Ville, Mathiez concluded, he changed his assessment of his chances, saw a reasonable hope of armed resistance to the Thermidorians, and was then prepared to appeal to the army and the populace, in the name of the French people.

Michelet can be forgiven his wrong interpretation of the evidence.[41] He wrote on Robespierre's end a year after his own dismissal from the archives because of his refusal to swear fealty to the dictatorship of Louis-Napoléon. He had taken refuge in Nantes to survive on his sharply reduced income and, no longer having the original documents to puzzle over, seems to have based his account on Lamartine's *Histoire des Girondins*.[42] Yet it is striking how closely his interpretation of Robespierre's end reflected his own principles at the time of his purging, when confronted with the street demonstrations of his supporters: "To begin a war against the Law, was it not at this moment to deny his entire life."

Michelet emphasized the importance of Robespierre for his identity in a moving fragment he wrote after concluding his book: "The largest emptiness at this table . . . from which my book now goes forth and at which I remain alone, is no longer to see my pale companion, the most faithful of all, who from '89 to Thermidor had not left me: the strong-willed man, laborious like me and poor like me with whom, every morning, I had such harsh discussions. The greatest fruit of my moral and physiological study is exactly this dispute, it is to have seriously anatomized Robespierre."[43]

If Michelet's portrayal was a factual error, that error leads us back to a double reality: the reality of his austere republican values, which he projected into the Incorruptible, and the larger reality of

the needs of the moment. Many of the democrats of the second
French republic were in 1853 imprisoned, proscribed, or, like the
purged historian, in voluntary exile, and the legend Michelet em-
broidered of a Robespierre who died "a great citizen" helped keep
their hearts from freezing over during the winter of the Second
Empire.[44]

CHAPTER 20

THE WARMTH BELOW:
LOVE AND POPULISM

Robespierre's republican purity, accepted by Michelet after years of denouncing it as a priestly asceticism, corresponded to only one side of the historian's complex character, the stoical self-chastising side that guided his youth and reemerged after his father's death. The Dantonist side, the mystical appreciation of human fraternity, of the mutually nurturant sociability inherent in the federations, the love of nature and the vision of France as the "good mother," was more important; it reappeared gradually through his popular writings of 1851, in his adumbrations on the religious and social revolution in the last volumes of the *History of the French Revolution* (1852–53), and finally in *Le Banquet* (1854). This was the side of Michelet that continued to make him popular with the often impoverished and bohemian student radicals for most of the Second Empire.

Though Michelet renounced their protests, the students did not feel rejected by him. Chassin, who accidentally encountered him a second time on the day of his suspension in the office of *L'Evène-ment,* asked his assistance in writing a history of his instruction in the Collège de France.[1] Even the skeptical Vallès, who detested the conformist atmosphere of the radicals at Michelet's lectures and shrugged at the professor's hyperbole, had said that "Michelet is one of our own and we have to defend him."[2] This attitude of trust did not change after the rejection. Apart from a temporary decline in Michelet's reputation in the late 1850s, because of his turn toward natural history and his moralizing books on love and women, the journalism of young radicals during the republican revival of the 1860s was replete with acknowledgments of Michelet as one of the Left's titular deities.[3]

Michelet's life and ideas in the period after his suspension were, after all, in a certain harmony with the embittered idealism of the young radicals who had defended him. Immediately after his ouster, he began working on the popular "legends" he had long been contemplating to bring the revolutionary message home to the half-educated urban masses. In spite of the reactionary tide that had purged him, he maintained his faith in the European revolution, as well as in the chances of democratic propaganda in France, and quickly began publishing relatively short articles in the Paris press, particularly in Hugo's *L'Evènement.*[4]

One of these essays, on J.-B. Cousin de Grainville's prose poem, "Le Dernier Homme," is particularly revealing. Grainville was an ex-priest turned revolutionary in the 1790s who was hounded out of a teaching job by the "white" reaction at the end of that decade and lived in poverty and isolation until he committed suicide in 1805. His only known writing was an allegorical vision of the last days of mankind, replete with a returned Adam, volcanic eruptions, and the resurrection of the dead; its basic message was that the survival of humanity through the bitterest of times can be assured only by love but that as long as one man loves one woman, the world could not end.

Clearly, Michelet's enthusiasm for Grainville's poem arose both from an identification with the purged schoolteacher and from passionate agreement with the idea that salvation began with an act of devotion. Now, when his career and the Republic were jointly foundering, the model for salvation would be his love for Athenaïs.

In his commentary on Grainville, Michelet showed the two directions of his love, both based on evocations of the period of his birth, when Grainville wrote his poem. One direction was away from the splendor of the Revolution, toward death and disillusion and the redeeming symbiotic tie to the wife-mother:

> Many men who are still alive, in assembling the memories of their youth, recall without difficulty the infinite sadness of these times. The immensity of the ruins, the loss of so many illusions, the sorrow of so many victims, the mourning for principles that had been immolated and betrayed, the immense legislative Saint-Bartholomew[5] of the best institutions of the Revolution, the Republic itself thrown out the windows of Saint-Cloud . . .
>
> . . . The time of the great destructions of men had begun . . . From victory to victory, from carnage to carnage, the world made its way on the downward slope to nothingness. Some developed a taste for it, raised death to a doctrine. De Maistre

taught us that extermination was the favored doctrine of God. Sénancour wrote on a tombstone his desolate *l'Amour.*

This is the moment when Grainville took up his pen. His book was for him an adjournment of suicide[6] . . . His wife often recounted the evening when Grainville's last pupil left his house. The two old people were seated by the fireplace and from time to time glanced abjectly at each other. The wife's eyes finally filled with tears she could no longer dissimulate. Grainville seized her hand and, striking his forehead as though to hold in place a sudden illumination, said: "Reassure yourself. Give me this useless paper, this ink that they will not use again . . . I will answer to you for the future."[7]

The other direction of Michelet's love was a social extrapolation from it. He saw the physical miseries, the famines of the late eighteenth century, as the consequences of poor agricultural methods, a "sterilization of the soil" that began under Louis XIV. The agrarian reforms of the Revolution laid the basis for a new fertility, but that was felt only after the Revolution itself was dead, with the result that famines, struggles over "the maximum," and bloody grain riots tainted popular memories of the revolutionary years. In reaction to this condition, which seems also to have affected England, there arose a genre, exemplified by the work of Thomas Malthus, that Michelet called the "economy of despair." To avoid the curse of excess population, to "disencumber the rich and the property owner, legitimate inhabitants of the world," Malthus counseled the poor "to live alone, die alone, forbid themselves the consolation of marriage, not to unite, not to love." In opposition to Malthus's "impious" notion that love was an iniquitous luxury, there rose "a hundred voices . . . that were the cry of nature," the first of which was Grainville's. Michelet summarized his poem as "the sublime and tender idea . . . that love is the very life of the world, its entire justification, the *world cannot die as long as man still loves.*"[8]

Clearly, he did not use Grainville's poem simply as an excuse for turning his back on society to enjoy the pleasures of his second marriage (in any case less than abundant). In concluding his article on Grainville, he returned to the stoic posture of his earlier work that would subsequently reappear in his pages on Robespierre's end. Addressing the schoolteachers of the Republic, Michelet wrote that he had been thinking of their miseries while writing of Grainville's. He urged them not to succumb to persecution and humiliation, and he pleaded with them as "the older sons of the Republic, its organs and its voice," to "teach la Patrie," to view their profession as a magistracy and an altar. He promised them "tomorrow

... the first dawn of humanity and justice." And in an obscure warning against the Catholic inclinations of their wives and daughters he closed by saying that when the Revolution returned "your enemies ... will be in your own house."[9]

Michelet's emphasis, in the discussion of Grainville, on conjugal love nonetheless had a strongly apolitical implication; it suggested a withdrawal to the marital bond as an answer to the ills of the world, and for close to a decade after 1854, this tendency was manifested in Michelet's works on feminine character and natural history. Even his resumed history of France showed an increasing obsession with the decadent, morbidly personal aspects of the French monarchy in its last two centuries. His son-in-law never shared his enthusiasm for Grainville. Because he had lost his home, his protector, and his father substitute to the amorous passions aroused by Athenaïs, Alfred probably sensed sharply the asocial implication of Michelet's celebration of those passions in the essay on Grainville and insistently opposed Michelet's plan to use the essay as the first chapter in his projected "Légendes démocratiques."[10]

In response to Alfred's opposition, Michelet dropped the idea of starting his legends with Grainville; instead, he began with a chapter on the generals of the Revolution.[11] Here, too, he made an important change. He had intended to start this chapter with an essay on his favorite military hero, Lazare Hoche, after whom he had named his son.[12] But now he realized that this would reinforce the popular tendency to hero-worship that underlay both the Napoleonic and the Christian legends, and he decided to include Hoche only as one of a "pleiade" of nine or more revolutionary generals; the idea was to emphasize "the plurality, the collectivity."[13] He even imagined a revolutionary monument, constructed from the debris of the Bastille, with "the people" up on top, visibly the only real "hero," and, around its base as defenders of the people, "the glorious garland of the generals of the Revolution, of the ones who, among those made famous by the sword, were nonetheless enemies of military government, sincere servants of the law."[14]

Michelet was thus not only replacing Grainville, celebrator of personal love, with the political legends of revolutionary generals; he was also recasting his propaganda concept to oppose the menace of Napoleonic hero-worship, the "idolatry" or "Messianism" that was gradually replacing his concept of the clerical threat as the most serious danger to the Revolution, as it long had in the realities of French politics. This reflected two deeper-lying changes in his ideas and attitudes after his suspension.

On an ideological level, he was now less gloomily fixed on the double idolatry of the "old" and the "new" church[15] and more inclined to fight them by propagating his ideas of popular revolution; in particular, he emphasized the fraternal, nurturant aspect of those ideals. Hinted at in his Grainville essay, this development is clearly visible in his elaboration of the "religious and social revolution" in the *History of the French Revolution* and *Le Banquet*.

Though too little and too late to stem the Bonapartist tide, this was an important step in the right direction, for a major part of the socialist and working-class Left was taken in by Louis-Napoléon's flirtation with socialist ideas. In the months before the coup, the prince-president played this card strongly, with the conscious intent of winning over or neutralizing the socialist opposition. On the day of the coup, Proudhon sarcastically noted six major issues in which the parliamentary socialists were in complete accord with Louis-Napoléon.[16] And on the same day, Victor Hugo reported a hurried visit from Proudhon, on leave from the prison of Sainte-Pélagie, warning him that Bonaparte's socialist pretenses were taken too seriously by the lower classes for armed resistance to be effective.[17] Indeed, Hugo himself had been taken in by Napoléon's nephew in 1848, George Sand still was, and as to the working-class militants, the exiled republican Victor Schoelcher reported to Quinet in 1852 that the Paris workers deported after the June rising of 1848, "refuse all assistance from Republicans or Montagnards, *considering that they have been and always will be Bonapartists.*"[18]

On a totally different level, roughly from the moment Michelet realized the purge machinery was moving against him, early in 1851, there is a nearly complete stop to the complaints about Athenaïs's sexual unavailability, which—with the exception of a few months around the time of Lazare's birth—were a frequent refrain in the journal. Thus, in the four and a half months before February 1851, there are seven expressions of what he called on October 16, 1850, a "famine d'amour."[19] They then stop abruptly for seven months. In the two years following his suspension, he made only three such complaints.[20] On the contrary, from the time of his suspension we find frequent expressions of happiness and satisfaction with his wife: "perfect unity of my hearth", "our complete unity,"[21] and so on.

Athenaïs's vaginismus had not been miraculously cured. Occasionally Michelet records unexpected sexual pleasures,[22] but more often he gives the impression of being happy with her "purity" and too engaged in his new labors as historian-feuilletonist to feel the absence of sexual satisfaction as a problem. On June 26, for example: "I will regret this time. Peace again! This pretty dwelling with this beloved wife, charm and wisdom incarnate . . . her extreme purity. All this happiness is nonetheless slipping away. I only enjoy the half of it by the excess of my preoccupation." The "preoccupation" refers to a preceding paragraph: "The execution of my new book left me in a worried state that gave me little chance to enjoy life." In August 1851, during a visit to Bordeaux to see Athenaïs's family: "Each time this angel of God descends to acts of tenderness I feel better for a long time, more pure, greater and as if sanctified . . . The more I approach her, the more it seems to me that I am at one with myself and with God. The vain thoughts and vain sadnesses leave me."

Again, what this suggests is not that Michelet's sexual famine had ceased but that it was no longer bothering him much. In fact, the expressions of sexual dissatisfaction had probably been symptomatic of a broader dissatisfaction with his position for which he may have held Athenaïs responsible in ways he could not admit. If he was sick of the bourgeois entourages that came with his status and longed to descend to the plebs, a part of his irritation may have derived from the feeling that it was his "pure angel" who was cutting him off from social contacts, with the "people" in general and with his daughter and son-in-law in particular. The alacrity with which he acceded to Alfred's suggestion that he reduce the importance of his essay on Grainville could be one sign of this; another could be the eager combativeness with which he shifted his intellectual efforts from the bourgeois precincts of the Collège de France to the populist offices of the left-wing press. Characteristic for the year 1851 was his comment on the publication of his manifesto to the purged *maîtres d'école* in *L'Evènement,* which seems to have led to a charged atmosphere at the archives: "The end of *Grainville* ('to the schoolteacher') appeared on the 20th in the evening. *Alea jacta est.*[23] I entered this day into the polemic of the age."[24]

Michelet's suspension at the Collège de France—and above all his secret willingness to *be* suspended—signified a radical break with the university milieu on which he had earlier counted to soften the social conflict and lead the revolution. Yet the break was the prelude to a new and more serious effort to reach the common people with his ideas and values. In the entourage of Eugène Noel and Alfred Dumesnil, a similar rupture combined with a similar new commitment was taking place.

Noel and Dumesnil had long been the center of a group of young republican idealists in Rouen—several of them ex-pupils of Michelet's disciple and friend Adolphe Chéruel.[25] Two years after Michelet's marriage, paralleling the broader disintegration of revolutionary fraternity after June, this group collapsed amid violent quarrels, deaths, and departures. Only the close tie between Dumesnil and Noel remained, together with the love these two felt for Michelet and their desire to help him in his new effort. That love was reciprocated. It was reconfirmed by Michelet's efforts to me-

diate during a quarrel that separated Dumesnil from his friends in
Rouen.[26] On New Year's Day 1851, Michelet reassured Noel that
he would find a way to "retie our triple unity," and as a token of
his independence vis-à-vis Athenaïs, he urged Noel to write him
confidentially at the archives.[27]

In a letter of April 17, Noel reaffirmed to Dumesnil their faith
and their friendship, despite all losses. It is characteristic of Michelet's influence that Noel did so in terms that combined an appreciation of the historian's new enterprise with an implicit evocation
both of his matriarchally tinted populism and of his ideal of per-
sonal-historical resurrection:

> Like you, I would sacrifice everything for the legends. Believe
> that the world has to start up again through them. Believe that
> it is time to make the new philosophy into porridge [*bouillie
> pour l'enfant*]. The centuries have sown, the harvest is ready.
> Let the *maternal geniuses*[28] prepare the meal for the little ones,
> the ill, the weak. The new world is still in its cradle. Let's give
> it its legend.
>   But let's also give the world this great history of the
> Revolution. Let it be for every soul the law and the prophets.
>   Breath into the souls of all a little of our hope and our
> faith, a little of the soul of my father. May your mother too,
> . . . may all those whom we have loved be raised from the dead
> by us! For there is no death!
>   . . . Providence has decreed that for the past six months
> we have been shaken to our foundations, but by these storms
> and destructions it has shown us that the fraternity between
> us allowed us to withstand these tempests. This has been a
> year of tears for us, but at the end of all this anguish we have
> refound holy friendship, eternal and unchangeable, we have
> refound invincible hope and, everywhere, a paternal smile.[29]

It was with just such "invincible hope" that Michelet wrote his
way through the year 1851. His first comprehensive plan for the
"legends" was dated March 20, the day of the student riots protesting his suspension.[30] With the exception of his essay on Grainville and several short pieces on the generals of the Revolution,
most of his work that year was directed against the czarist oppression in eastern Europe.[31] This emphasis followed from his appreciation for the military heroism and the foreign reception of the
first French revolution, and it reflected his post-June despair about
the chances of the Second Republic. But the fact that he was publishing in the popular left-wing press, indeed, that he had as early
as February 1851 promised his support to a new inexpensive paper

for the workers, shows how seriously he took the possibilities of popular education once he had decided to "descend."[32]

A sign of the probable direction of Michelet's popular writings if the coup d'état had not at year's end cut off all hope of revolutionary renewal, appears in a letter of Noel to Dumesnil dated June 16, 1851. In it, Noel, Michelet's rural alter ego, listed as subjects he wanted to write about:

—History of the conspiracy of worker tailors against the clothing stores.
—banks and merchant commerce, or murder and cannibalism among the civilized, a sequel to "property is theft" of citizen Proudhon.
—adventures of a proletarian: a contemporary true story ...
—on the disappearance of the middle class in France, of what ought to follow it and how it will be replaced.[33]

But the coup did occur; plans for it were being perfected at the end of November while Michelet was denouncing the barbaric treatment of Bakunin by czarist despotism.[34] Long apprehensive of the mass "idolatry" for Louis-Napoléon, he was nonetheless taken unawares by the Bonapartist seizure of power.[35] The seriousness of what had happened seems only slowly to have penetrated him: as late as December 7, he was planning a *Histoire de la France populaire,* and even while accepting in mid-December a cousin's offer to shelter him until the military had stopped making life unsafe for the regime's opponents, he began writing drafts for this history.[36] By month's end, however, he realized that the period of uplifting republican histories for the masses was closed, and he began to review his notes for the next volume of his history of the Revolution.[37]

CHAPTER 21

REPRESSION AND EXILE IN 1852—TERROR AND SOCIALISM IN 1793

Apart from a few pages in the spring on Charlotte Corday and the Siege of Nantes,[1] Michelet's work on the Revolution remained at the note-taking stage for the first half of 1852. The effects of the coup were being felt everywhere. Seventy-two republican deputies were exiled, including Quinet, Hugo, and Victor Versigny, who had received the student petition protesting Michelet's suspension in March 1851.[2] The military dictatorship demoralized the remaining French democrats, completing the purges begun toward the end of the Republic and destroying the most innocent reminders of the February Revolution, like the liberty tree in the courtyard of the National Archives.[3]

In February 1852, anticipating dismissal from his position in the archives, Michelet sent his wife to look for cheaper lodgings.[4] On April 12, he, Quinet, and Mickiewicz were dismissed from the Collège de France; the charges against Michelet were that his course had "given rise to the most scandalous scenes" and that his teaching was "of a nature to trouble the public peace."[5] On May 19, he and Athenaïs moved to an inexpensive flat in Montmartre, but they stayed there only three weeks. Ten days after the move, his Bonapartist boss at the archives, Chabrier, asked him to take an oath of loyalty to the new regime. He refused on June 3 and the next day moved out of the archives after twenty-two years of service.[6] On June 12, at the end of a week of farewell visits and making traveling arrangements, he left Paris for Nantes, where the reduced living costs kept him from the poorhouse and the historical archives could be of use to his work on the civil strife of 1793.

In the fifteen months since his course had been suspended, Michelet had proven to himself that he could break away from the academic status and routine in which he had spent his entire life, and, through his new orientation, he had begun to reach out both to a broader public and to some of the radical writers he had come to admire but had not yet—or hardly—met. This was highly important in the case of Pierre-Joseph Proudhon. In spite of similar personal backgrounds, their different career paths—Proudhon, an autodidact, was contemptuous of academic status—led to mutual incomprehension in the 1840s. Michelet, like others, identified Proudhon with "property is theft" (not really the socialist's position) and rejected him for it. Proudhon viewed the historian as an establishment figure with bizarre pretensions. On January 4, 1848, for example, at the time of Michelet's first suspension, Proudhon had written sarcastically in his Carnet: "The government suspends the course of Michelet. Thus is the trinity laid low: *Mickiewicz, Quinet, Michelet,* three mystics, veritable confidence men of the simpleminded: the first a visionary crank, the second, harebrained, the third, insane."[7]

The course of the Second Republic led to a complete reversal of these attitudes. From the spring and summer of 1851, Michelet and Proudhon began exchanging friendly and highly appreciative letters. Good relations began after Michelet, on March 4, 1851, defiantly answered the suspension hanging over his head by sending the imprisoned socialist the published volumes of his history of the Revolution. Proudhon wrote the historian on April 11 that he had read them "with extraordinary satisfaction" and, three weeks later, in response to Michelet's offering him his courses of 1848–49, told him, "You have formulated, better than I . . . my long study and my entire thought."[8] Proudhon seems to have developed the germ of his *De la justice dans la Révolution et dans l'église* (1858) from Michelet's antithesis of grace and justice.[9] In August 1851, Michelet was reading Proudhon's *Idée générale de la Révolution au XIXe siècle.*[10] Four days before the coup, on November 29, Michelet visited him in the prison of Sainte-Pélagie.[11]

Thus, in spite of their initial mutual hostility and difference in status,[12] the persecuted revolutionary theorist and the suspended professor discovered they had much in common: artisan backgrounds and work ethics, respect for small property, an austere, sometimes puritanical morality, intense anticlericalism, hatred of Robespierrist Jacobins, and a dislike of literary romanticism. Proudhon was a sharper theorist, Michelet, more visionary, more open to nature. Although Michelet never agreed with Proudhon's decentralist position, there can be little doubt that his increasing sympathy for socialist ideas in the years leading up to *Le Banquet* was a result of his friendship with Proudhon.

His relation to George Sand was older and more complicated.

He had read and praised a number of her novels in the 1840s, had exchanged letters with her, but only visited her after his second marriage.[13] He particularly liked in her novels the influence of Pierre Leroux, the dissident Saint-Simonian whose writings he admired. During the Second Republic he developed an additional interest in Sand's work: her use of theater to convey ideas to the masses. This was an aspect of his broad awareness of the need for popular republican propaganda which, in part under his friend Noel's influence, he had discussed in *L'Etudiant*, and he looked to Sand, despite her Bonapartist inclinations, as someone who had the instinctive capacity to nurture the masses or, lending her his own sobriquet of 1842, possessed the "génie maternel." After seeing "Le Mariage de Victorine" on November 27, 1851, for example, he appealed to her in a letter the following day (one day before he visited Proudhon in prison) to use her talents to portray heroes of thought and action, defenders of revolutionary France: "Nourish yourself, oh powerful mother, charming and fecund nurse, on the national idea. Give to this good and great people a food as strong as it. Remember that tomorrow it will have to save the world."[14] A similar rhetoric emerged during a conversation he had with her three months after the coup, on March 7, 1852. Though he disapproved of her private life and argued against her equation of the Bonapartist victors with the vanquished republicans,[15] he nonetheless thanked providence for bringing him to "this illustrious and unfortunate person who nourished all the earth with her rapid production, her charming fecundity." And he said at the end, in praise of her role in France's cultural leadership of the world: "We think and we give the food of our thought. All the nations collect from under our table the crumbs of our banquet." All these images of spiritual nurturance point in the direction of the brief, incomplete, but highly important book Michelet wrote two years later: *Le Banquet.*

On the day of his move to Montmartre, May 19, in anticipation of his dismissal from the archives and his self-chosen exile to Nantes, Michelet summarized his life since his marriage to Athenaïs. After listing his writings and courses in those three years and making a ritual bow to "this young treasure of virtue," his spouse, he noted that he looked forward eagerly to a coming personal "renewal": "To change habits, to break one's routines is no doubt a step toward divesting oneself of the old man and creating a new one, more fecund perhaps, better, more useful." His long-felt dissatisfaction with the limits his bourgeois milieu imposed on his effectiveness was confirmed for him and his intellectual colleagues, he felt, by the coup d'état: "I am angry with myself for December 2d. I reproach both myself and the entire literary class, writing or speaking, the men of letters, the press, and the parliament. We did nothing for the people and we are punished. Let us mend our ways, if possible." He said that he had come to fear most "the sterility of routine, the soporific uniformity of bureaucratic habits, the choking pile-up of science, of erudition," and then, metaphorically grasping the reification of knowledge, he wrote: "I often compared the souls of scholars to these lushly green islands that become invaded by coral, a beautiful and rich production for which one searches out these islands; but as time progresses, this coral covers everything with a dry, hard, impermeable surface: not a blade of grass can grow there."

Escaping the beautiful but moribund coral islands, the historian looked forward to another vita nuova of hope and rejuvenation and reiterated his love for the French common people, "whatever you have done to me, whatever you have done to yourself." For, he said, returning to his pedagogical mission, all of France's misfortunes were caused "by our fatal delay in enlightening those who remain in the shadows of ignorance." He appealed to God to show him the way to "a better and more popular science," and he added, in Rousseauian accents, "May I, in my new solitude, the better interrogating my heart, better understand the heart of man and find the language of crowds. I hope to hear it in the desert rather than in the crowd itself."

He and Athenaïs found their solitude in a charming, inexpensive eighteenth-century house overlooking the Erdre just outside Nantes, replete with fruit trees, vegetable garden, and chicken coop, such that Michelet could tell Noel, in a metaphor that perfectly reflected his new frame of mind, that he felt himself "suspended like a suckling babe at the breasts of nature."[16] Before settling into this new Eden, however, he was subjected to a Catholic feast-day procession in Nantes on June 20 that awakened both his revulsion for the pompous military culture of the new regime and his old hunger for genuine popular festivities: "*Des fêtes, donnez nous des fêtes,*" he implored, asking where the sailors and the traditional *confrèries* were that belonged in such a procession. What he found especially detestable was the rigid, policelike control of the priests over the procession and, above all,

> the rude discordance of the military music, violent, imperious, and barbarous ... This rude voice of Moloch, roaring in the ambulant paradise of the procession, seemed to me a blasphemy ... If it were just the easygoing National Guardsmen, themselves family men, the thing would be tolerable. But it's the regular army, our rough regiments of Africa and December 2d, it's the policemen and the mounted gendarmerie who prance around at the risk of crushing the faithful![17]

On July 2, the day Michelet wrote to Noel about his feeling of sucking at the breast of mother nature, his propensity for such fantasies was powerfully stimulated by a report that Adèle was pregnant again and, as if competing with her fecundity, he resumed—after a lapse of some sixteen months—his narrative of the Révolution.[18] To emphasize the harsh, relentless rhythm of the revolutionary terror (and, incidentally, to exploit his newfound talent as feuilletonist), he decided to write in a more abbreviated style.[19] As a result, the final eleven parts of the narrative he was to complete in the following year (books XI–XXI) averaged a third the length of the previous ten such sections, and the chapters were half as long.[20]

The following year was one of breathless labor on his magnum opus, interrupted only by occasional letters and visits with such democ-soc friends as Ange Guèpin, the Nantes republican chief, or Maria and Constantin Rossetti, who had come to Nantes from Paris when he did.[21] His work routine was very different from what it had been in the French capital, since he no longer had either the social circuit or his position as archivist as respite from his writing. He described his daily life in a letter to Alfred of October 18, 1852: "I write myself to death until noon: I go to Nantes for the Archives or household matters. From three to six, I read the newspapers of the Revolution to write the next day. We sleep at 9, most often at 10."[22] He was probably rising at 5 A.M. to start work, as he had since his youth.

Michelet's writing in Nantes during that year—the last two volumes of his *Révolution*—was on the Terror, the deaths of his protagonists and of his ideals: it was frequently a torment to him. After four months of keeping a reduced diary, hardly more than a line a day, he surrendered that daily companion as well, and for most of the next nine months he struggled alone in the hecatomb of revolutionary heroism, describing the long year that stretched from the purge of the Girondins to Thermidor, trying to transform the leaden grief of the Terror into the precious metal of historical understanding. In those nine months from November 1852 to July 1853, he opened his journal seven times to write a page about his life and work, and then closed it. A glance at his personal letters for the period, most of them to his son-in-law, shows better than the journal what was going on within him: "My book . . . makes me cross and re-cross the styx" (to Alfred, August 1, 1852); "Robespierre eats my marrow and my bones" (to Noel, undated, 1852); "I have refound in the catacombs some prodigiously tortured souls" (to Alfred, undated); "I make haste, the time may be too short. It burns, I feel it, and the earth disappears under me, life, the earth of la patrie" (to Alfred, October 18, 1852); "I march in my book as if on a volcanic field, frightfully scarred and pierced by pits of fire" (to Alfred, December 6, 1852); "I am hurrying in my work and am nearly at the death of Danton. I have traversed immensities of thorns. The terrible forest of Dante at the beginning of the Inferno is nothing next to it. I touch here the very bottom of this hell where *morality* makes men commit crimes. Robespierre and Saint-Just were harsh moralists" (to Alfred, January 14, 1853).[23]

Occasionally, we glimpse in the journal another side of Michelet's work on the Terror: the increasing importance to him of what he saw as the lost opportunity for the social and religious revolution, embodied in the men and policies of the Commune of 1793. Radicalized by his "descent," made more open to socialist ideas by Proudhon, and sobered by the coup, Michelet was on the point of broadening his republican populism to allow a rapprochement with the socialism of the age. Despite the horror of the military takeover in contemporary France and the wretchedness of the Terror he was dissecting in 1793, a renewal in his social ideas as well as in his life was pulsing within him, waiting to be born, and the site of its gestation was in his ideas on the Paris Commune of Cloots and Chaumette.

On August 22, for example, he tells us what he saw as "the dominant idea" of book XI, which he was struggling to complete. With all respect for the "heroic fathers" of the Revolution, he had to admit their insufficiency: "Their revolution [was based] on a single rail, without width or depth, neither social nor religious. The two great foundations were missing." The month before, as one of the first chapters in his restarted history: "I write a thing of religion, inspired by the registers of the Commune and Chaumette." And at years's end he wrote, "Absorbed entirely and without breathing in the very core of the book: *November 93: The Religious attempt and the papacy of Robespierre.*"[24]

The socialism Michelet was moving toward did not deny property: on the contrary, it was built on the material foundations of property and the family, and he usually condemned those who, like Babeuf, pleaded for agrarian communism. But like his new friend, Proudhon, he saw that property was a problem as well as a principle.[25] He endorsed only property justified by the needs of individual labor and sanctified by sacrifice; banks and the large landholdings of idle rentiers he condemned. (Industrial capitalism, still in its infancy in France, was for him a secondary question.)[26] And he saw clearly that the abstract individualism preached by the eighteenth century had to be replaced by a fraternity of the producing class, a humanitarian politics of mutual care and nurturance that for him was a legitimate socialism. He was convinced that this socialism had to be founded on a new religion of sacrifice and

brotherhood and that efforts to carry on the republican cause without it or against it doomed the revolutionary tradition to sterility.
This was as true of the First Republic as it was for the Second: we
glimpse the parallel in the "thing on religion" he wrote on the third
day of his return to the description of 1793, July 4, 1852. He then
cited Desmoulins's invocation of the great unknown—"terra in-
cognita"—that the revolutionaries dimly perceived beyond the left-
wing demagogue, Marat, and he described its location and its meaning:

> From Lyons ... the revolutionary mysticism of Chalier. To-
> ward the North, in Picardy, the great divider Babeuf ... In the
> center, a world surges under our feet, a bold attempt of a new
> religion ... the cult of reason ... Paris.
>   Could the political Revolution persist without becoming
> a social and religious revolution? Will the classical Revolution
> of Rousseau and Robespierre live in safety ... without taking
> account of the other, the romantic Revolution that roars con-
> fusedly outside its walls, like the voice of the ocean? ... The
> Montagne felt instinctively that to put the Revolution in the
> pure hand ... of the Jacobin dictatorship was to reject an in-
> finity of living forces ... which, if one suffocated them, by
> their death or their absence would sterilize the Republic, leav-
> ing it without blood and without life.[27]

Scattered through the five hundred-odd pages of the last two
volumes of his history were the signs of this "infinity of living
forces" that announced the "romantic Revolution" destined to follow the "classical" one. In contrast to the domination of the Con-
stituent Assembly by "the anglo-American school of laissez-faire,"
for example, the Convention opened the "great era of social fraternity," and, because of its humanitarian legislation (family assistance,
orphanages, and so on), he ascribed to it "the inexhaustible fecundity of nature."[28] More important than the Convention as
sources of the new social doctrine were certain revolutionary
seedbeds in Paris: the Cordeliers Club, the Commune, and the section of Gravilliers.
    Michelet had already—in 1847—designated the Cordeliers
Club as the site of a rebirth of the Joachimite évangile.[29] More than
any other of the Paris clubs, it continued the exalted voice of the
federations of 1790, the voice that heralded what he then called "the
social and religious age of the Revolution."[30] In book XIV, which
he described in his journal as the "very core of the book," the first
chapter, "The Revolution Was Nothing without the Religious Revolution," contains his most important reflections on the social and

religious revolution, the Cordeliers Club, and the Commune. Both the Girondins and the Jacobins, he wrote, were incapable of moving beyond the "classical," political revolution, which was doomed if not supported by "the religious revolution, the social revolution . . . its power and its depth." The most advanced of the Jacobins, Saint-Just, he complained, "does not dare to touch either religion or education or the very basis of social doctrines; one barely glimpses what he thinks about property."[31] Echoing once again a Saint-Simonian theme, he wrote that the Revolution "was required . . . not only to codify the XVIIIth century but . . . to *realize as a living affirmation* what was negative in it . . . It had to show that its negation of an arbitrary religion of favors for the elect contained *the affirmation of the religion of equal justice for all*; to show that its negation of privileged property contained *the affirmation of nonprivileged property, extended to all.*" Precisely on these two vital questions, the Revolution failed: "It closed the Church for a moment and didn't create the temple. It let property change hands but left it as a monopoly; the privileged were reborn as . . . speculators manipulating the assignats and the national domains."[32] Faced with inevitable discontent, the regime resorted to authoritarian repression. But the only real remedy was left untried: "The relation of man to God and of man to nature, religion, property, had to be constituted on a new and strong dogma, or the Revolution had only to await its death."[33]

The Girondins, Michelet argued, were unaware that there was a problem, and the Jacobins were capable only of an uncreative "judging, purging, weeding out." Only among the doomed tribunes of the Cordeliers Club could one find the germs of a solution. But, he pointed out, the Cordeliers were in a state of permanent insurrection against themselves: "The only party that momentarily dreamed of ways to fecundate the Revolution was the one which, as a living anarchy, was infertile."

The Cordeliers, thought Michelet, contained both the best and the worst elements of the Revolution—scoundrels and embezzlers like Hébert and his friends, the "black angel" of the Cordeliers, and as their "white angel" counterpart, Anacharsis Cloots: "the innocent, the pacific . . . the orator of the human race, man of the Rhine, brother of Beethoven, French, alas! by adoption." The "alas" was because the white angel, Cloots, who had adopted France as his home because of the Revolution, was guillotined in the Terror, a monstrous ingratitude that clearly reminded Michelet of his own purged, exiled existence, the basis of much of his account of 1793: "Oh France! What are you then, and how will I name you? . . . Dearly beloved! . . . How many times you have pierced my heart! . . . Adored mother, mistress, stepmother! . . . That we should die through you is proper! If you break us, it is yourself; you will not hear a sigh. But these others, so confident, who voluntarily threw themselves in your arms . . . innocent souls who had seen no frontiers, . . . oh! their destiny leaves in me an abyss of eternal sorrow."[34]

As mediator between the black and the white angels of the Cordeliers, Michelet identified Pierre-Gaspard Chaumette, who in 1793 was at the head of the Commune. Decisively influenced by Cloots, who anticipated the "romantic heresy" by identifying the Deity with the human race, Chaumette's administration of the Commune was a model of humanitarianism. Michelet filled three pages with examples of its measures for the poor, the aged, and the young and its protection of the libraries and museums of Paris.[35]

In the last six months of his writing on the Revolution, Michelet recurred to the major points of his chapter on the abortive religious revolution of the Commune and the Cordeliers. Chaumette, who had sealed his doom by pleading for a mitigation of the Terror, was, he said, "in himself not much, but significant as a magical symbol of Paris." Indeed, increasingly it was Paris itself whom the Incorruptible was emasculating through the purges. Michelet described the section of Gravilliers—the area where he was born, four years after Thermidor—as "the deep, agitated bowels of industrial Paris, which wept for Jacques Roux[36] and had been shaken to its roots by the preaching of Chaumette and Léonard Bourdon." Since two of these three had been martyred by Robespierre, the sansculottes of this section marched for the Convention and against the Jacobin leader at Thermidor.[37]

Michelet invoked his special tie to the French capital in the chapter "The Death of Chaumette and of the Commune"; he prided himself on having had "the honor of being born in the sacred mud of the metropolis of the world" and vaunted "the power of this astonishing crucible in which races and ideas transform and create themselves without end."[38] After describing the miserable end of Chaumette, who crawled before his accusers and denied his friendship with Cloots, Michelet indicated both his identification with the martyrdom of his native city and the political direction of his thought.

> The real heretic, the unbeliever, the martyr of liberty, was not so much Chaumette or Clootz as Paris itself. It was Paris that one struck down in them, it was the audacious avant-garde of human thought, of the free genius of the earth, which had its Precursor [*sic*] in the great Commune. After this crushing blow, Paris, delayed a moment (a half century is a moment), left the paths of religion and philosophical initiation, to return to them later by the circuitous route of Socialism.[39]

Michelet again brought up the question of property. If he had earlier shown hostility to the communist preachings of Jacques Roux and Babeuf, at the end of his book he was more inclined to condemn those who, like Robespierre, Saint-Just, and Marat, representatives of the "classical revolution," defended property and martyred those who demanded its division.[40] With the help of the demagogic journalists Marat and Hébert, Robespierre attacked the "dividers" in the section of Gravilliers, "until the formidable heart that subsisted in the Gravilliers was extinguished in the blood of Jacques Roux." The Cordeliers, too, under the pressure of Robespierre and Hébert, abandoned Roux and Chaumette and thereby lost their special influence in the artisanal heart of Paris, where Roux had been revered.

But the greatest of the Cordeliers' orators whom Robespierre brought down was Danton, who was also Robespierre's greatest competitor in the Jacobin Club. Michelet's final word on Danton points clearly to his own central concerns:

"Danton," says a man who knew him well . . . "had embraced pity like an altar on which everything can be expiated . . . He would have saved Robespierre." The great dream of Danton (this singular fact is in the registers of the Commune) was an immense table where all of France, reconciled, would be seated to break, without distinction of classes or parties, the bread of fraternity.

Three things remain about the Dantonists. They overthrew the monarchy and created the Republic; they wanted to save it by organizing the only thing that makes for life: justice, an effective justice because it would have been human; they loved one another to the moment of death. The fine Greek inscription is their own: "inseparable in war and friendship."[41]

Humanitarian justice, friendship, mutual nurturance, and limitations on property rights, all these would reappear as key elements of the unfinished *Le Banquet.* Rarely in describing the bleak passion of 1793 did Michelet have cause to write explicitly about nature. In one place that he did, the chapter on the marquis de Sade and the decadent libertinism that accompanied the Terror, he invoked the crawling, destructive world of vipers, reptiles, scorpions, and termites; the biological metaphor with which he summed up the season of fear and mutual denunciation was "moral cholera."[42] This may have been his principal reaction to the events he was describing between July 1852 and June 1853, but it was by no means his only one, no more than his bitter outcry "Mère, maîtresse, marâtre adorée!" was his last word on the France of Louis-Napoléon.[43]

Not long after thus condemning his native land as a step-mother, no better than the Catholic church he had renounced as *mère terrible* six years earlier,[44] Michelet plumbed the depths of his disenchantment and found new sources of belief in nature, in his country, and in himself. A month after the founding of the Second Empire, as he was preparing to describe the executions of all the great tribunes of the Revolution, he wrote into his history this personal note:

> I plunge with my subject into the night and into the winter. The furious winds of the storms that have pounded my windows on these hills of Nantes for the past two months, accompany with their voices, sometimes grave, sometimes piercing, my *Dies irae* of '93 . . . Many things that were incomprehensible to me became clear in the revelation of these voices of the ocean . . . These menaces of winter, all these semblances of death, were . . . life, the profound renewal. From the destructive powers, from the violent metamorphoses in which you thought yourself ruined, escapes, elastic and smiling, the eternal irony of nature.[45]

The assimilation of France to nature, implicit in *Le Peuple,* signaled here a double direction of Michelet's work in the decade to come: first, *Le Banquet,* in which he would draw equally on his experience of nature as a basic force for renewal and on his concept of the social and religious revolution; second, the subsequent turn from the political, his coming preoccupation with natural history and feminine nature. But it signified some things more basic as well: his notion of cyclical recurrence, of the inextricable connection of death and rebirth, what he and others had called "accouchement."[46]

There are various signs that in the years 1852–53, after his planned "descent," Michelet was moving through his social death toward another act of rebirth. Although on one level he was politically more engaged than ever, in his personal life he was clearly in a phase of return, of regression. In part this was mandated by the conditions of his existence. His isolated life with Athenaïs constituted a return to the situation of his childhood, when he learned his letters alone with his mother and when his father lost his employment as a result of the first Napoléon, just as he himself did through the second.[47]

Another kind of return is suggested in the warmth of his extensive correspondence with Alfred, with whom he had not been on such intimate terms since the mid-1840s.[48] In fact, in spite of the apparent closeness of Michelet and his young wife, and whatever the justification of his heavy writing schedule, the scarcity of journal entries during the period in Nantes suggests a weakening of the marital bond. This raises the possibility of other emotional attachments.

There may indeed have been one for Michelet, and it strengthens the argument that he was looking for a new mother as a prelude to his rebirth. He seems to have been considerably attracted to the half-English, half-French woman Maria Rossetti, who, with her Rumanian husband, had followed the Michelets to Nantes.[49] He memorialized her in *Légendes démocratiques du nord*; and her heroically maternal qualities, described in the book, contained more than a hint of Madame Dumesnil.

Like Madame Dumesnil, Madame Rossetti (born in 1818) attended Michelet's lectures at the Collège de France, and like Athenaïs, she read his book with enthusiasm. In *Legèndes démocratiques*, she combines the traits of Joan of Arc and the mother of God.[50] In his first letter to her of January 1850, he obliquely suggested his marital problems when he referred to the fact that a periodical article had called him "an old monk lost in the XIXth century" and added, "Monk? agreed." She may have been the reason for the English course Michelet took in Nantes from January to June 1853.[51]

Michelet was also friendly with Madame Rossetti's husband, and there is no evidence that his relationship to her was more than an admiring friendship. But the extent of the admiration—especially for her maternal qualities—could well have irritated Athenaïs, still childless in 1852, caused estrangement, and short-circuited his journal, which since 1849 had been written for her. In December 1861, the suppressed erotic component surfaced in a dream: "My bizarre dreams on the death of my grandmother and Mme Rossetti, who comes to console me and forgets herself [. . .] [*sic*]. I was touched by her blushing and her embarrassment."[52]

Independently of this likely infatuation, a retightening of the biologically based ties with Adèle and Charles, with his grandchildren, and indirectly with Alfred is plausible in light of the hypothesis argued above: that Michelet's abstract ideas on freedom as liberation from natural "fatality" corresponded to and justified his own guilt-ridden abandonment, for the sake of his rapidly ascending career, of his lower-middle-class biological origins.[53] This could explain his adoption of Alfred to replace Charles in 1841 and his adoption of Athenaïs to replace both Adèle and Alfred in 1849.[54] The ascent was over, the descent had begun, and it would be comprehensible if, now perhaps less overwhelmed by Athenaïs's purity and more pained by the rarity of her carnal passion, he should have sought warmer relations with his "children."[55]

CHAPTER 22

ITALY, LAMENNAIS, AND MICHELET'S "DESCENT" TO THE PEOPLE

In the last five months of his work on the Revolution, Michelet complained frequently of an intestinal disturbance,[1] probably induced by the impossibility of heating his ramshackle quarters outside Nantes.[2] Having finished the book, he began to look into alternative living arrangements. After two trips to Paris in the summer and early autumn of 1853 to arrange for publication of his recent work and a brief visit to his consumptive son, Charles, in Strasbourg, he attempted to improve his health by taking sea baths in Brittany. Not completely recovered and fearful of spending another winter in unheatable quarters in Nantes—perhaps frightened from having seen the wasted condition of Charles—he decided to seek a warmer climate and entered genuine exile in Italy. He left for Genoa on October 29. The decision seems to have been a sudden one, motivated by a desire both to restore his health and to escape the depressing political situation in France.[3] He had an exhausting year of writing behind him and was looking forward, he told Noel, to moving his "nomad chariot" to Italy. He arrived in Genoa on November 7 and remained in Italy for eight months.

While in Italy, Michelet planned to extend his history of the Revolution to cover the post-Thermidorian period[4] and to resume his *Histoire de France,* which he had abandoned at the fifteenth century a decade earlier.[5] These plans, however, were postponed: the post-Thermidorian history to 1869, and the resumption of the *Histoire de France* to his return to Paris in summer 1854. The reasons seem to have been a combination of continuing poor health, lack of archival resources, and a frame of mind that precluded serious history writing. The only publication he completed in Italy was his *Femmes de la Révolution,* a pastiche of chapters from his *Révolution* cemented with bits of narrative mortar. After finishing this in January 1854, he worked sporadically, and then for two weeks (between February 23 and March 7) intensively, at his post-Thermidor book, but from March 11, his work on this competed with a flood of ideas he was developing for *Le Banquet,* which he had twice mentioned in his journal since arriving in Italy. In fact, from that date on, as far as his post-Thermidor book is concerned, Michelet seems primarily to have been interested in pursuing the role and ideas of Babeuf, the "great divider," who continually brought him back to the terrain of *Le Banquet.* On April 1, he postponed further work on the Revolution indefinitely to write on "*Le Banquet* and the religious concentration";[6] it became his exclusive preoccupation for the next two months.

Le Banquet is an excellent example of Michelet's capacity for psychological rebirth and renewal, both social and religious. The conditions for it were in general set by the painful "descent" he had put himself through in the previous years and in particular by the physical debilitation he had experienced in 1853 and by the social-cultural circumstances of exile, of prolonged immersion in a new culture. The trigger of this renewal, however, was probably a specific event: the death on February 28, 1854, of Félicité de Lamennais. Lamennais had become part of his conscience, a model for his populist idealism; Michelet's unconscious, as well as his political values, had been bound up with the aging Christian radical.

Lamennais (born in 1782) had been a conservative, Ultramontane theologian in the 1820s, but his *Essai sur l'indifférence,* published between 1817 and 1823, won him the attention of the young Michelet, who was impressed by Lamennais's honest attempt to combat the egotism of the age and to reformulate the Christian faith for the nineteenth century.[7] In the early 1830s, Lamennais's journal *L'Avenir,* directed by his disciple Montalembert, wrote in praise of Michelet's austere view of Christianity in his "Introduction à l'histoire universelle"; and Jean-René Derré, Lamennais's biographer, suggests that the papal encyclicals directed against the liberal social Catholicism of the *Avenir* group may have led Michelet to a more questioning attitude toward Christianity in volume III of his *Histoire de France.*[8] Derré also indicates that Michelet was among a group of writers present at Lamennais's lectures of 1831.[9] This is entirely possible, since Michelet knew Lamennais's features well enough to find them in a portrait by Antonio Canova that he saw in 1834. His attitude toward Lamennais is reflected in the terms he used to describe the portrait: "Full of an exquisite gentleness, a charming penetration, and a passionate sense of beauty."[10]

The year 1834 was the beginning of Lamennais's radical phase, in which he responded to papal encyclicals against his liberal ideas by turning socialist in his *Paroles d'un croyant.* He quickly gained a reputation as a firebrand.[11] The young Proudhon revealed the contribution of the ex-priest to the revolutionary mood of the unemployed in 1839: "I have seen some who, upon reading the latest work of Lamennais, demanded guns and wanted to march immediately."[12] By 1843, Lamennais was commenting enthusiastically on Michelet's and Quinet's denunciations of the Jesuits.[13]

The tone of Lamennais's Christian radicalism in the *Paroles d'un croyant* and in his *Livre du peuple*—though not the specific ideas—is strikingly similar to Michelet's in his *Peuple* of 1846. Perhaps precisely for this reason Michelet, who was reluctant to offend his juste milieu friends before his own radical phase had begun in 1843, did not mention Lamennais in his journal during the decade 1834–44. From then, however, until Lamennais's death in 1854, Michelet referred to him about fifty times, and some of these references are important, particularly looking back from Michelet's reaction to the theologian's death.

His first, brief reference, for example, after a decade of silence, was: "A l'institut pour m. de Lamennais, contre Cousin." Michelet was protesting the absence of Lamennais's name on a list of proposed new members of the Academy of Moral Sciences, and that he related this protest to his antipathy to Victor Cousin is interesting. Michelet had long been a rival of his old teacher Cousin and had directed his "Introduction" of 1831 against Cousin's Hegelian determinism.[14] He was probably aware that Lamennais too detested Cousin, though whether he knew that the Christian revolutionary had called Cousin "the Plato of the guillotine," because of his support for judicial repression of the Left early in the July Monarchy,[15] is unclear. What he did not miss was the "hostile joy of the Cousin school" in the institute when he was suspended from the Collège de France in 1851.[16] As to Lamennais's reaction to that suspension, Michelet not only knew he could count on him but, at just the time he was planning his descent to the people and his metamorphosis to revolutionary feuilletoniste, he visited the theologian, probably to ask advice.[17] For Michelet's dreams of reaching the masses with the message of social romanticism had been associated with Lamennais from the beginning. I mean his literal dreams.

On September 27, 1846, the day after Michelet, sensing a new 1789 in the offing and convinced of the need of public enlightenment on the subject, started writing his *Révolution,* he reported in his journal: "Vu M. de Lamennais. Rêvé une réunion de Lamennais, George Sand, Béranger, Quinet, Eugène Sue."[18] Two weeks later, he visited Béranger, with whom he had long had close personal contact, and asked him, apparently without results, about a "réunion des gens de lettres."[19] In the thickets of his first month of writing on the Revolution, Michelet postponed further action on his dream until November 2, when he again visited Lamennais, this time with Alfred: "He would like a meeting, but only to supervise the young people, who would make little books that one would peddle through the compagnonnage. Poor propaganda of the communists: the workers rejecting a book because of the word God."

Lamennais's proposal was the first sign in Michelet's journal of his coming preoccupation with popular legends—the initial step in his descent of 1851 to the people. The situation is typical of the period and of the men involved. For one thing, Lamennais's proposal signaled clearly the threshold Michelet would have to cross during the Second Republic, from a traditional politics of notables talking among themselves to one that required the intellectuals to confront popular needs and tastes. For another, Lamennais had enormous prestige in such matters: his *Paroles d'un croyant* had sold tens of thousands of copies among common artisans, he had spent a year in Sainte-Pélagie for his convictions, and, as Michelet knew, the masthead of *La Fraternité de 1845*—*organe de communisme* was adorned with a quotation from Lamennais's *Livre du peuple*.[20] If anyone could stimulate Michelet's populist impulses at this time it was Lamennais, and this is probably why Michelet brought his disciple Noel with him to Lamennais[21]—Noel was also thinking about reaching the masses through *colportage*.

The more theoretical side of Michelet's work was also indebted to Lamennais. Not only does *Le Peuple* betray the prophetic spirit of Lamennais's popular books of the 1830s, but his Collège de France lectures in the spring of 1848, like those at the Ecole normale twenty years earlier, revealed the influence of Lamennais's *Essai sur l'indifférence,* in particular the placing of Christianity in a much broader pre-Christian theogony.[22]

After the June uprising Michelet complained that neither Béranger nor Lamennais had heard his plea for republican propaganda to counter Bonapartism. He seems, however, to have unjustly joined two positions. Béranger was never willing, apart from his poetry, to do anything concrete for the masses; their salvation, he said, would have to come from themselves. Lamennais seems merely to have emphasized journalism rather than the varied forms of publicity Michelet had wanted. And when the time came for Michelet's descent, it took precisely the form advocated by Lamennais: popular journalism. On the question of the revolution outside of France, moreover, Michelet and Lamennais thought exactly the same way. In the summer of 1851, when Michelet was busily preparing his "legends" on the revolutions in eastern Europe, Lamennais, as the chairman of a committee to support the revolution in Spain, Italy, and France, was writing a manifesto on that subject.[23] Two years earlier, Michelet, bringing Lamennais the proofs of the first part of volume III of the *Révolution,* had "consoled him about France by showing him Europe." The old Christian radical had answered, "Yes, undoubtedly God does what he can. He saves life. But honor?"²⁴

Ten days after this conversation, Athenaïs Mialaret visited Michelet and a new chapter began in his life. But his relationship with Lamennais continued to be what it had been: warm and influential. In December 1848, Michelet compared Athenaïs's literary style—"simple, lively, and strong"—to that of Lamennais.²⁵ On January 21, 1849, in planning their new life, Athenaïs's fiancé agreed to an isolated existence except for three friends: one was Lamennais. As one of half a dozen old friends invited to the wedding, Lamennais accepted, blessed them, and added, "When you already have but one soul, it is also good to have only one hearth. Yes, undoubtedly you will draw new power from this gentle community of life and work. Defender of the cause of the people, of the future of justice and fraternity that we see dawning on the horizon, happiness will be for you one more means of accomplishing the holy duty which is the true, the unique goal of human destiny."²⁶

In the year after his marriage, as I have noted, Michelet included in his history of the Revolution several depictions of the people—or specific revolutionaries—as Christlike in their suffering. Although these ideas were common in the "romantic heresy" of the time, there was no one with whom they were more associated than with his benign wedding guest.²⁷ More generally, Michelet's imagination was haunted throughout the martyrdom of the Second Republic by the idea of the fusion of the religious and social revolutions, and again, if any one figure could be viewed as incarnating that idea, it was Lamennais.²⁸ Michelet had often visited him on a Sunday and listened to him read from his translations of the New Testament and Dante. The last time he saw Lamennais was in October 1853, during his round of farewell visits before his move to Italy.

On December 14, 1853, Michelet wrote Lamennais from Nervi, a seaside village to which he had moved from Genoa. He waited impatiently for an answer alongside the "terrible, white, and savage" ocean. On December 30 he reported: "Dreamed a book: *Le Banquet.*"

More than a month later, in February, he received a letter from Lamennais dated January 7, 1854.²⁹ The old revolutionary wrote of the harsh winter in Paris and the cold and hunger of the poor. People of all classes were complaining, he said, but fear of worse, of the unknown, kept the government in the saddle. Lamennais nonetheless did not believe that the present silence would last: "As

suffering increases, fear will decrease, and a day will come when
. . . any future, whatever it may be, will not be frightening . . . When
liberty is reborn, those who imagine they will find themselves where
they were three years ago will be strangely surprised." Toward the
end of this warm, lengthy letter, Lamennais reiterated the "joyous
faith" of the 1848 Revolution, "that progress, despite the varied
resistances it encounters, will be accomplished infallibly." He urged
his friend not to be disappointed by the slowness of a movement
that was global in scope: "It's the entire world that is in motion. It
could not go like a train from Paris to St-Germain."[30] In conclusion,
Lamennais asked Michelet and his young wife to "take care of your
frail health during this harsh season and return to us in the spring."
No one, he wrote, would be happier to see them than he.

By the time Michelet received this letter, he could not but have
been touched and shaken by his friend's concern, for he knew that
he would never see him again. He had heard from Paris that Lamennais was mortally ill, and on January 28, he wrote to Armand
Lévy, the young leftist he had sheltered in June 1849 and who was
now, with others, taking care of Lamennais, that he was shaken to
the core by the news. Who was looking after Lamennais and his
papers, he wanted to know. The dying man had been writing "a
book on (that is, against) all religions," and Michelet urged Lévy
to save it. He said he was frightened and desolate at the thought
of "the vultures"—presumably the Jesuits—hovering over his
friend.[31] He then gave Lévy a last message for Lamennais:

> If M. Lamennais is still alive and can understand, tell him that
> I feel it as a misfortune in my life to be so far from him at this
> moment. Tell him we are and always will be his children. This
> great man, so badly off, is himself the painful and cruel birth
> that is letting the world pass from the last limbo of the Middle
> Ages to the modern light. Ten years ago he said, "I have no
> more books; when I want one, I borrow a Virgil." This sum-
> mer, I saw only one book in his house, Voltaire.[32]

Lamennais died on February 27. When Michelet heard the
news on March 4, he wrote immediately to his son-in-law, Alfred,
"I shall miss the man, I shall miss this word of steel in which I
found new strength; I shall miss this austere house where I used to
go with you and, more recently, with my wife, especially on Sundays, to communicate with this great heart, to nourish myself from
his discourse. My own is full of tears, thus little worthy of him who
has just given us such examples. May he pardon me if he sees it. I
embrace you all in this common grief."[33]

CHAPTER 23

LE BANQUET;
REBIRTH IN ACQUI

"On Sundays, to communicate with this great heart, to nourish myself from his discourse." "We are and always will be his children." These words betray much.

I have indicated above (Introduction) the useful Freudian distinction between two kinds of internalization of the paternal model, which support two aspects of conscience. Superego is the negative, punitive side of conscience; ego ideal, the positive, exemplary model used as a guide to life. In Hugo's *Les Misérables,* for example, the relentless police inspector Javert represents the punitive superego of the hero Jean Valjean; the saintly Bishop Myriel, his ego ideal. The superego is generally viewed as more primitive, more based on unconscious drives, so that the mildest father can be felt as a superego source, since the punishment a child's conscience deals him is automatically associated unconsciously with the father and has little to do with the father's actual behavior.

Thus the death even of a gentle father like Furcy Michelet, never described by his son as punitive, and materially dependent on him, could trigger in the son a storm of reproaches—in Michelet's case, because of his earlier affections for the Christian Middle Ages, offensive to the father's Voltairean views.[1] And it is also comprehensible that the first anniversary of his father's death should have provoked in him a new flood of self-reproaches, denunciations of his sensual pleasures and artistic self-indulgence, from which he could find relief only in his stoic affirmation of republican ideals of self-sacrifice.

Lamennais had been Michelet's ego ideal, his adopted model, something like Bishop Myriel for Hugo's Jean Valjean. The loss of such a positive model might be compared with the loss of Madame

Dumesnil twelve years earlier. It unleashed a work from the recesses of his feelings and imagination that combined the naturalist populism of *Le Peuple* with the ex-priest Lamennais's social radicalism and devotion to the common people, attitudes that Michelet adopted as his own in the months after the death of his *père adoptif.* Also similar to the period of Madame Dumesnil's death was the flood of reflections and autobiographic notes during and just after the composition of *Le Banquet.*

The relationship between Michelet's emotional and intellectual worlds was frequently mirrored in the notes for his books and lectures as well as in his journal.[2] Before the encounter with Madame Dumesnil in 1840, these sources betrayed his difficulty in connecting those worlds: he wrote as a Robinson Crusoe, with only his own developing personality, his intellect, and his conscience to communicate with. Pauline was no more than his "moi sensuel." The explosion of notes linking life and work after 1840 reveals that his personality, through love, was merging with that of Madame Dumesnil. The death of his father in 1846 added another inner voice to his thinking and writing. This voice, which had initially taken the harsh tones of revolutionary justice in the polemics against Christianity of his first volumes on the Revolution, gradually became reconciled with that of Madame Dumesnil, the voice of maternal love and nature. We have seen this reconciliation in his joining of the principles of justice with those of fraternal love and nurturance, both in the chapter on the federations and in his concept of the social and religious revolution.

The Revolution of 1848, which led quickly to the class war of June, broke Michelet's idealism, based precariously as it was on those voices of the dead. In 1849, finding love incarnate to replace the purely spiritual love that had died in him, he supplemented the voices of the departed with a living one, Athenaïs's. Through her, he recovered his social idealism, but he realized that the renewed embassy of love and reconciliation she had inspired in him was impotent without the charismatic power to speak directly to the masses. He sensed that his young friend Eugène Noel had that power, but Noel's talents were buried in the Norman countryside; he *knew* the famous Lamennais had it, and that was why, as père adoptif, as ego ideal, the Christian revolutionary invaded his dreams even before the Revolution of 1848. And that is also why, just after Lamennais's death, *Le Banquet* represented Michelet's last effort to write a revolutionary "legend" for the people.[3]

Michelet's "descent," begun in 1851, had taken him to the fishing village of Nervi, where, in contact with nature and the common people, he reached bottom. Poverty, cold, and illness were the conditions in which the Christian socialist message of Lamennais fused with his belief in the necessity of the religious and social revolution. The literary result was *Le Banquet*; the psychological one, profound sentiments of rebirth and renewal.

Guided by the spirit of the departed Lamennais, Michelet celebrated in the spring of 1854 his own festival of federation. Underlying the new direction was his recuperation of vital, half-forgotten memories of Madame Dumesnil, his father, and his childhood. These memories solidified his ties to nature and to the doomed religious and social revolution of 1793, and they gave new meaning to his more recent recollections, of Alfred—and of Athenaïs. For though he was breaking out of the strict control his fidelity to Athenaïs had placed on his memories of earlier feelings and attachments, he was not forgetting her either.

His first written reflections on *Le Banquet*—a note dealing with it and a letter to Alfred—mirror this new integration of life and work. Both were written on March 12, 1854, eight days after Michelet heard of Lamennais's death. March 12 was also his fifth wedding anniversary, which linked Athenaïs as well to the new work. The note began with a tribute to his five years with his young wife and then, through a description of his life in Nervi, moved into the subject of the book; the letter to Alfred, without reminding his sensitive son-in-law of the anniversary, broached the rest:

> This life of silence, of inaction, of meditation, has not been without an extension of my horizon; a thousand ideas have come to me, of which we will talk. This miserable, dried out little edge of the Apennines ... has told me several things I didn't know about human destiny. Everything here is poor, thirsty, or hungry (except for a couple of dozen walled and privileged gardens) and everything reveals so much the more the idea of the times: the dream of the universal banquet. Oh! The ideas of Chaumette and the Commune on the necessary and the sufficient life seem neither base nor materialist here. The plants themselves tell ... the too real identity of the needs of the soul and the body. However distinct the two substances may be, the first undergoes almost fatally the servitudes of the other.[4]

The only important aspects of the hastily scribbled note on *Le Banquet* left out of the letter to Alfred—apart from the one about his marriage—were references to his childhood, to other, grossly materialist interpretations of the "sufficient life," and to the political exiles of the period. The first two references merged in the note. He denied he had suffered real hunger in his impoverished childhood, said he only encountered it in Nervi, and then a bit further on, in connection with "the sufficient life," he wrote:

—materialist point of view? Not at all.
—for you, egoistic gluttons [*mangeurs égoistes*] it's a solitary pleasure.
—for us, serious workers, it's life in the family, fraternity; it's the banquet (regrets of my grandfather for being unable to buy me a Bavarian cream on the Boulevard du Temple).[5]

The last was followed, on a line with another margin, by "sacred renewal, wanted by nature." At the end, he wrote on his persecuted republican brothers: "And the others? Where are they? . . . Cayenne,[6] Algeria, Siberia! and all the earth is exile, famine . . . when will it begin, the great, the universal banquet?"

The title chosen by Michelet for his new book refracts a multitude of oral aspects of his life at the moment. In the first place, as he indicated on March 12, he saw real hunger all around him; he may have suffered it himself, and he held responsible for this hunger not so much the niggardliness of nature as the greed of men living outside of fraternity, and thus against nature. Some of the fifty pages of notes for *Le Banquet* published by Eric Fauquet[7] are suffused with oral obsessions, particularly his first sketches of the work's three main divisions.[8] Later, in May, these three sections took the titles under which Fauquet has published them: book I, "Le Jeûne" (the fast), dealing with the intimate banquet of his personal existence in Nervi and the social situation there; book II, "Le Banquet socialiste," which, on the basis of the contrast between socialist and Catholic districts in Lyons, summarized the fundamental opposition between the two principles they represented; and book III, "Du banquet socialiste et républicain de la république du monde." This last is largely a theoretical essay linking contemporary socialism to the traditions of the French Revolution. A month earlier, however, in the first outline of this tripartite division, the sections bore the following titles: "1. ma famine personnelle—1er banquet 2. ma famine locale . . . les devorans [the devourers], *banquet de partage* de l'eau 3. ma famine universelle. banquet socialiste!"[9] And on April 2, in a note that began with the dates he had conceived "the idea of *Le Banquet*" and an expressive "on the 18th I felt my entire life converging toward it," he seven times used the words *famine, devourers,* and *starving,* as in his elaboration of section 2, "famine locale":[10]

—*the devourers* . . . Genoa bankers
—*the devourers* . . . little princes, priests
—*the devourers* . . . Russia etc. successors of primitive crocodiles.

A similar note from this time has six further variants on "devouring," followed by "history of insects . . . princes . . . small states . . . Italian budgets: Parma, Modena, Rome!!! history of insects . . . priests parishes eat people, religious congregations [*oratoires*] bite on the parishes."[11]

These abundant signs of oral needs and fears are more likely to have been psychologically than physiologically founded, however difficult Michelet's material circumstances in Italy. At this critical point in his life, he reached back into his past to reexamine primitive fears and joys and fuse them to present hopes. The devouring and biting of the church and the petty despots of Italy were projections, as in his "Introduction" of 1831, of the maleficent power of the *mère terrible*, now unveiled in an orgy of oral sadism, but he refused to associate this sadism with mother nature. On April 26, he stated unequivocally, "—nature a stepmother? Made children to starve them? Blasphemy."[12] And on May 5, he pointed to the real source of the famine: "Don't accuse nature, but the devouring insects. Ex[ample] private property so well taken care of . . . communal property so neglected, violated."

All this is moving toward a triumphant reassertion of the matriarchal vision of nature he had developed under Madame Dumesnil's influence. He had quoted her as saying in 1841, in the course of a discussion about the possible influence of nature on his work, "She is coming to you with full breasts and her hands full of flowers,"[13] and he had come to accept this optimistic naturalism unreservedly in the years before his father's death. Now, working out the first part of *Le Banquet,* he invoked again "the great mother . . . who everywhere offers the cup filled to the brim."[14] In mid-May, he completed the chapter "La philosophie du jeûne" with a striking echo of Madame Dumesnil's augury: "Nature is coming everywhere to man as a good and rich wet nurse with full breasts."[15]

The beginning of the chapter that ends with this resonance of his earlier love elucidates the vocabulary of oral anxiety Michelet had used in his notes. Alluding to his intestinal illness of the previous year, he said that for a long time he could digest nothing more than a little milk each day and was unable to work: "a complete change of habits, a true death for the laborer." From this personal experience, he went on to discuss the social sources of material dearth, in Italy and elsewhere, and the Christian hostility to nature that found the highest good in fasting. Against that asceticism, which he saw as characterizing medieval thought, he upheld the revolution in attitudes toward nature of the Renaissance. This last prefigured the volume of the *Histoire de France* on the sixteenth century that he was to begin a few months later; moreover, it was a continuation of the theme of his "Grainville." Columbus's discovery of a new world with a new nature, he argued, put an end to the medieval conviction that the world was closed and dying. The new concept of nature as youthful and abundant constituted a violent denial "of the theory of the exhaustion of the world, of the dogma of fasting and abstinence . . . Life surges obstinately, untamable, and invincible, against the religion of death . . . The Hussites no longer want to open their mouths for nothing; they cry out openly: *The cup to the people!* So does Rabelais, the great prophet and host of the Abbey, who slakes the thirst of the Renaissance and lets it see at the bottom of the glass the secrets of the future."[16]

Also pointing to a later work (*La Mer,* 1861) was Michelet's description of the beneficence of nature in great bodies of water, which brings us remarkably close to the pre-Oedipal significance of Freud's "oceanic feeling":

> More fecund still is the sea. Its innumerable children who nourish all of nature are themselves nourished by it; it cradles and supports them; they cannot breathe without being nourished at the same time; they swim in the infinity of this perpetual banquet.
>
> I had sometimes felt this growling sea who, by her voice, one is tempted to think savage. I used to see her come to me, on a certain northern shore, full of life, fecundity, nourishing for its own, and no less so for those who live on dry land.
>
> Those memories of the ocean, of the nutritive forces of the North, came back to me in what seems the least likely place to recall them, on the arid shores of a sea that was luminous but nearly a desert. There my heart conceived *Le Banquet.* The universal fast of the world against the effort of nature to envelop its infant with life and nutrition . . . filled me with sorrow.[17]

These first chapters of *Le Banquet* are Michelet at his most materialist; the book began with genuine experiences of hunger and deprivation, and the core chapter of the first part, on the judge of Nervi, concerns a saintly, Lamennais-type Christian socialist who attempted to divide land for the local peasantry. In the last part, however, on socialist theory, the materialism is muted in favor of Michelet's communitarian religion. Unfortunately, he was able to incorporate only a fraction of what he had outlined in his notes. Running sympathetically, if briefly, through the socialist traditions of his time from Babeuf and Cloots through Saint-Simon and Fourier, he was looking for a socialism that would combine brotherhood with heroic sacrifice in the traditions of the federations and the armies of the Revolution. Many themes he had earlier stressed—

the need for revolutionary festivities, theater, and secular civic institutions to found the Republic—are recapitulated here.[18] There is also in these chapters an emphasis on class antagonisms, as in the judge of Nervi's struggle against the big landholders of the area and his effort to establish communal agriculture for the poor peasants. And the critical attitude to property of the last part of the *Révolution* is sustained. But the theory of socialism, so avidly discussed in the notes, is not worked out. The only thing that is clear about Michelet's socialist sympathies is that, through his orality, he was capable of linking the most material foundations of humanity's existence to its most sublimely spiritual attainment—brotherhood in communion.[19] This is all Michelet leaves us with, since ten pages of highly interesting notes on Proudhon, Fourier, Saint-Simon, and the antecedents of modern socialism were left largely unused in the text of *Le Banquet*.[20]

That these notes were not worked out is significant. It shows that the idea of the social and religious revolution, which Michelet should have explicated in this work, was losing its grip on him. What is perhaps more significant for his future than these unwritten pages on the bugbears of nineteenth-century capitalism was the conclusion of the chapter "Le Banquet intime." There he wrote of the true communion of the family meal, where "the woman is the mother and wet nurse of the man." The chapter concerns his gradual recovery from his stomach ailment, and he is full of praise for Athenaïs's care for him: "I rejuvenated; it seemed to me that in this beloved nourishment I was leaving behind centuries of history and of work, above all the bitterness of my last book, the terrible '93, which had eaten my entrails, drunk my blood, absorbed my life to the marrow of my bones. The sacred bread of Italy, received from she who in this solitude represented for me la patrie . . . also began to increase my forces and raise my spirit."[21]

At the end, he described a lovely outdoor dinner under the luminous sky on January 30, 1854, together with "she who in this solitude represented *la patrie*": "We had a moment of silence and our looks became profound . . . What they looked at was neither the heavens nor the sea—another infinity, less visible. A word broke the silence and I don't know which of us uttered it. 'But *the others*, where are they?' What have they experienced? Are they alive? Are they dead? We returned in silence, not daring too much to interrogate these thoughts blacker than the night."[22]

There was only one "other" about whom Michelet had cause to ask with alarm on January 30 whether he was living or dead: Lamennais. The report of his death, received on March 4, was followed a week later by the first sketch of *Le Banquet*.

If the death of Lamennais was the catalyst of Michelet's new work, a puzzle confronts us: Why is there no more than a fleeting mention of Lamennais in the fifty pages of notes for *Le Banquet* and none at all in the text? Michelet's feud with the church was the probably reason. Lamennais, though cast out of the church, had always viewed himself as a Christian, and Christian theology was his point of departure.

His career aborted by the dictatorship, which the clergy had supported, Michelet was extremely sensitive to any possibility of further attacks on him, particularly on the religious issue. His outspoken sympathy for Christianity in the early 1830s had become an embarrassment twenty years later, because, he feared, his clerical enemies might use it to sneer at his subsequent violent attacks on the church and Christianity. That was the reason for his excision, when he republished the first parts of the *Histoire de France* in June 1852, of passages that could obviously be used against his present position: that Christianity was historically, and properly, doomed to death. A sentence that said, "It [Christianity] may change its clothing, but perish, never" was cut; another that said, "This sign of the passion is that of the triumph of moral liberty," was changed to refer simply to "the triumph of the soul" ("moral liberty" was viewed as Michelet's own supreme value).[23]

In the winter of 1854, Michelet learned that Alexandre Dumas, exiled in Brussels, was planning a chapter of his *Mémoires* to deal with Michelet and had delegated it to his "slave" and fellow exile, Alphonse Esquiros.[24] This made Michelet extremely nervous, because he knew that Esquiros, a friendly, radical disciple of Lamennais,[25] thought the Revolution to be the continuator of Christianity, not its mortal antagonist, as the historian believed. Anxious, he wrote to Quinet, also in exile in Brussels, asking him to remind Esquiros of Michelet's view that the Christian dogma of grace "led fatally to the reign of the privileged"; furthermore, he wanted Quinet to tell Esquiros that "from the second volume of the *History of France* . . . I posed the necessity of a transitory death of Christianity . . . There is no contradiction in my past of 1833 and 1846."[26]

Under these conditions, it was impossible to say anything positive about Lamennais, Esquiros's master, without encouraging the camp of those who tried to see socialism as based on Christian principles, and without reminding everyone that in the early 1830s, he had enthusiastically defended the faith he now attacked—indeed, that he had possibly absorbed this faith at Lamennais's feet in 1831.[27] And, of course, saying anything pejorative about him was out of the question. So, apart from his intimate letters, he kept silent about the personal meaning of the older man's death. The one fleeting mention of Lamennais in the notes for *Le Banquet* also had an intimate character. Michelet named him parenthetically, together with

Alfred Dumesnil, his autre moi, in the context of their sensitivity to the cultural resonances of music.[28] Adding to the personal implications of the reference is the fact that Michelet's paternal ancestors had been musicians: his grandfather had been the *maître de chapelle* (music master) to the bishop of Laon.[29]

In fact, there is one clear sign of a Catholic presence in his book that may have been the main reason that Michelet did not dare invoke his dead friend's name, indeed, that he never completed his book for publication: His theme of the spiritual banquet was directly appropriated, without acknowledgment, from the Eucharist of the Catholic enemy. Even though Michelet linked the banquet to Rabelais and Danton, his readers would have immediately connected the idea with the Last Supper. Joseph de Maistre, one of the most reactionary Catholic thinkers of the nineteenth century, had a half-century earlier expressed and wholeheartedly endorsed this thesis: "Men have not found any more expressive symbol of union than that of assembling next to each other to take common nourishment. This symbol has appeared to exalt union to the point of unity . . . This sentiment [of solidarity] being universal, religion has chosen to make it the base of its principal mystery."[30]

Le Banquet not only represents the most extreme celebration of what its author had called "romantic socialism," it also shows the first, intellectual and spiritual, phase of the rebirth that followed his social descent and his completion of the *History of the French Revolution*. After several months in Nervi and Turin spent linking his past, his ideas, and his existential condition, Michelet went for his health to Acqui, a small town between Genoa and Milan, where he supplemented his psychological experience with the physical sensation of rebirth through restorative mud baths.

Michelet was still ill when he reached Acqui. The stomach affliction, which he had hoped to shake off by moving to Italy, though lessened, had not been cured.[31] On leaving the coach late in the afternoon of June 5, he fainted.[32] His treatment, begun after two good nights of rest, gradually induced regression.

On June 16, he was thinking of his experiences as an adolescent in the clinic where his father worked and where son and father moved after the mother's death. The sanatorium reminded him of "many of the scenes of harshness, indifference, and frivolousness" he had witnessed at eighteen. He also had the same complaints about peer pressures that he had expressed as a youth in his autobiography. As a schoolboy, he had written in his *Mémorial*,[33] he was so sensitive to the raillery of his friends that "I decided to isolate myself entirely, to talk to no one, to see no one." When he went to the lycée, "the least look from anyone upset me, and the idea that I could appear ridiculous, an object of scorn, aroused in me a violent rage." In June 1854, midway through his treatment, he saw a similar feeling in Athenaïs: "Last night, the fifteenth, she was very upset by the criticisms of those who don't like it that one wants to be alone." And, thinking back to the unpleasantness they temporarily left behind on a brief mountain climb, he wrote: "The world hates those who are not its own. Nobles, wealthy, priests, they feel instinctively those whose hearts are with the people ... I accept willingly the hatred of my natural enemies."[34]

Between June 20 and 28, the intensified mud baths imparted a literal sense of rebirth from the bowels of mother earth. On the twentieth, he wrote: "Places such as this ... are the paths through which the maternal life of the earth communicates again with its children, restores their fatigued strength, revives their exhaustion, brings them back to action and hope." On June 21, describing "the pleasures of burial [in] *terra mater,*" his language suggests uterine symbiosis or ("cradle," "diaper bed") the echo of it in the first postnatal months: "Here, no reflection. The identification was too perfect between me and nature; I didn't distinguish myself from her in any way ... Woods, fields, prairies, disappear! Let us see the subterranean laboratory of the great universal mother." On the twenty-fourth, feelings of rebirth: "Disinterment ... from the shapeless mass, dark, funereal in appearance, but in no way malevolent, far from that: gentle and sympathetic ... the earth, supreme bed of repose."

His last treatment, on June 28, began with "quietude and beatitude, the maternal embrace of the earth," and ended with the restoration of his youth, the consummation of his rebirth: "Forget the ones that are under the earth. This day, pliable earth, really very clean, comes off easily with a little water. You emerge shining with a gleam of youth; the years and the sorrows seem to remain behind at the bottom of the bath basin."[35]

In *La Montagne,* he summed up the experience in Acqui, which he viewed as the source of his books on natural history, on love, and on the Renaissance: "Nature, forgotten for the sake of the ferocious labor that had so blindly evaded happiness ... reopened her arms and awaited me."[36]

Thus healed and reborn in the Italian earth, Michelet entered his vita nuova.

CONCLUSION: PERSONALITY, MENTALITY, AND HISTORY

It is as a historian of social structures that I present myself
... but as a historian who, placed before human facts and
recognizing in them, by their nature, psychological facts, tries
more and more in his works ... to explain them from within.

MARC BLOCH
"Projet d'un enseignement d'histoire comparée
des sociétés européennes"

Michelet's will to descend socially may have been motivated by
politics, but as we have seen, the frontier between the political and
the personal was as unguarded in his case as that between past and
present. In the "dark wood" of his nineteenth-century inferno, he
experienced the spiritual death of revolutionary idealism in 1793 as
an echo to the demise of the Second Republic. The death of Felicité
de Lamennais in February 1854 was in a sense the material symbol
of both those disasters. He recovered from these losses through the
reintegration of his personality into his historical vision in *Le Banquet* and through a literal sensation of rebirth at Acqui. These experiences were typical of his capacity to overcome political and
personal traumas by a "descent" into his intimate history, a descent
that psychoanalysts of the creative process call regression in the
service of the ego.[1]

We have seen this capacity in his two prior rebirths—the one
accompanying his relation to Madame Dumesnil in 1841–42 and
the other inspired by his love for Athenaïs Mialaret in 1848–49. In
all these cases, Michelet displayed an ability that was rare among
historians (though not among poets) to cathect his intellect both
with his "primary processes," his basic emotional constitution, and
with relived and reformulated affects of childhood and adolescence.

Thus, to penetrate to the psychological sources of community and social solidarity in *Le Peuple* and in *Histoire de la Révolution française,* our historian used the *rameau d'or,* the golden bough given him by his experience with Madame Dumesnil. Through it he recaptured feelings of symbiosis with his mother and with nature; through it his adolescent love for Paul Poinsot became a model for revolutionary fraternity. This recaptured emotional life became in turn the basis of the humanitarian social religion he envisaged in *Le Banquet.*

In developing this argument, I have repeatedly emphasized that Michelet's ability to join his analytic capacities to his emotional experience occurred in the specific setting of the social-romantic mentality of the July Monarchy. That it outlived this setting is not surprising if we bear in mind that Michelet was a half century old when the June uprising showed the futility of the romantic dream of social harmony and that his dismissals in any case placed him outside the institutional framework in which the hard-nosed positivistic scholarship of the second half of the century would evolve. Yet if Michelet's unique capacity for social-psychological insights—an almost uncanny proto-Freudianism—received support from an important part of the elite culture of his time, this raises a more general question: Why social romanticism? Why the common denominator of reverence for nature, the common people, and la patrie that tied Michelet to figures as diverse as Eugène Sue, Victor Hugo, Pierre Jean de Béranger, Edgar Quinet, George Sand, and Pierre Leroux? What empowered so many of the poets and thinkers of the July Monarchy to break through the boundaries that usually separated analytic, poetic, and religious discourse, to fantasize new syntheses and cosmogonies?

I have suggested a part of the answer above. The French Revolution remained until 1871 on the agenda of French republicans as unfinished business. As long as a stable republican solution was unattained, dissatisfaction with the undemocratic regimes that generally governed France between 1814 and 1870 led bourgeois radicals to seek a renewal of the revolutionary alliance of plebs and elite that had made 1789 possible. Under the Second Empire, both the repressive authoritarianism of the regime and the bitter memories of the June uprising prevented any major revival of the revolutionary alliance until 1869, and the Commune quickly ended that. But before 1848 and especially after 1840, the political perspective of renewed revolution was clear, and republican ideologues of national unity, supplemented by romantic prophets of social, sexual, natural, and cosmic harmony, sprang from the ground like wildflowers.

Jerrold Seigel links the bohemian romanticism of the July Monarchy to the "party of Movement," the left-wing bourgeois current that lost out in the power struggle after 1830. This group favored "a politics open toward the lower tiers of society"—that is, toward the shopkeeper-artisan strata that had manned the plebeian battalions in 1789 and 1830 and would do so again in 1848.[2] The link that Seigel indicates between the party of movement and bohemian romanticism is even more evident for bohemianism's more respectable older brother: the social romanticism of the July Monarchy. During the Second Republic, Michelet supported both the activist wing of the party of movement, embodied in the electoral committee he joined in March 1848, and the heterogeneous group of social romantics whose meeting he had dreamed of when he began his *History of the French Revolution*: Lamennais, Sand, Béranger, Quinet, and Sue.

Michelet, who combined plebeian origins with bourgeois status, personified the harmonious alliance of social classes that was the goal of both the party of movement and the social romantics, and his efforts to bring the common people into history by reliving their fate were made possible by psychological returns and regressions to his own childhood and adolescence. Without the popular origins, many other social romantics undertook a similar exercise of social-psychological "descent." Novels of Sue, Sand, and Hugo that sympathetically portrayed the lot of the lower orders, an opera like Hector Berlioz's *Benvenuto Cellini* that celebrated the evolution from master artisan to artist, journalistic efforts such as those of Pierre Leroux, even the social utopian fantasies of the Saint-Simonians and Fourierists all bear witness to the intense preoccupation of the social romantics with forging political and cultural links between high and low in France.

This brings us to a more general observation about the evolving relation between elite and popular mentalities after the Renaissance. It is important to see the social romantics—and Michelet—within this context, which in recent decades has been illuminated by the theories of Bakhtin, Elias, and Foucault and by the historical research of Burke, Muchembled, Agulhon, and others. In these terms, the social romanticism of the July Monarchy constitutes a rupture with the centuries-old tendency of the elite culture to distance itself disdainfully from the popular culture and to suppress it with moralizing rigor and bureaucratic efficiency.

Norbert Elias's notion of a "civilizing process," the diffusion in the royal courts of early modern Europe of norms of increasing control over affect and bodily functions has been extended by Peter Burke and Robert Muchembled to the strategies of the Catholic and Protestant churches of this period, which with state support propagated similar norms to transform, subordinate, curtail, or suppress the traditional, mostly rural, popular cultures.[3] This pattern of repression has perhaps been best studied in France, but it was a European phenomenon. What church and state opposed in the popular culture was the anarchic violence that frequently erupted in its festivities, its recalcitrance to central control, its widely varying sexual and marital practices, and the powerful residue of pagan beliefs, condemned as superstitions, beneath its superficial acceptance of the rituals and holy days of the Christian faith.

Underlying these abhorred aspects of the popular culture was a cyclical style of life, based on the seasons, that contrasted sharply with the implicit assumptions of linear progress: increasing wealth, a more powerful state structure, and movement toward the kingdom of God. Such assumptions were shared by the secular and religious powers of the early modern era. The rural culture's proximity to nature and its dependence on natural forces also bred attitudes that were usually distant from Christian asceticism's disparagement of the natural world in favor of purely spiritual values and aspirations.

Conflicts between the elite and the popular cultures were rarely fought out directly. On the whole, the reforming "civilizing offensive" of the early modern church and state took the form of prohibitions of objectionable aspects of rural customs or festive rituals, such as charivaris, carnivals, and veillées, and vigorous efforts to replace uncontrollable local organizations like the abbayes de jeunesse by churchsponsored confréries. The peasant and town cultures rarely opposed such reforms directly; normally they adapted to them, internalizing much of the new morality and compromising overtly with the rest. On the basis of the newly internalized Christian norms, many of the older rituals and magical beliefs were now suppressed and feared as anti-Christian, the work of the Devil. Isolated women who continued the old beliefs and practices, for example, were stigmatized by their more "enlightened" neighbors as diabolically inspired witches and reported to the inquisitorial arm of the church.

The relation of the hegemonic powers to the popular classes entailed a triple suppression of low by high. First, the culture and consciousness of the lower orders became increasingly controlled, penetrated, and colonized by norms and values of their social superiors. Second, this control took the form, within the psychic structures of the traditional peasant and town cultures, of an internalization of norms that mandated increasing control over and repression of lower bodily functions and instinctually based impulses of sex and aggression. Perhaps most important, such control also implied a general control over personality development, which had vast implications for modes of thought and concepts of time. I will explain.

William Sewell has noted that the modern concept of property developed by the social philosophers of the Enlightenment presupposed an absolute ownership that contrasted sharply with the earlier assumption that an object could be subject to a wide variety of ownership rights.[4] Sewell's example suggests two social universes. The older notion of property mirrored a premodern social structure in which powers and authorities were diffusely present in such institutions as corporations, estates, and confréries. This social structure in turn reflected the compromises that mediated between the absolutist ambitions of church and state and the decentralized, often archaic reality of traditional urban and rural societies in the early modern era.

In fact, the ambitions of religious and secular absolutism, which went beyond the halfway houses that characterized the corporate structures of the old regime, were only to be realized in the bourgeois civilization of the modern era. They were formulated in the essential sphere of character formation by Père Maldonnat, who argued in the seventeenth century that the will should command the desires "like the father his son, the pedagogue his disciple, the lord his servant, and the king his subjects."[5] There is no room for mediating agencies in such a perspective. Freud, who constituted both the culmination and the repudiation of this line of thought, unwittingly offered a psychoanalytic translation of Père Maldonnat's dictum when he said that the rational ego should master and direct the id drives just as a rider masters and directs his horse.[6]

This personality ideal implied more than the dominance of higher over lower faculties. Freud saw the individual evolution toward this dominance as passing through the stages of psychosexual development from oral to genital, and from pre-Oedipal symbiosis with the mother to post-Oedipal identification with the father; his ideals in this respect cohered fully with those of the "civilizing offensive." The founder of psychoanalysis labeled "pathological" any recurrence to earlier stages of development.[7] Similarly, the secular and religious ideologists of absolutism opposed, in the festive culture of the people, recurrences to anal and oral pleasures and aggressions, which they viewed both as morally obscene and dangerously disruptive of social order; in the carnivals, charivaris, and folktales of the early modern era, the powers of the day often smelled rebellion.

These are precisely the aspects of popular culture that, according to Mikhail Bakhtin, constituted in Rabelais the grotesque humor of a world turned upside down and made of him one of the last syntheses before absolutism of popular and elite cultures.[8] In fact, the picture of premodern peasant mentalities that emerges from such studies as Emmanuel Le Roy Ladurie's *Montaillou* and Robert Darnton's "Peasants Tell Tales" is one of a continual moving back and forth in adult life among cultural expressions of anal, oral, and genital, pre-Oedipal and Oedipal levels of experience.[9] Such movement between varying levels of psychosexual development is consonant with the cyclical pattern of growth in nature-bound rural societies and with their cyclical notion of time. It is, however, completely inconsistent with the personality ideals propagated by apologists of the new absolutism, such as Père Maldonnat, or with the values of bourgeois inheritors of their cultural hegemony in the modern era.

Bourgeois hegemony, however, as we know, was mediated in the modern world by revolution, in France by the Revolution of 1789. That revolution crystallized into stable form only with the Third Republic, more than eighty years later. During much of the intervening period, and especially during the July Monarchy, bourgeois impulses to continue the Old Regime's cultural agenda of disciplining and moralizing the lower orders were counterbalanced by the need to forge a common front against the bastard remnants of monarchy. This need, incarnated politically in the party of movement and culturally in the social romantics, constituted the supportive framework for the many returns and regressions that inspired Michelet's historical vision—to the common people, to nature, to the recalled emotions of childhood and youth, and to previously repressed feelings of pre-Oedipal symbiosis with the mother.

Michelet's vision of popular culture does not match Bakhtin's. He was far too ambivalent about his plebeian background, far too schooled in an austere lower-middle-class morality of work and achievement, for that. Yet there is another side to the mature Michelet, the side that attempted to recapture a link to nature and especially to his own nature, that longed to "descend." He tried repeatedly to write in an idiom popular enough to inspire in the mass of his compatriots the same love for the ideals of the Revolution that infused his complex, brilliant, and visionary history writing. In fact, it is precisely his divided attitude toward the common people, his ineradicable affection and yearning for them, combined with his desire to make them what they were not, that moves us in his confrontation of their fate under the new powers of "machinism" and Caesarism.

It was with an uncommon mixture of self-knowledge, sincerity, and intellectual power that Michelet posed in *Le Peuple* questions of the alienation of men and women from their own nature and from their fellows that social theorists are still struggling with. In his history of 1789 to 1794, his analysis of the collapse of the principles of justice and fraternity had as its point of departure a transfigured vision of plebeian brotherhood in the federations of 1790, and it was this vision to which his intellectual descendants

Marc Bloch and Jean Guéhenno appealed in the black days of 1940 as a source of national pride and resistance for the years ahead.

If Michelet is admired by many in the present generation of French historians as the greatest of their nineteenth-century predecessors, it is not because he was a faultless practitioner of his craft. Indeed, his exalted nationalism and his carefree attitude toward sources often lead modern historians to reject him as a model. Yet this is the dross; we must be careful when discarding it that we do not lose the gold he bequeathed us. For in the very excess of his subjectivity, Michelet posed questions that spilled over all disciplinary boundaries and that foreshadowed an integration of the fractured study of human culture.

Roland Barthes wrote of Michelet that "his subjectivity . . . was only the earliest form of that insistence on totality . . . of that attention to the most insignificant detail of the concrete which today mark the very method of our human sciences." Barthes continued: "It is because Michelet was a discredited historian (in the scientist sense of the term) that he turns out to have been at once a sociologist, an ethnologist, a psychoanalyst, a social historian . . . He truly anticipated the foundation of a general science of man."[10] For several decades, this integrationist goal was interpreted by Marc Bloch's successors in the editorial board of the *Annales* to signify primarily studies of long-term economic and social processes, preferably quantifiable. Essays on individuals were denigrated as studies of mere "events," in spite of the resurrection of "insignificant detail" as a new heuristic golden bough by Carlo Ginzburg and others. Recently, however, in a most important editorial statement, the editors of the *Annales* recognized the potential significance of the event for understanding the broader frameworks and called for "new methods" that would, among other things, relate "the individual to the group and the society." Thus, to return to the idiom of our subject, the circle completes, and the grandfather's soul appears indeed to be reborn in his grandchildren.

APPENDIX A:
MICHELET'S
SECOND WIFE

Michelet's second wife, Athenaïs, has been systematically deni-grated as "veuve abusive" by the scholars who have taken charge of Michelet's papers since her death in 1899.[1] She has been held responsible for mutilating his journal, for publishing falsified ver-sions of his uncompleted manuscripts, and for misusing, bowdler-izing, and distorting his brief manuscript biography of her, as well as their love letters, in her edition of their correspondence. More generally, she has also been accused of distracting him from the more "serious" political perspectives of his histories of France and of the Revolution to the foggily romantic disquisitions on natural history and feminine nature of his later period.

During her widowhood, Athenaïs was undoubtedly guilty of most of the specific outrages against scholarship with which she has been charged; yet the terms of her condemnation, the lack of consideration for the circumstances of her effort to continue her husband's intellectual posterity, seem to me sometimes no less culp-able than her own arbitrariness. For one thing, she lacked any schol-arly training that might have equipped her properly to administer and publish her husband's manuscripts; the source of that lack lay neither in inadequate intelligence nor in the absence of professional training institutes, such as those that trained her critics, but in the exclusion of women from any education more advanced than train-ing as governesses and elementary school teachers.

For another, accusations that she bowdlerized his texts, elim-inating from the letters and other documents she published any overt sexual references, fail to take into account the literary con-ventions that prevailed until the mid-twentieth century and that prevented unexpurgated editions of most important autobiographical documents—such as the Goncourt *Journal* and the letters of Flaubert—until recent decades. The prudery one assumes to have been behind some of Athenaïs's excisions was common to the vast majority of men in her class and period. Her only seemingly inexcusable offense is the occasional mutilation and destruction of unpublished documents, but even here there are mitigating factors: she left untouched enough striking information on her husband's sexual tastes and dreams to fill a virtual encyclopedia of perversions;[2] and he had, after all, given her carte blanche with his papers (see chapter 3, note 15).

As to her editing of his posthumously published works, the charges against her have been exaggerated. Her editing of Michelet's *Le Banquet,* for example, though ideologically slanted and doubtless missing a passage on infant baptism that was indirectly critical of her, did present the world, shortly after her husband's death, with a reasonable version of an important Michelet manuscript at a time (1879) when his work was being ignored or belittled by the new historical positivism of the Third Republic. And her edition of their love letters, which she prefaced only a month before her own death, whatever its defects—she joins the letters by passages of pseudo-Michelet drawn in part from his 1861 biography of her and in part from her imagination[3]—at least had the advantage of printing her letters as well as his. In the scholarly edition of these letters (an appendix to volume 2 of the journal), Paul Viallaneix gives a more complete version of the historian's side, but Athenaïs's missives are reduced to meager excerpts in footnotes, so that one usually has little idea of just what Michelet was responding to.

As for Athenaïs's influence on her husband's scholarship, she can no more be held responsible for a deterioration of his political and social engagement than for his absorption in matters of natural history and feminine nature and his sexual obsessions. The fascination with nature and women was rooted in the Michelet of the early 1840s and the withdrawal from politics in his disillusionment during the Second Republic. If any one figure is responsible for the apolitical direction of Michelet's work after 1850, it is Louis-Napoléon. When the authoritarian empire became liberal in the late 1860s and the republican tide again ran high, Athenaïs resolutely supported her husband's resumption of political engagement.

APPENDIX B:
THE SUPPLEMENTS TO
MICHELET'S JOURNAL
INTIME, *1849–1854*

Michelet's published journal is composed of two sorts of documents. One is the—frequently interrupted—day by day account of his work and life which filled the four volumes bearing the title *Journal intime* that were sealed after Athenaïs's death and deposited in the Institut de France until 1950. Editors Viallaneix and Digeon wisely chose to supplement these often summary entries with various unpublished notes of clearly autobiographical significance found in Michelet's papers at the Bibliothèque Historique. After a struggle with purists at the institute who wanted to publish only the bound and sealed *Journal intime,* their point of view, militantly supported by their patron at the institute, Lucien Febvre, prevailed. Some of the materials at the Bibliothèque Historique were travel notes that belonged in the personal record (such as the extensive account of the visit to Germany in 1842), but many notes were either reflections on Michelet's spiritual and emotional condition of the moment, jotted down outside the journal, or ideas for a book he was working on that revealed something of his personal condition.

The frequency of such notes, especially of the second sort, is an index of the extent to which Michelet's scholarship was mixing with his personal life, which meant, from 1849 on, his relationship to Athenaïs. After that year, as his social hopes waned, as the purity of his young bride became an irritant, perhaps also as he realized the hurt he had caused to his own family by marrying her, ambivalence about Athenaïs led him to write less and less on the tie between his work and life. Not only his journal but his notes for his books reflected this emotional attrition.

Viallaneix's tables on the manuscript sources of his edition are eloquent. In 1849, the year of Michelet's remarriage, Viallaneix found eleven such notes. In 1850, five. In 1851, just three (seven additions in 1851 from papers that had come into the possession of the Rist family are generally brief journal entries reporting progress on the *Légendes démocratiques du nord*). In 1852, there were two. In 1853, *none.* And in 1854, none until March 12. In fact, in the entire twenty months' exile in Nantes and Italy, during which Michelet wrote his last two volumes on the history of the Revolution, *Les Femmes de la Révolution,* and prepared the *Légendes démocratiques du nord* for publication, Viallaneix saw not one scrap of paper in the notes for his literary production of the period as directly relating that production to Michelet's intimate existence. In the less than four months from March 12 to July 4, 1854, Viallaneix found thirteen such notes, most of them highly significant for the link between *Le Banquet* and Michelet's personal condition. Eric Fauquet, in his edition of *Le Banquet* for the *Œuvres complètes,* includes even more of them. The sudden flood of these documents testify to the "breakthrough" character of Michelet's work on *Le Banquet.*

ABBREVIATIONS
USED IN NOTES

BHVP   Bibliothèque Historique de la Ville de Paris
AN   Archives Nationales
OC   Jules Michelet, *Œuvres complètes,* ed. Paul Viallaneix
            (Paris, 1971–)
HRF   Jules Michelet, *Histoire de la Révolution française,* ed.
            Gérard Walter, 2 vols. (Paris, 1952)
J1, J2   Jules Michelet, *Journal,* ed. Paul Viallaneix (Paris,
            1969 and 1972), vols. 1 and 2
EJ   Jules Michelet, *Ecrits de jeunesse, Journal (1820–1823),*
            ed. Paul Viallaneix (Paris, 1959)
Ollivier Emile Ollivier, *Journal I, 1846–1860,* ed. Theodore
            Zeldin and Anne Troisier de Diaz (Paris, 1961)
P   Jules Michelet, *Le Peuple,* ed. Paul Viallaneix (Paris,
            1974)
PE   Jules Michelet, *The People,* trans. and intro. John P.
            McKay (Urbana, 1973)
S   Jules Michelet, *Lettres inédites (1841–1871),* ed. Paul
            Sirven (Paris, 1924)
LI   Jules Michelet, *Lettres inédites addressées à Mlle
            Mialaret (Mme Michelet)* (Paris, ± 1900) [*Œuvres
            complètes de J. Michelet*]
Voie royale   Paul Viallaneix, *La Voie royale, essai sur l'idée de
            peuple dans l'œuvre de Michelet* (Paris, 1959)
Vie et pensée   G. Monod, *La Vie et la pensée de Jules Michelet
            (1798–1852),* 2 vols. (Paris, 1923)

NOTES

INTRODUCTION: BIOGRAPHY AND THEORY

1. Fernand Braudel referred to his master, Lucien Febvre, as "since Michelet . . . the greatest, perhaps the only historian writing in the French language" (cited by H. Stuart Hughes in *The Obstructed Path: French Social Thought in the Years of Desperation, 1930–1960* [New York, 1968], 21).

2. See William R. Keylor, *Academy and Community: The Foundations of the French Historical Profession* (Cambridge, Mass., 1975), 55–74; Pim den Boer, *Geschiedenis als Beroep: De Professionalisering van de Geschiedsbeoefening in Frankrijk (1818–1914)* (Nijmegen, 1987); Charles-Olivier Carbonell, *Histoire et historiens: Une Mutation idéologique des historiens français, 1865–1885* (Toulouse, 1976).

3. Hughes, *Obstructed Path*, 21–26. Febvre devoted two series of lectures at the Collège de France during World War II to Michelet, published after the war a 75-page introduction to a short book of selections from Michelet (*Michelet, 1798–1874: Introduction et choix par Lucien Febvre* [Geneva and Paris, 1946]), supervised the preparation of the "Journal intime" for publication (Paul Viallaneix and Claude Digeon were assigned the task by Febvre), and took such extensive notes on it himself that he seems, in the years before his death in 1956, to have been preparing a book on his predecessor (Febvre papers, private archives of Henri Febvre).

4. Jules Michelet, "Introduction à l'histoire universelle" (1831), in *Œuvres complètes*, vol. 2 (Paris, 1972) (hereafter, *OC*); *Histoire de la Révolution française* (1847–53), in édition de la Pleiade, 2 vols., ed. Gérard Walter (Paris, 1952) (hereafter, *HRF*); *Nos fils* (Paris, 1969).

5. Michelet wrote on witchcraft and popular religion in *La Sorcière* (1862); on women in *La Femme* (1858) and *L'Amour* (1859); on children, working people, and sociability in *Le Peuple* (1846) and *Nos fils*.

6. See Peter Gay, *Freud for Historians* (New York, 1985); Peter Loewenberg, *Decoding the Past: The Psychohistorical Approach* (New York, 1983); George Devereux, *From Anxiety to Method in the Behavioral and Social Sciences* (The Hague, 1967); H. Stuart Hughes, *Consciousness and Society: The Re-*

orientation of European Social Thought, 1890–1930 (New York, 1958); Dominic La Capra, "Is Everyone a *Mentalité* Case? Transference and the 'Culture' Concept," *History and Theory: Studies in the Philosophy of History* 23:3 (1984): 297–311.

7. The historiographical current is principally that of the *Annales*. Gabriel Monod, Michelet's disciple and biographer, was the dissertation supervisor of Lucien Febvre, one of the two founders of the *Annales*. Although Febvre's monographs (on Rabelais, Luther, etc.) rarely break out of a traditional history of ideas approach, he did write important articles on the integration of ideology and emotion into the historian's vision (e.g., "Comment reconstituer la vie affective d'autrefois? La sensibilité et l'histoire," in *Combats pour l'histoire* [Paris, 1953]). The other founder, Marc Bloch, was the pupil of Charles Seignobos, who, detested for his positivism by Febvre, nonetheless published two good anthologies of Michelet's work (*Extraits historiques de J. Michelet* [Paris, 1887] and *Anthologie des œuvres de J. Michelet: Extraits littéraires* [Paris, 1889]). Bloch himself, from his *Les Rois thaumaturges* (Strasbourg, 1924) to his death in 1944, has been the principal stimulator of the interest in mentalités. Among the successors of Bloch and Febvre, medievalist Jacques Le Goff and historian of early modern mentalities Robert Mandrou have particularly celebrated Michelet's influence (cf. their contributions to the French radio round table "Resurrection de Michelet," published in *Michelet cent ans après: Romantisme* 10 (1975). Michelet's quite conscious reflection on the relation among his background, personality, and historical perspective has been continued by historians as dissimilar as Philippe Ariès (*Un Historien de dimanche* [Paris, 1980]) and Emmanuel Le Roy Ladurie (*Paris-Montpellier, C.-S.U. 1945–1963* [Paris, 1982]). See also Maurice Agulhon, Pierre Chaunu, et al., *Essais d'ego-histoire,* ed. Pierra Nora (Paris, 1987).

8. A partial exception to this criticism is the pioneering work of the dean of current Michelet studies, Paul Viallaneix, *La Voie royale: Essai sur l'idée du peuple dans l'œuvre de Michelet,* 2d ed. (Paris, 1971) (hereafter, *Voie royale*); Viallaneix also edited and annotated the first two (of four) parts of Michelet's *Journal* (vol. 1: Paris, 1959; vol. 2: Paris, 1962—hereafter, *J1* and *J2*), and his *Ecrits de jeunesse* (Paris, 1959) (hereafter, *EJ*); he is the general editor of the new edition of *OC* (Paris, 1971–). Yet Viallaneix, too, has his credentials from the discipline of French literature, not history. The same holds true for most of the other major writers on Michelet: Roland Barthes (*Michelet par lui-même* [Paris, 1954]); Claude Digeon (editor of vols. 3 and 4 of Michelet's *Journal* [Paris, 1976] and author of *Note sur le journal de Michelet, années 1870–1874* [Saarbrücken, 1959]); Linda Orr (*Jules Michelet: Nature, History, and Language* [Ithaca, 1976]; Edward Kaplan (*Michelet's Poetic Vision: A Romantic Philosophy of Nature, Man, and Woman* [Amherst, 1977]); Jacques Seebacher ("L'Education ou la fin de Michelet," *Europe* [Nov.–Dec. 1963]: 132–45); Jean-Louis Cornuz (*Jules Michelet: Un Aspect de la pensée religieuse au XIXe siècle* [Geneva, 1955]); Jeanne Calo (*La Création de la femme chez Michelet* [Paris, 1975]); Thérèse Moreau (*Le Sang de l'histoire: Michelet, l'histoire et l'idée de la femme au XIXe siècle* [Paris, 1982]); Paul Bénichou (*Le Temps des prophètes: Doctrines de l'âge romantique* [Paris, 1977], 497–564). Stephen A. Kippur (*Jules Michelet: A Study of Mind and*

Sensibility [Albany, 1981]) does have historical training, and his work does
integrate Michelet into the historiographical tradition; it lacks, however,
the subtle understanding of the relation between Michelet's work and his
personality of many of the literary studies.

9. Skilled workmen have occasionally written autobiographies, but
such documents are of dubious reliability for the precision of emotional
experiences that occurred decades earlier.

10. Sophisticated arguments for the use of psychoanalysis by historians may be found in Peter Gay and Peter Loewenberg (works cited in
n. 6) and Saul Friedländer, *Histoire et psychanalyse* (Paris, 1975). For useful
reformulations of psychoanalysis to fit social and cultural phenomena, see:
Erik Erikson, *Childhood and Society*, 2d ed. (New York, 1963), and Gérard
Mendel, *La Révolte contre le père* (Paris, 1968). There are also excellent
critical articles on psychohistory by Joseph M. Woods ("Some Considerations on Psycho-History," in G. Cocks and T. Crosby, eds., *Psycho/His-
tory: Readings in the Method of Psychology, Psychoanalysis and History* [New
Haven, 1987]), and by Thomas A. Kohut, "Psychohistory as History,"
American Historical Review 91:2 (1986): 336–54.

11. On the various socially given significances of pregenital phases,
see Erikson, *Childhood and Society*; Erich Fromm, "Psychoanalytic Charac-
terology and Its Relevance for Social Psychology," in *The Crisis of Psychoanalysis* (Greenwich, Conn., 1970); and my "The Civilizing Offensive:
Mentalities, High Culture, and Individual Psyches," *Review of Social History*
20:4 (1986): 663–87.

12. On Freud's hazy distinction between "superego" and "ego ideal,"
see James Strachey's introduction to Freud's *Ego and the Id* (New York,
1960), xv–xvi, and Freud, *New Introductory Lectures on Psychoanalysis* (Har-
mondsworth, 1977), 96.

13. The following pages refer to ideas of Robert Muchembled, Emmanuel Le Roy Ladurie, Michel Vovelle, Willem Frijhoff, Peter Burke,
Robert Darnton, and Norbert Elias.

14. Max Weber assumed this relationship in discussing the difference
between the Calvinist doctrines of seventeenth-century Puritan divines,
which were a creative response to theological and psychological pressures,
and the "iron cage" of worldly asceticism these doctrines had become in
the modern world. His work on the Protestant ethic can be viewed as an
attempt to reassert the primacy of subjective over objective mind. See my
The Iron Cage: An Historical Interpretation of Max Weber (New York, 1970).

15. Alan Spitzer, *The French Generation of 1820* (Princeton, 1987).

CHAPTER 1: MICHELET'S WORLD

1. For an excellent summary of the French and Anglo-American
research on the anthropological "otherness" of nineteenth-century France,
see Ted W. Margadant, "Tradition and Modernity in Rural France during
the Nineteenth Century," *Journal of Modern History*, 56 (1984): 667–97. For
a view of nineteenth-century European culture and society as a whole from
this perspective, see Arno Mayer, *The Persistence of the Old Regime: Europe
to the Great War* (New York, 1981).

2. F. W. J. Hemmings, *Culture and Society in France, 1848–1898* (London, 1971), 221–27. There was, of course, an earlier Wagnerian vogue in France, in the 1860s, but it was more limited to the cognoscenti than the later one. See Gerald D. Turbow, "Art and Politics: Wagnerism in France," in D. Large and W. Weber, *Wagnerism in European Culture and Politics* (Ithaca, 1980), 134–66, and Léon Guichard, *La Musique et les lettres en France au temps du Wagnerisme* (Grenoble, 1967), 30–49.

3. See below, chap. 9, esp. nn. 1, 2.

4. Spitzer, *French Generation*, 28f., 180f.

5. Ibid., 173.

6. Ibid., chap. 7, and Marc Bloch, *Apologie pour l'histoire* (Paris, 1974), 150: "Les hommes nés dans une même ambiance sociale, à des dates voisines, subissent nécessairement ... des influences analogues ... Leur comportement présente ... des traits distinctifs ... jusque dans leurs désaccords, qui peuvent être des plus aigus ... Cette communauté d'empreinte, venant d'une communauté d'âge, fait une génération." See also Karl Mannheim, "The Problem of Generations," in *Essays on the Sociology of Knowledge* (London, 1959): 276–322.

7. Paul Viallaneix quotes a most revealing letter from Michelet to Quinet, written two weeks after the Revolution of 1830 had brought French liberals to power: "Il faut venir sur-le-champ, mon ami, tout s'organise. Les places vont être enlevées rapidement. La vôtre se trouvera sans peine si vous arrivez à temps. Vos amis sont au pouvoir, Guizot à l'interieur et à l'instruction ou Villemain ... ou Cousin? Hâtez-vous donc. Voilà le seul conseil que je crois devoir vous donner maintenant." *Voie royale*, 30n.

8. David Pinkney, *Decisive Years in France, 1840–1847* (Princeton, 1986), 93f.

9. Bénichou, *Temps des prophètes*, 330–58, 381–422.

10. Louis Girard, *Etude comparée des mouvements révolutionnaires en France en 1830, 1848 et 1870–71,* fasc. I, Cours de la Sorbonne (Paris [1970?]), 32. See also Mark Traugott, "The Crowd in the French Revolution of 1848," *American Historical Review* (June 1988): 638–52, and, on 1848 in Provence, Maurice Agulhon, *La République au village* (Paris, 1970).

11. Wm. Sewell, Jr., *Work and Revolution in France: The Language of Labor from the Old Regime to 1848* (Cambridge, 1980). A comparable study for Germany in 1848 is T. S. Hamerow, *Restoration, Revolution, and Reaction* (Princeton, 1958). See also G. Rudé, "The Motives of Revolutionary Crowds" and "The Generation of Revolutionary Activity," in his *The Crowd in the French Revolution* (London, 1959), 191–231; David Pinkney, *The French Revolution of 1830* (Princeton, 1972), 252–73; Edgar Leon Newman, "What the Crowd Wanted in the French Revolution of 1830," in John Merriman, ed., *1830 in France* (New York, 1975), 17–40.

12. Newman, "What the Crowd Wanted."

13. George Sand heard that the Saint-Simonians were going to bestow this honor on her in 1832, but nothing came of it; see her *Correspondance* (Paris, 1966), 2:120. On the Saint-Simonians, see Robert B. Carlisle, *The Proffered Crown: Saint-Simonianism and the Doctrine of Hope* (Baltimore, 1987). On Saint-Simonian feminism, see Marguerite Thibert, *Le Féminisme dans le socialisme français de 1830 à 1850* (Paris, 1926). See also Claire

Goldberg Moses, *French Feminism in the Nineteenth Century* (Albany, N.Y., 1984); R. Picard, *Le Romantisme social* (New York, 1944); Alexandrian, *Le Socialisme romantique* (Paris, 1979); Jehan d'Ivray, *L'Aventure Saint-Simonienne et les femmes* (Paris 1928); Maria Teresa Bulciolu, *L'Ecole Saint-Simonienne et le femme: Notes et documents . . . , 1828–1833* (Golliardica-Pisa, 1980).

14. Bénichou, *Temps des prophètes,* 423–53.

15. Spitzer, *French Generation,* 182; A. Mitzman, "The Unstrung Orpheus: Flaubert's Youth and the Psycho-Social Origins of Art for Art's Sake," *Psychohistory Review* (Summer 1977): 27–42.

CHAPTER 2: THE YOUNG MICHELET

1. From a student's notes, quoted in Gabriel Monod, *Michelet à l'Ecole normale* (Paris, 1895), 9 (reprinted in Monod's *Portraits et souvenirs* [Paris, 1897]).

2. Paul Bénichou, *Les Temps des prophètes: Doctrines de l'âge romantique* (Paris, 1977), 29f.

3. Michelet, "Introduction à l'histoire universelle," in *OC,* 2:229, 255.

4. Michelet, *Le Peuple,* ed. Paul Viallaneix (Paris, 1974), 200 (hereafter, *P*).

5. Here, as elsewhere in this book, I touch on matters discussed by Lionel Gossman in a brilliant essay, "The Go-Between: Jules Michelet, 1798–1874" *Modern Language Notes* (1974): 503–41. Gossman's study, however, attempts to make one structural unity, valid for all periods in his life and work, out of Michelet's antitheses man-nature, male-female, reason-emotion, etc. I find such an attempt—premised on the assumption of a permanent and unchanging ambivalence in Michelet, and thus on the rejection of fundamental change over time in his choice of values—to be unreasonable. Although ambivalence may often underlie Michelet's valuations, at any moment, of one side or the other of these antitheses, close reading of his texts imposes a sense of basic change over time in those valuations that can best be correlated with demonstrable evolution of his personality. The recent introduction to Michelet's *L'Amour* (by A. Govindane and P. Viallaneix in *OC,* vol. 18 [Paris, 1985], 19f.) traces just as I do the reversal of Michelet's values concerning nature, India, and human brotherhood between the "Introduction" of 1831 and *Le Peuple* but attributes it to Michelet his readings in Indian culture. I find the change too decisive and profound to have depended simply on the hazard of literary formation. See below, chap. 10, for my assessment of Michelet's reading on Indian philosophy and of his use of it in *Origines du droit français* (1837).

6. Michelet, "Mémorial," in *EJ,* 179–218.

7. Ibid., 183.

8. Ibid., 184.

9. Gabriel Monod, *La Vie et la pensée de Jules Michelet (1789–1852),* 2 vols. (Paris, 1923), 1:15 (hereafter, *Vie et pensée*). According to Arimadavane Govindane, Michelet also owed his sexual initiation to this mother replacement ("Il n'y a point de vieille femme," in *Michelet cent ans après: Etudes et temoignages recueillis par Paul Viallaneix* [Grenoble, 1975], 197–202).

10. Cited in *Voie royale,* 13f.

11. Ibid., 15.

12. Freud, "Analerotik," in *Gesammelte Werke,* vol. 7 (London, 1941).

13. On Villemain as Michelet's teacher: *Vie et pensée,* 1:14. With the exception of Villemain, Michelet later turned against these men, but it was Cousin who helped with his first important work on Vico, Guizot who made him his replacement at the Sorbonne after 1830, and Thiers who used Michelet's "Précis de l'histoire de France" as the introduction to his *Histoire de la Révolution française.*

14. *EJ,* 203.

15. In the "Mémorial," Michelet precedes mention of his mother's precarious state of health at one point (199) by a reference to the closing down of his father's presses by the government, and at another (207) by mention of his desire to take revenge on his teasing comrades, like "Marius on the ruins of Carthage." Marius, however, said he was in the ruins of Carthage only to mislead the Roman government; he actually went elsewhere, which suggests the tactics of Michelet père in evading possible arrest during the Revolution by moving to another address.

16. *EJ,* 261. On the riots, see Spitzer, *Generation,* 55–60.

17. *EJ,* 182. A year later, when Michelet visited the grave of Poinsot in June 1821, he also stopped at the tomb of the student Lallemand, killed during the demonstrations of June 1820 (ibid., 151).

18. Poret assisted Cousin in translating Greek philosophy (*Vie et pensée,* 1:48).

19. Ibid., 28.

20. See Donald R. Kelley, *Historians and the Law in Postrevolutionary France* (Princeton, 1984), 102–10; Charles Rearick, *Beyond the Enlightenment: Historians and Folklore in Nineteenth-Century France* (Bloomington, 1974), 84–103.

21. *Voie royale,* 177, 202, 237f.; *Vie et pensée,* 1:55; Bénichou, *Temps des prophètes,* 505f.; for an overview of Michelet's relations with his students in this period, see F. Berriot, "Michelet à l'Ecole normale (1827–1836)," in Berriot, ed., *Jules Michelet: Leçons inédites de l'Ecole normale . . .* (Paris, 1987), 9–86.

22. G. Monod, "Une Election au Collège de France en 1830," *La Revue bleue,* Nov. 3, Dec. 8, 1906.

CHAPTER 3: THE BACKGROUND OF AN AFFAIR

1. *OC,* 4:702. That Michelet's incarnation of the grammatically feminine "la liberté" is the very masculine Hercules requires us to replace his "she's" by "he's." Michelet excised the passage from the definitive edition of 1861.

2. *J1,* 119, July 13, 1834.

3. Ibid., 255, July 14, 1838.

4. Ibid., 306, July 24, 1839.

5. Ibid., 318, Sept. 12, 1839.

6. Viallaneix's note in ibid., 803.

7. Ibid., 804.

8. Ibid., 330, June 23, 1840. There is no evidence that the lady in question was Madame Dumesnil; she might have been. Viallaneix suggested it might have been Madame Aupèpin, the wife of a doctor who treated Pauline at the end, with whom Michelet had a long affair in the mid-1840s.

9. *J1*, 352f.

10. Ibid., 804, 810f.

11. Ibid., 359. The "serious comforts" refers, according to Viallaneix to Madame Dumesnil.

12. Quotations in this paragraph are from ibid., 359–61.

13. Michelet, *Lettres inédites (1841–1871)*, ed. Paul Sirven (Paris, 1924), 15 (hereafter, *S*); *J1*, 811.

14. Ibid., 366.

15. Michelet subsequently gave his second wife carte blanche to eliminate, after his death, what she found inappropriate for the eyes of posterity (*J2*, 355, Sept. 24, 1857); scholars agree that she took advantage of it. For the entire important year of 1841, only nineteen pages appear in the printed edition, considerably less than the average, and there is nothing at all for May, when he wrote an important draft on the Renaissance, sent it to Alfred, and visited the Dumesnils in Rouen. It is, of course, also possible that he did not confide this experience to the journal or that he later destroyed it himself.

CHAPTER 4: JOAN OF ARC AND THE RESURRECTION OF NATURE

1. *J1*, 247, July 16, 1837.

2. *OC*, 6:12.

3. See also Eugène Noel, *J. Michelet et ses enfants* (Paris, 1878), 30.

4. *J1*, 367, Aug. 21, 1841.

5. Viallaneix in *OC*, 7:10.

6. Ibid., 7:11–12.

7. *Vie et pensée*, 2:42–50.

8. The brief "L'agneau de Van Eyck toutes enceintes" is based on *J1*, 340f., Aug. 1, 1840.

9. A cautionary note; Michelet's celebration of seemingly conservative religious and nationalist symbols—the Virgin and Joan of Arc—should not lead us to anachronistic judgments. French nationalism, born in 1789, was for nearly a century a left-wing credo. The shift from Left to Right began in the 1880s (cf. Zeev Sternhell's *La Droite révolutionnaire* [Paris, 1978]), but even in its most reactionary phase, French nationalism of the Right was counterbalanced by a no less patriotic nationalism of the Left, as the martyrdom of Marc Bloch, an admirer of Michelet, made evident in 1944.

10. "Comment Jules Michelet inventa la Renaissance," in Lucien Febvre, *Pour une histoire à part entière* [Paris, 1962], 717–29.

CHAPTER 5: DEATH AND HISTORICAL RECURRENCE

1. *S*, 20–24.

2. *J1*, 281.

3. Noel, *J. Michelet et ses enfants* (Paris, 1878), 95f.

4. *Ji*, 379, Feb. 22, 1842.

5. Ibid., 380f., Mar. 16, 1842.

6. Ibid., 381f., Mar. 18, 1842; cf. Bloch, *Apologie,* 126, 129, for similar formulations.

7. *Ji*, 386, Mar. 28, 1842. On Leroux: D. O. Evans, *Le Socialisme romantique: Pierre Leroux et ses contemporains* (Paris, 1948); A. LeBres Chopard, *De l'égalité dans la différence: Le Socialisme de Pierre Leroux* (Paris, 1986); P. F. Thomas, *Pierre Leroux: Sa vie, ses œuvres, sa doctrine, contribution à l'histoire des idées au XIXe siècle* (Paris, 1904); On Leroux and Michelet: Jacques Viard, "George Sand et Michelet, disciples de Pierre Leroux," *Revue d'histoire littéraire de la France* 75 (1975): 749–73.

8. *Ji*, 387, Mar. 30, 1842. On Reynaud, see David Albert Griffith, *Jean Reynaud: Encyclopédiste de l'époque romantique* (Paris, 1965); D. G. Charlton, *Secular Religions in France, 1815–1870* (Oxford, 1963), 79f., 130; Paul Bénichou, *Les Mages romantiques* (Paris, 1988), 415f., 421f., 499f.; Mario Proth, *Depuis 89* (Paris, 1891), 197–238; and Ernest Legouvé, *Soixante ans de souvenirs,* pt. 2 (Paris, n.d.), 281–323. See also Reynaud's "Ciel," in *Encyclopédie nouvelle,* vol. 3 (Paris, 1837), 296, 356, 809.

9. M. Nathan, *Le Ciel des Fouriéristes, habitants des étoiles et réincarnations* ... (Lyons, 1981), 186.

10. See Pierre Albouy, *La Création mythologique chez Victor Hugo* (Paris 1968), 386f. The basic scholarly study of the illuminists is Auguste Viatte, *Les Sources occultes du romantisme, illuminisme, théosophie, 1770–1820,* 2 vols. (Paris, 1928). For a lively overview of nineteenth-century occultism, with special attention to Hugo and Michelet, see Philippe Muray, *Le 19e Siècle à travers les âges* (Paris, 1984).

11. See Robert van der Elst, *Michelet naturaliste* (Paris, 1914), and Edward Kaplan, *Michelet's Poetic Vision: A Romantic Philosophy of Nature, Man, and Woman* (Amherst, 1977), 21–45.

12. *Ji*, 495f., May 30, 1842, and Dumesnil to Noel, Aug. 22, 1847, in BHVP, MS 1587, fol. 348v.

13. *Ji*, 388, April 1842, day unspecified.

14. Jean Guéhenno, *L'Evangile éternel, étude sur Michelet* (Paris, 1927). According to Anne-Marie Amiot, the term *accouchement,* to which Michelet recurs, was "an image in vogue in this period (Ballanche, Saint-Simonians) to express simultaneously violence, rupture, and birth," and she gives an example of it in Victor Hugo. See her "Fondements théologiques de la Révolution française dans *La Fin de Satan* de Victor Hugo," in *Philosophies de la Révolution française* (Paris, 1984), 162. See also below, chaps. 10 and 17, 3d sec.

15. On the 'romantic heresies' of the period, see Paul Bénichou, *Le Temps des prophètes: Doctrines de l'âge romantique* (Paris, 1977).

16. *Ji*, 398–402.

CHAPTER 6: GRIEF AND INCESTUOUS LONGING

1. Alfred's journal, BHVP, MS 1496, fol. 118f., and Viallaneix's note to *Ji*, 835.

2. Examples are Wagner's *Die Meistersinger* and Berlioz's *Benvenuto Cellini* (on the latter, see François Piatier, *Benvenuto Cellini de Berlioz, ou le mythe de l'artiste* (Paris, 1979). On the enthusiasm of French romantics for Agricol Perdiguier and the artisan compagnonnages, see Emile Coornaert, *Les Compagnonnages en France* (Paris, 1966), 72–75; on incest in romantic life and literature, see Rudolph Binion, "Notes on Romanticism," *Journal of Psychohistory* 11 (Summer 1983).

3. See Alfred's journal entry for June 4, 1842, BHVP, MS 1496.

4. *J1,* 416, June 24, 1842: "J'ai voulu seulement souffler sur eux l'esprit de la vie."

5. Ibid., 417.

6. On Michelet's journey of 1842, see: G. Monod, "Voyage d'Allemagne, 1842," in *Jules Michelet: Etudes sur sa vie et ses œuvres* (Paris, 1905), 130–218; Oscar A. Haac, "A Spiritual Journey: Michelet in Germany, 1842," *Proceedings of the American Philosophical Society,* 94:5 (1950): 502–9; Jean Seznec, "Michelet in Germany: Journey in Self-Discovery," *History and Theory* 16 (1977): 1–10.

7. Viallaneix writes, "En apprenant à composer, dès douze ans, dans l'atelier de la rue de Bondy, il devient, pour la vie, un artisan," and describes "le culte que Michelet voue au travail" (*Voie royale,* 81). Only after Madame Dumesnil, however, did Michelet reconnect with, and idealize, his artisan origins—another aspect of his "rebirth" through her.

8. *OC,* 6:185–92. See also *J1,* 358, Mar. 11, 1841, and Michelet to Madame Dumesnil of Apr. 1, 1841 (he is finishing vol. 5 of the *Histoire de France* and hopes to have a copy for her in two months): "I've touched in passing on your Flemish school, Madame, work in the family, the *béguinages,* and many other handsome subjects on which a more delicate hand, one less heavy with erudition, would have been preferable" (*S,* 2). Viallaneix's point that Michelet's description of the Lollards' singing at work goes back to a "confused memory" of his paternal grandfather, former *maître de chapelle,* in the family printing shop, may well be so, but it is likely that this memory was mediated by the second mothership of Madame Dumesnil, which in so many ways reopened his childhood for him (*Voie royale,* 51). Perhaps that is why the Lollard chants brought back to him "those of a woman rocking a child."

9. *OC,* 6:187f. In a footnote Michelet became even more personal and then, fearing he was revealing too much, switched back to a historical perspective: "Infinite pleasures of work in the family! He alone feels them well whose hearth has been broken. This tear will be pardoned (the man? no), the historian at the moment when this labor is going to end, when the factory is going to suppress our flax spinner and those of Flanders." In a journal entry of about the same time, he spelled out his identification with the weavers he was writing about and, by implication, with Madame Dumesnil: "Sympathy for solitary labor, for the weaver, consoled by God in his shadows. And me too, by imitation. I am one of them. Sympathy for happy and pleasant labor in the family. I knew it too, when my hearth was not yet broken" (*J1,* 358f., Mar. 11, 1841).

10. Alfred's journal, MS 1496, fol. 169v, June 25, 1842. Michelet's

comment on Madame Dumesnil's tapestry work in his journal was similar but less sharp (*J1*, 455, July 18, 1842).

11. *J1*, 453, July 18, 1842.

12. Ibid., 458, July 21, 1842. See the reproduction and text on this painting in F. Anzelewsky, *Albrecht Dürer: Das Malerische Werk* (Berlin, 1971), 159f., pl. 57. Michelet had seen himself, during his mourning for Pauline as bearing a funeral urn through history (*J1*, 317).

13. *OC*, 6:188.

14. *J1*, 478, Sept. 21, 1842.

15. Ibid., 479–80, Sept. 30, 1842: "Il me semblait que je disais à ma mère mon indigence d'amour. Elle disait: *Eh bien! prends ici, mon enfant*" (italics in original; Michelet's indication of a quotation). Apparently he needed reassurance about the state of his soul, or mental health, after this dream, which he seems to have had before: he could not forebear telling the dream to his daughter, who said with a smile, "If it's the second time you won't die of it" ("Je ne pus m'empêcher de conter le rêve, et l'on dit seulement en riant: *Si c'est la seconde fois, on n'en meurt pas*" [ibid.]). Adèle indicated that she was the "on" in her letter to Alfred of Sept. 30, 1842 (BHVP).

CHAPTER 7: WAR ON THE JESUITS

1. The relation to Marie lasted from 1842 to 1844; that with Victoire began as soon as he dismissed Marie, who had become an embarrassment, and lasted until 1848. On the problems with Marie, see below, chap. 17, n. 2.

2. *J1*, 469, Aug. 11, 1842. See also *OC*, 6:298.

3. Jeanne Calo, *La Création de la femme chez Michelet* (Paris, 1975), 422, 462.

4. *Les Jésuites*, 402f.; *Le Prêtre, la femme et la famille*, 49, 81, 199, 244f., in Michelet, *Œuvres complètes* (Paris [± 1900]). On Alfred's role as his mother's "director" during her last days, see his letter to Noel, chap. 5, above.

5. *Vie et pensée*, 2:81–84; René Rémond, *L'Anti-clericalisme en France de 1815 à nos jours* (Paris, 1976), 61–122; G. Weill, *Histoire de l'idée laïque au XIXe siècle* (Paris, 1925), 11–33; Paul Thureau-Dangin, *Le Parti liberale sous la Restauration* (Paris, 1876), 319–99, and *Histoire de la Monarchie de juillet*, 7 vols. (Paris, 1892), 1:228–59.

6. Louis Blanc, *Histoire de dix ans* (Brussels, 1846), 2:192.

7. Thureau-Dangin, *Monarchie de juillet*, 5:459–525.

8. *Le Monopole universitaire, destructeur de la religion et des lois* (Lyons and Paris, 1843), discussed in José Cabanis, *Michelet le prêtre et la femme* (Paris, 1978), 29.

9. *Le Prêtre*, 257.

10. Quoted in Eugène Noel, *J. Michelet et ses enfants* (Paris, 1878), 31.

11. *Le Prêtre*, 261.

12. Ibid., 263.

13. According to Madame Dumesnil in a letter to Alfred of May 5, 1840 (Noel, *Michelet*, 18f.).

14. *EJ*, 203.

15. *Le Prêtre,* 271.

16. *J1,* 481, Oct. 20, 1842.

17. Excerpts from the letters of Charles and Alfred are in Noel, *Michelet,* 112f.

18. Michelet to M. Dumesnil père, Sept. 24, 1842, in *S,* 37.

19. *S,* 39.

20. *J1,* 484, Nov. 10, 1842, and *S,* 47.

21. Noel, *Michelet,* 80, and *J1,* 485, Nov. 14, 1842.

22. *J1,* 501, Mar. 25, 1843.

23. *La Revue indépendante,* unsigned article, Apr. 10, 1843.

24. Ibid., 458. This forgotten account seems to be the only one to illuminate the significance of machinism and popular legend in these lectures. Title of the lectures is given in *J1,* 497.

25. "Cette desymbolisation des Templiers" (*J1,* 501).

26. Cited in ibid., 845.

27. See John Gillis, *Youth in History* (New York, 1974), esp. chap. 1: "Like a Family and a Fraternity." On the meanings given to "fraternity" in the rhetoric of the Revolutionary era: Marcel David, *Fraternité et Révolution française* (Paris, 1987).

28. See R. Muchembled, *Culture populaire et culture des élites (XVe–XVIIIe siècles)* (Paris, 1978).

29. Wm. Sewell, Jr. (*Work and Revolution in France: The Language of Labor from the Old Regime to 1848* [Cambridge, 1980]), has outlined this evolution from old to new brilliantly, as has E. P. Thompson in *The Making of the English Working Class* (New York, 1963).

30. Natalie Zemon Davis, "The Reasons for Misrule," in her *Society and Culture in Early Modern France* (London, 1975), 97–123; Yves-Marie Bercé, *Fête et révolte* (Paris, 1976).

31. Jean-Claude Schmitt and Jacques Le Goff, eds., *Le Charivari* (Paris, 1981).

32. Without making a special search for this kind of relationship, I have stumbled across it in the cases of Flaubert and Le Poittevin, Du Camp and De Cormenin, Dumesnil and Noel, Zola and Cézanne, Gide and Louÿs, and Michelet and Poinsot.

33. Gillis, *Youth in History,* 73, 76, 81, 89. Gillis sees a curtailment of this possibility with the greater regimentation of youth in the second half of the nineteenth century. It is arguable that pressure from above only increased the opposition of certain circles of intransigeant youth.

CHAPTER 8: THE ORIGINS OF LE PEUPLE

1. *J1,* 517, Aug. 4, 1843.

2. Above, chap. 5. Although Michelet informally adopted Alfred after Madame Dumesnil's death, he was secretly relieved that Alfred was kept in Rouen by inheritance problems in autumn 1842, and Alfred complained of Michelet's lack of warmth and unwillingness to talk about the wedding after his return to Paris in December 1842 (Michelet to Noel, Nov. 5, 1842, and Dumesnil to Noel, Apr. 2, June 22, 1843, BHVP).

3. *Vie et pensée,* 2:121ff.

4. Alfred indicated the connection between the lectures on the Jesuits and his marriage to Adèle in a letter of May 8, 1843: "M. Michelet était dans un extrême affaiblissement. [He had received the marriage request a month earlier] Je craignais beaucoup de ce découragement moral dans un si grand état de fatigue; mais les Jésuites sont venus à point; depuis huit jours, plus que jamais il est vivant, actif, il parle, écrit" (*Vie et pensée*, 2:122); also in his note on Michelet's conversation with the duchesse d'Orléans in August 1844: "Il [Michelet] lui disait qu'il avait marié sa fille, que faisant la guerre, il ne voulait point avoir une femme dans ses bagages" (Dumesnil journal, MS 1497, fol. 7, Aug. 19, 1844). Michelet was reversing the causal sequence to make the best of a bad situation.

5. Oedipal and pre-Oedipal are not necessarily opposed dispositions; Oedipally based quarreling with a concrete father figure over a concrete mother figure depends on some feeling (or fantasy) of having been symbiotically attached to such a mother figure in the first place, which was in Michelet's case true only for Madame Dumesnil. There is no sign of this symbiotic relationship with Pauline or with his adolescent substitute mother, Madame Fourcy, and any possible early experience of it with his biological mother seems to have been buried under the weight of her puritanism.

6. Eugène Noel, *J. Michelet et ses enfants* (Paris, 1878), 76.

7. See Chéruel's letters on his marriage in his correspondence with Michelet (BHVP).

8. *J1*, 785.

9. Michelet Corr., BHVP, A4765 fols. 45, 67; F. Berriot reprints the letter for Flaubert (*Jules Michelet: Leçons inédites de L'Ecole normale . . .* [Paris, 1987], 62).

10. Dumesnil's letters (in Noel, *Michelet*) of 1841 mention Baudry as Michelet's guest.

11. *S*, 42–50, and the letter of Oct. 26, 1842 (*J1*, 839f.).

12. Viallaneix's note, *J1*, 841.

13. *S*, 55.

14. *J1*, 488, Dec. 10, 1842.

15. *S*, 57.

16. *Les Jésuites*, 339.

17. Ibid., 334, and *J1*, 506.

18. *J1*, 507, 514, 850f., May 16, 26, July 30, 1843; *S*, 68.

19. Madame Edgar Quinet, *Cinquante ans d'amitié, Michelet-Quinet, 1825–1875* (Paris, 1899), 136.

20. See below, chap. 10.

21. During this long reexamination, Michelet wrote on the connection between historian and history: "De quoi l'histoire s'est-elle faite sinon de moi?" and "L'histoire: violent chimie morale où mes passions individuelles tournent en généralités, où mon moi retourne animer les peuples" (*J1*, 382, 362, Mar. 18, 1842, June 18, 1841).

22. I have translated "la patrie" as "nation," because the more literal "fatherland" gives a false impression (the French noun is feminine in gender).

23. The surviving notes for these lectures are often incoherent, but

not, as Monod thought (*Vie et pensée*, 2:188), because Michelet was inserting too much of his oversensitive personality into them, but because they contained the germ of three major works; his history of the Revolution, *Le Peuple*, and another work he never did write, on the history of the popular classes since the Middle Ages.

24. *Vie et pensée*, 2:189. Enfantin wrote Michelet at length on Feb. 2, 1845: Enfantin, *Correspondance philosophique et religieuse, 1843–1845* (Paris, 1847), 33–52.

25. *Vie et pensée*, 2:194.

26. Ibid.

27. Ibid., 195.

28. Laurens van der Heijden, "Rossi's Missie: Politiek en Jezuïten-angst in de Julimonarchie," *Skript, Tijdschrift voor Geschiedenisstudenten* (June 1981): 81–94.

29. *Vie et pensée*, 2:202.

30. *J1*, 542, Nov. 27, 1843.

31. Ibid., 83, Aug. 6, 1831.

32. Ibid., Aug. 7, 1831.

33. Ibid., 111, 316. In 1860, five years after Adèle's death, he also wrote it into *La Mer* (pp. 111, 316 in the 1923 ed.).

34. *S*, 90.

35. *S*, 93 (letter to Dumesnil of Nov. 12, 1845), and *P*, 112.

CHAPTER 9: LE PEUPLE AS AUTOBIOGRAPHY

1. George Dupeux refers to them as "this *conservative mass*, this re-assuring force on which the bourgeoisie will rely when a new revolutionary menace will appear, the organized proletariat" (*La Société française, 1789–1970* [Paris, 1974]).

2. *P*, 95, 113f. Wm. Sewell, Jr., *Work and Revolution in France: The Language of Labor from the Old Regime to 1848* (Cambridge, 1980), 154, cites a study that "estimates that the industrial population employed in artisan industry in France was twice the population employed in large-scale industry even as late as 1876." Sewell sees the predominance of artisans as "even greater in the first half of the century," and writes that "the typical French worker of the nineteenth century lived in an old city with long-standing artisan traditions, not in a new factory town."

3. Louis René Villermé, *Tableau de l'état physique et moral des ouvriers employés dans les manufactures de coton, de laine et de soie*, 2 vols. (Paris, 1840).

4. *P*, 80f.

5. *P*, 38 ("examen du texte"). Dumesnil's letter to Noel of Nov. 24, 1845—accompanying a copy of the first chapters that Michelet wanted Noel's comments on—is critical of this version; Dumesnil explains that Michelet had agreed to return to the original version ("Si nous voulons etc."); BHVP, MS 1586, fol. 230.

6. *P*, 89.

7. *Vie et pensée*, 2:195. The word *Jew* was used among liberals and radicals under the July Monarchy as a synonym for *banker* to strengthen the negative connotations of that profession, as in "Prince Juif" in the

subscript to one of the Daumier cartoons depicting Louis-Philippe as a pear in the satirical daily *Le Charivari,* as in Alphonse Toussenel's *Les Juifs rois de l'epoque* (1847). This kind of open, casual anti-Semitism was dropped by the French Left only after the Dreyfus Affair indicated its xenophobic and reactionary implications.

8. David Pinkney, *Decisive Years in France, 1840–1847* (Princeton, 1986), 135.

9. *J1,* 597, 621, Apr. 1, Aug. 23, 1845.

10. Ibid., 598f., Apr. 8, 10, 1845.

11. Ibid., 888.

12. Ibid., 612f., Aug. 3, 1845.

13. *P,* 101.

14. See the long note in ibid., 95f.

15. *The People,* trans. and introd. John P. McKay (Urbana, 1973), 46 (hereafter, *PE*).

16. See n. 3, above.

17. Frédéric Le Play, *La Réforme sociale* (Paris, 1864), and *L'organisation de la famille* (Paris, 1871); Karl Bücher, *Arbeit und Rythmus,* 3d ed. (Leipzig, 1902).

18. *PE,* 50. The idea is extended in *J1,* 627, Sept. 28, 1845. See below in chap. 9, 3d sec.

19. See chap. 6, n. 9, above. For the harsh realities of artisan life and labor in nineteenth-century France, see Jacques Rancière, *La Nuit des prolètaires* (Paris, 1981).

20. *P,* 100.

21. Ibid., 197; *Le Prêtre,* 253.

22. *P,* 113. For the second half of the quote I follow *PE,* 61.

23. *J1,* 405f.

24. MS 1586, Sept. 22, 1845.

25. Ibid., Dusmesnil to Noel, Sept. 28, 1845, fol. 173.

26. *J1,* 627.

27. Ibid., 119.

28. Three dots in the original; deletion not attributable to Athenaïs.

29. "Ecrit peu et mal sur l'ouvrier" (*J1,* 631, Oct. 20, 1845).

30. The cryptic phrase "Windsor, le serment de la Jarretière" appears in an unused version of this chapter (*J1,* 630, Oct. 14, 1845). See *P,* 41.

31. *Vie et pensée,* 2:195, and chap. 8, above.

32. Dickens (not to mention Balzac, Zola, and other novelist-moralists of the past century and a half) similarly condemned the parvenu: see *Hard Times, Great Expectations,* and *Our Mutual Friend.*

33. *PE,* 89.

34. *P,* 139. The point would be amplified in *L'Etudiant* (below, chap. 16).

35. Ibid., 140.

36. *PE,* 91, with slight changes in the translation. Michelet's suggestion to Noel that he himself might incarnate "this bond we are seeking between the people and the bourgeoisie" would point the passage in Noel's direction but for the evidence mentioned in the next paragraph. Dumesnil's letter to Noel of Oct. 19, 1845, suggests that Michelet was looking chiefly

to his son-in-law at this moment. Just as Michelet was writing the lines I have quoted, after returning from Fontainebleau in October, Dumesnil wrote his friend: "Je me suis ouvert tout entier à M. Michelet, je lui ai demandé conseil pour l'avenir, sur mon état . . . Ce qu'il m'a dit aura décidé de mon avenir . . . Ce voyage de Fontainebleau est un des grands événements de ma vie. Suis-je digne de la vie nouvelle où il me fait entrer?"

37. "L'état moins la patrie."

38. *PE,* 97, modified by author.

39. With one modification from *PE,* 98. Compare Camus's "The Artist as Witness of Freedom:" "But what is the mechanism of polemics? It consists in considering the opponent as an enemy, consequently in simplifying him and refusing to see him. We have no idea of what the man we are insulting looks like, or whether he ever smiles, or how. Having become three quarters blind by the grace of polemics, we no longer live among men but in a world of silhouettes . . . No wonder that these silhouettes, henceforth blind and deaf, terrorized, fed by ration tickets, their entire lives summed up in a police questionnaire, can then be treated as anonymous abstractions" (*Journal for the Protection of All Beings* [San Francisco] 1 [1961]: 33).

40. *P,* 147.

41. *PE,* 99.

CHAPTER 10: LE PEUPLE, PART II

1. For theoretical approaches to projection in history writing, see Dominic La Capra, "Is Everyone a *Mentalité* Case?: Transference and the 'Culture' Concept," *History and Theory: Studies in the Philosophy of History* 23:3 (1984): 297–311, and George Devereux, *From Anxiety to Method in the Behavioral and Social Sciences* (The Hague, 1967). Michelet was aware of the extraordinary character of part II. His *autre moi,* Dumesnil, wrote Noel that "the second part [is] the most difficult and the core of the book" (MS 1586, Jan. 20, 1846).

2. For a survey of this literary influence on bourgeois perceptions of the lower orders, see Louis Chevalier, *Laboring Classes and Dangerous Classes in Paris during the First Half of the Nineteenth Century* (New York, 1973). More recent studies, which deal more subtly than Chevalier with the literary and intellectual perceptions of "le peuple," are Pierre Michel, *Un Mythe romantique: Les Barbares, 1789–1848* (Lyons, 1981), and Gérard Fritz, *L'Idée du peuple en France du XVIIe au XIXe siècles* (Strasbourg, 1988).

3. Viallaneix's note to *P,* 164. On Couture and Michelet, see Albert Boime, *Thomas Couture and the Eclectic Vision* (New Haven, 1980), 79. Boime exaggerates the influence of Cousin's eclecticism on Michelet but gives a comprehensive picture of Couture's life and oeuvre.

4. *PE,* 120, modified by author.

5. *P,* 167f.

6. Ibid., 168.

7. Ibid.

8. *PE,* 123.

9. *P,* 169. On the reflections of these beliefs in nineteenth-century popular culture, see below (chap. 17, n. 79).

10. *Ji,* 393, Apr. 4, 1842. Emphasis before the colon is mine, after it, Michelet's.

11. *P,* 169. Michelet refers his readers back to his original citation of this passage in his *Origines du droit française,* but the above quotation differs in five respects from the one in that work (*OC,* 3:607), and, considering how he was clearly basing his ideas on his journal entry of Apr. 4, 1842 (in which the modified version of the quotation appears), there can be no doubt that the entry was his point of departure. (See chap. 5, above.)

12. *OC,* 2:236; *P,* 172.

13. E. Le Roy Ladurie, *Montaillou: Village occitan de 1294 à 1324* (Paris, 1976); Carlo Ginzburg, *The Cheese and the Worms* (Baltimore, 1980), and *Night Battles* (Baltimore, 1983); R. Muchembled, *Culture populaire et culture des élites (XVe–XVIIIe siècles)* (Paris, 1978); Mikhail Bakhtin, *Rabelais and His World* (Cambridge, Mass., 1968).

14. *PE,* 131.

15. *P,* 177.

16. Ibid., 177f.

17. *PE,* 134.

18. Ibid., 136f. At roughly the same time, Alfred Dumesnil described his and Michelet's reaction to the course given by Geoffroy Saint-Hilaire's son on the same subject: "We emerge from it so enlivened that we are almost always practically inebriated afterward. What an immense labor of love. Everything appears there. All of nature" (letter to Noel, MS 1586, fol. 264v).

19. *PE,* 140.

20. Ibid., 143.

21. *Ji,* 590, Feb. 4, 1845.

22. *Ji,* 592f. Michelet dismissed the idea that rejection of great individuals might lead to the impotence of every individual before the dominance of machinism and science with an optimism characteristic of the social romanticism of the 1840s: "The part of labor that is subject to machines is still the exception and will always be so. Science is more accessible than you think ... The individual, who was immobile and impotent in the period foolishly called that of heroic individualism, has today, to the contrary, a thousand handles on society, on nature. Your time will be the heroic time if you want it" (*Ji,* 593, Feb. 22–23, 1845).

23. *PE,* 152.

24. Ibid., translation modified by author.

25. *P,* 196.

26. *Ji,* 821n.

27. Theodore Zeldin, *France, 1848–1945,* vol. 1 (Oxford, 1973), 654–60.

CHAPTER 11: LE PEUPLE, PART III

1. *PE,* 158.

2. The principal study is Margaret Mahler, *On Human Symbiosis and*

the Vicissitudes of Individuation: Infantile Psychosis (New York, 1968). See also Matthew Besdine, "The Jocasta Complex: Mothering and Genius," *Psychoanalytic Review* 56:4 (1968–69): esp. 590–94. On Lacan's "mirroring" concept, see Sherry Turkle, *Psychoanalytic Politics: Freud's French Revolution* (New York, 1978), 57.

3. *P,* 200.

4. In *HRF,* 1:123f., one of these generals, Hoche, is described in terms that could have been used to refer to the young Michelet's search for knowledge and hard-working character; the "soldier" and the "citizen" are seen as "two children of the same mother" who "fall into each other's arms"—a paraphrase of Michelet's description of his and Quinet's origins and friendship in the open letter to Quinet that precedes *Le Peuple.* The passage on Hoche was written less than a year afterward. In 1850, Michelet named his son Lazare after Hoche.

5. *PE,* 177.

6. Ibid., 166. Viallaneix relates this paragraph to Victoire (*P,* 206n).

7. *PE,* 166.

8. Ibid., 167.

9. On the "bad mother," a concept of post-Freudian psychoanalysis, see Gérard Mendel, *La Révolte contre le père* (Paris, 1968), 78–91.

10. *PE,* 183f.

11. *J1,* 135, Aug. 17, 1834.

12. Ibid., 162.

CHAPTER 12: THE BOOK OF THE FATHER

1. Monod (*Vie et pensée,* 2:212) sees Michelet as preoccupied since 1843 with plans for the *HRF.* Whatever vague ideas he may have had on it, I do not believe the execution of the work can be separated from the specific political and personal circumstances of the year of its origin, 1846.

2. For an extensive discussion, see Paul Thureau-Dangin, *Histoire de la Monarchie de juillet* (Paris, 1892), 5:459–582.

3. E. Regnault, *Histoire de huit ans,* 3 vols. (Paris, 1851–52), 3:49.

4. Eugène Noel, *J. Michelet et ses enfants* (Paris, 1878), 163.

5. E. Brisson, "L'enseignement de Quinet au Collège de France," in *Edgar Quinet, ce Juif Errant,* Colloque de Clermont Ferrand (1978), 104; *Voie royale,* 345.

6. Regnault, *Huit ans,* 3:141, 202.

7. MS 1587, BHVP. See below, chap. 17.

8. *S,* 102.

9. *J1,* 658.

10. W. Fortescue, "Poetry, Politics and Publicity, and the Writing of History: Lamartine's *Histoire des Girondins* (1847)," *European History Quarterly* 17 (1987): 259–84.

11. Thureau-Dangin, *Monarchie de juillet,* 7:45–51; G. Gooch, *History and Historians in the Nineteenth Century* (Boston, 1954), 215f.

12. Michelet's quarrel with Blanc anticipated the early twentieth-century one between Alphonse Aulard (pro-Danton) and Albert Mathiez

(pro-Robespierre), as well as the current one between the Marxist and anti-Marxist interpretations, respectively, of Michel Vovelle and François Furet.

13. For this and the quotations on the following pages: *HRF,* 1:1–3.

14. Ibid., 5.

15. Ibid., 7. See also *Le Peuple*: "La chaleur est en bas" (141).

16. *Nos fils.*

17. *P,* 168.

18. See chap. 6, n. 9, above.

19. R. Muchembled, *Culture populaire et culture des élites (XVe–XVIIIe siècles)* (Paris, 1978); Yves-Marie Bercé, *Fête et révolte* (Paris, 1978).

20. Michelet tacitly acknowledged these points: "Je souffrais d'ailleurs bien plus qu'un autre du divorce déplorable que l'on tache de produire entre les hommes, entre les classes, moi qui les ai tous en moi" (*P,* 73).

21. *J1,* 658.

22. *HRF,* 1:203.

23. According to G. Walter (note to the *HRF*), this passage referred to Michelet's depiction of peasant misery in book V of *Histoire de France* (*OC,* 5:226).

24. Further efforts to rewrite his past occur in 1852–54. See chap. 23, below.

25. *HRF,* 1:26.

26. Ibid., 31.

27. Ibid., 32.

28. Ibid., 63.

29. Ibid., 55; Cocks trans., 57.

30. Ibid., 54.

31. Ibid., 59, Cocks trans., 61.

32. Ibid., 76.

33. *OC,* 2:241.

34. *EJ,* 216, cited by Jeanne Calo, *La Création de la femme chez Michelet* (Paris, 1975), 431f.

35. *HRF* 1:76.

36. Ibid. The reference to "Justice my mother" is the only one in which justice is given a feminine attribute, a sign that Michelet was being swept away by his own hyperbole.

CHAPTER 13: FEDERATION AND EPIPHANY

1. *HRF,* 1:412.

2. See R. Muchembled, *Culture populaire et culture des élites (XVe–XVIIIe siècles)* (Paris, 1978), and Yves-Marie Bercé, *Fête et révolte* (Paris, 1976).

3. See M. de Certeau, D. Julia, and J. Revel, *Une Politique de la langue: La Révolution française et les patois; l'enquête de Grégoire* (Paris, 1975); E. Weber, *Peasants into Frenchmen* (Stanford, 1976).

4. Marcel David, *Fraternité et Révolution française* (Paris, 1987).

5. Mona Ozouf, *La Fête révolutionnaire, 1789–1799* (Paris, 1976), 260–316.

6. *HRF,* 1:382.

7. Ibid., 396; Cocks trans., 324f.

8. BHVP, Papiers Michelet, Collège de France III, fol. 53 (Mar. 11, 1847).

9. *J1, 574.*

10. "Where the spirit of the Lord is, there is liberty.—The first age was an age of slaves, the second of free men, the third of friends; the first, age of old men, the second of men, the third of children" (*Les Jésuites,* 359–60). See also Z. Markiewicz, "L'Evangile éternel de Joachim de Flore et les romantiques," *Revue des études italiennes* (Apr.–Sept. 1959): 149–60.

11. *Les Jésuites,* 360.

12. Edgar Quinet had already linked the évangile éternel to the idea of revolutionary justice in *Le Christianisme et la Révolution française* (1845; reprint ed., Paris, 1984), 274.

13. *J1, 677.*

14. Marc Giraud, "*Correspondance (1847–1862) Jules Michelet. Emile Ollivier,*" ed. Paul Viallaneix (typescript, n.d.), 12f. (My thanks to M. Viallaneix for transmitting this excellent memoire.)

15. *J1, 579.*

16. *HRF,* 1:298.

17. Ibid., 300.

18. BHVP, Papiers Michelet, Collège de France III, fol. 79.

19. *HRF,* 1:429.

20. Ibid., 430.

21. Ibid.

22. Ibid., 493.

23. Ibid., 497, 499, 505.

24. Louis Blanc and Jean Jaurès give the federations a chapter, Edgar Quinet, two pages. Mathiez, who only has a page on them in his history of the Revolution, gives them six in his *Origines des cultes révolutionnaires (1789–1792)* (Paris, 1904), in which he also pays handsome tribute to his predecessor: "Michelet consacre de belles pages lyriques aux Fédérations, qu'il considère avec raison comme la première manifestation d'une foi nouvelle. Mieux qu'aucun autre, il a soupçonné le caractère religieux des grandes scènes de la Révolution" (7). Mathiez distances himself from Michelet's skepticism about the later revolutionary festivals, which, basing himself on Durkheim, he sees as the foundation of a new republican religion. My thanks to Peter Jelavich for this reference.

25. Ozouf, *Fête révolutionnaire,* 42.

26. Ozouf says Michelet is "almost exclusively attached to the Parisian scene" (ibid., 23). In fact, he wrote thirty pages in book III on the federations in the villages, towns, and provinces and fewer than ten on the Paris Festival of Federation.

27. *HRF,* 1:329, 497, 410–12, 423.

28. Victor Turner, *The Ritual Process* (Ithaca, 1969), 95.

29. Victor Turner, *Dogmas, Fields, and Metaphors* (Ithaca, 1974), 274.

30. Turner, *Ritual Process,* 140–53; *Dramas, Fields, and Metaphors,* 166–230.

31. See Alphonse Dupront, *Du Sacré: Croisades et pèlerinages, images et langages* (Paris, 1987), 406: "La société de pèlerinage est une société ...

sans catégories ni différences, où ages, sexes, hiérarchies, et même clercs et laïcs se retrouvent dans une communion panique de ferveur, d'espérance, de lumière et de joie." Dupront discusses festive and even orgiastic aspects of pilgrimages (often condemned by the priestly class) on pp. 407–12.

32. "He who is high will be low, he who is low will be high" (*HRF,* 1:418). Michelet noted that the version of 1790 was considerably milder than that of 1793.

33. "Society and its structures are always present in the form of the family institution and the father, the representative of the law of society" (Anika Lemaire, *Jacques Lacan* [London, 1977], 92).

34. Turner, *Ritual Process,* 96.

35. Ibid., 95, 96.

36. Turner, *Dramas, Fields, and Metaphors,* 182.

37. Ibid., 185.

38. *HRF,* 1:327, 310.

39. Ibid., 407.

40. Ibid., 410–12.

41. Ibid., 305, 327.

42. Papiers Michelet, Collège de France III, fol. 79.

43. *P,* 200.

44. J. Guéhenno, *L'Evangile éternel (étude sur Michelet)* (Paris, 1927).

45. Jean Guéhenno, *Journal des années noires* (Paris, 1947), 84. My thanks to Marleen Wessel for calling my attention to this and the following reference.

46. Marc Bloch, *Etrange défaite* (Paris, 1957), 210.

47. Mikhail Bakhtin, *Rabelais and His World* (Cambridge, Mass., 1968); Bercé, *Fête et révolte*; Jean-Claude Schmitt and Jacques Le Goff, eds., *Le Charivari* (Paris, 1981); E. Le Roy Ladurie, *Le Carnaval de Romans* (Paris, 1979); Alain Faure, *Paris Carème-Prenant, du carnaval à Paris au XIXe siècle* (Paris, 1978).

CHAPTER 14: NOEL, THE STUDENTS, AND THE RETURN TO REVOLUTION

1. See Michelet to Noel, Aug. 20, 1845, in *S,* 90.

2. The inner circle around Dumesnil and Noel included, in 1847, their *douanier* friend Alphonse Delaunay, Delaunay's associate Charles Levavasseur, who became a republican club leader in Rouen in 1848, and the eighteen-year-old lycéen Jules Levallois, later Sainte-Beuve's secretary and a literary critic in his own right. Family relations also brought close to Michelet by these five were Delaunay's wife, Emma, and sister-in-law Clémence Roty (with whom both Noel and Levavasseur were in love in 1847), and Noel's father. There was in addition a floating periphery of young men in Rouen. Michelet had of course his own circle of disciples and admirers in Rouen, centered around the historian Chéruel and the republican ex-*carbonaro* Lefèvre.

3. BHVP, Lettres de Michelet à Noel I, fol. 30, Feb. 13, 1847; *S,* 105, contains an incomplete version.

4. Noel to Michelet, Feb. 15, 1847, copy in MS 1587, fol. 47. Noel

has probably just read Michelet's reference to his generation having been born in the Revolution (above).

5. MS 1587, fol. 46, Feb. 19, 1847.

6. Ibid., fol. 62vf.

7. Ibid., fol. 493, Nov. 24, 1847.

8. Ibid., fol. 495, Dec. 1, 1847.

9. Ibid., fol. 112, Mar. 29, 1847.

10. Ibid., fol. 513, Dec. 1847.

11. *La Fraternité de 1845* (January 1848) estimated two thousand at the first lesson, probably an exaggeration.

12. "L'homme *fatal* qui doit nous le donner" (*S*, 90, Michelet to Noel, Aug. 20, 1845).

13. Michelet means by *Cité* the Latin *civitas,* closer to "society" than to "city."

14. "Il ne faut qu'un grand caractère."

15. MS 1587, fol. 31, Feb. 3, 1847.

16. *L'Etudiant* (Paris, 1968), 67f.

17. Ibid., 86, 88, 67. On the image of the *barbare,* see Pierre Michel, *Un Mythe romantique: Les Barbares, 1789–1848* (Lyons, 1981). For the celebration of the oppressed trinity of child, woman, and people, see the popular novels of Sue, Sand, and Hugo (*Les Misérables,* for example, begun in 1845, though not finished until 1862).

18. MS 1587.

19. Ibid., fol. 438.

20. *J1,* 683.

CHAPTER 15: MICHELET'S POLITICAL ENGAGEMENT AND DISAFFECTION

1. Proudhon reported this in his *Carnets,* vol. 3 (Paris, 1968), 11.

2. On Senard, president of the National Assembly at the time of the June uprising, see: J.-P. Chaline, *Les Bourgeois de Rouen: Une Elite urbaine au XIXe siècle* (Paris, 1982), 349–51; Jean Joubert, *Jules Senard de la défense de Flaubert à la défense de la Republique, 1800–1885* (Paris, 1984). Senard had important ties to both Michelet and Flaubert. Alfred Baudry, schoolmate of Flaubert and former secretary of Michelet, married Senard's daughter in the 1840s, and in 1857 Senard successfully defended Flaubert against government charges that *Madame Bovary* was an offense to public morals. Flaubert dedicated the novel to him.

3. John Merriman, *The Agony of the Republic: The Repression of the Left in Revolutionary France, 1848–1851* (New Haven, 1978), 1–24.

4. "A broad coalition of skilled workers was joined by a small but appreciable admixture of members of the commercial and professional classes" (Mark Traugott, "The Crowd in the French Revolution of 1848," *American Historical Review* [June 1988]: 651).

5. BHVP, MS 1588, fol. 150v, Noel to Dumesnil, June 29, 1848. Noel added, in his report to Dumesnil, that the National Guard of Rouen shouted "Vive la République" for the first time with enthusiasm at the return of the volunteers who had helped crush the June uprising in Paris.

6. See chap. 16, below. In many respects, Michelet mirrored his

proposal on the methods of the Bonapartists themselves. Compare Robert-Pimenta, *La propagande Bonapartiste en 1848* (Paris, 1911), 41–74.

7. For more than two decades, historians have demonstrated the post-June spread of republican and socialist ideas outside Paris: Ph. Vigier, *La Seconde République dans la région Alpine: Etude politique et sociale* (Paris, 1964); Maurice Agulhon, *La République au village* (Paris, 1970); Merriman, *Agony of the Republic*; Edward Berenson, *Populist Religion and Left-Wing Politics in France, 1830–1852* (Princeton, 1984); Ted Margadant, *French Peasants in Revolt: The Insurrection of 1851* (Princeton, 1979).

8. Pierre de la Gorce, *Histoire de la seconde République française,* 2 vols. (Paris, 1904), 1:141.

9. *HRF,* 1:965.

10. *J2,* 74, Oct. 27, 1849.

11. Ibid., 95f., Apr. 5, 10, 1850.

12. "The peasants are waking up ... Who would have imagined it could be so rapid ... Instead of these shocking images, debris of the Gothic world that even after February carpeted the rural markets, I see today the lithographs (not too bad) of Ledru-Rollin, Raspail, Béranger. The Holy Virgin herself has disappeared. What is serious is that with these portraits, the ideas are arriving ... A thousand small but excellent papers are circulating" (BHVP, MS 1589, 47, Apr. 30, 1849). In the elections of May 1849, Noel's friend, radical lawyer Eugène Manchon, doubled the left-wing vote in the Rouen area (40,000 instead of 20,000 a year earlier), and Noel expected him to be elected the next time (ibid., fol. 80, May 19, 1849).

13. Peter H. Amann, *Revolution and Mass Democracy: The Paris Club Movement in 1848* (Princeton, 1975); Merriman, *Agony of the Republic.*

14. Merriman, *Agony of the Republic,* xvii.

15. Agulhon, *République au village.*

16. Papiers Michelet, Collège de France III, fol. 138, May 12, 1848.

17. Flaubert, *Correspondance* (Paris, 1929 [Conard ed.]), 5:347 (to George Sand, Dec. 18–19, 1867). Flaubert's letter to Sand of October 1868 (ibid., 412) shows the influence of Michelet's antinomy of grace and justice in his further tirade against Buchez and Roux.

18. MS 1589, fol. 71f., Noel to Dumesnil, May 10, 1849. The "brothers in religion" were Dumesnil and Auguste de Gerando, son of the philosopher, joint recipients of the letter. On the democ-soc propaganda of Joigneaux, see Edward Berenson, *Populist Religion and Left-Wing Politics in France, 1830–1852* (Princeton, 1984), 138–40, 150f., 217f.; Merriman, *Agony of the Republic,* 41–44.

19. Jean Tulard, *Les Révolutions de 1789 à 1851* (Paris, 1985), 334f.

CHAPTER 16: FRATERNITY TO FRATRICIDE

1. *J1,* 683, Feb. 23, 1848.

2. Ibid., 922. Adam and Narcy were shoemakers, Savary an engraver, according to J. Maitron, ed., *Dictionnaire biographique du mouvement ouvrier.* Michelet may himself have suggested opening the committee to the *Fraternité* people: he had praised their views in *HRF,* 1:287, and they had reported sympathetically on the suspension of his course in their number

of January 1848. Their "communism" signified that they were dissident followers of Cabet: Marx was unknown to the French Left at the time. On *La Fraternité*, see Christopher Johnson, *Utopian Communism in France* (Ithaca, 1974), 112f., 119f., 148, 221, and Aart H. Bakker, "La Fraternité: Een arbeidersblad in Frankrijk" (doctoraalscriptie, University of Amsterdam, 1988).

3. *J1*, 925. In the April elections, Paris voters chose 34 nominees from a list of 2,000. See Louis Girard, *La IIe République* (Paris, 1968), 114.

4. Copy in Dumesnil's hand in BHVP, MS 1588, fol. 30, Feb. 28, 1848. On Sand, see chap. 21, below.

5. MS 1588, fol. 35, Mar. 3, 1848, and fol. 33 (n.d.). Michelet had probably heard about the peasantry's state of mind through Noel's letter to Dumesnil of Feb. 28, 1848 (fol. 24): "The peasants are a little frightened of this word ['republic'] and there will be no lack of *curés* to tell them that all is lost, that we are back to the Terror, bad harvests, pillage, and arson."

6. *J1*, 685: "Jusqu'ici je faisais la révolution; maintenant je la subis ... passif."

7. In a letter accepting Michelet's request that he run, Dumesnil said he and Noel would do so to represent Michelet's position in the National Assembly (MS 1588).

8. On the elections, the Left wanted time to organize; Michelet feared time would be to the advantage of the Reaction. He opposed democratization of the National Guard as premature, sure to alienate those unsure about the Republic (*J1*, 684, Mar. 17, 1848).

9. Ibid., 688, May 18, 1848.

10. Ibid., 683 (Feb. 6, 1848), 696 (June 21, 1848), and 920n.

11. Ibid., 692, June 16, 1848.

12. Pierre De la Gorce, *Histoire de la seconde République française* (Paris, 1904), 1:339f., 359f.

13. Eugène Noel, *J. Michelet et ses enfants* (Paris, 1878), 229f.

14. BHVP, Papiers Michelet, Collège de France III, fol. 138.

15. Ibid., fol. 139.

16. *HRF*, 1:652.

17. These two chapters were planned on July 26, 1848, and completed on Aug. 28, 1848 (*J1*, 698, 701).

18. *HRF*, 1:655–58, 660–64.

19. Jeanne Calo, *La Création de la femme chez Michelet* (Paris, 1975), 205; Viallaneix, in *J2*, xix.

20. *HRF*, 1:662.

CHAPTER 17: EROS AND DISCORD

1. *J2*, 659 (note to Mar. 23, 1849). Michelet had written off Charles in 1847 ("La mort de mon père, de Charles en un sens" [*J1*, 8-26-1847]); in 1850, when Charles announced his desire to marry, his father warned him he would be on his own. Michelet believed that only daughters merited support in marriage; sons were to fend for themselves (*Voie royale*, 16f.). He subsequently relented and gave Charles an annual allowance of between Fr 1,200 and 1,400 per year. See Henri Hauser, "Jules Michelet:

Lettres inédites sur la mort de Charles Michelet (1862–1866)," in *Revue bleue* 52 (1914): 421–23.

2. Dumesnil's journal for 1844, BHVP, MS 1497, fol. 24. Both the sexual exploitation of household personnel and the paternalism were common among nineteenth-century bourgeois males. P. Guiral and G. Thuillier, *La Vie quotidienne des domestiques en France au XIXe siècle* (Paris, 1986), 33f., 136–42.

3. See appendix A on the role of Michelet's second wife in his publications.

4. Michelet, *Lettres inédites addressées à Mlle Mialaret (Mme Michelet)* (Paris [± 1900]), 15 (hereafter, *LI*).

5. *J2*, 603 (letter of Oct. 30, 1847).

6. Michelet's letter of March 19 reached Athenaïs five days later, on March 24 (*LI*, 25).

7. *J2*, 577, Nov. 12, 1847.

8. Ibid., 604.

9. *LI*, 24.

10. *J2*, 605. The sequence of the letters is difficult to reconstruct. Athenaïs omitted Michelet's letter of June 9, 1848, from her *LI*; in it he refers both to her mentioning "vos souffrances *morales et physiques*" and to his transmitting "de vos nouvelles à M et Mlle Gronlier"—suggesting she had asked him to do so. Neither reference appears in her letter of March as she printed it. Either she had excised them from the published letter (Gronlier was an early suitor and she may have felt diffident about her complaints). Or there may have been additional letters between his of June 9 and hers of March 19; the latter is suggested by Michelet's letter to Noel about her of Nov. 29, 1848: "Plusieurs lettres vives en février, mai" (MS 1587, fol. 319).

11. Her reference to the "riot of the 15th" must have been to the tumult in the National Assembly on June 15, when LouisNapoléon's letter—"Si le peuple m'impose des devoirs, je saurai les remplir"—was read and provoked a furious response. See Pierre De la Gorce, *Histoire de la seconde République française* (Paris, 1904), 1:315.

12. Letter to Noel, *S*, 119, July 21, 1848.

13. For Michelet's visits between July 16 and Oct. 16, 1848, see *J1*; in *S*, there are thirteen personal letters for this period, three for the two weeks since he had received her letter.

14. *J2*, 607.

15. Apparently, Michelet did not abandon the journal in November and December, since excerpts from it appear in Athenaïs's edition of their letters, but either she destroyed the originals or they were subsequently lost. Athenaïs died only weeks after signing the preface to *LI*, after which Monod took over the Michelet papers.

16. R. J. Rath, *The Viennese Revolution of 1848* (Austin, 1957), 346–65.

17. Athenaïs erroneously calls him Fürster.

18. Michelet's "Mémoires" of 1861 allude to lesbian practices among the women of the Austrian aristocracy, specifically, to the unchaste desire for Athenaïs of her employer, Princess Cantacuzène: "Elle eût voulu un abandon complet et toutefois appréciait la réserve de la jeune fille" (*J2*,

578). The epistolary fragment, probably of February 1849, urged her to "take distance from these miserable pinpricks, these remnants of a world from which you have suffered so much and which I thought you had left forever." It concluded: "If I'm writing you this long letter, painful and humiliating for me, it is . . . because it was necessary sooner or later to discuss this" (*J2*, 642).

19. Michelet's "Mémoires" of 1861 have her arriving on the evening of November 7 (*J2*, 588); the pseudo-Michelet that she composed for *LI* fifty years after the event has her arriving at 5 A.M. on November 8 at her hotel (68).

20. "Mémoires" in *J2*, 590.

21. Ibid.

22. Ibid.

23. Although Michelet calls it "le nouveau volume," the actual volume III, containing the chapters on these heroines in book V together with book VI, was published only the following year. But Michelet was accustomed to having his (half-volume) "books" printed as he completed them, and it is likely that he gave her, as a mark of esteem, one of these preprints. (The first half of volume III—two thousand copies—was printed in October 1848; see David Bellos, "Edition de l'histoire / histoire de l'édition: Le Cas Michelet," *Romantisme* 47 [1985]: 76.)

24. *J2*, 591. According to Athenaïs's pseudo-Michelet (*LI*, 72), this visit occurred on November 16, and *he* visited *her*. The earlier account in Michelet's hand is almost certainly the correct one.

25. *J2*, 607f.

26. *LI*, 76.

27. Ibid., 74–77.

28. His and her accounts of his discovery of that skirmish differ. In her pseudo-Michelet, she has him finding out about it only through his visit of the twenty-second, when he saw her, in her window, reading a final letter of surrender from the Abbé Caulery, and asked her about it (*LI*, 78). He claims he knew about it beforehand through the Gronliers, whom he apparently visited during the two weeks he kept himself from going to her (*J2*, 592).

29. *J2*, 592.

30. Ibid., 593.

31. Ibid.

32. Copies made by Noel of this letter, long considered lost, are in BHVP, MS 1560.

33. MS 1560, fol. 319.

34. *LI*, 94–98. Her reconstruction is almost certainly a pastiche based largely on her letter of acceptance, in which she cited literally a number of phrases from his proposal.

35. Athenaïs's letters to him in *LI* were considered reliable enough by Viallaneix to cite them in his notes to Michelet's letter to her in *J2*.

36. *LI*, 101f.

37. Ibid., 403. Noel's copy is in MS 1560, fol. 324.

38. Michelet to Noel, Dec. 7, 1848, MS 1560, fol. 330.

39. The dossier MS 1560, which contains copies in Noel's hand of

Michelet's letters to him of the period (the originals have largely disappeared), seems to have been established for possible publication of this *correspondance à trois.*

40. MS 1560, fol. 330.

41. MS 1588, fol. 292.

42. Ibid., fol. 298.

43. Michelet to Noel, Nov. 12, 1848, MS 1560, fol. 332.

44. *LI,* 108. Unlike other passages she attributed to Michelet, this one was probably not fabricated by her, though she may have "improved" his telegraphic style and omitted parts that made her uncomfortable. In Michelet's letter to Noel of December 11, for example, which is quoted in the journal entry she gives of that day, she cut out a reference to Madame Dumesnil, and it may have been a plethora of such references that led her to "lose" the journal entries of November and December after using them for *LI.*

45. A copy is in Dumesnil to Noel, Dec. 13, 1848, MS 1588, fol. 292.

46. MS 1588, fol. 298.

47. MS 1559, fol. 467.

48. MS 1588, fol. 307.

49. BHVP, Papiers Michelet, "Lettres de Michelet à Eugène Noel," 1:48.

50. Dec. 23, 1848, MS 1588, fol. 324.

51. Ibid., fols. 318, 324.

52. "Lettres de Michelet à Eugène Noel," 1:52.

53. See his letter to Athenaïs of Jan. 3, 1849: "Living from the great soul of the people, nearly always escaping individual attachments, giving little to myself, I went through life without or *nearly without love*" (*J2,* 628). And to Noel, Dec. 11, 1848: "This very somber life, without personal compensation (except for having heard for an hour the dying Mme D[umesnil])" (MS 1560, fol. 332).

54. *LI,* 125.

55. "Lettres de Michelet à Eugène Noel," 1:52 (Dec. 26, 1848): "Vivre ensemble est impossible"; ibid., fol. 54, Dec. 29, 1848: "Au 1er avril je déménage, et vivrai à la campagne tout près Paris, s'il est possible." On January 10, he was inquiring about housing in the faubourg Saint-Honoré, on the twentieth, about the Château des Ternes and Neuilly. On the twenty-sixth, he was planning the furnishings of their rented quarters at no. 43, rue Villiers (*J2*).

56. *LI,* letters 39, 40 (Jan. 8, 13, 1849).

57. Jules Barthélemy Saint-Hilaire undoubtedly "played the part of the Reaction" in the subsequent (March 1851) purging of Michelet, but his hostility was probably based on his close ties to Michelet's old and powerful rival, liberal philosopher Victor Cousin: Cousin had long argued for a reconciliation of church and state and opposed Michelet's confrontationist tactics. See Georges Weill, *Histoire de l'idée laïque en France au XIXe siècle* (Paris, 1925), esp. 286. For a violent contemporary attack on Cousin and his followers—including Barthélemy Saint-Hilaire—as corrupt opportunists, see Joseph Ferrari, *Les Philosophes salariés* (Paris, 1849), recently republished by Slatkine, with an introduction by Marc Vuillemier (Paris,

1980). Considered too liberal under the Second Empire, Barthélemy Saint-Hilaire was, like Michelet, purged from the Collège de France: his official request, after 1870, for compensation, has been preserved in the Archives Nationales in the same dossier as that of Michelet's widow (AN, F17 12746). Unlike Michelet, he survived long enough to play an important role under the Third Republic. In 1895, he published a three-volume homage to his mentor: *M. Victor Cousin: Sa vie et sa correspondance.*

58. *LI,* 159f.

59. Ibid., 160, Jan. 6, 1849.

60. *J2,* 634f., Jan. 9, 1849.

61. Ibid., 636f.

62. Jeanne Calo, *Création de la femme,* 338.

63. Michelet, who had been anxiously consulting doctors about Athenaïs's health since December, was probably aware before the marriage of a clear connection between her chronic constipation and her vaginismus. There is a long, reflective journal entry of Mar. 5, 1849, on the general link between the bowels and the womb that could well have been inspired by this awareness. In it, Michelet attacked eighteenth-century corsetry for "this cruel strangulation of the womb and the bowels." Toward the end, he rejected Voltaire's contrast between the womb, "sanctuaire de l'amour," and the adjacent "laboratoire chimique de l'alimentation." The common goal of the two is "life. One supports it, the other reproduces and renews it." The relation between the two functions is "a major problem. The organs there are so close and mixed that mutual influence must be infinitely strong" (*J2,* 28–30).

64. Speculation on the possibility of psychoneurotically induced frigidity is useless in the absence of more information about Athenaïs's upbringing and superfluous in the light of the plausibly somatic basis of her vaginismus.

65. "Elle a achevé de s'ouvrir . . . dans un moment si critique pour la jeune fille, combien je l'ai épargnée, aimant mieux souffrir, attendre que l'obstacle anormal fut résolu" (*J2,* 66, Sept. 3, 1949). It was the anniversary of her father's death and Michelet imagined how "he would have loved me if he had seen with what tenderness I treated his princess." He added, "All moral or physical contact is an exquisite pleasure, often (and then still exquisite, like this morning) seasoned with suffering." Though they may have conceived a child the following month (Lazare was born July 2, 1850), Viallaneix finds evidence of consummation only on November 1, 1849: "Je pénétrai entièrement" (*J2,* 75, 670).

66. *J2,* 627.

67. Ibid., 633f.

68. In *LI,* Athenaïs avoided the appearance of rupture in the second half of January by including five long pseudo-letters, the origins of which can be found in numerous passages of the journal from January 20 on, in which he addresses her. That this period was marked by quarrels and that she found them compromising, is shown by a mutilated passage from the journal of January 22 that she used in the pseudo-letter of January 20 (*LI,* 182–86): "Beyond the hatreds of races, peoples, classes, the hatreds of families, there are the hatreds of lovers, the *hatreds of love.* This last word

appeared so cruel that I feel my pen breaking between my fingers . . . Polar ices, piled up, etc." Athenaïs followed, with minor alterations, the journal entry, but her three dots censor an explicit reference to their quarreling: "Oh! If the feeble appearance of a moment of indifference on the way back from Saint-Cloud made me feel the coldness of death, what does that mean?" Generalizations about lovers' quarrels were permitted; a specific allusion to one was not.

69. The completion of volume III of *HRF* on January 19 was also essential for this resumption. In *J2* (Feb. 14, 1849), he said that January 20 was "the day in which I was able to devote myself to my ideas" (*J2*, 6, 20).

70. *J2*, 8, Jan. 21, 1849. For an example of Saint-Simonian invocatory prose that was remarkably similar to Michelet's, see Charles Duveyrier, "La Ville Nouvelle, ou le Paris des Saint-Simoniens," in *Paris, ou le livre des cent-et-un,* vol. 8 (Paris, 1832).

71. *J2*, 8f. A study of Bismarck's insomnia show that at least one nineteenth-century physician shared Michelet's notion about the need of rigid personalities for mothering and made a therapeutic success of the material "envelopment" of the iron chancellor in "friendly warmth." See Otto Pflanze, "Towards a Psychoanalytic Interpretation of Bismarck," *American Historical Review* 76 (1971): 419–44.

72. *J2*, 11.

73. The faithful were actually in short supply on the only day of civil strife on which he had lectured in 1848: on May 15, 1848, he noted in his journal that the hall was a "desert" (*J1*, 687).

74. "Lettres de Michelet à Eugène Noel," 1:60. See also *J2*, 13, 653n.; *S*, 127.

75. See chap. 2, above.

76. *J2*, 19.

77. Ibid., 652.

78. Ibid., 11, Jan. 22, 1849.

79. Jacques Gélis, *L'Arbre et le fruit: La Naissance dans l'Occident moderne, XVIe–XIXe siècle* (Paris, 1984), 104f. It is highly probable that Michelet picked up this belief from the popular culture he had inherited from his parents but, realizing how the educated public deprecated folk wisdom, cited it in the more acceptable packaging of Indian philosophy, transmitted to him by his friend and colleague Eugène Burnouf.

80. See the concluding pages of chap. 12, above.

81. *J2*, 30f.

82. Dumesnil to Noel, Mar. 12, 1849, cited in *J2*, 657.

83. Ibid., 656f.

CHAPTER 18: TOWARD THE COUP

1. *J2*, 658.

2. Ibid., 33–40, 659n. He printed an open letter replying to his superiors on March 28 (ibid., 38).

3. See the introduction to the edition of *L'Amour* by Govindane and

Viallaneix, and to that of *La Femme* by Thérèse Moreau, both in *OC,* 18:22, 368.

4. BHVP, Papiers Michelet, Collège de France III, Mar. 4, 1847, fol. 54; italics Michelet's.

5. Ibid., fol. 53. Compare John 2:4, 13–21. Michelet's antimaternal animus at this point, his equation of the oppressive weight of history, both in the case of Judea and of the Catholic Middle Ages, with the "terrible mother," is evident in his linking together chap. 2:4, in which Jesus dissociates himself from Mary, and verses 13–21, in which he is challenged by the Jews in the Temple. The two passages have no connection.

6. The *cri de cœur* a week after the wedding, "physiquement il est impossible d'être moins marié," though modified the next day, recurred, less blatantly, until autumn 1849. Compare *J2,* 34, 36, 40, 42, 48, 55f., 59. See also chap. 20, below.

7. See N. O. Brown, *Life against Death: The Psychoanalytic Meaning of History* (New York, 1961), 140: "Freud formulates the relation between repression and sublimation extremely ambiguously . . . the sexual curiosity of childhood . . . (1) . . . can be simply repressed, resulting in a general intellectual inhibition and lack of curiosity; (2) it can be replaced by intellectual investigation, which is then sexualized by association with the repressed sexual investigation impulse, with the result that the intellectual investigation is compulsive; (3) there is perfect sublimation."

8. *J2,* 35f. By contrast, his diatribe of 1830 against SaintSimonian "pantheism" attacked the notion that "sensual nature" should be "at peace with the soul" and insisted the body should be "vanquished"—more like the position he subsequently opposed in Christianity. See chap. 2, above.

9. *J2,* 51.

10. Ibid., 35, Mar. 23, 1849: "Elle me demanda au sujet des Jésuites et de ce qu'on leur reprochait. La nuit, difficultés insolubles."

11. "Le prêtre, la femme et la Vendée" (written in October 1849), *HRF,* 1:1144–71.

12. *HRF,* 1:1078 (written in June 1849).

13. Ferdinand Guillon, imprisoned after the rising of June 1849 (*J2,* 53); Armand Lévy, sheltered in Michelet's home for three nights after the same incident, then fled to Belgium (54, 663); a year later, Michelet visited Guillon and another of his disciples, Georges Douhet, in the political prison of Sainte-Pélagie (131).

14. Auguste de Gérando, Noel's "brother in religion" (above, chap. 17, n. 18). *HRF,* 1:1225.

15. *Voie royale,* 505. M. Cadot discusses the sources of Michelet's interest in European nationalism ("Introduction," *Légendes démocratiques du nord* [Paris, 1968]).

16. The reference to himself (above) as Athenaïs's mother is not casual. On May 28, 1850, Michelet wrote: "Her true mother has married her" (*J2,* 104).

17. Paul Bénichou, *Le Temps des prophètes: Doctrines de l'âge romantique* (Paris, 1977).

18. *HRF,* 1:1134.

19. Ibid., 1141.

20. Ibid., 1143.

21. Ibid., 1229. See also chap. 13, 3d sec., above.

22. *HRF,* 2:68 (written April 1850).

23. *J2,* 117, Aug. 13, 1850. In what must have been a writing error, he also wrote: "female religions prepare individuality [he probably meant "fraternity"] by grace."

24. *HRF,* 1:281–302.

25. See the discussion in chap. 13, above, on the anthropological evidence for viewing the federations of 1790 in terms of the pre-Oedipal mother-child relation and Michelet's understanding of them in terms of his "matriarchal" principle.

26. *HRF,* 2:121f., 204f., 348, 408f., 659f., 893f.

27. Ibid., book XIV, chap. 1, "La révolution n'était rien sans la révolution religieuse."

28. The single exception to his fairness was his treatment of Hébert. Even Marat, Hébert's precursor as bloodthirsty rabblerouser, ends with a human face (at his death).

29. *HRF,* 2:815, 970–76; for a comprehensive supplement to Michelet's assessment, see Walter's note, ibid., 1131–37.

30. Michelet introduced his discussion of corruption in 1793 with a reference to the increasing apathy of the urban masses: "The people hardly goes any more" (ibid., 23).

31. During the prerevolutionary decades, the duke, nearly bankrupt, had had this complex of cafés and shops built along the colonnades of his palace, as a means of recouping his fortunes. See ibid., 1492n., and R. Héron de Villefosse, *L'Anti-Versailles, ou le Palais-Royal de Philippe égalité* (Paris, 1974).

32. *HRF,* 2:25.

33. He first refers to the chapter on Mar. 10, 1850: "Le matin, écrit *Les mœurs de la terreur.*" Then on April 7: "Tous ces jours-ci je poursuivis le second chapitre (Palais-Royal, Sade Robespierre)." Finally on April 26 he decided to revise it, deleting Sade and setting up Robespierre and the Jacobins as chapters 3 and 4 of book IX.

34. *J2,* 92.

35. Ibid., 95.

36. Ibid., 95f. See chap. 17, above. Apart from Dupont, Michelet was approached for the candidacy by Alfred and by Armand Lévy (above, chap. 18, n. 13). Dupont appealed to him to prevent the opportunist editor Emile de Girardin from obtaining the candidacy; Dumesnil and Lévy's argument was "Voulez-vous donc que le pape subsiste?" Probably they meant that he could oppose, from the Assembly, military support for the pope in Rome. On the struggle for this candidacy, see Pierre De la Gorce, *Histoire de la seconde République française* (Paris, 1904), 2:314–17.

37. De la Gorce, *Seconde République,* 2:317–36.

38. *J2,* 120, Aug. 25, 1850.

39. Compare *P,* part II, chap. 2.

40. *J2,* 118f., Aug. 25, 1850.

41. He anticipated a "great blow which, tomorrow, will be delivered to property" (*J2,* 125).

42. Ibid., 126. The implication that the ascetic idée fixe of Catholicism could be combined with the asceticism of antiproperty socialists was not far-fetched in 1850. Louis-Napoléon drew support from both groups.

43. He wrote afterward: "I was preoccupied with the deplorable reaction of the times and I tried to sketch a *Popular History*. I made little headway" (*J2*, 130, Sept. 6, 1850).

44. Ibid., 127f.

45. *J1*, 692f., June 17–19, 1848. The unpublished sketch of "L'ancienne et la nouvelle église," partly in *J1*, 692, is in BHVP, Papiers Michelet, Collège de France III, fol. 205.

46. *J2*, 123–31.

47. *HRF*, 2:18.

48. Ibid., 205.

49. *Voie royale*, 221, 335–37, 345; Linda Orr, *Jules Michelet: Nature, History, and Language* (Ithaca, 1976), 6, 10.

50. *HRF*, 2:444, for this and the preceding quote. Drafted on Jan. 5, 1852, a month after the coup. See *J2*, 181.

51. Jeanne Calo, *La Création de la femme chez Michelet* (Paris, 1975), 387ff.; L. Orr, "Les Alternatives bizarres de Michelet," *Europe* (Nov.–Dec. 1973): 117–31.

52. *HRF*, 2:446f.

53. Also noted by Calo, *Création de la femme*, 103.

54. *HRF*, 2:774f.

55. Ibid., 446.

56. Ibid., 893f; italics added.

CHAPTER 19: DISMISSAL AND RIOT

1. He noted writing on Danton's marriage in Nantes on July 3, 1852 (*J2*, 201).

2. The police reports are in AN, F17 12746.

3. Jules Vallès, *Le Bachelier* (Paris, 1955); Charles-Louis Chassin, *Felicien, ou souvenirs d'un étudiant de 48* (Paris, 1904). Both are autobiographical novels. See also Jules Levallois (in 1851 a young member of the Noel-Dumesnil circle), *Mémoires d'un critique* (Paris, 1896). Chassin wrote his book around 1885, probably as a response to that published in 1881 by his old friend Vallès. Their two accounts differ in details. Paranoia about note-taking Jesuits appears in all three accounts.

4. Levallois says the hall was intended for 800 auditors (*Mémoires*, 80). *La Fraternité de 1845* was probably exaggerating when they wrote of 2,000 in January 1848. Just before the suspension, a police report mentioned 1,200 (John Merriman, *The Agony of the Republic: The Repression of the Left in Revolutionary France, 1848–1851* [New Haven, 1978], 125). In any case, given Michelet's weak voice, keeping spies out of the front end of the amphitheater was a practical defense against hostile note-takers.

5. Chassin, *Felicien*, 201f.; *J2*, 700.

6. Vallès, *Bachelier*, 86f. On Ollivier (b.1825) and Michelet, see chap. 15, n. 14.

7. Merriman, *Agony of the Republic*, 121.

8. One of the police reports on his lectures in February went even further, alleging that more than half his audience were "clubistes" rather than students: AN, F17 12746.

9. *J2,* 151. He does not say who made them.

10. Ibid., 151, 701. On Jules Barthélemy Saint-Hilaire, see chap. 17, n. 56, above.

11. Ibid., 700.

12. Ibid., 701. For details of the administrative actions against Michelet, see Stephen A. Kippur, *Jules Michelet: A Study of Mind and Sensibility* (Albany, 1981), 131–33. The censure vote of Michelet's colleagues was 17–4 against him.

13. The burial was of Quinet's wife, Emma.

14. Chassin, *Felicien,* 202. Levallois wrote that he had to get in line in the morning to be sure of a place and was warned by a fellow student to watch his words, "since there are 3000 police spies" (*Mémoires,* 80). The following account conflates Chassin and Vallès.

15. Chassin, *Felicien,* 203. Vallès confuses this demonstration with the one a week later (*Bachelier,* 90).

16. I follow Chassin's more convincing account. Chassin says the two deputies who met them were Victor Versigny and Noël Parfait; Vallès, Versigny and Adolphe Crémieux.

17. Chassin, *Felicien,* 205f. The other papers were *La Presse, Le Siècle, Le National,* and *La République.*

18. Ibid., 207. The quotation represents the view of Michelet's hostile colleague, administrator of the Collège de France, Jules Barthélemy Saint-Hilaire (see chap. 17, n. 57, above).

19. Above, chap. 8; Chassin, 212. The students wanted to persuade Quinet, then in the National Assembly, to resume his Collège de France lectures. They considered his replacement—Dumesnil—overly "pacifique."

20. Chassin, *Felicien,* 209–14. Chassin was released without trial ten days later, March 30 (243).

21. *J2,* Mar. 31, 1851: "Visite du jeune homme sorti de Mazas." It would have been logical for Chassin to visit Michelet, since he had just been let out of prison and probably still had the undelivered letter to him. *Felicien* is silent on this, but Chassin, writing thirty-five years later, could easily have forgotten the visit.

22. Adèle must have heard the news from Alfred, Quinet's replacement in the Collège de France.

23. *J2,* 173 (Oct. 24, 30, 1851) and nn., 709, 710.

24. Kippur, *Jules Michelet,* 132f.

25. *Voie royale,* 32. Viallaneix cites a letter with a similar tone from Michelet to his son Charles written just before Michelet was dismissed as archivist in 1852.

26. Emile Ollivier, *Journal I, 1846–1860,* ed. Theodore Zeldin and Anne Troisier de Diaz (Paris, 1961), 79 (hereafter, *Ollivier*).

27. Two such plans (of Mar. 20 and 26, 1851) are printed in *OC,* 16:93ff. Michelet did not await his dismissal before formulating them. Ideas for "popular legends" on the federations of 1790 and the revolutionary

armies of 1792, as well as on the Italian and Hungarian heroes of 1848, appear both in his plans after the suspension and in *Ollivier,* Feb. 20, 1851, the day of his lecture on *livres populaires.*

28. I have collated information on Michelet's income and expenses around 1850 from three sources. Government documents from the 1870s on compensation to his widow for his dismissals (AN, F17 12746) list his annual salaries in 1851 as Fr 5,000 for each of his two positions. A detailed sketch of his investments and the interest on them in October 1842 (BHVP, Papiers Michelet, Biographie III, fol. 80) gives his capital as Fr 60,000 and interest on it as 3,000, with two-thirds of this sum promised to his children and his father. Third, in his will (printed copy in AN, F17 12746) he says that he increased his payments to Adèle after his second marriage ("lorsque nous habitâmes à part") to Fr 2,700. Even assuming that the capital and interest of 1842 were, through wise investments of book royalties and salary savings, more than doubled in 1851–52, income from investments after his dismissals would have been too low to support anything but an impoverished existence. Flaubert's income from interest, Fr 7,000 in the 1850s, has been declared by his biographer Benjamin Bart to be "not large … yet … enough to keep him from want if only he consented to live sensibly" (*Flaubert* [Syracuse, 1967], 454). The annual expenses of Balzac seem to have varied from over Fr 25,000 in the palmy 1830s to about Fr 7,000 in the relative austerity of his last years (R. Bouvier and E. Maynial, *Les Comptes dramatiques de Balzac* [Paris, 1938]). At the other end of the social ladder, laborers during the Second Empire could receive as little as Fr 2.50 per day (about Fr 750 a year), whereas the most skilled craftsmen— porcelain workers, engravers, and watchmakers—might earn Fr 10–12 a day, or about Fr 3,000 a year (G. Duveau, *La Vie ouvrière sous la Second Empire* [Paris, 1946], 306).

29. *P,* 141.

30. *EJ,* 84.

31. *J1,* 683, 921.

32. Ibid., 687.

33. See chap. 16, above.

34. J. Godechot, *France and the Atlantic Revolution of the Eighteenth Century, 1770–1799* (London, 1971), 175–78; G. Lefebvre, *The Thermidorians* (London, 1965), 1–20.

35. During the recapture, Robespierre received a bullet in the jaw, either from one of the arresting police or in a suicide attempt. Accounts differ.

36. Cited by Walter, *HRF,* 2:1138.

37. Ibid., 2:979 (written in 1853).

38. A. Mathiez, "Robespierre à la Commune le 9 Thermidor," *Annales historiques de la Révolution française* 1 (1924): 289–314.

39. Ibid., 290.

40. Ibid., 309.

41. Blanc reproduced enough of the original documents to have come to the conclusions later reached by Mathiez but, in spite of his frequent attacks on Michelet, chose instead to follow his (and Lamartine's—see below) interpretation: " 'In whose name?' Sublime word, under the circum-

stances! Such hesitations lose a man but immortalize him. In the middle of the cannons and the pikestaffs, amid the noise of the tocsin, when success depended only on *Force,* Robespierre thought only of saving the idea of *Right*" (Louis Blanc, *Histoire de la Révolution française,* vol. 13 [Paris, 1876], 267). Michelet, reformulated by a Jacobin pedant! On Blanc's *Histoire,* see Leo Loubère: "Essentially subjective ... the product of much labor ... generalizations ... not really intended to serve the cause of history, but rather that of Jacobin Socialism" (*Louis Blanc: His Life and His Contribution to the Rise of French Jacobin Socialism* [Chicago, 1961], 169). Michelet's preface to the 1868 edition of *HRF* answered Blanc's running critique of his work (*HRF,* 1:15–20).

42. Alphonse de Lamartine, *Histoire des Girondins,* vol. 8 (Brussels, 1847), 259.

43. *HRF,* 2:992–96. Previously published, posthumously and separately, only in 1888.

44. Justification of history as legend seems a violation of the historian's obligation to seek the truth: in a certain sense it is. But this professional standpoint overlooks: (1) The lack of a clearly independent historical profession in Michelet's day and the related intertwining of nineteenth-century history writing with the ideologies and values of the period, particularly with those of nationalism, liberalism, and a reformulated Christianity. None of the great historians of the age—Macaulay, Tocqueville, Burckhardt, Mommsen, and even Ranke, "wie es eigentlich gewesen," notwithstanding—escaped this intertwining (cf. Peter Gay, *Style in History* [New York, 1974]). And (2) The inevitable shaping of intellectual discourse and interpretation by the mentalities, ideologies, and "paradigms" of the times, as the present *Historikerstreit* in Germany and the quarrel in France between "liberals" and "Marxists" over the French Revolution (Furet v. Vovelle) demonstrate. See T. S. Kuhn, *The Structure of Scientific Revolutions* (Chicago, 1960), and Wm. McNeill, *Mythistory* (Chicago, 1985).

CHAPTER 20: THE WARMTH BELOW

1. Chassin, undated letter in BHVP, Papiers Michelet, Correspondance XIII, fol. 412f. Internal evidence suggests it was written between the two student protests of Mar. 13 and 20, 1851.

2. Jules Vallès, *Le Bachelier* (Paris, 1955), 83.

3. Most of the many references to Michelet by young writers in the 1860s in Luc Badesco's *La Generation poétique de 1860: La jeunesse de deux rives* (2 vols. [Paris, 1971]) are highly positive. Hippolyte Taine mentioned a Collège de France lecture of Renan in 1862 as being preceded by forty-five minutes of shouts of "Vive Quinet, Michelet, Prevost-Paradol, Laprade ... à bas les Jésuites" (*Correspondance,* vol. 2 [Paris, 1908], 227). In 1870, Vallès successfully appealed to Michelet to try to rescue Blanquist comrades from a military firing squad (*L'Insurgé* [Paris, 1884]). His open letter for clemency appeared in *Le Temps* of Sept. 2, 1870 (*J4,* 487).

4. Details of Michelet's 1851 publications in *L'Evènement* are in *OC,* 16:19–21.

5. A reference to the festival-day massacre of Huguenots by Catholics in 1572.

6. Michelet had considered suicide himself after Madame Dumesnil's death. He admitted this in his confession of Nov. 2, 1844, which he referred to as "mon histoire de cette année, mes dégouts" (*J1*, 581). Viallaneix thought this document to have been "perdue ou détruite" (ibid., 881), but it was retained by Alfred in the pages of his own journal (MS 1497, fol. 32).

7. *OC*, 16:53f.

8. Ibid., 54; Michelet's emphasis.

9. Ibid., 58–60.

10. *J2*, 161, May 28, 1851—an early title of *Légendes démocratiques du nord* of 1854. On the first title he gave for this work, *Légende d'or*—a play on the medieval *Légende dorée* (on the saints) of Voragine—see *S*, 162 (to Noel, Apr. 14, 1851).

11. *J2*, 162, May 29, 1851.

12. *S*, 151 (to Dumesnil, July 3, 1850).

13. *J2*, 162, *May 29*, 1851.

14. Michelet's text reflects the close ties that were thought to exist between the army and revolutionary republicanism during the restoration and the July Monarchy. Alan B. Spitzer has cast doubt on the idealism of most of the soldiers and generals of the period—retired or not (*Old Hatreds and Young Hopes: The French Carbonari against the Bourbon Restoration* [Cambridge, Mass., 1971] 20–24).

15. Christianity and Bonapartism. See 177, above.

16. *Carnets de P.-J. Proudhon*, vol. 4: *1850–51* (Paris, 1974), 380.

17. K. S. Vincent, *Proudhon and the Rise of French Jacobin Socialism* (Oxford, 1984), 202f.

18. Edgar Quinet, *Lettres d'exil*, vol. 1 (Paris, 1885), 22 (to Michelet, Nov. 23, 1852).

19. Sept. 15, Oct. 16, 31, Nov. 26, Dec. 17, 26, 1850, Jan. 28, 1851 (*J2*).

20. Sept. 1, Nov. 9, 1851, Feb. 11, 1853 (ibid.).

21. Mar. 24, Apr. 17, 1851 (ibid.).

22. Aug. 22, Oct. 21, 1851, Jan. 17, 1852 (ibid.).

23. "The die is cast": Caesar on crossing the Rubicon and beginning the Civil War.

24. *J2*, 169, Aug. 22, 1851.

25. See above, chap. 14, n. 2.

26. The Dumesnil-Noel correspondence (MS 1591) does not reveal the cause of the rift.

27. BHVP, Papiers Michelet, "Lettres de Michelet à Eugène Noel," 1:99, Jan. 1, 1851.

28. Sic! Noel's underlining.

29. MS 1591, fol. 75, Noel to Dumesnil, Apr. 17, 1851.

30. *OC*, 16:93f.

31. He tied czarist despotism too closely to Russian national character for the taste of Alexander Herzen, who replied to Michelet in a long open letter, abridged in *L'Evènement* of Sept. 19, 1851 (*OC*, 16:327–345) and, in

English translation ("The Russian People and Socialism"), in *My Past and Thoughts: The Memoirs of Alexander Herzen,* vol. 4 (London, 1968), 1647–79. According to Sidney Monas, in a personal letter to the author, "Herzen's personal crises . . . and their relation to his public and ideological role are strikingly analogous to Michelet" and Herzen's "letter," basically an adaptation of Michelet's populist ideas to a Russian context, is "central to the history of the Russian revolutionary movement." Herzen's program for a uniquely Russian socialism depends, Monas writes, on "the union of intelligentsia and peasantry (common people, *narod*)."

32. *J2,* 150, 151, Feb. 18, 22, 1851; also Michelet to Noel, Jan. 22, 1851, in MS 1591, fol. 103: the new paper *Le Bien-être universel,* was backed by Paul Meurice of *L'Evènement* and financed by *La Presse.*

33. MS 1591, fol. 129.

34. *J2,* 176, Nov. 27, 1851.

35. "Ma femme m'apprend l'étonnante nouvelle"; ibid., 176, Dec. 2, 1851.

36. Ibid., 177, Dec. 14, 1851. He was writing on Sainte-Geneviève, patron saint of Paris.

37. *J2,* 178, Dec. 29, 1851.

CHAPTER 21: REPRESSION AND EXILE

1. *J2,* 189, *Mar. 23, Apr. 1,* 1852.

2. Eugène Ténot, *Paris en décembre 1851* (Paris, 1868), 284, and above, chap. 19, n. 16.

3. *J2,* 182, Jan. 12, 1852.

4. Ibid., 185. Shortly before, ready "for any eventuality," he had destroyed, from his papers, "an enormous mass of insignificant things . . . a kind of *last judgment*" (*S,* 172f., Michelet to Noel, Feb. 2, 1852). One wonders if certain parts of his journal, dealing with Madame Dumesnil or with his carnal relations of the 1840s, then disappeared.

5. The document of revocation is in AN, F17 12746.

6. *J2,* 718n. The note is unclear as to whether he resigned or was fired.

7. Proudhon, Carnet VI, 187f., cited in Pierre Haubtmann, *Pierre-Joseph Proudhon: Sa vie et sa pensée, 1809–1849* (Beauchesne, 1982), 612.

8. *J2,* 705.

9. *Carnets de P.-J. Proudhon,* vol. 4: *1850–51* (Paris, 1974), 198f. Proudhon also connected his federative principle to the federations of 1790, which he had probably learned about from Michelet's *HRF,* in his *De la justice dans la Révolution et dans l'église,* pt. 3: *Les Biens,* new ed. (Brussels, 1860), 180.

10. *J2,* 167.

11. K. S. Vincent, *Proudhon and the Rise of French Jacobin Socialism* (Oxford, 1984), 212. See also: Pierre Palix, "Proudhon, un ami méconnu de Michelet," *Revue d'Histoire littéraire de la France* 77:2 (1977): 206–26, and, in the same number, "Michelet et Proudhon: Lettres inédites," 246–61. Edward Hyams says that Michelet's *History of the French Revolution* "influenced

all that Proudhon wrote after 1850" (*Pierre-Joseph Proudhon: His Revolutionary Life, Mind and Works* [London, 1979], 204).

12. J. Hampden Jackson, compares their careers in *Marx, Proudhon and European Socialism* (New York, 1962), 28.

13. G. Monod, "Michelet et G. Sand," in *Jules Michelet: Etudes sur sa vie et ses œuvres* (Paris, 1905), 356.

14. *J2*, 711 (Michelet to Sand, *Nov. 28*, 1851).

15. "She felt little difference, both groups saying 'the end justifies the means.'—*and justice, Madame? Is it no factor between the two camps?*" (*J2*, 187, Mar. 7, 1852).

16. See the letters to Dumesnil (June 17, 1852) and to Noel (July 2, 1852), in *S*, 173f., 179. From the letter to Dumesnil we learn that the rent was a modest Fr 600 per year.

17. *J2*, 199. See *S*, 176f. (to Dumesnil, June 24, 1851).

18. *J2*, 201. His grandson's birth had triggered the writing of *Le Peuple* in 1845 (chap. 8, above).

19. *S*, 178f. (to Noel, July 2, 1852).

20. Fifty-two pages per "book" against 160 pages on average in the first ten "books" and 8½ pages per chapter against 16 for the earlier volumes (*HRF*, Pleiade ed.).

21. Maria Rossetti would be memorialized in *Légendes démocratiques du nord* ([Paris, 1968], 208–38). Her Rumanian husband had been an important figure in the 1848 revolution in his country.

22. *S*, 188.

23. Ibid., 181–98 passim.

24. *J2*, 201, 209.

25. Proudhon's "property is theft" was widely misunderstood in the 1840s. It only meant the use of large holding by the idle rich as a source of revenue. Like Michelet, Proudhon valued the artisan or peasant working his own property (Vincent, *Proudhon and French Socialism*, 63f.).

26. See 81f., above.

27. *HRF*, 2:408.

28. Ibid., 402.

29. See above, .

30. *HRF*, 2:430.

31. Ibid., 2:622f. *Ollivier* summarizes, on the basis of conversations with Michelet in June 1853, as follows: "Robespierre perished . . . from having coddled the priests, from not having wanted to attack property, and from having repressed socialism" (160).

32. On the *assignats* and the *biens nationaux*: J. Godechot, *Les Institutions de France sous la Révolution et l'Empire* (Paris, 1968), 174–87.

33. *HRF*, 2:623f.

34. Ibid., 625.

35. Ibid., 627–30.

36. Jacques Roux was a communist ex-priest.

37. *HRF*, 2:768.

38. Ibid., 822.

39. Ibid., 828.

40. Ibid., 766.

41. Ibid., 807.
42. Ibid., 842.
43. Ibid., 625, written in December 1852. See chap 21, above.
44. See chap. 18, 1st sec., above.
45. *HRF,* 2:696.
46. See above.
47. Claude Digeon, editor of volumes 3 and 4 of Michelet's *Journals* (Paris, 1976), suggests this when he writes that the essence of Michelet's later life was "the extraordinary possession of this man by this woman. The relations of Michelet and his wife are based on a narrow dependence: this unique woman is able to give him precisely the physical and spiritual happiness he needs and he thinks that she alone can give it" (*Note sur le journal de Michelet, années 1870–1874* [Saarbrücken, 1959], 34).
48. Michelet's letters to Alfred clearly convey the impression of increasing warmth after his "descent." See *S,* 165–95 passim.
49. *J2,* 198–204, 720n.
50. *Légendes démocratiques du nord,* 228, and Jeanne Calo, *La Création de la femme chez Michelet* (Paris, 1975), 187f.
51. *J2,* 215.
52. Digeon, *Journal,* 3:90. The connection to the "grandmère" appears in the fact that at the time he first met Madame Rossetti, April 25, 1850, his aunt Vannestier was dying and had to be moved to a hospital. She died a month later (*J2,* 99, 104).
53. See 133f., above.
54. See chap. 17, above.
55. Michelet's less frequent complaints about Athenaïs's unavailability probably did not reflect any diminished interest on his part. In 1857, he commented in his journal on the frequency of intercourse advocated by various ancient sages: "Every 10 days is too infrequent: one forgets. Little intimacy." There is no indication he reached the ten-day frequency advised by Solon (*J2,* 325).

CHAPTER 22: ITALY, LAMENNAIS, AND
MICHELET'S "DESCENT" TO THE PEOPLE

1. *S,* 200, 205; *J2,* 213.
2. *S,* 200 (to Alfred, Mar. 3, 1853).
3. Ibid., 207 (to Noel, Oct. 17, 1853).
4. Ibid., 208, 210 (to Noel, Oct. 17, 1853; to Dumesnil, Nov. 14, 1853).
5. Ibid., 210 (to Dumesnil, Nov. 14, 1853).
6. Ibid., 240.
7. *Voie royale,* 147. Viallaneix also points out Lamennais's influence on Michelet's first lessons at the Ecole normale in 1827 (169f.).
8. Jean-René Derré, *Lamennais, ses amis et le mouvement des idées à l'époque romantique* (Paris, 1962), 585–97. On Michelet and Montalembert, see Jean-Marie Carré, *Michelet et son temps* (Paris, 1926), 99–120.
9. Derré, *Lamennais,* 341n.
10. *J1,* 127, Aug. 10, 1834.

11. Paul Bénichou sees him at that point simply as a "humanitarian publicist" (*Le Temps des prophètes: Doctrines de l'âge romantique* [Paris, 1977], 158).

12. E. Dolleans, *Histoire du mouvement ouvrier, 1830–1871* (Paris, 1947), 181.

13. "Impudently slandered, they have defended themselves nobly . . . They have not said too much; they have not even said enough" (Lamennais, *Correspondance, textes reunis . . . par Louis le Guillou*, vol. 8 [Paris, 1981], 280f.).

14. See chap. 2, above.

15. Derré, *Lamennais*, 181.

16. *J2*, 155.

17. Ibid., 146.

18. *J1*, 650; to Noel, Sept. 26, 1846, in ibid., 910.

19. Ibid., 651.

20. On *La Fraternité de 1845*, see chap. 16, n. 2, above.

21. *J2*, June 1, 1845, Jan. 30, 1846, Jan. 5, 1848. In the last entry, between his suspension and the 1848 Revolution: "causé des livres populaires."

22. On this aspect of Lamennais's work and its influence on Victor Hugo, see Pierre Albouy, *La Création mythologique chez Victor Hugo* (Paris, 1968), 40, 82.

23. *J2*, 169, 708n.

24. Ibid., 702, Oct. 29, 1848.

25. Michelet to Noel, Dec. 11, 1848, in BHVP, MS 1560, fol. 332.

26. *J2*, 657f.

27. Bénichou, *Temps des prophètes*, and R. Journet and G. Robert, *Le Mythe du peuple dans Les Miserables* (Paris [1964]), 108f.

28. See *Voie royale*, 461–64, for an excellent comparison of Michelet and Lamennais.

29. The letter arrived Feb. 2, 1854; the delay was probably because of Lamennais's illness.

30. Lamennais, *Correspondance*, 8:840–41; also in *J2*, 733.

31. The church did indeed try to persuade Lamennais to confess as he lay dying. See the document signed by friends at his deathbed (Armand Lévy and others), in *Correspondance de Béranger, recueillie par Paul Boitou*, vol. 4 (Paris, 1860), 280–83.

32. *S*, 215–16. Viallaneix (*J2*, 736n.) is mistaken in saying this letter was addressed to Dumesnil: a letter from Dumesnil to Noel (MS 1592, fol. 261) containing a copy of it, says it was sent to Lévy. (My thanks to Peter de Back for this information.)

33. *S*, 217f.

CHAPTER 23: LE BANQUET; REBIRTH IN ACQUI

1. Above, chaps. 12, 13.

2. See appendix B.

3. See the epigraph to *Le Banquet* in the Fauquet edition (*OC*, 16:591): "*Exulibus!* N'ayant rien, je convie ce grand peuple à mon banquet."

Some of the chapters, such as the one on the Judge of Nervi, remind one of *Légendes démocratiques du nord.*

4. *S,* 218.

5. *OC,* 16:680.

6. Cayenne was the penal colony in French Guiana.

7. Fauquet published Michelet's notes for *Le Banquet* in *OC,* 16:678–727.

8. Ibid., 684 (9) and (10).

9. Ibid., 684 (9). This plan is probably the one referred to in the journal entry of April 2 as having been written on March 31.

10. Ibid., 685.

11. Ibid.

12. Ibid., 701.

13. *J1,* 366.

14. *OC,* 16:709.

15. Ibid., 602.

16. Ibid., 601f.

17. Ibid., 602. Freud described the "oceanic feeling" that accompanied religious enthusiasm as an echo in adult life of a pre-Oedipal state (*Civilization and Its Discontents* [New York, 1961], 11–20).

18. A clear indication that Athenaïs's baptism of their dying child remained a life-long source of friction between them is that in the posthumous edition of *Le Banquet* that she published, she excised an implicit criticism of her, a plea for republican baptism to replace the "barbarous absurdity" of Christian dogma (*OC,* 16:641f.).

19. See Michelet's note in *OC,* 16:712 (also in *J2,* 254): "Communism is a sentiment, not a system—as in Saint-Simon's hierarchy, Fourier's harmonious diversity, Proudhon's anarchy. What we always need is communism of the heart."

20. *OC,* 16:695–98, 708–20 passim, nn. 22–24, 34–36, 38–42.

21. Ibid., 612.

22. Ibid., 613.

23. *OC,* 4:669, 679. In the following edition, the cuts were massive. See the survey of the two later editions by Robert Casanova in ibid., 639–41, and the "examen des remaniements," of 2:642–83. See also Jacques Le Goff, "Les Moyen Ages de Michelet," in *Pour un autre Moyen Age: Temps, travail et culture en Occident, 18 essais* (Paris, 1977), esp. 32.

24. Dumas did this frequently. After his first years, it was difficult to tell what he had written and what he had had written by his "assistants."

25. See Jacques van der Linden, *Alphonse Esquiros: De la Bohème romantique à la république sociale* (Paris, 1948).

26. *J2,* 737. The letter was dated Feb. 10, 1854. Six months later, in a letter to Noel, he dated his belief "in the necessity of a temporary death" of Christianity only back to 1845 (*S,* 222).

27. See above, this chapter.

28. *OC,* 16:706.

29. *Voie royale,* 61f.

30. From Maistre's *Soirées de Saint-Petersbourg,* cited in *Voie royale,* 146f. At the end of Michelet's chapter of *Le Banquet,* "Des fêtes, donnez-

nous des fêtes!" he repeats that title and adds: "Que le peuple y voie, y écoute sa propre pensée, s'y nourisse de sa jeune foi, y communique de lui-même, de son cœur, soit sa propre" (*OC,* 16:640).

31. *J2,* 273.

32. Ibid., 262, and Michelet, *La Montagne* (Paris, 1887), 110. The account of his experience in the mud baths in the latter work, written over a decade after it happened, may be romanticized; I shall restrict myself to the journal for the period he stayed in Acqui.

33. *EJ,* 206.

34. *J2,* 267.

35. Ibid., 269–74.

36. Michelet, *La Montagne,* 115.

CONCLUSION: PERSONALITY, MENTALITY, AND HISTORY

1. See Ernst Kris, *Psychoanalytic Explorations in Art* (London, 1953).

2. Jerrold Seigel, *Bohemian Paris: Culture, Politics, and the Boundaries of Bourgeois Life, 1830–1930* (New York, 1986), 8.

3. Norbert Elias, *Über den Prozess der Zivilisation: Sociogenetische und Psychogenetische Untersuchungen,* 2 vols. (Basel, 1939); Peter Burke, *Popular Culture in Early Modern Europe* (New York, 1978); R. Muchembled, *Culture populaire et culture des élites (XVe–XVIIIe siècles)* (Paris, 1978).

4. Wm. Sewell, Jr., *Work and Revolution in France: The Language of Labor from the Old Regime to 1848* (Cambridge, 1980), 114–42.

5. G. Snyders, *La Pédagogie en France aux XVIIe et XVIIIe siècles* (Paris, 1965), 264.

6. Freud, *The Ego and the Id* (New York, 1950), 15. Freud acknowledged that the will borrowed the forces with which it directed the affects from the affects themselves. Nonetheless, Freud's desire to replace id impulses by ego controls was essentially the same as Père Maldonnat's dominance of the will over the desires.

7. In *Civilization and Its Discontents* (New York, 1961), 13. Erik Erikson relatived Freud's perspective to fit an anthropologically neutral point of view (*Childhood and Society,* 2d ed. [New York, 1963]).

8. Mikhail Bakhtin, *Rabelais and His World* (Cambridge, Mass., 1968).

9. Robert Darnton, *The Great Cat Massacre and Other Episodes in French Cultural History* (London, 1984), 9–72. My point is implicit, not explicit, in his essay.

10. Roland Barthes, *Critical Essays* (Evanston, Ill., 1972), 115.

APPENDIX A

1. See Anatole de Monzie, *Les Veuves abusives* (Paris, 1936). Monzie was minister of education in various radical governments of the 1920s and 1930s and the patron of Lucien Febvre in the publication of the *Encyclopédie française.* His book dealt with widows who, he thought, abused their husbands' legacies: Athenaïs was a prime example. Febvre and Viallaneix, both

involved in the publication of Michelet's journal, seem to have shared Monzie's opinion of her.

2. See Jeanne Calo, *La Création de la femme chez Michelet* (Paris, 1975).

3. See Viallaneix's detailed listing of her misdeeds in his edition of the letters, *J2*, 601f.

INDEX